PETER SHAFFER

PETER SHAFFER

Roles, Rites, and Rituals in the Theater

Gene A. Plunka

Rutherford ● Madison ● Teaneck
Fairleigh Dickinson University Press
London and Toronto: Associated University Presses

Associated University Presses
440 Forsgate Drive
Cranbury, NJ 08512

Associated University Presses
25 Sicilian Avenue
London WC1A 2QH, England

Associated University Presses
P.O. Box 488, Port Credit
Mississauga, Ontario
Canada L5G 4M2

The paper used in this publication meets the requirements
of the American National Standard for Permanence of Paper
for Printed Library Materials Z39.48-1984.

Library of Congress Cataloging-in-Publication Data

Plunka, Gene A., 1949–
    Peter Shaffer : roles, rites, and rituals in the
theater.

        Bibliography: p.
        Includes index.
        1. Shaffer, Peter, 1926–   —Criticism and
    interpretation.   I. Title.
        PR6037.H23Z8   1988   822'.914   87-46010
        ISBN 0-8386-3329-3 (alk. paper)

Printed in the United States of America

To My Parents, Harry and Hannah

Contents

Acknowledgments

I would first like to thank Peter Shaffer for providing insight, information, and support for my project and for conducting an interview with me in New York City on 19 April 1986. From 1985 to 1987, my letters and telephone calls followed him around the world, constantly reminding him of my persistence. Although intermittently hounded from New York to London, Mr. Shaffer always remained the polite gentleman. Without his cordial assistance, this book could not have been written.

However, I believe that I did strain the patience of those faithful employees of the Lantz Office, Peter Shaffer's agent in New York. I am indebted to Robert Lantz for acting as an intermediary between me and Peter Shaffer. Mr. Lantz tirelessly passed telephone messages to Mr. Shaffer and sent my letters to him overseas. In addition, I would like to thank the Lantz Office staff members—Melinda, Mark, and Allison—for constantly relaying my messages to Robert Lantz and for tolerating my numerous telephone calls to their office.

A 1985–86 research grant from Memphis State University enabled me to finance the trip to New York to interview Shaffer. I also gratefully acknowledge the release time given to me by Professors Joseph K. Davis (spring 1985), John Lasley Dameron (spring 1986), and William O'Donnell (spring 1987), successive chairmen of the English Department, Memphis State University.

I want to express my appreciation to Deborah Brackstone and Brenda Woods of Memphis State University's interlibrary loan office. These two women virtually became detectives in trying to track down every available article written on Peter Shaffer. I will even forgive them for the long delays in getting microfilm copies of British newspaper articles from the Library of Congress.

With regard to assistance on the research of the manuscript, I want to thank Professor Dennis Klein of the University of South Dakota, who, at the time of this writing, had written the only published book on Peter Shaffer. Our numerous telephone chats and my conversations with him at the Modern Language Association Convention in 1986 provided me with valuable insight on Shaffer and his plays. In addition, I would like to

9

acknowledge the assistance of Sir Peter Hall and the staff of the National Theatre in London for their information on Shaffer's latest play, *Yonadab*.

Part of chapter 6 of this book first appeared in the Summer 1986 edition of *Ball State University Forum*. I am indebted to Dr. Frances Mayhew Rippy and Dr. Bruce W. Hozeski for giving me permission to reprint this material on *The Royal Hunt of the Sun*. Some of chapter 9 (*Equus*) was originally published in a different form in the Fall 1980 edition of *Kansas Quarterly*. My thanks to Harold Schneider and the editors of *Kansas Quarterly* for granting me permission to reprint much of the article on *Equus*.

Permission to quote from Shaffer's plays has been kindly granted from Peter Shaffer and the Lantz Office. I wish to acknowledge André Deutsch for permission to quote from *Shrivings*, as well as Harper & Row, Inc., for permission to reprint quotations from *Amadeus*.

I would also like to express my gratitude to Harry Keyishian, director of Fairleigh Dickinson University Press, for his honesty and integrity. During the initial stages of the review process, Mr. Keyishian was able to move the book through to publication efficiently and effectively. In addition, I also want to acknowledge the superb editing done on the manuscript by Ms. Paula Wissing of Associated University Presses; her close attention to detail is a trait that I strongly admire.

Finally, I want to thank my colleagues in the English Department at Memphis State University, my friends, my brother and his wife, and my parents for their encouragement and support. By constantly inquiring about the status of my research, my friends and relatives made the book much easier for me to complete.

PETER SHAFFER

Introduction

PETER Shaffer is one of the most successful playwrights in the world today. With Harold Pinter, Tom Stoppard, Edward Bond, Joe Orton, John Osborne, and other contemporary West End playwrights, Shaffer has brought new life into a previously inert post-Shavian British theater. Shaffer's plays have had long runs in England, West Germany, Austria, France, Sweden, the United States, and many other nations that have appreciated his unique style of drama. The awards have been numerous and frequent; Shaffer has won the Dramatist Award of the London *Evening Standard* (1958, 1980), the Best Play Award by a New Playwright (1958–59), the New York Drama Critics' Circle Award (1960, 1975, 1981), the Antoinette Perry "Tony" Award (1975, 1981), the Outer Critics' Circle Award (1975), and an Academy Award for screenwriting (1985). Many of his plays seem to be popular with audiences of all ages, and his most significant dramas are frequently staged by all types of theater companies, including amateur repertory groups, dinner theaters, college ensembles, and professionals worldwide. Most of Shaffer's dramas are readily available in bookstores everywhere, and his most celebrated works (*The Royal Hunt of the Sun, Equus,* and *Amadeus*) are fast becoming standard fare for many college theater and literature reading lists on campuses throughout England and the United States. In addition, *Five Finger Exercise, The Private Ear, The Public Eye, The Royal Hunt of the Sun, Equus,* and *Amadeus* have all been made into films.

Although Shaffer's reputation among theatergoers has been outstanding, the response among scholars and theater critics has often verged on the vitriolic. Much of the criticism has to do with Shaffer's search for a suitable theatrical form to express his ideas. His early plays were criticized as "kitchen-sink drama" in the style of Terence Rattigan or Arthur Pinero.[1] The later plays were deemed "too theatrical": they were stylized presentations whose success was attributed to Peter Shaffer's talented directors— Peter Wood, John Dexter, and Peter Hall—or to scenic designers such as John Napier (*Equus*) and John Bury (*Amadeus*), who make the productions come to life. Even notable actors and actresses—Sir John Gielgud, Brian Bedford, Roland Culver, Jessica Tandy, Maggie Smith, Kenneth Williams, Colin Blakely, Robert Stephens, Christopher Plummer, Albert Finney, Ian

McKellen, Derek Jacobi, Alec McCowen, Peter Firth, Richard Burton, Anthony Hopkins, Paul Scofield, Tim Curry, Jane Seymour, Alan Bates, Patrick Stewart, and F. Murray Abraham, among others—have all been credited with providing the necessary talent to transform one of Shaffer's "mediocre plays" into a viable production. Instead, Shaffer has developed a reputation as a playwright adept at theatrical gimmicks and stage conventions of all sorts yet one whose ideas are shallow, muddled, or trite.[2]

One purpose of this study will be to present Peter Shaffer as a consummate playwright who has the unique capability of effectively combining form, content, and *mise-en-scène*. Hardly anyone would argue with Shaffer's ability to create drama that is *visually* effective. From the spectacle of climbing the Andes in Peru to Alan Strang's midnight ride on Nugget to the lavish Viennese court of Emperor Joseph II, Shaffer has created elaborate scenarios that have been stunning and colorful, even breathtaking at times. The language frequently matches such scenic design and is often poetic, rhythmic, or incantatory, depending on the need. His plays are not only pleasing to the eye and to the ear, but also present stimulating ideas concerning such sociological and philosophical questions as the nature of Time and immortality, the existential search for identity in a society based on role playing, and the dialectical struggle between the Apollonian and Dionysian forces of one's psyche. In addition, Shaffer's canon reflects the philosophy that "form follows function." Basic sociological issues are explored in a naturalistic style, whereas the more metaphysical/philosophical themes found in the later plays are presented in a type of ritualistic/cathartic drama of the unconscious defined by Antonin Artaud in *Le théâtre et son double*.

Shaffer's unique form of theater, his ideas, and his use of the *mise-en-scène* will be explored in detail in subsequent chapters. It is important, however, to begin this study of Shaffer's writings by examining first the biographical details available so as to learn what motivated him to become a playwright and then to formulate how this vision led him to develop his own strong ideas and theories concerning stage conventions and techniques.

Peter Levin Shaffer was born into an Orthodox Jewish middle-class family in Liverpool, England on 15 May 1926. His brother, Anthony (author of *Sleuth* and other plays), is Peter's fraternal twin, born five minutes earlier. Peter jokes about his birth: "It was all very smooth as I first heard it. Tony says that he is older than I, but I cling to the possibly Talmudic notion that since I was the second to emerge I was the first to be conceived."[3]

Psychiatrist Jules Glenn has done extensive research on twinship and has stated that the intense rivalry between Peter and Anthony carries over into their writings as well.[4] Other noted psychiatrists have continued Glenn's investigation, particularly with regard to the later plays, especially *Equus*.[5]

More will be written on twinship studies in chapter 1; for now, let us hear from Peter Shaffer on the subject:

> We were always dressed alike when we were children. I think now that that's a very bad idea. It's hard enough to have another one *like* you without having the similarities stressed. The nightmare of being a twin is always being asked, "Which one are you?" I'm afraid I'm very dull because I cannot remember the famous sibling rivalry and all that sort of thing which psychiatrists to this day assure me I must have felt.[6]

Shaffer's father, Jack, worked in real estate and with his wife, Reka, managed to provide a comfortable home for the family, which included Peter, Anthony, and Brian, the youngest child. Peter went to prep school in Liverpool, the city in which he lived until he was nine years old. His family was always closely knit, yet some critics have pointed out that marital tensions in his plays perhaps stem from problems within his own family life. Shaffer, when asked if his family life as a child had been successful, responded with, "Yes, I think so. We get along well; the family has worked."[7] In another interview, Shaffer noted that "Tony and I have always gotten on extremely well, although we're very different. He's married and has a family and is keen on sport and I'm just an old bachelor. We live only about a mile apart in London and we see a great deal of each other, of our parents . . . and of our younger brother, Brian, who is really the clever one in the family."[8]

During those formative years, Shaffer developed an interest in solving puzzles—a preoccupation that he will pursue through the writing of his detective novels to the unraveling of the pieces of the puzzle that would force a seventeen-year-old boy to blind six horses or a celebrated Viennese musician to poison his hated rival. Anthony Shaffer explains the twins' early interest in putting together the pieces of the puzzle to form a coherent whole:

> Well, we had a grandfather who was a great one for that [solving puzzles, riddles]. We could scarcely visit him, but there was a puzzle to figure out or mathematical equation to solve. I confess we rather hated him for it. Well, you are under pressure to solve them; they aren't all that difficult, but if you *don't* solve them, then you look a fool.[9]

Shaffer's family moved to London in 1936 and remained there until the outbreak of World War II; from 1939 to 1942, the Shaffers moved from one refuge to the other, and finally they left London to keep the children safe. Peter recalls that "children love moving about and we never suffered. Our parents were very protective."[10] The family remained closely knit even during those arduous times. Peter was raised in the traditional Orthodox manner, was taught Hebrew, and was bar mitzvahed at the age of thirteen.

The education that he received was the finest available, considering the circumstances surrounding the turmoil in England during the war. Peter was even able to take piano lessons:

> As a boy I had a succession of piano teachers and eventually reached the point where I could play the sonatas of Haydn and Mozart and the less-demanding works of Chopin with a fair degree of proficiency. And I still do play whenever I can.[11]

This early appreciation for music, to be discussed in detail in chapter 2, has stayed with Shaffer throughout most of his lifetime and will influence his desire to create a rhythmic effect in the language used in his more mature plays. Not only will Shaffer seek to create this ordered musical structure in a number of his dramas, but also he will fill his plays, from *Five Finger Exercise* to *Amadeus,* with motifs relating to music.

In 1942, the family settled in Crowthorne, a village bordering on Berkshire and Hampshire, so that the twins (aged sixteen) could attend St. Paul's School. Peter described the public school as having a "fine academic reputation, comparable to Eton but with none of that English public school snobbery."[12] Peter did well there and won an "exhibition" to Trinity College, Cambridge University, but could not matriculate until he had completed a required stint for war service. So, in 1944, Peter and Anthony were drafted to work in the coal mines as Bevin Boys in Kent and Yorkshire. The "award" of servitude, named after Britain's Minister of Labor, Ernest Bevin, consisted of laboring in the nation's undermanned coal mines instead of serving in the army. Shaffer describes his memories of those war years:

> Bevin boys were called up on the basis of the last number or last two numbers of their identity card—it was an alternative form of conscription. I suppose like most boys of that age I would rather have been a soldier than go down a coalmine, but it was not to be. I found myself one day doing PT and then training on Pontefract racecourse. The next day I was down a mine, being initiated into the mysteries of haulage. For two and half years I was down Chislet colliery in Kent. I can't say it was pleasant. I worked some of it underground, but my eyes are very bad and I finally ended up on the surface doing haulage. That involved emptying ten ton trucks of carbide and rock, very good for the muscles, not very good particularly for anything else. It must have been a tense period because I finally got a duodenal ulcer.[13]

The experience in the mines made a lasting impression upon Peter Shaffer and was perhaps the impetus for his decision to turn to playwriting and escape the "drudgery" of manual labor that did not suit him well, considering the fact that this was not normative behavior in his middle-class Jewish family: "My three years in coal mining gave me an enormous sympathy and feeling of outrage in contemplating how a lot of people had to spend their lives."[14]

In 1947, Shaffer went to Trinity College on the scholarship he had won at St. Paul's. In an interview for *Horizon,* Shaffer discussed his impressions of postwar life at Cambridge University:

I'll never forget the extraordinary contrast of those two worlds—the world of industry and slave labor, so to speak, and the immense world of learning and freedom that I tasted as an undergraduate. The Cambridge I entered was the Cambridge of Wittgenstein, E. M. Forster, Bertrand Russell, G. M. Trevelyan. It was an amazing time. But I remained on the fringes. And I never came in contact with anyone connected with the theater, though both Peter Hall and Peter Wood (who would later direct Shaffer's plays) were there at the same time. I was very much a loner. In those days I never quite trusted myself, and I slightly bought the lie that there is something essentially indulgent about being connected with the arts. . . I felt there were lots of Peter Shaffers living all together in one body, and I still do feel this.[15]

At Cambridge, Shaffer read history, yet was very much inclined to a literary career. He helped brother Anthony edit *Granta,* the school newspaper, and during the summer of 1947, wrote a radio play about Alexander Cruden, the eccentric author of the standard concordance for the King James Bible. Shaffer was quite surprised when the British Broadcasting Company (BBC) accepted the script, thus whetting the aspiring writer's appetite and giving him the impetus to continue his creative urge to write. In addition, he collaborated with Anthony on a couple of detective stories that would later be published as novels.[16]

Shaffer graduated from Cambridge in 1950 with a baccalaureate in history. At the age of twenty-four, he was now faced with the reality of having to earn a living yet not knowing which career to choose. Shaffer preferred a literary career, but because of social pressures imposed on him by his family and his environment, he reneged on a commitment to literature:

I knew it had something to do with literature, something indeed to do with the theatre, but I think I was a Puritan of an extreme kind. By that I mean that somehow along the line I had absorbed the belief that if I really wanted to do something, the theatre for example—I was passionately devoted to the theatre—that was somehow frivolous and wrong and bad for me. I should do something respectable and "serious" like one of the professions and the theatre in my spare time. As a result I think I denied myself the pleasure of writing plays for a very long time. Foolish, very foolish.[17]

Shaffer unsuccessfully made the rounds of the London publishers, hoping to obtain an entry-level position. For a short time, he worked in his father's business but realized that it was not his calling in life. Becoming more and more depressed with how difficult it was for him to find a career position in London, Shaffer, beginning to see himself as "unemployable" in British society, decided to venture to New York to look for work.

In 1951, Shaffer arrived in New York and discovered almost immediately that jobs were fairly easy to find there. His first job was as a salesman at Doubleday's bookstore in Grand Central Station. He disliked the work immensely, chiefly because he was asked to throw himself on the public so as to keep the customers moving in an orderly fashion if they were not buying. He also recalls absurd conversations that a Cambridge honors student might find difficult to accept:

> One day a woman sailed up and asked, "Have you anything in red?" This seemed such an odd request that I thought I had misunderstood it for "Have you anything I haven't read?" But no. It turned out that she needed red books to go with a new color scheme in her living room.[18]

During the early 1950s, Shaffer lived in a small apartment on West Forty-seventh Street (a section of Manhattan referred to as "Hell's Kitchen") and also in a "rather foul little place on West 113th Street."[19] This period of his life was miserable for him; he quit work at Doubleday's and then labored in an airlines terminal and later in a department store. Consequently, he developed an ulcer which, Shaffer says, was "like all ulcers, brought on by pure frustration."[20] He lived with friends on Long Island until he was able to regain his strength. Then he took a job in the acquisitions department of the New York Public Library. Shaffer spent most of his time at the library copying titles out of catalogs, thereby boring himself to tears: "You begin each day ready to conquer the world and end up having filed dozens of invoices and answered mail about other people's business. You become part of a regulated ant heap."[21] After a year and a half of this type of mundane office work, Shaffer was ready to return to London. In an interview with Tom Buckley in 1975, Shaffer summed up his initial reaction to his first stay in the United States:

> The whole period is almost unreal to me. Whole weeks would go by that I just couldn't account for. Although I took rather a large step in flying the coop, I think I chose the very worst city if one was unsure of oneself, shy, convinced that one was unemployable. I might have been much happier in a smaller, less brutal place.[22]

However, the one bright spot during Shaffer's New York escapade was the availability of professional theater. Living in Hell's Kitchen, on the fringe of New York's theater district, Shaffer was able to see all sorts of plays from Off-Broadway to Broadway musicals. What he saw in the theater inspired him to write his first play, *The Salt Land,* a television script about the conflict between two immigrant brothers in an Israeli kibbutz.

Shaffer returned to England in 1954 and through friends of his family, was able to secure a position with music publishers Boosey and Hawkes in London. The job required him to publicize symphonic sheet music. His bosses were Erwin Stein, a disciple of Schoenberg, and Ernst Roth, friend of Richard Strauss; Shaffer liked the job and enjoyed working with his superiors. He remembers that he "shared an office with Malcolm Williamson [an Australian composer, now Master of the Queen's Musick] and happily filled my days compiling catalogues and doing whatever editorial chores came my way."[23] Shaffer hated office work and was only earning ten pounds per week, but his love of music outweighed the negative aspects of the job: "I was working with material I understood and the feeling of being relatively useless and unemployable began to vanish a bit."[24] He did so well in the firm that after a year on the job, Ernst Roth called him into the office and revealed to him that although the publishing side of the business was shrinking, the directors liked his work and "were prepared to offer me a really promising position in the band instrument division. But somehow I didn't see my future managing a factory, even one making trombones and trumpets, so I thanked him very much and quit."[25] What prompted Shaffer to leave his secure job and turn to a literary career was the decision by the ITV, a new independent television station in Manchester, to produce *The Salt Land* on British television: "It brought me £350, a fortune in those days, and it suddenly occurred to me that I might be able to earn my living as a writer. So I thanked Dr. Roth very much and quit my job."[26] This was also the year (1955) that Shaffer had his last detective novel, *Withered Murder,* published in London under the name "A. and P. Shaffer."

Encouraged by the success of *The Salt Land,* Shaffer was urged to write for a living. From 1956 to 1957, he worked as a literary critic for *Truth* magazine where he developed a more sophisticated interest in literature. During an interview that I conducted with Shaffer, he discussed his duties as *Truth*'s literary critic:

> I reviewed novels, which I found to be rather a chore because I had to read four massive novels a week. Sometimes when the novel was long . . . I was very hard put to it. But to reflect on what one was reading and then to review it—well, this is hard . . . I went through quite a number of interesting books at that time. I didn't do it for very long; I did it for only about six months.[27]

In the late 1950s, Shaffer became quite a prolific writer. *The Prodigal Father,* a radio play, was aired by the BBC on the "Saturday Matinee" program of 14 September 1957. Later that year, Shaffer followed with *Balance of Terror,* a television play about spies, which was presented by the BBC on 21 November 1957, and was subsequently shown on *Studio One* on 27 January 1958. The script is no longer available due to a contractual agreement with the BBC that required them to erase the tape, destroying the text.[28]

The major breakthrough came in 1958:

> I sat down and wrote a play, *Five Finger Exercise,* and sent it to a girl I knew who worked for H. M. Tennent. It ended up on the desk of John Perry, a director of Tennents [*sic*]. This took about six months. I had virtually forgotten all about it, then one day I got a phone call from John Perry asking to go and see him [*sic*]. In those days they had offices in the Globe Theatre, in that circular bit, in Shaftesbury Avenue. He said, "Would John Gielgud suit you as a director?"[29]

Five Finger Exercise was produced by the firm of H. M. Tennent, whose two directors, Hugh Beaumont and John Perry, had previously staged some of London's best West End theater. The play opened at the Comedy Theatre in London on 16 July 1958, where it ran for over a year before it debuted at the Music Box in New York on 2 December 1959. Although Shaffer's later dramas have more depth, *Five Finger Exercise* has enjoyed more critical success (see chapter 4) than any of Shaffer's works. In Shaffer's own words, the attitude of the critics was that Shaffer was "a Tory playwright, an Establishment dramatist," who would bring theater back to the drawing room where it belonged:

> Here is one of the men we have been waiting for, who will lead British drama out of the kitchen and back into the comfortable areas of the house. . . . Here at last is someone who denies that slum attics in the Midlands are the sole temples where truth can feel at home, who knows that she can lie just as easily on a Shaftesbury Avenue sofa as on one of those awful Stratford East truckle beds, and that our dearly beloved French windows can, after all, become the doorways of perception.[30]

Five Finger Exercise was voted the Dramatist Award of the London *Evening Standard* and Best Play by a New Playwright (1958–59) and then went on to win the New York Drama Critics' Award for Best Foreign Play of 1959–60. In 1962, a film was made of the play. Shaffer recalls how the success of his first full-length play affected him:

> Suddenly my life changed totally. I know this may sound falsely naive, because I was thirty-two years old then. But it really *was* a new world for me, a world of work and frivolity, of desperation and lightheartedness, which *is* the theater and which absolutely captivated me, an extraordinary world to which I semi-consciously always wanted to belong. My sense of being on the other side of a pane of glass watching life go by began to disappear. I became real to myself for the first time.[31]

Shaffer, who, due to his repressive environment, had cowed himself into believing that business was reality and art was pretense, now was becoming more confident with literature:

> Success of that sort has a way of turning the cobweb strands of self-confidence into good stout ropes, for a while, at least. But partly, too, I was surprised by the readiness of other people who cared about the drama to tell me who I was—artistically and socially—when I had no idea myself.[32]

The success at home and abroad convinced Shaffer of making a full-time commitment to drama: "I was started and it seemed there was no going back, that I was a playwright."[33]

Shaffer next served a brief stint as music critic for *Time and Tide* magazine in 1961–62. Shaffer's job was quite enjoyable for such a music aficionado as he was. He attended operas and concerts and wrote reviews of the performances so that the layman could appreciate the music as much as the connoisseur. Shaffer recalls that the experience was quite pleasant, particularly in working for such a high-quality magazine as *Time and Tide* and in introducing a young audience to the wonders of music.[34]

Shaffer scored his second major theatrical success with the double bill, *The Private Ear/The Public Eye*. Again, H. M. Tennent produced the plays under the direction of John Wood. The debut was 10 May 1962, at the Globe Theatre in London, and then the plays transferred to Broadway on 9 October 1963, at the Morosco. The London version had a long run, but, as Shaffer explains it, the New York production "was curtailed almost at the start by the assassination of President Kennedy some seven weeks after the play opened. The prevailing mood of the city was scarcely conducive to comedy, and though *The New York Times* hailed *The Public Eye* as soaring like an unfettered bird, the grim mood of the time soon shot it down to earth, along with its romantic companion."[35] Both plays were relatively well received by the London reviewers and by the New York press; *The Public Eye* was popular enough that a film version of the play was done in 1972.

In 1963, Shaffer had another busy year. His sketch for the American television series *That Was the Week That Was* eventually was included in the New York production of *The Establishment*. Shaffer also began to sharpen his literary acumen by working on his first screenplay, an adaptation of William Golding's novel, *The Lord of the Flies*. After months of work on the project, Shaffer turned the script over to director Peter Brook who freely adapted the text for the screen.[36] Brook's work on ritualistic drama and his ideas on Artaud's Theatre of Cruelty impressed Shaffer:

> Brook was the most innovative and brilliantly articulate man I had ever met. He had already produced his grandly ritualistic *Titus Andronicus,* and

he was embarked on his experiments with the Theatre of Cruelty. His relentless chameleonism impressed me almost as much as his profound aestheticism.[37]

Shaffer also spent part of 1963 working on *The Merry Roosters' Panto,* a fairy tale for children that opened at Wyndham's Theatre on 17 December 1963. This innocuous Christmas piece, no longer extant, was a collaboration between Shaffer; Lionel Bart, who wrote the lyrics; as well as Stanley Myers and Steven Vinaver, who set the lyrics to music for director Joan Littlewood and the Theatre Workshop Company.[38] Shaffer's divertissement was a new version of the Cinderella fairy tale, completely rewritten for a contemporary British audience.

Shaffer's next play, *The Royal Hunt of the Sun,* completed in 1964, after years of work that had begun before Shaffer wrote *Five Finger Exercise* in 1958, was a major breakthrough for him. Shaffer had hoped that H. M. Tennent would stage the play, but they refused. Actually, this may have been a stroke of luck for Shaffer because John Dexter, then a theater director for Laurence Olivier's newly formed National Theatre, discovered the play among a stack of old manuscripts submitted for possible production. Shaffer recalls the experience:

> When I first showed *The Royal Hunt of the Sun* to H. M. Tennent, the firm clearly regarded it as unproduceable and me as an eccentric for having written it. People did not climb the Andes Mountains in Tennent productions. They did, however, in Mr. Dexter's. My play, in fact, was precisely what this extraordinary man had been looking for. He found it in a pile of neglected scripts at the National Theatre office and immediately offered to direct it—and we advanced together through the spring of 1964 into the by-then nearly abandoned kingdom of epic theater. The result made a special kind of theatrical history.[39]

Shaffer's association with Peter Brook and John Dexter was to lead this aspiring young British playwright, trying to find a suitable form for the expression of his philosophical thought, into an exploration of ritualistic and archetypal drama.[40] Dexter, in particular, would go on to direct *The Royal Hunt of the Sun, Black Comedy*, and *Equus*, while influencing Shaffer's style, tightening the dialogue, making the plays flow coherently, and assisting him to determine what will and will not work "on the boards."

The Royal Hunt of the Sun, produced by the National Theatre, opened at the Chichester Festival on 6 July 1964, and transferred to the Old Vic in London on 8 December 1964. The expensive production moved to New York where seven producers financed the opening on 26 October 1965, at the ANTA Theatre. This type of "total theater" in the London and New York productions was Shaffer's realization of the sort of drama that he longed to create:

I do not think that I ever enjoyed doing anything so much as *The Royal Hunt of the Sun*—and the wonderful thing was that hordes of people shared my intoxication. I still recall the extra chairs being carried into the large Chichester Theatre and placed right across the dividing aisle of the auditorium to appease the crowds waiting outside. In the sunburst of the play's success, which certainly owed as much to the authority and passion of Dexter as to my own dream of what theater should be like, I felt my last inhibitions dissolve. I knew then that it was my task in life to make elaborate pieces of theater—to create things seen to be done, like justice, yet also to invoke the substance of things unseen, like faith.[41]

In early spring 1965, Kenneth Tynan asked Shaffer if he had a one-act play to accompany *Miss Julie* on a twin bill to be presented later that year at Chichester. Shaffer told Tynan that he was toying with the thought of reversing light and dark on stage (actors performing in total darkness that is represented by white light so the spectators could see while the actors supposedly could not), an idea that came to him after viewing the Peking Opera perform such a play years before at London's Palace Theatre. Tynan dragged Shaffer to see Sir Laurence Olivier, and when he arrived, Shaffer assured Olivier that he had no play in hand, just a vague idea of a play in mind, and had to go to New York to write a film script: "Olivier simply looked through me with his own Chinese and unseeing eyes, said 'It's all going to be thrilling!' and left the room."[42] Shaffer's deadline was met, and on 27 July 1965, *Black Comedy* was presented by the National Theatre Company at the Chichester Festival. It ran successfully to mostly favorable notices and had its New York debut, almost like clockwork, a year and a half later at the Ethel Barrymore Theatre on 12 February 1967. To accompany the one-act play, Shaffer wrote a companion piece, *White Lies,* originally titled *A Warning Game*.[43] Shaffer was not pleased with the play, although the reviews overall were favorable: "But I am afraid that I did not manage to get it quite right. The dramatic pulse was too low, and the work came out a little mechanically."[44] So he rewrote the play, now titled *The White Liars,* and subsequently staged it in London with *Black Comedy,* this time directed by Peter Wood for the 21 February 1968, opening at the Lyric Theatre. Although this version of the play was also successful, Shaffer said the play still was not right, particularly because of the use of an offstage tape recording of the voice of Vassili, Sophie Harburg's husband. A second rewrite remedied the problem, and it was this third version of the play, directed at London's Shaw Theatre by Paul Giovanni, with which Shaffer was satisfied.[45]

Shaffer spent considerable time in the United States while attending rehearsals and performances of his early plays in New York. Since 1975, he has spent as much or more time in his penthouse on Riverside Drive than in his London apartment, and he now calls New York home. In his preface to *Shrivings,* Shaffer stated that flying from Kennedy to Heathrow Airport felt like flying out of the twentieth century back to the nineteenth. A truly multi-racial society would be receeding [*sic*], in all the torment of its birth: approaching would be one chiefly insular, condescending, and frigid. This impression was of course unfair, and confessing it makes one seem self-righteous, but I was never happy in swinging, satirical London: the constant drizzle of put-down and small-minded preoccupation tended to dampen my spirits far too often.[46]

With Shaffer harboring such fond passion for New York and the United States, one wonders why the British playwright has not debuted any of his plays first in New York and *then* in London or another city. In a 1965 interview with George Oppenheimer of *Newsday* (Long Island), Shaffer discussed his hesitancy to "open" in New York: "I love New York and love living here, but one thing militates against it. I do not want to and will not initiate a play here. The opposing odds are too great. Above all there are the economics of Broadway. My play has to make $40,000 a week in order to break even. This fact automatically strikes terror into every heart connected with the enterprise."[47]

After Shaffer's work on *Black Comedy* and *The White Liars,* he spent more time in the United States during 1968 and 1969. Shaffer, however, recalls that these sojourns were slightly different and more distinct than previous trips to New York because the "streets were choked with raging protesters against the Vietnam War, newspapers were filled with the killings at Kent State University, and there drifted through our midst the fantastic army of Flower People, now already turned into ghosts."[48] Inspired by the turmoil with regard to the peace demonstrations that he witnessed in the United States, Shaffer wrote *The Battle of Shrivings.* Produced by H. M. Tennent, directed by Peter Hall, and starring John Gielgud as Gideon Petrie, the play looked like a surefire success on paper when it opened at London's Lyric Theatre on 5 February 1970. The critics found the ideas contained in the play to be shallow, the characters cold, and the flavor of the play to be a bit foreign for a London audience. After two months of running time, the play closed. It was the first time in his career that Shaffer had experienced a majority of unfavorable reviews with regard to one of his plays, and he acknowledged that "I was deeply depressed by the failure of this piece and by the derisory quality of the notices which greeted it."[49] Shaffer was determined to improve the play and reworked it into a new version titled *Shrivings:* "I invested more sheer effort into this play than any other. It is really covered with the fingermarks of struggle."[50] As of this writing, however, the play has yet to be staged in the United States—Shaffer's only drama that has this infamous distinction.

With the failure of *Shrivings* behind him, Shaffer, who learns well from his shortcomings in the theater, made sure that his next play would be an improvement. Working closely with John Dexter, Shaffer went through rehearsals of *Equus* at the Old Vic. He recalls that the experience was thrilling:

> Throughout this time of rehearsal, I felt a good and sustaining tension but, curiously, no anxiety. The power of the play seemed to be constantly inside me, telling me where to go with it. I think the director would agree that it largely told him also. The excellence of Dexter's achievement lay in controlling that power—avoiding from beginning to end the slightest sense of absurdity, which can easily arise when actors perform as animals—and allowing giant specters to appear on stage. *Equus* was his barest production and yet his most unnerving. It contained, toward its close, the most explicit and prolonged scene of nudity the British theater had so far witnessed; yet because it was entirely suitable and appropriate, this scene caused no affront at all.[51]

Equus premiered at London's Old Vic Theatre on 26 July 1973, and soon enjoyed a long run there. On 24 October 1974, the play had its Broadway debut at the Plymouth Theatre and eventually ran for over a thousand performances before the production went on tour across the United States. Shaffer acknowledges that although some critics condemned the play for its nudity, its depiction of cruelty to horses, and its belittlement of the psychiatric profession, the overall response was quite positive:

> For the only time in my life I was accorded a standing ovation—on the first night at the Plymouth Theatre—an event no playwright is likely to forget. Approval of this kind, poured from an American bottle down a European throat, is an elixir of youth. I experienced the undeniable euphoria of feeling psychically younger at fifty than I had at thirty. Strangely, this optimism has persisted with me for years. It sustained me all through the long period of time I spent working on *Amadeus*.[52]

Equus went on to win the Outer Critics' Circle Award, the New York Drama Critics' Award, the Antoinette Perry "Tony" Award, and the Los Angeles Drama Critics' Award. The play was made into a movie in 1977.

It took Shaffer five years to complete his work on *Amadeus*. One may safely surmise that *Amadeus* presented Shaffer with his greatest challenge in the theater. Serious work on the play did not begin until 1977, and Shaffer, admitting that the play was difficult to write, spent "a whole year attempting a different opening scene every week."[53] With the assistance of director Peter Hall, musical arranger Harrison Birtwistle, and scenic designer John Bury, Shaffer was able to get the play ready for its 2 November 1979 opening on the National Theatre's largest stage, the Olivier Theatre. The play was an immediate success and had an extensive run before transferring to the West End's Her Majesty's Theatre. Shaffer, in his preface to the play, was elated that one year after the premiere of *Amadeus,* "the *Sunday Times* of

London reports that audiences began lining up at six o'clock in the morning to buy the few tickets which are sold only on the day of performance. This is hardly a usual practice with the Great British Public."[54] After *Amadeus's* trial run in Washington, D.C., Shaffer rewrote the play to achieve greater clarity, to link Salieri more directly with Mozart's ruin, and to remove characters and scenes Shaffer thought were extraneous. The result was that a more streamlined version of the play opened in New York at the Broadhurst Theatre on 17 December 1980. The public flocked to see it, and *Amadeus* proved to be as much of a hit in New York as it was in London. The play, popular with many critics as well as with the public, received many accolades, including the 1981 Tony Award for Best Play of the Year. Since then, *Amadeus* has played successfully on tour in the United States and in virtually every capital city in Europe.

One of the many admirers of *Amadeus* was film director Milos Forman, who was so impressed with the play that he urged Shaffer to work with him on the film version. Shaffer's experiences with film scripts was a bitter one, since most of the screenplays of his dramas had been unfairly distorted by film directors who ignored Shaffer's material and freely adapted it for their own purposes. At first, Shaffer refused to work with Forman; however, the Hollywood mogul, already a winner of an Academy Award for his direction of *One Flew Over the Cuckoo's Nest,* convinced Shaffer that this would be a joint effort and that the film would be faithful to Shaffer's intentions. Shaffer's bad experiences of handing a script over to an aloof, uncaring director were over.

On 1 February 1982, Shaffer and Forman began work on the film version of *Amadeus.*[55] They spent four months together in Forman's colonial farmhouse in Warren, Connecticut—five days per week, twelve hours per day. They eventually hammered out a workable script, taking a bit more liberty with the historical events than did the New York or London versions of the play. Shaffer supervised some of the filming in Prague, and was quite pleased with the $18 million product that he and Forman turned out. The movie was completed for distribution in fall 1984. By 25 March 1985, Shaffer had pocketed an Academy Award for Best Screenplay (Adaptation), and Milos Forman had won his second Academy Award for film directing; the film garnered a total of eight Academy awards, including best picture, best art direction, best actor (F. Murray Abraham), best costume design, best sound, and best makeup.

Shaffer's latest play, *Yonadab,* premiered at the National Theatre under Sir Peter Hall's direction on 4 December 1985 and has enjoyed a successful run. The play is based on Dan Jacobson's novel, *The Rape of Tamar,* depicting the biblical account of Amnon, King David's son, who raped his sister Tamar. Shaffer, however, is not satisfied with the play and plans to rewrite it extensively before it debuts in New York.

1

Peter Shaffer: Sociologist of the Theater

PETER Shaffer has acquired a reputation that does not do him justice. He is perceived by critics as being an accomplished technician, a master of stagecraft, and an exploiter of sensationalism. Because Shaffer is meticulously concerned with vivid descriptive details regarding scenic design, costuming, musical accompaniment, and spectacle, he has been stereotyped as a skilled craftsman with little to say. Shaffer's plays do dazzle the spectator; as we watch his plays, we are awed by his middle-class British dialogue (a particular fascination for middle-class American audiences), epic scenery, elaborate costumes, classical music, exquisite sounds, mood lighting, a fair amount of well-placed comedy, and also some nudity to titillate the senses. Most audiences would agree that their first impressions of one of his plays would lead them to surmise that Shaffer writes for the eye and ear but does little to make us think in the theater. In addition, because Shaffer in his early plays was excessively concerned with precise characterization and carefully contrived plots, he was accused of writing "well-made plays." In short, Shaffer again was classified as a playwright who was concerned with dramatic structure, as well as with stagecraft, but not necessarily with ideas. The purpose of this chapter will be to present a general discussion concerning the content of Shaffer's plays and to prove that he is indeed a playwright with a significant, carefully formulated sociological viewpoint.

Shaffer's plays deal with the development of an individual's sense of awareness. His protagonists are indecisive adults who can exist only in a secure world of roles, rules, and regulations. Their worlds are filled with illusions, lies, and make-believe, but they cling to these artificialities for fear of losing everything. Shaffer's protagonists would like nothing better than to break out of their isolated shells, but because they are steeped in years of role playing, it is difficult for them to alter their staid existence.

Shaffer can be described as a sociologist working in the theater, much in the tradition of Henrik Ibsen, Arthur Miller, John Osborne, and Edward Albee. His theater is primarily concerned with the nature of role playing. The major conflict that dominates almost all of his plays is the dialectic between sanctioned, normative behavior accepted in society and a sense of

individual consciousness that opposes any type of formally channeled lifestyle. His protagonists—Clive Harrington, Bob, Tom, Brindsley Miller,
Charles Sidley, Francisco Pizarro, Gideon Petrie, Martin Dysart, and Antonio Salieri—feel trapped in their often stuffy roles, yet they cannot adjust
to change: they are in the process of finding themselves but never will unless
they destroy their roles, thereby freeing themselves from being dependent
on what others think of them. Shaffer, as a sociologist, is also critical of
some institutions such as church and state (particularly in *The Royal Hunt of
the Sun*), but he is not per se apprehensive of the family as an institution.
Shaffer, however, does not, much like Brecht or Weiss, concern himself
with political issues. He is critical of institutions when they work as bands
to codify role playing and sanction individuals into proper channels of
behavior. The nature of his criticism is always concerned with the sociological, not the political or the methods of administration of governmen-
tal policy.

Almost all of Shaffer's plays present a dialectic between a threatened,
often isolated, individual trapped in a world of roles and codified behavior
and his alter ego, an independent person who is not controlled by the desires
and wishes of others. These alter egos or foils for the protagonist—Walter
Langer, Julian Cristoforou, Atahuallpa, Mark Askelon, Alan Strang, and
Wolfgang Amadeus Mozart, to name a few—are often seen as primitives
who create their own microcosm and answer to no one but themselves.
They may be "primitive" and unsocialized by society's standards, but they
definitely have a strong sense of identity and can think and act for themselves without relying on the acceptance and sanctions of others. These
independent individuals teach Shaffer's misguided protagonists that they are
living in a phony and artificial world. Shaffer's principal characters learn
from their alter egos—they see their "doubles" living a life of unfettered
freedom without having to conform to established and often pretentious
roles and norms. The protagonists secretly wish that they could feel free in
their own environments; they identify with their alter egos, want to be like
them, and often have an unconscious desire to merge with them (or *be*
them), existing as a corporate godhead of Self and Other. However,
Shaffer's protagonists are not to be confused with existential heroes who
might rebel or revolt to initiate change. His main characters gain a new sense
of understanding from their alter egos, but they never act on this newly
acquired knowledge. They are passively conscious of their new awakening,
yet they never take the final step and change from their former staid
existence to a more liberated state of awareness; they certainly want to make
the change, but they are incapable of doing so.

Shaffer himself can be compared to Dr. Dysart, Pizarro, Clive, Bob,
Sidley, and many of his other protagonists, despite the fact that the portrait
presented is not too flattering. Shaffer was raised in a traditional middle-

class Orthodox Jewish family and was educated in well-established conservative institutions. Yet he often expresses a desire to break free from his
traditional background and follow through with many of his unconscious
or secret desires that would be considered unacceptable by family or peers.
Much of Shaffer's life has been an attempt to reach out and explore artistic
forms and personal choices that are not considered to be traditional.

It was difficult for Shaffer to choose playwriting as a career. He had taken
a number of socially "acceptable" office jobs, had read history at Cambridge, and had even tried writing detective novels before forcing himself to
admit that the theater was like a temple to him—a source of inspiration.
Shaffer explains why his success as a playwright came so late in life:

> I was quite old, as these things go, to be making my debut, but I had
> spent my earlier life being cowed, and this accounted for my tardy
> appearance as a dramatist. I mean by this that as an adolescent I had
> bought the lie, assiduously circulated by the world that I was born into,
> that business is reality and art pretence. . . . The theater was much too
> seductive a place to be a proper habitation, and the only true space for real
> work had to be an office.[1]

Forced by his employers to make a decision—whether to remain at
Boosey and Hawkes or to try his hand at drama—Shaffer chose to make his
living as a playwright. But his first few plays were traditional in form and
content, not at all what he wanted theater to be. It was not until 1964, with
the debut of *The Royal Hunt of the Sun,* that Shaffer broke with conventional
notions of the stage and turned drama into "total theater" or, as Artaud
would have it, a ritualistic Theatre of Cruelty. As Shaffer has said on
numerous occasions, a rhythmic theater is the type of drama that he prefers,
as opposed to his earlier plays where he tried to conform to a more
acceptable notion of what others thought British drama should be. In
Shaffer's later plays, we see him shying away from conventional theater,
forcing himself to obtain positive reinforcement for his efforts from directors Peter Hall and John Dexter.

In the preface to his collected works, Shaffer wrote: "The truth is that I
have always experienced difficulties in following the immediate promptings
of my spirit. I regret this deeply, although I have some cause to be thankful
for it as well. Repression, properly used, can be a beneficial force."[2] Indeed,
this motif concerning the search for identity and the repression of individual
desires and dreams forms the foundation of Shaffer's sociological theater.

Shaffer is continually torn between opposing forces. On the one hand, he
is a product of his family, his environment, and his formal educational
training—the author of "well-made plays"; on the other hand, he is the
unconventional experimenter searching for a suitable form to embellish a
theater of the unconscious with sociological themes—the author of *The*

Royal Hunt of the Sun and *Equus*. He is constantly faced with the challenge of conforming to roles, thereby writing the conventional type of British drama to which family and peers could respond or experimenting with form and stagecraft to create his own theatrical innovations. In a revealing statement made during an interview with *The New York Times*, Shaffer said:

> When I was younger, I often was invaded by this feeling of invisibility: of having no definite outline to myself and others. There seemed to be so many people inside me, all of them contradictory. I could not imagine the shape which could contain them all, and so assumed that there was none.[3]

Shaffer's life had been determined by the influence of those around him, although he secretly yearns to act according to the conventions that he has created for himself. In "Labels Aren't for Playwrights," Shaffer discussed the two conflicting sides of his personality:

> There is something about a man who won't dream that compels respect. It is the same constancy that makes one admire people who are always the same in any company, and remain uninfluenced by anyone they meet. I am terribly impressed by such people; I wonder how they manage it, and end up being slightly irritated by their rigidity. As a playwright, I'm scared of the too well-defined identity—of being either publicly or (even worse) privately its prisoner. I rather believe my totem animal to be the chameleon.[4]

Shaffer says that he admires people who know and understand themselves and who are not pulled in different directions by opposing forces.[5] He compares himself to a chameleon because his sense of identity is amorphous and is constantly in flux.[6]

This constant polarity between social forces that have an impact on Shaffer's life, and consequently on the ideas presented in his plays, has been internalized by Shaffer as psychoanalytic as well:

> There is in me a continuous tension between what I suppose I could loosely call the Apollonian and the Dionysiac sides of interpreting life, between say, Dysart and Alan Strang.
> . . . I just feel in myself that there is a constant debate going on between the violence of instinct on the one hand and the desire in my mind for order and restraint.[7]

This tension that Shaffer feels between two opposing forces—the Apollonian and the Dionysian—has been explored extensively by psychiatrist Jules Glenn. (See Introduction.) Dr. Glenn believes that this polarity between the protagonist and his alter ego, the basis for all of Shaffer's dramatic conflicts, stems from Shaffer's childhood and his relationship with his fraternal twin, Anthony. Glenn asserts that when twins are raised together, as Peter and

Anthony were, they often develop an intense rivalry combined with strong affectional bonds.[8] In other words, the twins develop a love-hate relationship with each other: each twin competes with his brother yet unconsciously longs to become "one" with his rival. Frequently, each twin has the fantasy of being half a person and seeks to merge with his alter ego. The love-hate relationship is, at times, intense; each twin feels guilty that his brother has deprived him of his mother's love. Although the desire is strong for the twin to become "one" with his brother, thereby becoming a more complete person, this sense of revenge is instinctual (libidinal) and is often directed at the mother, father, or brother.[9]

Twinship studies may be important to psychiatrists but perhaps not to English literature students or drama critics. However, Glenn's research does tell us quite a bit about the origins of Shaffer's own search for identity and how this theme is manifested in virtually all of the plays. Peter and Anthony were raised together as twins, were dressed alike, went to the same schools, worked together as coal miners, went to the same college, coedited the school newspaper, and coauthored two detective novels; eventually, each turned to playwriting.[10] When they wrote their detective novels together, the name of the author cited turned out to be "Peter Antony," a combination of both writers' names.[11] Dr. Glenn also finds it unusual that Peter Shaffer often presents his plays as "twin bills," or two plays that, when taken together, form a coherent whole.[12] *White Lies* was presented with *Black Comedy,* the latter being a play where light and dark were contrasted and presented as opposites (a dark stage was illuminated brightly, and Brindsley's lighted apartment at the end of the play was depicted in total darkness). *The Private Ear* was originally staged with *The Public Eye:* the latter play is about a private eye.[13]

Shaffer, as might be expected, takes a dim view of this sort of criticism of his plays. One must be aware that psychiatrists such as Dr. Glenn obviously have little knowledge of literary criticism and never seem to interpret the play in question as a piece of literature. Instead, Shaffer insists, psychoanalytic approaches to drama often appear limited and biased. Shaffer, who has discussed theater with Dr. Glenn, finds his research to be arrogant, one-sided (he applies the same ideas to every play), distorted, and parasitic.[14]

Almost all of Shaffer's plays dramatize this conflict (whether it is sociological or psychological in origin) of the conservative role player at odds with his rival, his "twin" or double. Shaffer's dramas become a psychological tug-of-war between the liberated half of the "twin" and his staid alter ego who wishes to conform to roles with which he feels comfortable yet would love to abandon. The conservative role player, feeling secure in a world that has been positively sanctioned and approved by others, actually longs to become one with his rival because his alter ego, often seen as a primitive (Atahuallpa, Alan Strang, Mozart), has achieved a sort of independence which is envied by the staid role player.

Shaffer's plays are built upon this conflict between the staid conservative and his liberated alter ego. The role player is often like Shaffer himself. On stage we see an artist or musician (Clive, Bob, Brindsley, or Salieri) trying to find his identity and, at the same time, defend his art/vocation or justify it to others. In the later plays, the conflict between the role player and his primitive "twin" becomes more glaring. Michael Gillespie has noted that the dialectic focuses on an older man's conflict with his younger rival.[15] He goes on to argue that these younger characters—the primitives such as Atahuallpa, Alan Strang, and Mozart—are closer to God than their alter egos are and experience an ecstasy that is equivalent to a spiritual state. Meanwhile, the older role players are excluded from worship and from many other of life's pleasures. These older gentlemen—the characters in whom Shaffer is much more interested than the young, independent free spirits—have lost hope and faith. The result is that they exist in a world of illusion, a spiritual void, with time running out to rejuvenate their "lost" spirits. In essence, many of Shaffer's plays are concerned with this sense of "loss" and how to avoid ending up like such spiritually hollow individuals as Pizarro, Dysart, and Salieri. Shaffer's plays, in effect, deal with "Paradise Lost" or the condition that we all face when we conform to values that are not our own instead of seeking our own sense of identity for ourselves.[16]

In virtually all of Shaffer's plays, those individuals who lack a strong sense of identity find themselves living not only in a world of illusion and artifice but also in a world of lies and hypocrisies. Most of these role players turn out to be liars, and the lies that they tell tend to destroy themselves as well as others. Some of Shaffer's protagonists base their identities on a lie while others try to create a false image of themselves to become the kind of person they secretly yearn to be. At times, these insecure individuals will lash out with lies or learn to live in the lie when their stable environments are threatened. Their alter egos, however, are capable of controlling their own fate and therefore do not have to resort to hiding behind lies. As we will see in the early plays (e.g., *The Public Eye* and *The White Liars*), when the protagonist is completely free as an individual in control of his own life, the lies will cease.

In addition to these social problems that plague Shaffer's insecure heroes, they suffer from sexual inadequacies as well. All of these miserable hypocrites who play roles and lack a strong sense of identity for themselves find that they have sexual problems that often lead to sterility or homosexuality.[17] The single males experience problems when they are near women; most of them have never had a positive sexual relationship with a woman. The married men (Sidley, Dysart, and Salieri) discover that their marriages are simply not working and have wound up being psychologically and physically sterile relationships. Those who have no sense of identity find that sex controls them, rather than vice versa. In contrast, their alter egos believe that "normal" sexuality is whatever is right for them. They are not inhibited in their sexual behavior (Mozart is an obvious example) but "freeze up" when they must sexually perform according to the expectations of others (e.g., Alan Strang). Unfortunately, the role players often set sexual standards that they cannot meet, and sex consequently loses any stimulating value it once had for them. Thus, Shaffer's protagonists, socially isolated individuals, become literally sterile, socially *and* physically, as a graphic representation of their horrible plight.

Shaffer's theater is essentially an investigation into the nature of conformity; it is the single theme that unites all of his major plays. Individuals who conform to roles, social pressures, codified sanctions, and formalized institutional behavior are subject to scrutiny and, ultimately, ridicule. The models of behavior are the "free spirits," the young primitives often engrossed in their own meaningful ritualistic means of communication or worship that is so important to them but is insignificant to anyone else. These alter egos—the Atahuallpas, the Alan Strangs, the Mozarts—create meaning for themselves and are free from the sanctions of peers, parents, or institutions.

At first glance, it would appear that Shaffer is critical of institutions and their oligarchic methods. The critics who argue this point base most of their evidence on Shaffer's only formal attack on institutionalized behavior: *The Royal Hunt of the Sun*. On the surface, the play seems to be a harsh indictment on the usurping powers of church and state. Shaffer, in various interviews, has criticized both institutions for the demeaning way that they debase and control individual behavior.[18] Renee Winegarten even claims that Shaffer, a Jewish writer, is making a statement in *The Royal Hunt of the Sun* not against Christianity per se but against organized religion.[19] The same idea could be applied both to Alan Strang's rebellion against the religious views of his parents in *Equus* and to Salieri's absurd pact with God in *Amadeus* (an ironic situation that intensifies when Salieri confronts Mozart, an irresponsible reprobate who seems to be "beloved by God"). Shaffer is not attacking organized religion nor is he assailing business, industry, or government; instead, the focus is on how certain individuals insist on conforming to established guidelines. Shaffer never explores the inner machinations of established organizations. However, he is interested in how *individuals* conform to group or peer pressure, and whether or not institutions are involved in the relationship is of secondary importance.

Critics may argue that Shaffer's plays are an attack on marriage as an institution. Many of Shaffer's marriages, as seen in his plays, do not work: Stanley and Louise (*Five Finger Exercise*), Sidley and Belinda (*The Public Eye*), Dysart and Margaret (*Equus*), and Salieri and Teresa (*Amadeus*) are the unhappy couples. However, Sophie and Vassili (*White Lies*), Mark Askelon and Giulia (*Shrivings*), and Mozart and Constanze (*Amadeus*) are couples whose marriages were effective. In still other plays—*The Private Ear, The Royal Hunt of the Sun,* and *Black Comedy*—we see the same sort of problems where male-female relationships break down, yet marriage and the family play no part in the drama. Shaffer is not criticizing marriage; instead, the family is seen as a viable institution, the balance often upset by one member's need to conform to a rigid code of behavior.[20] Shaffer's ideal prototype of the family is a "five-finger exercise," where all members of the group function as a well-meshed unit. Shaffer is not arguing that the family, as a unit, cannot work well. He is, however, depicting the breakdown of relationships (couples or families) that splinter because of one individual's stubborn refusal to conform to the mediocre, or to what others want him to be. The result, in Shaffer's microcosm, is that the protagonist is often reduced to sterility, thereby curtailing any normal sexual activity that would be so important in keeping a marriage or relationship active.

Shaffer's plays can best be understood if one grasps these sociological, and somewhat psychological, issues that form the foundation of his weltanschauung. His plays maintain a coherent philosophy and unity of purpose. Of course, even the greatest ideas would not work in the theater without a suitable medium to express them concisely and effectively. In chapter 2, we will see how Shaffer explores his craft to search for a suitable form for his sociological theater.

2

Form Follows Function

PETER Shaffer is constantly engaged in a search for the most appropriate form to convey his sociological messages to the public. Some of Shaffer's early plays seems to be lackluster and do not work well on the contemporary stage. However, because Shaffer has experimented with various forms of drama and with different stage techniques, he was able, through trial and error, to establish an effective ritualistic theater that would work well to dramatize the conflict between the Apollonian and Dionysian forces presented in his plays. Many of the world's great playwrights—Shaw, O'Neill, Williams, Brecht, and Albee, among others—have experimented with forms of theater (many of which did not work well at all) and have written atrocious plays because of such experimentation; in the process of writing plays that were not effective, these playwrights learned what did and did not work on stage. They were therefore able to produce the masterpieces that are universally accepted as great theater. This chapter examines Shaffer's views on theater as art and explores his search for form that culminated in his effective use of ritualistic theater.

Shaffer is a perfectionist. He is obsessed with the art of playwriting and treats it as a sacred and profane act. In the preface to his collected works, Shaffer discussed his obsession with accuracy and detail:

> This quality of *shape* is very important to me. I have always entertained the profoundest respect for art, meaning "artefact," and for the suffix "wright" in the word *playwright*. I hope that all the plays in this book are wrought properly and that they proclaim this fact sufficiently to give audiences a deep satisfaction in their form and their finish. I also hope that these qualities are not too assertively evident—because if a play irritates by seeming to be too well made, this surely means that it has not been well made enough: that the smoothness of the joinery is sealing the work off from the viewer. [1]

Although Shaffer admits to writing *The Private Ear* in just four days, most of his other dramas (e.g., *The Royal Hunt of the Sun, Equus,* and *Amadeus*) took years to write. [2] Shaffer is a slow writer; although he writes scenes quickly, he usually goes through twenty to forty rewrites, discovering a new aspect of the play with each revision.[3] He simply cannot leave well enough alone: "I tear up and I tear up. The waste-paper baskets are always full. It would be good for me if someone said, 'You open at the end of the month. Bloody well get on with it.'"[4]

As a meticulous craftsman of the theater, Shaffer has spent much of his career searching for a suitable form to convey his ideas. He has experimented with realistic drama similar to Ibsen's middle period, farce, one-act plays, melodrama, epic theater, modern tragedy, and musical/operatic theater. In an essay published in *Comparative Drama*, Michael Hinden compares Shaffer's theatrical experiments to O'Neill's search for form.[5] Hinden notes that Shaffer, like O'Neill, toyed with theatrical conventions such as thought asides (*White Lies*), extended monologues (*Shrivings, Amadeus*), mime (*The Royal Hunt of the Sun*), and split protagonists (*Equus*). Shaffer is not merely interested in dialogue, ideas, and character. He realizes, as Aristotle suggested in the *Poetics,* that there is more to theater than just words. Consequently, Shaffer is willing to collaborate with theater directors to do whatever it takes to make the play work "on the boards," including experimenting with lighting, scenic design, music, masks, choruses, sounds and sonority, incantations and rhythms, as well as rites and rituals. In an interview with Shaffer, I asked him which writers or literary artists inspired his work. Interestingly enough, playwrights or actors who work with a combination of the verbal and the mimetic intrigued Shaffer:

> Obviously, the greatest pleasure I've had in the theater is in Shakespeare because, apart from the language, which I glory in more than anything else, I've always enjoyed the variety of his characters and the immensity of his themes. . . . In the past, I've always been much more interested in the way the characters in Shakespeare reveal themselves in action, in what they do, rather than sitting around talking about the past all the time. . . . The people who stimulated my pleasure in the theater were people like John Gielgud and Laurence Olivier—the verbal excitement of one and the visceral excitement of the other. . . . I love the mimetic and gestural side of Brecht's theater, although I don't like the didactic side. Chekhov I like enormously. I don't think that he's influenced my writing, but I always adore seeing his four last great plays, particularly *The Cherry Orchard*—again because of the extraordinary way he mixes, with such apparent ease, the symbolic and the naturalistic.[6]

Perhaps Shaffer's theater is more closely akin to Brecht than to O'Neill. Brecht's political theater was based on a dialectic in which the audience, after viewing the play, would arrive at a consensus of opinion—the synthesis that developed from the thesis and corresponding antithesis of an argument. Brecht encouraged the audience to think or to make choices. His theater was a reaction to the illogical, often hysterical, response of the German people to

Hitler's Third Reich. Thus, Brecht tried to reduce empathy (Einfühlungsvermögen) in the theater and make drama more "scientific" wherein the spectator made up his or her own mind through a dialectic that supposedly presented both sides to the argument without regard to persuasive rhetorical techniques.[7] Brecht incorporated a number of theatrical conventions—filmstrips, newsreels, headlines, posters, masks, and songs—to reduce empathy for the characters on stage, thereby "alienating" the audience. He distanced the audience in time (often setting the play hundreds of years earlier rather than in modern times), in place (anywhere but modern Germany), and in action (just when the audience would begin to identify with the protagonist on stage, other characters would be introduced or a different plot would develop). Frequently, Brecht used a narrator to interrupt the play when he thought that the audience was becoming too familiar with the *characters* on stage. The narrator's function was to refocus our attention on the *ideas* presented on stage, without regard to the audience's identification with any particular character in the play.

Shaffer's major plays are Brechtian. The audience is forced to take sides in a dialectical struggle between two opposing forces. The protagonist, a staid and often sterile role player, is faced with his alter ego, a primitive spirit who is not controlled by roles, rules, or institutionalized behavior. Shaffer's audience is forced to think in the theater. We witness the struggle between the Apollonian and Dionysian forces of reason versus instinct, and we are asked to take sides objectively (with a little help from the author, again in the Brechtian tradition). At times, the audience is asked to assess the guilt of the protagonist based upon historical events (*The Royal Hunt of the Sun, Amadeus*). C. J. Gianakaris suggests that some of Shaffer's plays are like courtroom dramas, with the protagonist defending his conduct as if he were being tried by a jury.[8] In *Equus,* the setting is similar to a boxing ring (recall Brecht's ideal vision of drama as being "smoking theater" much like a prizefight) or some type of arena arranged for combat. Shaffer, however, does not use theatrical devices solely to create a distancing effect, nor is he interested in reducing empathy for the characters on stage. Shaffer, like Brecht, does use various stage techniques to remind us that we are in the theater, a place of magic and illusion that is not to be confused with reality. Although some of Shaffer's plays are Aristotelian, many are not, and there is often no unity of time or place. Some of the plays are set in the present, but most of what see on stage is a flashback to an earlier period. With regard to unity of place, *The Royal Hunt of the Sun* spans continents, and *Equus's* setting changes from scene to scene. Often, the protagonist functions as a narrator to talk directly to the audience (e.g., *The Royal Hunt of the Sun, Equus, Amadeus,* and *Yonadab*). In addition, Shaffer has used a chorus or choral element to repeat important information for an audience that is forced to make decisions by the end of the play. Moreover, the episodic structure of the later plays is similar to Brecht's idea of "gestus" where each scene stands alone as a separate piece of information, quite different from the Aristotelian notion of having each scene move the plot one step further along.

The core of Shaffer's drama, like Brecht's "parable" for the theater, is scientific: we are to think about what we see on stage and perhaps learn from it. However, the sociological/political (and, at times, didactic) nature of Shaffer's and Brecht's theater is often lost because of the heavy emphasis on stage techniques. Because Shaffer experiments with lighting, masks, choral elements, ritualistic gestures, stylized costuming, and scenic design, he has been repeatedly accused of being "too theatrical," thereby allowing stage conventions to overshadow any important ideas he presents on stage. Shaffer has a strong response to this sort of drama criticism:

> People who quite like one's work but want to put it down a bit say "well, it's very theatrical, of course." I always find that very odd. It's almost as if you are making a pejorative remark about a painter by saying of course it's painterly.
>
> My quarrel with a lot of London is that it's not theatrical enough, it does not use the medium of theatre nearly enough. I am tired of seeing a one-set play with two people whining at each other all night or delivering a sequence of lectures to the audience. It doesn't seem to me to be what the theatre is for.[9]

Shaffer, often stung by theater reviewers who refuse to judge his plays as total theater but instead insist on evaluating drama solely as a means of expressing beautiful language, reacts harshly to the accusations labeled against him:

> They are apt to say about a play, with a condescending inflection, "Well, that was certainly *theatrical*"—as if the word were an accusation. For a certain kind of limited mind, of course, it is an accusation. Such a mind cannot receive visceral experience, is blind to gesture, is deeply irritated by the sight of an audience being moved by a dramatic experience . . . and judges the worth of any play solely by the verbalized thoughts it can detach from it, as if they were cherries sunk in jam.
>
> Theater itself is actually a source of fear to this kind of man. He sometimes tries to exorcise this fear by working as a drama critic.[10]

Although Shaffer has learned over the years how to use stage techniques with flair and precision, underlying the *mise-en-scène* is a strong foundation built on the well-made play tradition. Shaffer learned the essentials of good plot construction when he wrote and polished his three detective novels in the late 1940s and early 1950s. Most of his dramas (major and minor), no matter how ritualized or ceremonial the effects may be, are carefully constructed in the tradition of a nineteenth-century Sherlock Holmes novel.

Shaffer is adept at telling a story or piecing the parts of a puzzle together to unravel a "whodunit." The construction may be Ibsen-like where one scene builds on the information contained in the previous scene, or it may consist of flashbacks that, when assimilated collectively, provide us with the necessary pieces to make the puzzle fit together. Shaffer insists on weaving a story with a beginning, middle, and end: "I'm afraid we're coming away from one of the main essentials of a good play, namely a story. Think of the great dramas of history and inevitably you come upon a narrative—*Hamlet, Lear, Electra, Oedipus.*"[11] Shaffer, the master at taking a historical incident or a newspaper clipping and turning it into a story for the stage (e.g., the Spanish conquest of Mexico, a young man's blinding of twenty-six horses, the Mozart-Salieri relationship), discussed why his ability to tell stories is essential to good playwriting:

> I remember when I was in Morocco some years ago, I went into that huge market square one evening, and there was an enormous crowd of people sitting on the ground, listening to an itinerant story-teller, and I'd never seen such an electric expectation on faces before, and I remember feeling—if only one could get that atmosphere into an audience in a theatre, one would be doing very good work. So many times, audiences can come out feeling, with modern plays—yes, the characters were very good, and that moment was wonderfully directed. But these appear to me to be subsidiary elements. What the audiences seem also to come out feeling is slightly starved, cheated. If you've ever had the experience of telling a child a bedtime story, and watching the way a child hangs on your suspension of its disbelief, I think you will receive a terrific lesson in playwriting. I know playwriting can't be taught, but there are all sorts of universities and colleges that do set out to teach it, and I think one of the pieces of homework they should set is actually to make up and convey a tale to an expectant child in bed at night.[12]

All of Shaffer's plays are carefully constructed and demonstrate an ability to develop logical plots with unified action and complex characters. However, in the early plays, there is less emphasis on total theater or ritualistic drama, partly because Shaffer was learning his trade and did not have the confidence to experiment with the more innovative forms of theater. What he knew and understood was the well-made play tradition, so that is what he practiced. Furthermore, Shaffer, because of family constraints that had forced him to consider career avenues other than playwriting, was more apt initially to begin writing conventional rather than experimental drama. Later in his career, when Shaffer became more confident of himself and when he learned more about the craft of playwriting, he was able to construct plays that more closely resembled total theater—the ritualistic catharsis Shaffer wanted to create on stage.

Although Shaffer's early well-made plays were successful, he was not pleased with them. Writing detective novels had helped Shaffer develop a logical structure that created the foundation for his early, carefully crafted plays. During my interview with Shaffer, he mentioned that "when I did my detective stories, I think it did help me. It stimulated a pleasure in deploying material to the best advantage in an artful and effective manner."[13] The early plays taught him how to construct plots, develop characters, and create a sense of time and place; yet these realistic dramas were not his forte: "I think I always wanted to do strictly nonnaturalistic plays. . . . And I always wanted to write plays involving total theatre. By that, I mean theatre that is, of course, a text fulfilled by gesture, and ritual and music."[14] For Shaffer, theater is a place of wonderment, a means of exploring the mind and the soul through ceremonies, rites, and rituals. In a 1975 interview with Tom Buckley of *The New York Times,* Shaffer commented on the contrast between his early and late plays:

> I had always wanted to do, I realize now, something dealing with the numinous, if that's the word. . . . but in terms of what is on the surface a rather doubting, provincial situation. To take, in other words, as in *Equus,* an electrical shop, a semidetached house, a riding stable, and conjure the same dark forces as in *The Royal Hunt of the Sun*.[15]

Shaffer views the theater as a means of psychoanalytically exploring sociological, philosophical, and metaphysical ideas. In addition, drama for Shaffer becomes a tool to probe the inner recesses of the mind: imagination, instinct, and intuition. In a 1974 interview with Glenn Loney, Shaffer discussed the current state of theater arts: "What's wrong with the theater is that it's still recording external appearances of people in situations. We've had enough of that. People pouring out drinks and spouting lines: what they *say* they believe. These are really external things. As opposed to what's inside their heads!"[16] Perhaps Shaffer's reference to "people pouring out drinks and spouting lines" is more of a critique of his early plays than it is of the Ibsenite social dramas of writers such as Albee or O'Neill. On a number of occasions, Shaffer has stated that the goal of theater is to incite the imagination and to fuel our inner drives, instincts, and archetypes.[17] Shaffer sees theater as an awe-inspiring place of entertainment and worship, much like a church or temple: "The theater should lead people into mystery and magic; it should give them a sense of wonderment, and while entertaining reveal a vision of life."[18]

In writing his mature plays—*The Royal Hunt of the Sun, Equus,* and *Amadeus*—Shaffer tried to create ritualistic/incantatory drama, his ideal vision of what theater should represent. According to Shaffer, rites and rituals were an essential element of total theater: "People go to the theater for many reasons, but mainly, I think to be surprised. Surprised *by* things and *into* things: by beauty and into beauty: by rite into reality."[19] To Shaffer, the theater is more than words or dialogue; it is a place for cathartic release of archetypal drives: "I passionately believe that people come to the theatre to be surprised, moved, illuminated. They're not interested simply in what they're *hearing*. They're receiving what you say viscerally."[20]

In his essay, "The Cannibal Theater," Shaffer describes his dramas as rituals in which the actors participate in a communal performance composed of rites and ceremonies: "The rehearsal of a serious play is an elaborate and quietly awful ceremony of fertilization; a ritual, despite its frequent appearance of disorganization and its very real air of friendliness, of sacrifice and rebirth."[21] Shaffer's essay views theater as archetypal, with the actors performing any play as a sort of exorcism for them, much more in line with the theoretical views of Artaud or Grotowski. Shaffer sees the actors as a primitive tribe rather than a fraternity, and he compares them to priests exorcising their demons.[22] Using language that would be familiar to readers of James G. Frazer's *The Golden Bough,* Shaffer cannot resist the emphasis on archetypal imagery:

> *For the actor dies between roles, and comes to work seeking his spring.* It is not an accident that we speak of the theatrical "season." Under that trivial word you may see primal planting, the earth wetted with lifeblood, the shoots emerging, thickening, talling, harvested, and eaten: a corn of text, and words becoming flesh.[23]

In a similar vein, Shaffer embellished the role of the playwright who is "accepted as God-King; he is felt to contain some truth without which the players cannot live. He is treated with deference, consulted, danced before. He speaks, or his interpreter speaks for him, and is eagerly obeyed."[24] The catharsis that culminates from this ritualistic drama affects the playwright as much as it does the actors or the audience: "He also seeks rebirth, and the only way for him to achieve it is to be liberated from his old play, to have the obsessional demon who first beat it from the cover of his unrest haled out of his body in the fullness of performance. The actor is the playwright's exorcist."[25]

Shaffer's early plays explored sociological ideas concerning role playing and one's need to establish a strong identity that is not dependent on societal pressures. However, there often was no clear-cut dialectic between the role player and his primitive alter ego. In Shaffer's mature plays, freedom from roles and social mores is depicted in the form of primitives (Atahuallpa, Mark Askelon, Alan Strang, Mozart) who worship according to their own needs, depending on no one for the source of their inspiration.

To dramatize the unique nature of these primitives, Shaffer abandoned his early well-made play style and ritualized the drama, creating a rhythmic structure throughout the play. The ritual or incantatory effect presented in Shaffer's plays provides the audience with an unconscious or intuitive appre-

ciation of the basic drives and instincts of these primitives in contrast to the
role player. In addition, the ritualistic form of worship that Shaffer's primitive heroes practice often serves to "unmask" the role player, making him
see life in its most liberated state. The ritualistic/rhythmic structure often
presents an educational experience in which the highly sophisticated, "civilized" individual learns from these "primitives," who frequently appear to
be coarse or barbaric persons. As Rodney Simard has stated in *Postmodern
Drama: Contemporary Playwrights in America and Britain,* "As it appears in all
of his [Shaffer's] major works, ritual affirms the necessity for subjectively
apprehending and ordering one's individual existence in an inherently cha-
otic world."[26] The learning experience is often a rite of passage from the
listless state of role playing to a state of awareness in which the individual
matures and begins to accept his alter ego's behavior as a superior alternative
to his own sterile existence. The ritual, as seen in the rhythmic structure of
Shaffer's plays and in the ceremonial nature of the primitive's lifestyle, is the
means of codifying the change that the sterile role player (and the audience)
experiences when confronted by this new awareness of identity exemplified
by the unfettered lives of Shaffer's primitives.

When one thinks of ritualistic drama and total theater, Artaud comes to
mind. It is important to understand Artaud's theories on drama because
perhaps no other playwright or theorist influenced the form of Shaffer's
plays more than this French *metteur en scène* did. It is no secret that *The Royal
Hunt of the Sun* is extraordinarily similar to Artaud's plans for the staging of
The Conquest of Mexico, the spectacle he proposed for the first production of
his Theatre of Cruelty. Numerous reviewers have mentioned the parallels
between *The Royal Hunt of the Sun, Equus,* and *Amadeus* and Artaud's
ritualistic drama. In addition, various directors associated with Shaffer's
dramas or screenplays—Peter Brook, Peter Hall, and John Dexter—are well
schooled in Artaudian stage techniques. In 1964, Shaffer even participated in
a roundtable discussion on Artaud with such notables as Brook, Hall,
Charles Marowitz, and Michel St. Denis. An understanding of Artaud will
provide us with a better insight into Shaffer's more mature plays.

In *Le théâtre et son double (The Theater and Its Double),* Artaud proposed a
theater of exorcism that would hypnotize the spectator and free his repressed unconscious state. The unconscious, the id, or archetypal images
form the core of Artaud's theater: "In the true theater a play disturbs the
senses' repose, frees the repressed unconscious, incites a kind of virtual
revolt. . . ."[27] Artaud's writing constantly emphasizes a Jungian theater that
explores rites, rituals, and rhythmic patterns associated with archetypes
ingrained in our unconscious:

> The theater will never find itself again—i.e., constitute a means of true
> illusion—except by furnishing the spectator with the truthful precipitates
> of dreams, in which his taste for crime, his erotic obsessions, his savagery,

his chimeras, his utopian sense of life and matter, even his cannibalism, pour out, on a level not counterfeit or illusory, but interior.[28]

Artaud's theories on his Theatre of Cruelty, germinated by his association with Roger Vitrac and Le Théâtre d'Alfred Jarry and by impressive performances by a Balinese dance troupe at the Colonial Exposition in Paris in 1931 and even earlier by Cambodian dancers who performed in Artaud's native city of Marseilles in 1922, were formulated in letters to André Gide, Louis Jouvet, Jacques Rivière, and Jean Paulhan. In *Le théâtre et son double,* a compilation of dramatic criticism written between 1931 and 1936, Artaud discussed the concept of cruelty, a term that is often misunderstood and only tangentially relates to violence. In a 1932 letter to Jean Paulhan, Artaud defined the term: "From the point of view of the mind, cruelty signifies rigor, implacapable intention and decision, irreversible and absolute determination."[29] He goes on to state that

it is a mistake to give the word "cruelty" a meaning of merciless bloodshed and disinterested, gratuitous pursuit of physical suffering. . . . In the practice of cruelty there is a kind of higher determinism, to which the executioner-tormentor himself is subjected and which he must be *determined* to endure when the time comes. Cruelty is above all lucid, a kind of rigid control and submission to necessity.[30]

Artaud believed that our repressed unconscious was dominated by violent and evil emotions ingrained in our minds since childhood. Artaud wanted to expose the spectator to the evils of his archetypal nature and then purge those latent drives and instincts from his psyche. Thus, the purgation effect of the Theatre of Cruelty is actually a catharsis that works first by subjecting the spectator to the Dionysiac side of his unconscious state and then releasing the tension through a dissipation of these destructive, and often frustrating, inner drives. In an essay on the Le Théâtre d'Alfred Jarry, Artaud described this type of catharsis:

The spectator who comes to our theater knows that he is to undergo a real operation in which not only his mind but his senses and his flesh are at stake. Henceforth he will go to the theater the way he goes to the surgeon or the dentist. In the same state of mind—knowing, of course, that he will not die, but that it is a serious thing, and that he will not come out of it unscathed. If we were not convinced that we would reach him as deeply as possible, we would consider ourselves inadequate to our most absolute duty. He must be totally convinced that we are capable of making him scream.[31]

Thus, according to Artaud, the theater is like the plague: it is communicative and it cleanses (the actor, the spectator, and even the playwright). Artaud wants the spectator to come face to face with the plague or with evil itself so he or she can be purged of it.[32] It is a theater of abreaction in which the spectator recognizes his own frustrations and anxieties by what he sees on stage, then is dissected, even tormented, before being healed.[33] The cleansing and purification were to lead to an intuitive perception of metaphysical ideas; to present this type of drama on stage, Artaud knew that he had to reform the nature of theater by transforming sociological and psychological plays popular in France during the 1930s into ritualistic drama similar to the oriental theater that so impressed him.

Although Artaud's Theatre of Cruelty is not to be confused with acts of aggression, Artaud is explicit when he states that a major goal of this type of theater is to release our latent sexual and evil desires: "If the essential theater is like the plague, it is not because it is contagious, but because like the plague it is the revelation, the bringing forth, the exteriorization of a depth of latent cruelty by means of which all the perverse possibilities of the mind, whether of an individual or a people, are localized."[34] The theater liberates or purifies in the same manner as a religious rite or ceremony. In order for drama to affect our latent unconscious drives in a vigorous way, Artaud insisted that the theater resemble rites and rituals—actually, the origins of tragedy in ancient Greece. The model was to be the ritualistic Balinese theater:

> The Balinese productions take shape at the very heart of matter, life, reality. There is in them something of the ceremonial quality of a religious rite, in the sense that they extirpate from the mind of the onlooker all idea of pretense, of cheap imitations of reality. . . . The thoughts it aims at, the spiritual states it seeks to create, the mystic solutions it proposes are aroused and attained without delay or circumlocution. All of which seems to be an exorcism to make our demons FLOW.[35]

Artaud believed that through signs, rites, and "sacred ceremonies," theater would be able to transform life into a series of elaborate rituals that would expand our awareness of ourselves: "The true purpose of theater is to create Myths, to express life in its immense, universal aspect, and from that life to extract images in which we find pleasure in discovering ourselves."[36]

Artaud proposed a ritualistic type of drama that would convey a carefully calculated rhythmic effect from start to finish: "The overlapping of images and movements will culminate, through the collusion of objects, silences, shouts, and rhythms, or in a genuine physical language with signs, not words, as its root."[37] The play itself must have a code of movement, including appropriate gestures, signs or hieroglyphs, intonations, lighting, music, and dialogue whereby words have an incantatory effect—all designed to create a unified rhythmic sensibility on stage.[38] The director is the doctor, the therapeutic agent or priest (one who forces the spectator to confess) controlling the ritual; the playwright may present a script, but it is the director's responsibility to make it flow as a unified rite.

Artaud's *mise-en-scène* is actually total theater. E. T. Kirby, in his book, *Total Theatre,* defined the term:

> Theatre as the place of intersection of all the arts, is, then the meaning of "total theatre." We most often find this totality indicated by a list of components such as music, movement, voice, scenery, lighting, etc. More important, however, is the understanding that there must be an interplay among the various elements or a significant synthesis of them.[39]

Artaud is interested in appealing to the senses—this is the essence of his theater, and whatever brings the spectator back to logical and rational thought processes is to be suppressed. Artaud hoped to create a form of poetry in space, and he believed that words were only one component of that calculated rhythm: "This very difficult and complex poetry assumes many aspects: especially the aspects of all the means of expression utilizable on the stage, such as music, dance, plastic art, pantomime, mimicry, gesticulation, intonation, architecture, lighting, and scenery."[40] In short, Artaud can never be accused of being "too theatrical"; these words have no meaning because, according to Artaud, stage convention is what makes the play flow. Sounds, cries, and groans are linked with movements, surprises of all kinds, incantational music, and rhythmic lighting effects to create a "total theater" that works on the archetypal or unconscious level. Artaud, echoing some of the ideas of Gordon Craig, Adolphe Appia, Bertolt Brecht, Vsevolod Meyerhold, Max Reinhardt, and Yevgeny Vakhtangov, believed that "the stage is a concrete physical place which asks to be filled, and to be given its own concrete language to speak."[41] In other words, drama is not merely dialogue or words; stage techniques can be just as important as language.

Artaud has been criticized, and often misunderstood, with regard to his ideas on the importance of language and speech in the theater. Artaud's criticism of playwrights who favor *only* the spoken language while eschewing gestures or signs, derives from the idea that denotative language addresses the mind rather than the senses: "I say that this concrete language, intended for the senses and independent of speech, has first to satisfy the senses, that there is a poetry of the senses as there is a poetry of language, and that this concrete physical language to which I refer is truly theatrical only to the degree that the thoughts it expresses are beyond the reach of the spoken language."[42]

In a draft of a letter to the director of the Alliance Française in 1935, Artaud explained the importance of language in the theater: "Not that speech is despised, but it is taken in its concrete state, for its vibratory and sonorous value. It gives rise to gesture and gesture has given rise to it; and gesture has ceased to be conditioned by it. And in this way a kind of new poetry appears in space."[43] Artaud was interested in using language in new ways—to produce physical shock, to create a musical or rhythmic effect, and to consider speech as a form of incantation. He was opposed to using language merely as argument and to advance conversation.[44] In his essay on oriental and occidental theater in *Le théâtre et son double,* Artaud insisted that "it is not a matter of suppressing speech in the theater but of changing its role, and especially of reducing its position, of considering it as something else than a means of conducting human characters to their external ends since the theater is concerned only with the way feelings and passions conflict with one another, and man with man, in life."[45] In short, language has its place in the theater, but it is merely one part of the codified rhythmic structure of a play. Language must function on the unconscious as well as the denotative levels: "It is not a question of suppressing the spoken language, but of giving words approximately the importance they have in dreams."[46]

Artaud stressed the *mise-en-scène* as much as he did the rhythmic effects of music and language. The goal was to surprise and shock the spectator into a new sense of awareness. Artaud advocated using musical instruments as part of the decor and to produce a wide array of vibratory ranges; arranging various lighting effects to move the spectator to anxiety, terror, love, or eroticism; abolishing the stage and replacing it with a single site or space for direct communication between actor and spectator; using ritualistic or ancient, not modern, costumes to capture the magic and mystery of the unknown; reducing the importance of words in favor of sign language, gestures, and hieroglyphs; replacing a set decor with props that are solely used as stimuli for archetypal responses; and creating masks to relate symbolically to the concrete language of the stage, much in the manner in which they were used in the ancient Greek theater.

Peter Shaffer's mature plays are comprised of many of these Artaudian ideas. The astute drama critic already familiar with Shaffer's canon will immediately conjure visions of ritualistic dances in *The Royal Hunt of the Sun,* pagan rites in *Shrivings,* Alan's orgiastic midnight ride in *Equus,* or the rhythmic structure of *Amadeus.*[47]

As was mentioned previously, Shaffer's early plays were realistic "kitchen-sink" dramas that Shaffer felt comfortable with at that time in his career. Later, when he developed more confidence as a playwright and as he experimented with various forms of drama, he rejected the well-made play tradition in favor of total theater. Ritualistic drama, in particular, allowed him to present the conflict between the protagonist and his "primitive" alter ego who existed only according to a code of behavior that he created for himself, not for other individuals.

The mature Shaffer is much like Artaud in that they have the same goals: to produce a type of theater that would unconsciously stimulate our basic drives, impulses, archetypes, or instincts. As we have already seen in his essay, "The Cannibal Theater," Shaffer considers drama to be ritual or ceremony, an elaborate rite (usually a rite of passage in which the protagonist matures and learns from his alter ego) in which there is a catharsis or purging of the audience's hidden, and often evil, drives. In an important interview in *Vogue,* Shaffer mentioned that he appreciates the work of Jung and seemed, in one line, to sum up this fusion of form and content in his plays: ". . . but the more one comes to realize that the cells of one's brain contain endless archetypal images that stretch back beyond the Stone Age, the more one can come to an immense and important sense of who one is, for himself, instead of just a little worried package of responses and reflexes, sexual drives and frustrations."[48]

In Shaffer's mature plays, the spectators, who identify with an ambitious, role-playing, often middle-class protagonist, are purged of their sins and "confess" their evils along with the protagonist. As the spectators watch the primitive rituals of Atahuallpa or Alan Strang, they are not only internalizing the cathartic pleas of the protagonist but are also intuitively developing their own assumptions through the rites, rituals, and rhythmic structures of Shaffer's plays.

Shaffer, who believes that theater must surprise the spectator and prey upon his or her imagination, has created in his later plays his own form of Artaudian total theater. Shaffer defined "total theater" in his introduction to *The Royal Hunt of the Sun,* also reproduced in a 1965 interview with *The New York Times:* "I mean by the word a theater that is gestural as well as verbal, hallucinatory as well as cerebral—*magical,* if that word isn't now too debased to use."[49]

Total theater plays a major part in the structure of Shaffer's later plays and is very similar to what Artaud had in mind. Artaud's desire to present violence, sexuality, and evil on stage so as to purge or heal the audience from the "sickness" from which it was suffering can be seen in Pizarro's guilt over the Spanish rape of the Incas in *The Royal Hunt of the Sun,* Alan's relationship with and subsequent blinding of the horses in *Equus,* and Salieri's jealousy of Mozart concerning job and career in *Amadeus.* Artaud was quite concerned with "sonorization" or incantatory sound effects; Shaffer often fills the stages with ritualistic or rhythmic chants, cries, or groans, and a chorus is sometimes used to reinforce the vibratory qualities of the words. Shaffer experiments with a single setting to unite spectators and actors (*Equus*), with mood lighting, with ritualistic or ancient costumes (*The Royal Hunt of the Sun*), with gestures and mime, and with highly stylized stage scenery that is far removed from a realistic or naturalistic setting but indeed serves to intensify the ritualistic quality of the drama.

Most importantly, Shaffer insists that his plays be built on a carefully calculated rhythm that unites all of these Artaudian elements. Artaud believed that the playwright was subservient to the director, the master of sacred ceremonies and the person who makes the play flow. Shaffer, however, views his role differently: "It's true that in the theatre there is a triumvirate. There are the director, the actors, and the playwright, and there could be deficiencies anywhere. But the playwright is still the most important. If he writes a bad play, nothing can be done."[50] Nevertheless, Shaffer has frequently turned his plays over to strong-willed directors who knew how to shape the play into the type of total theater for which Shaffer strived and who were more familiar than Shaffer with regard to choreographing the various rites and rituals.

Shaffer's forte is the distinct and precise ear that he has for the type of musical or rhythmic structure needed to make total theater flow. Throughout his life, Shaffer has been a connoisseur of music, classical as well as modern. His parents encouraged his musical talents, initiating him into a life-long appreciation of the arts. He learned to play the piano as a child, easily mastered the sonatas of Haydn, Mozart, and Chopin, and still plays in his leisure time. Shaffer's early training in musical arts eventually found its application in his plays: "Music has been a source of immense pleasure to me ever since, and hardly a day goes by when I do not spend at least an hour playing the piano. I find that ideas tend to rearrange themselves in the proper order at the keyboard, and this can be very helpful when one is in the throes of working out a plot."[51]

Shaffer, in the beginning of his career, spent as much time as a music critic than he did in literary circles. In the early 1950s, he worked for music publishers Boosey and Hawkes and in 1961 was music critic for *Time and Tide*. Occasionally, Shaffer felt the urge to write a piece of musical criticism himself rather than just edit catalogues or scores.[52] Shaffer acknowledges that music would have been a logical career choice for him had he not chosen playwriting. In an early interview with *Life,* Shaffer explained the correlation between music and playwriting, stating that he was interested in music as a career because "you don't need words. All the great effects in life are nonverbal—which is a galling thing for a writer to admit."[53]

Music plays a major part in most of Shaffer's plays either in the form of musical interludes reinforcing nonverbal communication in a particular scene or in determining the structure of the play itself, as in *Amadeus*. During my interview with Shaffer, he discussed the influence of music on the structure of his plays:

> I love the opera and operatic technique. . . . I think *Amadeus* is a very operatic play; I think *Equus* to some extent is. *Royal Hunt* unquestionably is. I don't just mean rhythmic in structure but also in its stylization. There's almost something choric about it. For example, the Venticelli in

Amadeus. They are like the overture in the beginning of *The Marriage of Figaro*. It's an overture to something but it's an operatic one and not naturalistic, obviously; and yet it is conveying how gossips operate and the effect they create.[54]

Five Finger Exercise, Shaffer's first major success, was originally conceived of as a sort of fugue for five "instruments," or characters in this instance. Piano music from Bach and Brahms is interwoven throughout the drama and plays an integral part in driving a wedge between the cultured tradition with which Walter feels at ease and Stanley Harrington, who has an inferiority complex when it comes to appreciation of the arts. In *The Private Ear,* Bob, a musician nicknamed Tchaik for Tchaikovsky, has met Doreen at a concert and has invited her to his apartment for the evening. The soirée is punctuated with conversations about Bach, Britten, and Tchaikovsky, with appropriate musical selections again moving the play along. In *The White Liars,* Shaffer depicts a relationship based on an intuitive understanding between Sophie, who was raised on Brahms and was inculcated by her father to appreciate the finest music in Austria, and Tom, a sensitive musician who is out of place in the band in which he performs. *The Royal Hunt of the Sun* is filled with musical interludes, ritualistic chants, Inca songs and dances, and stichomythic dialogue, producing a deliberate and continuous rhythm throughout the play. The same type of rhythmic pattern occurs in *Equus,* with the chorus creating a humming noise to illustrate the presence of Alan's horse-god. The Equus noise and the ritualistic chanting again serve to focus our attention on an archetypal communion with the primitive (Alan Strang) and his strange form of worship. With regard to *Amadeus,* Shaffer has written that "what I wanted to emerge clearly from the play is the obsession of a man, Salieri . . . with finding an absolute in music."[55] Mozart's music is essential to the underlying structure of both the play and the film. When the spectator hears Mozart's sonatas, arias, and operas, he or she is able to understand intuitively why Salieri was tormented and why he envied Mozart as he did.[56]

Despite the many similarities between Artaud and Shaffer, the two playwrights have fundamental differences of opinion concerning dramatic theory. Some critics argue that Shaffer is closer to a theater of sensationalism than to Artaud's concept of Theatre of Cruelty.[57] Other critics cite the fact that Shaffer's theater stresses psychological and sociological issues that Artaud so despised and wanted to eliminate from the modern stage. There are some important differences between the two styles of theater, but, on the whole, Shaffer's basic intention to create a theater of exorcism in which the struggle between Apollonian and Dionysian forces is intuitively perceived by the audience through a rhythmic structure unconsciously received by the spectator reflects the underlying thrust of Artaud's intentions.

One major difference between Artaud and Shaffer concerns the way language is used in the theater. Shaffer uses language to create a rhythmic, incantatory effect that would appeal to Artaud, yet Shaffer also views language as a functional tool to make us think and feel. In Shaffer's plays, we find a carefully calculated choice of words; he is meticulous about his vocabulary and is adept at reproducing variations in the English language that extend from a working-class cockney accent to the pomposity of the British tea room. During Shaffer's roundtable discussion on Artaud, already alluded to in this chapter, he was asked about his views on Artaud's vision of "the death of the word." Shaffer defended his denotative use of language in contrast to Artaud's position:

> It's remarkable, in fact, that a man who had declared that the word is totally meaningless spent so much of his time hammering away at words. . . . But one never attacks lethally the word itself, the idea of writing a play, the idea of destroying the basis on which drama exists, which is indeed a ritual, a celebration of something.[58]

Even more crucial than their differences concerning language is the fact that Shaffer's theater, its *raison d'être*, is sociological and psychological in its orientation. These sociological motifs, anathema to Artaud, are embedded in the dialectical nature of almost all of Shaffer's plays. In response to Artaud's diatribe on western theater's dependence on existential or psychological drama as opposed to the metaphysical, Shaffer remarked that "when he says the psychological drama is dead, this seems to me to be absolutely rubbish—it has hardly begun."[59]

Shaffer's awareness of the need to combine important sociological ideas with a type of ritualistic drama that would embellish the Apollonian-Dionysian dialectic makes him a more well-rounded playwright than Artaud was. Artaud, essentially a surrealist by practice, tradition, and orientation, was important in helping to mold the form of the modern theater but was not able to realize that surrealism, the juxtaposition of words and images in a random or unconscious manner, was not enough to make a play *work* on stage. Shaffer, however, is the consummate man of the theater who has paid particular attention to the most suitable coordination of language, form, content, and stage technique. He has the unique ability to combine Brechtian theater with Artaudian stage conventions. Using a Brechtian dialectic, Shaffer makes us think about existential and sociological issues concerning one's identity in society; at the same time, the Artaudian stage techniques make the plays work on a mythical or metaphysical level. Perhaps this is the main reason why Shaffer's plays have been so successful: they not only entertain, but they work on many different levels, appealing to a wide variety of interests, from the esoteric to the purely sensational.

3
The Early/Unpublished Works:
Minor Chords

THE information contained in Shaffer's early and unpublished works, including the detective novels, as well as the radio and television scripts, supplies the astute critic with the necessary keys to unlock the mysteries of Shaffer's more complex theatrical endeavors. A look at Shaffer's experiments with these minor works suggests that his apprenticeship enabled him to determine more readily what type of language and structures were most effective for his purposes.

I will provide a summary of the novels since they are not readily available, and very few readers will thus be familiar with them.

Shaffer's first novel, *The Woman in the Wardrobe*, written under the pseudonym of Peter Antony, was published in London in 1951.[1] The subtitle of this ten-chapter book described the novel as "a light-hearted detective story." Most of the novel is written in dialogue form, suggesting perhaps that drama might be the ideal medium even for the early works, much in the manner that Agatha Christie's fiction has worked on stage.

The setting of the novel is the town of Amnestie, a seaside resort in Sussex. Mr. Verity, described as a "laughing cavalier" sort of gentleman, is a well-respected, well-traveled sixty-six-year-old detective accustomed to solving murder mysteries between tea and supper. He is about to embark on one of the most tenacious assignments he has ever tackled.

Taking his morning stroll, Mr. Verity notices a man climbing into one of the windows of the Charter Hotel. Verity enters the hotel and informs the manageress, Miss Framer, of the incident. Just then, Mr. Paxton, the fellow climbing on the balcony, runs downstairs and tells Verity and Framer that Maxwell, a guest at the hotel, is dead. While all of this excitement is going on, another guest at the hotel, Mr. Cunningham, is caught by a constable while scurrying down the drainpipe after leaving Maxwell's room. Upon investigating, Verity and his cohort, police inspector Jackson, find that Maxwell's room is locked from the inside. The case becomes curiouser when Mr. Verity shoots off the lock and finds the key to the door on the carpet near a recently fired gun that obviously appears to be the murder weapon. The events become more complicated when the police also discover that Maxwell's window had been locked from the inside. The detectives soon notice that someone is in the closet: Alice Burton, a waitress at the hotel. Miss Burton claims that she had been bringing breakfast up to Maxwell's room when a masked man appeared and argued with Maxwell over money matters. Alice Burton fainted and woke up tied and gagged in the closet. Mr. Verity listens intently to Burton's story, but he hardly believes it because of the unexplained locked door and window.

Mr. Verity begins his investigation. He learns that Maxwell had been at the hotel for only five days, yet he knew everyone there. As Verity questions each person individually, he discovers that Maxwell was fond of collecting secret, often privileged, information about people, with the intention of bribing them. Everyone in the hotel hated Maxwell; Mr. Verity was not finding it difficult to find motives for the murder: any of the suspects could have committed the crime. Especially suspect is Mr. Cunningham, for it was his gun that was found in Maxwell's room.

Two other individuals are also interviewed. First, there is Richard Tudor, an eccentric guest at the hotel who claims to be King Richard the Fourth, the rightful heir to the throne of England—and he has documents to prove it. Perhaps a more viable suspect is Alice Burton's fiancé, Ted Winnidge, who had threatened to kill Maxwell if he did not stop pestering Alice, one of Maxwell's many bribe victims. In addition, Reverend Robertson saw Winnidge and Maxwell quarrel on the morning of the murder, culminating in Winnidge carrying the unconscious loser of the argument up the stairs to the hotel. Mr. Verity is not sure if Winnidge killed Maxwell and then carried the dead body up to the room or whether Maxwell was killed later in the day. The events become more complicated as Verity learns that on the alleged murder weapon were the fingerprints of Alice Burton, Paxton, *and* Cunningham.

As Mr. Verity and his associate Rambler examine each suspect individually, the detectives are told one lie after another. The remainder of the novel becomes a quest for the "truth," as Mr. Verity unravels all of these lies to find a logical solution to the murder. Later we will see how the question-and-answer motif to derive the truth becomes the basis not only for Shaffer's other novels but also for plays such as *Five Finger Exercise, The White Liars, Shrivings,* and *Equus.*

Mr. Verity, as his name implies, is the prototype of the Shafferian primitive. This self-made man, true to his own instincts and intuition, has a mind of his own. As a sort of eccentric genius, Verity lives by himself in a villa outside the city and is perfectly content to enjoy life without much contact from the mediocrities living in Amnestie. Shaffer describes Mr. Verity's living quarters:

He lives in his "villa" just outside Amnestie, on a windy hill overlooking the town: to be truthful, it was little more than three tiny fishing cottages knocked into one low, medium-sized house, but it charmed him. The whole had been whitewashed and named "Persepolis." Its living room, but for the smallest of kitchens, ran the length of the place, and resembled nothing so much as a sculptor's workroom. From the floor sprang a forest of pedestals, each bearing the head or torso (and very occasionally both) of some Ancient notable.[2]

Although Mr. Verity must live in the modern world, he prefers the security and orderliness of ancient Greece. Almost his entire life has been spent collecting artifacts from ancient civilizations, and he often uses his knowledge of Plato or ancient Greek terracotta to solve murder mysteries. Mr. Verity even goes so far as to judge people's facial expressions by comparing them with similar ancient or primitive visages among his archaeological treasures. Thus, Mr. Verity is certain that Alice Burton is not the murderer because when she was told that Maxwell was dead, she had a look of relief that reminded Verity of a smiling visage on one of the artifacts he had dug up.

Mr. Verity understands that he is trying to chase down the murderer of a man whom no one liked. Although Mr. Verity had never met Maxwell, the detective knew that Maxwell was evil just by seeing the dead man's face. Verity explains his prejudice by telling Reverend Robertson the following anecdote about his understanding of primitive cultures:

> I am a diabolist, parson: I once looked on the face of the devil. His face was black. Throughout a long life I have collected many statues, but never have I possessed the only statuary I fully understand: I mean the work of the great primitive civilisations that knew some of the truth about evil. The Greeks were foolish enough to confuse it with ignorance; the Romans even identified it with neglect of duty. But the Assyrians who took blunt instruments and hacked out those towering giants in stone— they knew evil. Their giants carry thongs: they grip savage beasts in their huge hands and glare as they tear them apart. The Phoenicians knew evil that put up Moloch, and fried babies between his legs. (134–35)

Mr. Verity prides himself on being different. The eccentric social isolate lives in a world all his own—an ideal state of existence akin to the independent, free-spirited citizens of ancient Greece. He is more at home with primitive rites and rituals than he is with the complexities of modern life, lamenting to Miss Framer that "life among the denizens of Amnestie must be very uneventful" (23). Mr. Verity lives in a villa overlooking the resort, yet he has no direct interaction with its inhabitants. His role is godlike: all seeing, all knowing, omnipotent, and capable of solving mysteries and administering justice. He is at ease with himself and refuses to be judged by anyone else. As the epitome of Truth, Verity notes, "How pleasant it would be—how really pleasant—just for once to be taken at one's face value" (232). In short, Mr. Verity is the precursor to Atahuallpa, Alan Strang, and Mozart—three independent spirits (perhaps geniuses) who are perfectly content to commune with their personal gods via rites and rituals or a lifestyle that they themselves have created.

As we will see in Shaffer's later plays, the protagonist—often a genius who is close to God or at least to a more primitive, less hypocritical way of life than those who exist in the modern "wasteland"—is frequently at odds with the mediocrities that he must come into contact with daily. Mr. Verity tries his best to avoid such unpleasant confrontations, reminding us perhaps of F. Scott Fitzgerald's Dr. T. J. Eckleburg who "looked down upon" the wasteland from above. Mr. Verity occasionally comes down from his lofty villa, provides "amnesty" for the populace's shortcomings, solves crimes that they are themselves incapable of unraveling, and then retreats into his own world of unfettered freedom. Although Mr. Verity is brilliant, he, like Shaffer's other independent spirits, was very much disliked. Shaffer explains this distrust of genius by stating that "it was partly because he [Verity] was so often right . . . the thing which no one could excuse this brilliant, lumbering, bearded giant was his amateur enlightenment—the fact that his words spoke so much louder than everybody else's actions" (12–13).

Mr. Verity senses the envy that others, especially what Salieri might refer to as "mediocrities," have for creative talents or geniuses. Mr. Verity tells this story about envy to Inspector Jackson:

> There have been one or two men . . . I have met in my lifetime whom I felt I should never understand. No—not even if I devoted many years to it. One was a Sicilian who worked in the garden of my villa outside Naples. It was many years ago. I had unearthed and set up a most delicate little statue—a Priapus in clay. He was really delightful: a fat, laughing, rollicking little handful of terracotta. It made you happy just to gaze at him. Now my gardener hated that statue. Hated it, I firmly believe, for the joy in its grin, and the wrinkles round its little hands and feet. One morning he waited till he thought I was out; then he took his spade and smashed it. Just smashed it! And then buried the pieces among the laurel bushes . . . I shall never forget that: it made me very frightened. . . .
>
> That Sicilian gardener was a terrible man. I know that. A warped and envious soul. The frankness and pride of that tiny God of Procreation filled him with anger. (81)

The gardener, a "warped and envious soul," will later emerge as the Pizarros, Dysarts, and Salieris of Shaffer's microcosm. They will try their best to understand and even emulate their alter egos; if they are not successful, these misguided mediocrities may even try to destroy what they cannot be.

Shaffer's second novel, *How Doth the Little Crocodile?*, was originally published by Evans Brothers in London (1952) under the pseudonym of Peter Antony; in 1957, The Macmillan Company in New York published the book with the names A. and P. Shaffer on the title page. *How Doth the Little Crocodile?* is another detective novel meant to entertain and provides little gratification for connoisseurs of style and structure.

Mr. Fathom, England's greatest detective and a carbon copy of Mr. Verity (both even share a fondness for classical literature and rare archaeological treasures), is called upon to solve a unique murder mystery. The Beverley Club, an exclusive group of wealthy criminologists who are aficionados in studying the fine art of murder, are puzzled over a case that has the group stymied. They offer Mr. Fathom £300 to solve the mystery. After hearing the details of the murder, Fathom finds the case intriguing and, with the opportunity of pocketing some extra cash, agrees to investigate the murder.

The murder took place in Sussex, England, where Judge Derek Livingstone was living with his wife. The murder occurred around 2 P.M., and at 2:15 P.M., Zelda Carlisle, one of Derek's friends, found Livingstone on the floor with a knife in his back. She ran to get the police, and by the time she and the officers had returned, the police found the body in the garden with the gate locked. Later the police arrested Livingstone's best friend, Roger Hope, who had the keys to the locked gate and whose prints were on the dagger that was the murder weapon. In addition, Hope had the perfect motive for the murder: he had embezzled £20,000 from Livingstone. During the subsequent murder trial, however, it was discovered that Hope also had the perfect alibi: he had made a telephone call to Livingstone's house at approximately 2:15 P.M. and did not leave the company of his friends until 2:30 P.M.—well after the murder had taken place. Thus, Roger Hope was acquitted in court even though the evidence looked as if it were stacked against him. Approximately seven weeks after the trial, Roger Hope, a member of the Beverley Club and who, like Livingstone, dabbled in criminology as a hobby, wrote a letter to Club members stating that he had solved the mystery of Livingstone's murder. Unfortunately, he was run over by a car and killed two days before he was to reveal the murderer to the Beverley Club members.

Mr. Fathom investigates Livingstone's death and finds a number of interesting suspects, including Lady Livingstone, a cold, cruel woman who constantly argued with her husband; the maid Lottie; Zelda Carlisle, who was being blackmailed by Livingstone; Jean Lovelace, Livingstone's mistress, who, as her last name implies, had loose morals and was despised by Livingstone, who ironically enough, spent the majority of his days presiding in court judgment over people; Victor Spendel, Livingstone's shiftless friend who, as an actor, had no stable means of support and was forced to borrow money from Livingstone; Charles Raspe, Livingstone's nephew, who hoped to collect from his uncle's will; and George Couldson, a handyman whom Livingstone sent for the day of the murder and who was seen on the grounds just before the murder was committed. All of the suspects had motives for killing Livingstone. Mr. Fathom, working with the dead man's diary and his correspondence, tries to replay the scenario during the day of the murder to find the guilty party (or parties).

Detective Fathom proceeds with the case by trying to sort out the truth in a world filled with hypocrisy. As he questions each suspect individually, he begins to piece the puzzle together; however, although Fathom does obtain bits and pieces of the truth, he must wade through the lies that each of them tells. Mr. Fathom gives us a hint of what Shaffer will later turn into a dialectic between reason versus instinct, or the Apollonian versus the Dionysian:

> Surely it's the old crossword puzzle again? No one can shed fuller light on the identity of a murderer than his victim. In a case like this you almost have to take your pick among possible murderers, and so you must ask yourself: What kind of man was the victim? Then you'll be in some position to ask: What kind of person would kill such a man?[3]

This dichotomy of victim-executioner, found so often in existential absurdist dramas of the twentieth century (e.g., the plays of Sartre, Osborne, Beckett, Genet), will form the basis of Shaffer's theater. In Shaffer's plays, the protagonist and his alter ego tear at each other, hoping to find truth among a layer of lies; as the cross-examination continues, more of the pieces of the puzzle fit into place. The result of the battle of wills always varies, with some possible ramifications being an attempted suicide (*Five Finger Exercise*), humiliation (*The Private Ear, Shrivings*), education of one of the protagonists (*The Public Eye, Black Comedy, The White Liars, Equus*), and, of course, one of Detective Shaffer's favorite ploys, murder (*The Royal Hunt of the Sun, Amadeus*).

In his early writing efforts, Shaffer explored various genres that might be suitable for the presentation of this relationship between the two alter egos. Shaffer does not even begin to dabble in the theater until 1955, when he wrote *The Salt Land,* three years after the publication of *How Doth the Little Crocodile?* However, there are strong indications that Shaffer was beginning to believe that the extended dialogue format for his novels was not the ideal form for his ideas. *How Doth the Little Crocodile?* actually becomes Shaffer's first stage play, although it is written in the form of a novel.

As Mr. Fathom continues to investigate Livingstone's murder, he unravels the truth behind a series of lies. Livingstone and Roger Hope, both connoisseurs of murder mysteries, tried to arrange the perfect murder. Livingstone, in poor health and near death, arranged to have Hope kill him. Livingstone invited Jean Carlisle to his house at precisely 2:20 P.M.; when she arrived, she found his "dead" body. Livingstone, however, was not dead at all; instead, he faked his death, and while Carlisle was summoning the police, Livingstone had Hope commit the real murder. The idea was to implicate Roger Hope, knowing that he had a sound alibi and would be acquitted in court; Hope's alibi was that he had witnesses testifying that he had spoken to Livingstone at 2:15 P.M. when, according to Carlisle's testimony, Livingstone had already been stabbed in the back. Thus, Hope was "framed" for the murder and had to be acquitted, even though he was the actual murderer—the perfect crime had been committed! Of course, Livingstone made sure to scatter plenty of clues to implicate all of his enemies, each of whom had a motive for killing him.

As Mr. Fathom gathers all of the suspects together in one room to bring the investigation to a dramatic close and reveal the guilty party (a scenario that occurs in all three of Shaffer's novels), he describes the denouement of the "drama":

> I knew when first I set eyes on the garden at Selby House how it reminded me of an empty theatre—a stage where the curtain was still up three months after the audience had gone away. But unaccountably, the cast had remained: the wretched, horrible cast, tricked out in all the effects of a repellent game of charades. I mean, of course, all you people here today. All of you, by reason of your involvement in this business, cease to exist for the detective as human beings. You have no more reality for me than those monstrous Sicilian puppets on iron strings that prance heavily round loaded with paint and clearly recognisable Virtues and Vices, enacting the old, old dramas day after day for meaningless, sanctified reasons. . . .
>
> You'll find it hard to believe me, but I tell you you are all of you suspects: and as suspects, all of you are inventions—fabrications!—fictions!—stock props like those gilded puppets! Look at you! . . . Look! The Jealous Wife, The Other Woman. The Man in Need of Money. The Victim of Blackmail. Even the Psychological Misfit. Nothing has been left out. (171–72)

Fathom's initial impression upon observing the scene of the crime was that it was a fitting place for theater, with an appropriate cast of stock characters. Shaffer, perhaps ready to make the breakthrough to drama, offers this discussion between Fathom and his colleague, Inspector Sands:

> "Well, perhaps the others aren't what we think they are either. It could be that they're all acting."
>
> "I'm afraid I don't see—"
>
> "Always trust your first impression, Sands. And mine, if you recall, was a sense of the theatre!"

"In heaven's name!" said Sands, exasperated. "I don't understand a single word."

"Oh, but yes . . . yes . . ." Fathom gesticulated wildly. "Don't you see what confirms it? Don't you see?"

"Confirms what? That they're all acting? They can't be. It's absurd." (161)

Indeed, Shaffer's first attempts at creating character portraits, including Mr. Verity and Mr. Fathom, come closer to resembling the stereotyped roles of the commedia dell'arte than the well-rounded characters presented in even an early play such as *Five Finger Exercise*. Shaffer, however, at least recognizes that his early characters come from Renaissance stock figures and that he can poke fun at an often-simplistic dialectic which had its roots in the conflict between the Virtues and the Vices of the medieval morality plays.[4]

Withered Murder, Shaffer's third, and last, novel (his second with Anthony), was originally published in 1955 by Evans Brothers in London and then was reprinted by Macmillan in 1956. Shaffer did not use a pseudonym for this novel, which appears under the names "A. and P. Shaffer."

Detective Fathom, forever probing, as his name implies, has now filled the shoes that Mr. Verity once wore. Fathom's description—a corpulent satyr and a laughing sixty-six-year-old cavalier, well traveled in classical lands and a patron of the arts, particularly archaeology—is a carbon copy of Mr. Verity. Fathom, "the finest detective alive," was also quite disliked because "his words spoke so much louder than everybody else's actions."[5]

This time Mr. Fathom is off to Crab Point in the Cornish sea to buy some pieces of sculpture. While staying at the Barnacle Hotel—the only lodging in town—he gradually gets acquainted with the other guests vacationing there. The cast of characters includes former actress, Celia Whitely; third-rate artist Terence Germayne and his ex-wife, Hilary Stanton, now secretary to Miss Whitely; Colin Grey, a journalist who fancies himself to be quite a gallant; prudish Reverend Denis Radley and his wife, Alice, who had dreams of becoming an actress; archaeologist and ancient historian Meredith Blaire; Celia Whiteley's lawyer, George Potter; Professor Hans Richter; and Mary Arundel, a middle-aged spinster who distributes religious literature on London streetcorners. One evening, all of the guests (except Blaire and Reverend Radley) attend a performance of *Macbeth*. When they return, they begin to relax before dinner, scheduled for midnight. Reverend Radley wanders off near the fireplace and discovers Celia Whitely's body, faceless, with the flesh ripped and clawed away. Is there a lunatic running amok? The guests start to worry, but Mr. Fathom assuages their anxieties by promising to have the murderer in tow by early morning.

This third novel follows the same pattern as the previous two pieces of fiction. Detective Fathom investigates the murder by talking individually to each of the guests, as well as to the hotel's proprietress, Mrs. Poscol. As Mr. Fathom puts the pieces of the puzzle together, he learns that each person despised Celia Whitely for one reason or another, a fact that supplies the detective with plenty of suspects for the murder. Mr. Fathom stays up all evening and pries into each person's past, and by morning he has the case solved.

Shaffer's last novel explores the idea that we live in a world of deceit, hypocrisy, and artificiality. His characters are often much more at home with lies and pretense than they are with truth. In the early works, Shaffer uses Verity/Fathom to cross-examine each of these troubled individuals so as to separate fact from fiction and peel away one lie after another until the truth can be found.

What does Mr. Fathom learn during his investigation? He discovers these facts beneath all of the pretense: 1) Hilary Stanton is going to remarry an Indian officer, but actually she does not love him at all; 2) Celia Whitely does not want a secretary; instead, she wants to possess Hilary in a sort of lesbian-type relationship; 3) Mrs. Poscol was once Whitely's dresser and is now half-owner of the hotel with Celia; 4) Colin Grey claims to have no contact with Hilary or Celia but is actually in love with the former; 5) the irreproachable Meredith Blaire was being blackmailed by Whitely; 6) Terence Germayne fails to realize that his wife left him because of personal (sexual) and professional problems that he was experiencing; 7) Mrs. Radley has been having an affair with Professor Richter; and 8) Mary Arundel is actually Celia Whitely in disguise—the real Celia murdered a maid and disfigured the face beyond the point of recognition so that the guests would believe that Celia was the murdered victim. Celia, assuming the new role of Mary Arundel, then murders Hilary Stanton—she did not want to share Hilary with her husband—and escapes scot-free because Celia is presumed dead and cannot be suspected of killing anyone.

Mr. Fathom discovers that the guests staying at the Barnacle are role players: some are literally actresses while others are consciously acting to achieve some sort of identity. Almost all of these "characters" are playing roles for various secretive reasons of their own. As Fathom questions each person, we find out more about their ulterior motives, but we never seem to appreciate them as anything but cardboard figures steeped in artificiality.

The role playing goes hand-in-hand with hypocrisy, as we witness the hypocritical nature of virtually all of the suspects scrutinized by Detective Fathom. Mary Arundel, alias actress Celia Whitely, condemns the modern theater for being lewd and offensive. Similarly, Denis Radley claims that he hates stage performers, whom he believes are "deceivers of the people" who "have erected temples of their own" (60); of course, it is ironic that he married one of these despicable deceivers, an aspiring actress. Terence Germayne assumes the mask of an illustrious artist when, in reality, he fails to acknowledge that he never had any talent for painting. Meredeth Blaire, who prides himself on his expertise concerning archaeology and ancient history, has an amateurish knowledge of these subjects and gets his facts so scrambled when presenting some of the treasures in his pottery collection that he has to be corrected by Fathom. Prudish Alice Radley, wife of a minister, is actually having an affair with Hans Richter. Numerous examples of the artificiality of role playing are found in the novel, foreshadowing the most significant motif that we are to see in almost all of Shaffer's plays.

This sense of role playing results in sterile relationships and a sense of loneliness or despair among many of the characters in the novel. As is true of most of Shaffer's works, role players living in a world of lies and hypocritical values find that marriage does not work for them. With regard to the two marriages in the novel—Hilary Stanton/Terence Germayne and Reverend Denis Radley/Alice Radley—neither is successful, and both couples are childless. Shaffer describes the relationship between Hilary and her husband:

> The quarrels had been continual, violent and pointless. When the idea of divorce came—presented itself, as it were, like an angel of annunciation with lillies in her hand—there was a sudden joy between them. Terence had especially enjoyed it, because he could also play a part before the angel. He was cold, correct, long-suffering, quietly helpful. He apologised incessantly for his inability to give her money. He promised her his first six paintings. He was in his element. (20)

Mrs. Radley, like Hilary, was frayed from endless arguments with her husband, as would be expected of anyone who had to live with such a vocal religious zealot. Fathom's first impression of Mrs. Radley offers us a glimpse of her marital status:

> She was by no means the usual minister's wife, dowdy and inconspicuous; to the contrary, she was assertively feminine and delicate. "Assertively" is the word for her: she had what is vaguely known as "character," a kind of fierce determination in her to be delicate and softly winning at all costs, developed over the years of conflict with her husband, who cared little for the soft and yielding in this life, and nothing at all for the graces. Mrs. Radley's charm had sprung from self-defence: but it was now hers in her own right, and she used it as if she had truly forgotten the pathetically earnest reason why she had had to acquire it. (29)

Shaffer has been accused of ridiculing marriage as an institution. The point is, however, that Shaffer is not attacking marriage at all; instead, he is critical of individuals who fear being themselves and choose to wear masks so as to live in an artificial and illusory world. Whether or not these social perverts are married makes no difference. In Shaffer's works, sterility exists equally among the married and single adults. He depicts role players as lost souls, sexually sterile, and unable to develop contact or have meaningful relationships with others in any intimate way. Detective Fathom, an individual with a strong identity of his own, is forced to mingle in this world of masquerade as he searches for the truth beneath all of the lies. His summary of the case, as well as Shaffer's comprehensive statement about the shallow characters of the novel, is indeed a bleak portrait:

> *"Lonely, yes."* he thought. *Each of them: Blaire: Miss Arundel—even Radley. Most especially Radley. Lonely. And from loneliness reaching out into the world with their immoderate hands, seeking to create—even if it be only to reproduce their loneliness. The silence of the heart conjures the silence of the grave. With such lost people, murder itself becomes a form of reproduction. Out of their frenzied silence comes the sturdy solitude of the corpse. What matter the motive— the feebleness of the reason? The desire to own a hotel, to free a woman one can never have, to punish harlotry, to revenge earlier deprivation: how insufficient are such causes beside such awful truth as this!* (207–208)

In short, all of the characters in the novel who are play acting and are not true to themselves, whether they are married or unmarried, experience this sense of alienation and isolation that for each of them has gradually produced their own "withered murder."

In the mid-1950s, Shaffer probably realized that he could do little more with the detective novel than he had already done. *Withered Murder* repeats the plot, style, form, and content of the first two novels. In effect, Shaffer had been writing material more suitable for drama than for novels. *Withered Murder* was virtually all dialogue, and the idea of cross-examining each person individually should have been ideally suited for the theater. There is quite a bit in *Withered Murder* to suggest that Shaffer was thinking of theater when he wrote the book. The epigraph to the novel informs us that the phrase "withered murder" is from act 2, scene 1 of *Macbeth;* indeed, quotations from *Macbeth* precede each chapter of the novel, providing clues concerning plot and thematic development. Detective Fathom treats the murder as a crime with mythical proportions right out of classical drama or, as he tells Professor Richter, "as the ancients saw it, as we two perhaps saw it from the beginning. Possession, religious mania, rapacity, illicit love. . . " (148). Shaffer is not too far from being able to see the beginnings of modern tragedy, which will become ritualistic drama in his more mature works.

During the early 1950s, when Shaffer was living in New York, he was inspired by having the best theater in the world right on his doorstep. After experimenting with dramatic monologues in the novels, Shaffer, getting his first taste of professional theater, soon realized that drama would be a more suitable form for his dialectic. His next work, *The Salt Land,* was a television play written during his sojourn in New York. The play was eventually aired by ITV in London on 8 November 1955. A scenario in two acts and five scenes, *The Salt Land* concerns a father at odds with his two sons, Arieh and Jo, over the fate of the newly formed state of Israel. Unfortunately, Shaffer has not had the play published and retains the only available copy. He has no plans to publish it in the near future and currently does not wish to allow quotations from the play to be printed. Because most readers will be unfamiliar with the plot of *The Salt Land,* I will provide a summary of the play.

Act 1, scene 1 takes place on a boat bearing illegal Jewish immigrants to Palestine in autumn 1947. The "cargo" includes Mr. Mayer, a middle-aged businessman from Germany; his two sons, Arieh (the elder, twenty-seven years old) and Jo (age undetermined); an old rabbi named Jacob; Rivkeh, a middle-aged woman; Kulli, an intense young girl; Mr. Mordecai, a sophisticated German businessman; Max Galinsky, a young Polish lad; and Saul, the captain of the ship and a member of the Palmach, a military organization determined to bring Jews from Europe into Palestine. As some of the Jewish immigrants chant Sabbath eve songs, Saul warns them about noise that will alert patrol boats to their position. Saul's admonition leads to a discussion between the play's two protagonists, Arieh and Jo, about the fate of the immigrants. Arieh, who believes in Talmudic law and espouses a passive philosophy in which he views man's fate existing only in God's hands, is at odds with Jo, a nouveau-riche cosmopolitan whose only credo is to control his own fate through whatever means (legal or illicit) is available. Arieh, dressed in the Hassidic garb of long robes, expresses a sense of idealism as he states his opposition to the voyage to the Promised Land, preferring a sign from the Messiah to initiate the trek to Jerusalem. Jo, reflecting a contemporary lifestyle that he acquired while living in Paris in a conscious attempt to escape the Jewish ghetto, mocks his brother's conservative creed with a hearty dose of realism. Jo asserts that Arieh's experience is limited to a Jewish ghetto tradition that can be traced to the Middle Ages yet has no practical value for the modernized state of Israel. Mr. Mayer, however, defends his eldest son and criticizes Jo's materialistic values, which led Jo to illegal black market trading and an ensuing jail sentence.

Act 2, scene 2 occurs the following night on board the ship. Jo is talking with his friend and business partner, Mr. Mordecai. A prosperous Jewish businessman too immaculately dressed for the voyage, Mordecai complains about the accommodations on board and about the pettiness of his traveling companions. Like Jo, Mordecai has come to Israel to invest capital into a land ripe for new business ventures. Kulli, Arieh, and Rivkeh are appalled that Mordecai would be so eager to get rich quickly at the expense of Israel. Max Galinsky reminds the passengers that Mordecai would do unscrupulous deeds in Israel because in Europe he was arrested after the war for helping the Nazis run their black market operations. In short, Mordecai, a Jewish businessman, got rich from aiding and abetting the Nazis. He was sentenced to five years in prison, but he jumped bail and fled from Europe. Arieh, in particular, links Jo and Mordecai, claiming that because they have abandoned the traditional Hebraic values of the Talmud in favor of an effete brand of prosperity, they have no right to be called Jews. Arieh insists that these types of parasites will find modern Israel to be a sterile society, a salt land. Jo defends himself and his mentor by stating that it was Mordecai who paid for the Mayer family's trip to Palestine: certainly, no prayers to the Messiah made the voyage possible. The arguments cease as the boat approaches the Promised Land.

The last scene of act 1 (scene 3) occurs at a command post in the Negev during early October 1948. Arieh is the commander of a settlement of one hundred men and women who are fighting two thousand Egyptians for control of the land. Hopelessly outnumbered and without the needed planes, tanks, or artillery to muster a stand, the Jewish settlers seem to be waging battle supported only by their faith in a just cause and in the will of God. Arieh, who believes that he is defending sacred land and who has assumed command of the post because God bade him to do so, refuses to be cowed by the overwhelming odds against him. Jo, who has been trading on the black market in Tel Aviv, visits Arieh to strike a deal with him. Jo offers his brother artillery, tanks, jeeps, and ammunition in return for a favor that Arieh will grant once he becomes a leader in the state. Arieh, supported by Kulli, is opposed to accepting what he believes are tainted supplies obtained through the black market, but his dream for the Promised Land will go unfulfilled unless the war with the Egyptians can be won. Arieh accepts the offer, justifying his decision by reminding himself that he can always renege on his deal with Jo and by rationalizing that God sent Jo to him and used his brother as a means to provide the Israelis with the arms needed to win the battle for territorial rights.

Act 2, scene 1 occurs one year later in a Negev farm commune. Arieh, now married to Kulli, is the leader of the commune and spends most of his time trying to keep the kibbutz functioning. Backbreaking chores, such as clearing away rocks, planting fruit in the desert, and trying desperately to locate sources of water, keep Arieh and other members of the commune from attending religious services conducted by Mr. Mayer, who complains of a society in the throes of too much socialism and not enough religion. Jo, still living in Tel Aviv, was tried for profiteering but was acquitted when the witnesses refused to testify in court. Jo's luxurious lifestyle becomes a contrast to the frugal, hard-working, pristine efforts of the Jews in the commune who have to slave without proper machinery or manpower to irrigate their land. Thus, when Jo arrives at the commune, he is given an unfriendly reception. Jo tells his brother that the Israelis are losing their respect for Arieh, the self-imposed prophetic leader of the commune, and now even view him as an egotist searching for power. Yet Arieh has enough support to be able to repay the debt that he owes his brother; Jo is going to make sure that he collects the debt before Arieh becomes unable, in a political sense, to pay retribution. Jo and Mordecai plan to form a new conservative political party to modernize Israel. The party "platform" would include plans to reduce communal settlements, restrict immigration, and improve technology. In return for Arieh's support, Jo will provide Arieh with machinery, tools, and water to make his commune flourish. Arieh, opposed to any plan to restrict Jewish immigrants into a society that is supposed to be open to all people, prays to God for assistance. Jo, impatient with Arieh's ambivalence, slaps his brother, reminding him that it was Jo and Mordecai who paid for the family's trip to Israel. The scene ends with Arieh agreeing to allow the members of the commune to determine their own future with regard to Jo's proposition.

Act 2, scene 2 occurs in the same setting later in the evening. Mr. Mayer urges Arieh to accept Jo's proposal because the commune will prosper, much to the anticipation of Mr. Mayer who compares the current situation to the squalor he was familiar with in the ghettoes of Europe. As Jo presents his proposal to the members of the commune, he encourages them to accept his plan to modernize Israel with new capital and with proper management, including reducing the number of immigrants for economic reasons. Mordecai offers to make Arieh's kibbutz the focal point of the newly proposed party. However, Saul opposes the idea of restricting immigration, especially to Jews who are leaving Europe after living in fear and oppression during World War II. Saul views Israel as the land of hope for those persecuted during the Nazi regime, and he refuses to support a political party that suppresses any semblance of such idealism. Gradually, the other members of the commune agree to support Arieh, and they reject Jo's proposal. In an outburst directed against his sibling-tormentor, Arieh delivers an emotional speech about the intrinsic value of pastoral Israel, the land of biblical legend, without need of modernization. In a rage, Arieh hurls Jo across the room and then strangles him. Arieh is certain that God directed him to murder his brother, yet the other commune members are aghast at his rash behavior. Saul takes command and orders Arieh to his room to await the police. Mr. Mayer is stunned by Arieh's act of fratricide, and the play ends with the horror expressed on the old man's face as he realizes what has happened to his two egotistical sons.

The Apollonian-Dionysian dialectic manifested in the later plays is first represented in Shaffer's theater by the conflict between Jo and Arieh in *The Salt Land*. The sibling rivalry in the play is a precursor to the battle of wills between a role player and his liberated alter ego. Jo Mayer, a realist who tries to survive by his own wits and cunning, is constantly at odds with his brother Arieh, an idealist who refuses to accept change and relies on sanctioned values associated with the Judaic tradition. The two rivals compete for a share of the Promised Land, each motivated by an inculcated sense of pride and self-intoxication.

Arieh Mayer presumes to be a pious Orthodox Jew. On the surface, he wears a veneer of the traditional ghetto worshipper replete with long robes and side curls. Certainly, his discussions of the Talmud, Judaic traditions, and the Messiah, coupled with a firm belief that man is in God's hands, would lead one to believe that Arieh is a serious worshipper. However, Arieh's sense of religion is translated into idealism when he begins to rely on God exclusively and refuses to acknowledge the real world. He claims that individuals such as his own brother Jo who depend on man, not God, will inhabit a salt land or wilderness as the Promised Land. Unfortunately, Arieh's notion of determinism is archaic, and actually Jo, relying on his own instincts for survival, turns Israel into a "land of milk and honey." Arieh's insistence that God has willed the land to him in order to create a temple in the Lord's honor almost single-handedly precludes his downfall during the fight against the Egyptian army in October 1948. Arieh seems to allow his supposedly strong faith in God to exclude all other rational alternatives for decision making.

Although Arieh is not a role player per se, his exclusive value system contributes to his sense of tunnel vision. As a passive conformist existing merely at God's whim, Arieh has no identity of his own. He cannot think for himself and always seems to make the wrong decisions. Arieh is faced with three crises in the play: the trek to Palestine, the struggle with the Egyptians for control of the land, and the futile effort to irrigate the Negev. Arieh, relying on God to make decisions for him, refuses to acknowledge that Jo paid for his passage to Israel, provided him with the artillery and equipment to mount an offensive against the Egyptian army, and supplied the tools, fertilizer, and water to save the settlement in the Negev. Instead, Arieh insists that Jo was sent by God to free the Promised Land.

Arieh's sense of hypocrisy runs throughout the play as we witness how he uses God as a means of justifying his overwhelming pride and ambition. Arieh pays lip service to God yet is quick to insist that God serve him. When major decisions go in favor of Arieh, he acknowledges God's service, but when problems occur, Arieh loses faith in God and virtually becomes an atheist, claiming that the Lord has abandoned him and chooses instead to torment him. In short, God becomes a tool to justify Arieh's ascendance to power. As the play progresses, we witness Arieh's flimsy adherence to biblical doctrine. Each scene of the play takes Arieh on a progression away from God to a more satisfying state of egomania. Finally, in act 2, Arieh refuses to attend religious services, loses his temper among his friends, unbearably torments his wife, insults his father, and eventually murders his own brother. Through Arieh's hypocritical actions, the audience intuitively perceives his infatuation with divinity and his concomitant "holier-than-thou" behavior to be far removed from Talmudic doctrine.

On the other hand, Jo represents the realist who is in control of his own future. In act 1, we learn that he has decided to seek refuge in Palestine and vows that he will defend, to the death if need be, his right to emigrate. Jo has rebelled against a tradition and religion that would confine him to the Judengasse, a restricted ghetto for Jews. He has traveled all over Europe and has tried to improve his lifestyle by obtaining wealth and power, even if it meant working through the black market. Although Jo has become rich and powerful through his illicit contacts, he has not had to rely on others to confirm his existence. His independent spirit brings him much closer to Shaffer's "primitives" than Arieh could ever hope to be.

The Salt Land, however, does not depict relationships that are all black or all white. One of Shaffer's goals was to present a dialectic between a religious conformist who betrays God and the trust of his family, and a free-spirited gambler with a loose sense of morality. Of course, Jo's crimes become minuscule when compared with Arieh's fratricide. However, Shaffer makes it clear that Jo's involvement in the black market, his subsequent jail sentence, and his profiteering activities in Israel are repulsive to the other Jews in the play. In addition, Jo's association with Mordecai, an indirect collaboration with the Nazis, is abhorrent, especially to Mr. Mayer. Jo's isolation from his friends, family, and ancestry equates him with the pariahs of the later plays, yet his notorious business transactions do not make him the object of his alter ego's envy, even though both men aspire toward self-gratification through prestige and success.

The Salt Land is also noteworthy as an early attempt to create a musical rhythm to unify form and content. Music plays an important part in the play: Shaffer opens four of the play's five scenes with songs or musical interludes (the only exception is act 1, scene 2). The music personifies the spirit of Israel and the strong sense of worship that Arieh and Jo have abandoned. By intermingling the verses of "Ygdal" during Friday evening services, melancholic Israeli songs, Sabbath chants, and the great battle songs of the Israeli army ("The Song of the Signal Man," "We Have the Strength"), Shaffer tries to instill in the audience a carefully calculated rhythm throughout the play. The songs and chants unconsciously inculcate the audience with a sense of worship that we begin to associate with the traditional values of Mr. Mayer. The dialectic between Arieh and Jo, a battle of wills between two proud profiteers who have abandoned fundamental Yiddish ideologies, is in sharp contrast with the more important inner values that Shaffer wants to stress through musical interludes associated with Judaism. In the later plays, however, Shaffer will learn to merge Brechtian and Artaudian theatrical devices to produce a more discernible conflict between two directly opposing alter egos, thereby using music to disassociate the "primitive" from his envious counterpart.

Shaffer's next effort was *Balance of Terror,* a television spy drama about British intelligence operations against Soviet agents in Berlin. Its debut was in England on BBC television (21 November 1957) followed by a later showing in the United States on the CBS series, *Studio One* (27 January 1958). Shaffer recalls the difference between the two television airings:

> *Balance of Terror* was sheer fun stuff and, I think, well done. On American television it was rewritten and came out as hideously mediocre stuff. The good guys were clean-limbed, overgrown Boy Scouts. The bad guys were wicked, dreadful Communist agents. It was boiled down to the lowest common denominator of American television rubbish.[6]

The anonymous reviewer for *The New York Times* seemed to agree with Shaffer's assessment of the production; in the review the day after the *Studio One* showing, the play was described as an "inept production, presuming to deal with as important a subject as control of inter-continental ballistic missiles."[7] The play is no longer available because the BBC has erased the tapes; Shaffer assured me that no copy of the play exists.[8]

During that same year, Shaffer wrote *The Prodigal Father,* a radio play that was broadcast by the BBC for its *Saturday Matinee* program on 14 September 1957. The play basically reflects a generation gap between Leander Johnson and his son Jed, who lacks what Leander calls "class" and appears, to his father at least, to be useless as an individual. As Dennis Klein has noted, the conflict foreshadows family tensions in *Five Finger Exercise,* written one year later.[9] *The Prodigal Father* has never been published, and Shaffer does not plan to adapt it for the stage.

In 1963, Shaffer wrote two sketches for the British television series *That Was the Week That Was.* The first piece, "But My Dear," is a one-scene satire on sexual insinuations that can appear in a standard civil service letter. An insecure junior officer, shaking nervously, shows a letter he has just composed to his pompous and bullying boss. At first, the senior officer congratulates the young man for not beginning the letter with the repulsive and suggestive word "Dear." The senior officer then reprimands the subordinate for making such obvious sexual innuendoes as "Pursuant to your letter," "I am hoping for the favour of an early reply," "Thanking you in anticipation," and "Yours faithfully." The boss even suggests that the letter's close, "Your obedient servant," is "just plain perverted," obviously referring to some sort of kinky sex.[10] After a tirade on homosexuality, the senior officer asks for the junior officer's name, and the latter responds with "Fairy, sir" (51). Upon hearing this, the young man's employer says, "I don't think somehow you are going to go very far in Her Majesty's Service. Good morning" (51).

"But My Dear" shows the pomposity of staid businessmen who are set in their ways, at odds with their youthful coworkers. The senior officer, reminiscent of Charles Sidley of *The Public Eye,* seems to be overly concerned with image and roles. His nitpicking attitude, critical of the junior officer for not being more concerned with how the public will react to an innocuous business letter, demonstrates his unwillingness to be flexible with others. Later, as Shaffer's plays evolve, the same attitude degenerates into the Dysart–Alan Strang dialectic and the Salieri-Mozart rift between a free-spirited younger man and his staid alter ego.

Shaffer's second sketch, "The President of France," is a sarcastic speech delivered by a hypothetical French president in 1990. The French leader, newly elected as the Supreme Chief Spokesman of the European Community, gives an acceptance speech that is a parody of Marcus Antonius's famous eulogy in *Julius Caesar.* Shaffer notes that the French president is "a tremendous old man. In his delivery and gestures he is elaborate, theatrical, but forceful."[11] The comparisons to General de Gaulle seem obvious. The speech itself is the president's explanation of why he should be the Chief Spokesman for Europe. There are basically two reasons that he cites. First, he has been a successful soldier, ready to sacrifice lives for an ideal. Second, because the president's ancestors were great leaders, he feels that he is more than capable of carrying on the tradition of Charlemagne, Louis XIV, and Napoleon. He proceeds to attack various other nations because their heritage is not as illustrious and noble as French history and French ancestry.

The sketch mocks idealists who believe they are close to God. One of Shaffer's most important themes, the worshipping of idols and the need to create gods in order to pacify our desire for perfection, is found throughout the sketch. The president, who, as a successful soldier has slaughtered many individuals, admits that he cares only for ideals: "Europe has always worshipped her soldier-idealists, provided they are violent enough, and withdrawn enough from common sympathy. Even the sentimental English grovel at the feet of their Wellingtons, their Haigs, their Montgomerys" (95). The president, once a paid killer disguised as a soldier, realizes that the common man's own mediocrity creates heroes like himself: "St. Paul's Cathedral in London boasts a high altar dedicated to the memories of men whose sole distinction is that they practised murder. And this is as it should be. Under all that Protestant cant, Europe still worships force" (95). At the end of the parody, the president takes the crown and, like Napoleon, coronates himself as King of Europe who, as a model close to God, inspires awe and idolatry from the masses. The connection between the monarch and God is made quite clear in the closing lines: "And may God in His wisdom give fury to our missiles and power to our bomb [sic], that we may protect forever this final revelation of His divine will on earth!" (96). In essence, Shaffer's "The President of France" becomes a satire on the need to worship idols, even if they are artificial ones.

In 1963, Shaffer also wrote the text for *The Merry Roosters' Panto,* a play that is a Christmas entertainment (pantomime) for children. Stanley Myers and Steven Vinaver did the music and lyrics, and Joan Littlewood's Theatre Workshop Company initially staged the piece at Wyndham's Theatre on 17 December 1963; the play continued on matinees to accompany Littlewood's *Oh, What a Lovely War.* Shaffer used his poetic license to create a new version of the Cinderella tale:

> The show is presented as a running battle between the cast and the theatre's manager—a tyrant in red socks smoking a 12-inch cigar, determined to clear the actors off the stage and inflict a recital of Welsh folk tales on the audience. Once his back is turned, the company creep back and embark stealthily on the show, after posting look-outs in the audience to signal the return of the dreaded killjoy. [12]

In other words, the audience virtually participates in the stage production, a foreshadowing of the actor-audience relationship in *Equus.* Other innovations to the Cinderella story include Prince Charming as a cosmonaut who takes his bride to the moon on a rocketship, males playing Cinderella's ugly sisters, the Fairy Godmother as the Duchess of Margate, and Cinderella as a young Stepney ingenue.

Reviewers were divided as to the worth of the project. Critics for *The Times, The Guardian,* and *The Daily Telegraph and Morning Post* enjoyed the show, while their counterparts from *Financial Times* and the *Evening Standard* disagreed with them; Herbert Kretzmer of the *Daily Express* could not make up his mind, claiming that the production lacked magic and mystery yet could be recommended for children whose parents believed in progressive education. [13] Shaffer, however, is still quite proud of *The Merry Roosters' Panto,* and although the play has never been published, he would like to see it staged in New York. During my interview with Shaffer, he expressed a fondness for the play, as opposed to the unpublished radio and television scripts, simply because he found the piece to be charming theater that actually worked on stage. [14]

Although the detective novels and the radio/television scripts are not major writings, they allowed Shaffer to explore traditional structures to determine the most suitable form for his works. With his apprenticeship behind him, Shaffer was able to concentrate on writing serious theater, leaving the pantomimes, novels, radio plays, and television dramas to rest.

4

Five Finger Exercise:
The Sweet Music Begins

FIVE Finger Exercise, Peter Shaffer's first major play and his most successful in terms of positive critical appraisal, opened on 16 July 1958, at the Comedy Theatre in London. The play was produced by H. M. Tennent and directed by Sir John Gielgud, with a cast that included Roland Culver (Stanley), Adrianne Allen (Louise), Brian Bedford (Clive), Michael Bryant (Walter), and Juliet Mills (Pamela). At a time when British theater was mired in "kitchen-sink drama," critics were looking for a fresh approach to modern theater. Shaffer was hailed as the messiah with a solid background behind him and a good future ahead of him, even though the play is traditional in form and content. Shaffer recalls the reaction of the British press: "Here is a Tory Playwright, an Establishment Dramatist, a Normal Worker, in the sense that the weekend cottage or the flat in Knightsbridge is the norm of the Good British Play; all else is a departure to be regarded with great suspicion."[1]

Five Finger Exercise was given favorable reviews in *The Times, The Sunday Times, Evening Standard, The Spectator, Daily Telegraph, New Statesman,* and *Variety.*[2] Philip Hope-Wallace of *The Manchester Guardian* initially offered a somewhat neutral review on 17 July 1958, claiming that Shaffer's characters were shallow and did not elicit much sympathy from the spectators, although he stated that Shaffer analyzed them well enough.[3] After the play ran 450 performances, *The Manchester Guardian* ran a second review with W. L. Webb concluding that "above all, it is a remarkably fluent and well-constructed play; there are no real structural faults and very few loose ends of the sort that blur the impact of many an interesting first play, and it is this theatrical sureness that makes Shaffer a rare bird among the current flock of new playwrights."[4]

Most of the reviewers had very few negative things to say about the play and praised Shaffer's writing ability. Milton Shulman of the *Evening Standard* remarked that "although Mr. Shaffer fails to justify the mercurial emotional shifts of his characters, he writes with telling perception of this over-refined strata of the middle class."[5] In *Encore,* Ian Dallas summed up what most critics said about this talented young playwright: "The greatest qualities the play has are firstly, the way its author has marshalled the action into a clear, dramatic line and secondly, the way he deserts dialogue in favor of the long soul-searching tirades the like of which cannot be heard elsewhere on the London stage."[6] Patrick Gibbs of the *Daily Telegraph* offered an overall assessment of how the critics judged the H. M. Tennent production: "In the way of performance he [Shaffer] had the good fortune his play deserved, the casting being unusually happy, the acting exciting and the production by John Gielgud very smooth and vivid."[7]

The only negative opinion came from Kenneth Tynan of *The Observer.* Tynan's unfavorable review focused on what he thought was miscasting with regard to Adrianne Allen and Roland Culver and a stereotyping of Clive, the lad "made to suffer." Tynan did not believe that the play had an authentic ring to it: "Mr. Shaffer's trouble is that he can be good as well as glib: and it is the good lines, ironically, that make us most conscious of the surrounding falseness."[8] Strangely enough, Tynan enjoyed the play, praising it highly in his review of the Broadway production in 1959.[9]

After running for over a year in London, *Five Finger Exercise,* for which Shaffer had won the *Evening Standard* award for Best Play of the Year and accolades as the most promising young playwright in England, moved to New York under the sponsorship of H. M. Tennent, Frederick Brisson, and Roger L. Stevens of The Playwrights' Company.[10] Gielgud again directed with the original London cast except for Jessica Tandy now playing Louise in place of Miss Allen. The British text was hardly altered for its American staging.[11] Shaffer did consult with Gielgud to make the New York production's first scene less farcical than the London version, but form and content were hardly affected.[12] The New York premiere was on 2 December 1959, at the Music Box Theater.

Again, *Five Finger Exercise* scored favorably among critics, with Shaffer receiving strong reviews from *The New York Times, New York Post, New York Journal American, Daily Mirror, New York World-Telegram, New York Herald Tribune, The Reporter, Christian Century, The Nation, Variety, Theatre Arts,* and *Time.*[13] Richard Watts, Jr., of the *New York Post* particularly noted Shaffer's ability to create strong characters, stating that "the drama of the play stems entirely from them and their believable conflicts as individuals."[14] Brooks Atkinson of *The New York Times* had lots of praise for the play, concluding that "as an exercise in the art of expression, *Five Finger Exercise* is superb."[15] *Variety* mentioned that the New York version was "clearer, sharper, and more stimulating" than the London production.[16] The critics shared an optimistic feeling that Shaffer's best writing was ahead of him. Harold Clurman offered a consensus of opinion on Shaffer's potential talents: "The author will grow in stature when he has freed himself from the symmetry of conventional English theatrical forms and feelings."[17]

John Chapman of the *Daily News* supplied the only negative review of the play.[18] Praising the acting and the dialogue that was "intelligently written and gracefully spoken," Chapman claimed that the play lacks depth and "fails to strike a major chord."[19] His major complaint was that "there isn't much more to it when it is finished than there was when it was begun."[20]

In 1960, *Five Finger Exercise* won the New York Drama Critics' Circle Award for Best Foreign Play of the Year. In 1962, the play was turned into a film much less successful than the stage version.

Shaffer's first major play has all the features of a nineteenth-century conventional English drama. It is "kitchen-sink drama" in the well-made play tradition, far removed from Artaud and ritualistic theater. Shaffer explained the rationale for the form of *Five Finger Exercise:* "The scene was set that innocent way on purpose. I was using the stock properties of the artificial, untrue and boring family plays the English never seem to tire of in order that the audience should feel solid ground under its feet and so follow me more easily into my play."[21] The setting of the play is the naturalistic living room of the Harringtons' weekend cottage in Suffolk. The cluttered set reminds us more of Pinero than Pinter. Shaffer presents a sort of scientifically monitored background, similar to Ibsen's control of the set so that he could observe the human animals functioning as guinea pigs in an elaborate experiment that he had created to measure the interplay of heredity versus environment. In *Five Finger Exercise,* Shaffer does his best to suppress the creative urges of any director, not only by properly situating sofas at fixed angles to doors, but also by providing precise descriptions of each character and his or her mannerisms, as well as by describing, Shavian-like, how the decor affects those on stage. Stage conventions are realistic, not stylized as in ritualistic theater. The language is direct, not symbolic or based on incantatory rhythms. In short, *Five Finger Exercise* carries on the tradition of nineteenth-century realism and adds nothing new to drama in terms of form and structure.

Does Shaffer feel defensive about this first effort in the theater? He admits that the "well-made play" is the sort of style that he has been steadily moving away from, yet he feels that this was a good start for a playwright who was not quite confident enough to experiment with different forms of drama.[22] When asked if the play was old-fashioned, Shaffer said, "As far as the form being old-fashioned, I suppose it is. But *Look Back in Anger* is just as old-fashioned in form. Anyway form is dictated by content."[23]

There is some evidence available to suggest that Shaffer envisioned a musical structure for the play but did not know enough about dramatic structure at this stage in his career to experiment with ritualistic theater. In his preface to the play, Frederick Brisson, one of the New York producers, had enough insight into the drama to see its structure as a consciously arranged musical score: "It is like a Bach piano piece: seemingly simple, yet interwoven and enormously complicated."[24] As the title implies, Shaffer tried to create a tightly knit ensemble of five characters. In an interview with *Stage and Television Today,* Shaffer stated that he "wrote five equal parts, so that the play can be compared to a string quintet."[25] In theory, he wanted to create the type of fraternal ceremony that he described in "The Cannibal Theater," thereby turning the play into a Strindbergian battle of wills. Clive even warns Walter that "this isn't a family. It's a tribe of wild cannibals. Between us we eat everyone we can"(25). However, no matter what presumptuous ideas Shaffer had of turning the play into a ritualistic "battle of Shrivings," the *Walpurgisnacht* never fully develops as it might, simply because the realistic tradition negates the grostesque instead of accentuating it.[26]

At first glance, it would seem as if *Five Finger Exercise* focuses on why five characters fail to work as a unit, a well-knit family. In her analysis of the play, Joan F. Dean notes that the family deteriorates because each person is myopic and is concerned only with his or her individual needs.[27] Indeed, Shaffer has stated that the play is concerned with "non-communication among members of a family."[28] Perhaps we are witnessing on stage Shaffer's *Long Day's Journey into Night,* written at the beginning of his career instead of at the end, as was true of O'Neill. Shaffer's family is similar to the one in the play, a five-character study including his parents and two brothers. The Harringtons could easily pass for a middle-class Jewish family living in the suburbs of London. Moreover, when Shaffer wrote the preface to his collected plays, he commented that *Five Finger Exercise* "expressed a great deal of my own family tensions and also a desperate need to stop feeling invisible."[29]

During our interview, Shaffer admitted to me that he identified with Clive and that "what was autobiographical was the tension between my mother and father in which I was involved."[30] However, Shaffer also warned that it would be a mistake to assume that Clive is a young Peter Shaffer; indeed, Shaffer recognizes that Clive is very selfish and self-pitying. Shaffer explained that Louise is not quite like his mother, for she is much more pretentious than Reka Shaffer. Stanley Harrington is a model for Shaffer's father, Jack, who never did actually oppose his son's education at Cambridge but, as a businessman, did question the value of an arts education. By Shaffer's own admission, Jack, however, was much more eccentric than Stanley Harrington, whom Shaffer describes as fairly conventional.

The play is more than a sociological or scientific study of the family as an institution. Critics who have tried to press Shaffer into revealing strains in his own life so as to relate these frustrations to the play have been unable to do so.[31] Furthermore, the dissolution of the family is a theme that is not developed in any of Shaffer's other plays. The family is always seen as a viable institution, quite different from Albee's plays where the family is usually a tribe of wild cannibals forever tearing at each other. Shaffer envies "the delicate balance"; Albee cannot relate to it.

Five Finger Exercise, like virtually all of Shaffer's plays, is a study of role playing and, in this instance, is an examination of the influence of environment on the freedom of the individual. The protagonist, Clive Harrington, tries to develop a positive image of himself in an environment where people around him think and act for him. As a result of his lack of independence, Clive's world becomes artificial and phony, created *for* him, not *by* him. Lacking a strong sense of identity, Clive has retreated into a world of sexual sterility. Later in the play, Clive is found to be a liar, a characteristic common to all of Shaffer's inhibited protagonists. By not being true to themselves, Shaffer's heroes fail to be honest with others.

Pamela, Clive's younger sister, is the least developed character or the "pinky" of the "five finger exercise," yet she is essential to making the five fingers work. Pamela's function is to provide some comic relief from a highly tense play; she offers the audience a sense of release from emotionally charged exchanges. Not old enough to be concerned with her own sense of identity or to share in the battle of wills in which the other characters are engaged, Pamela, and her presence on stage, assures us that there will be a break in the dialectical struggle long enough for the audience to catch its breath.

In an interview with *The New York Times,* Shaffer said *Five Finger Exercise* was about "various levels of dishonesty."[32] Clive, who is controlled by others and has no identity of his own, is the center of this dishonesty. His parents, Louise and Stanley, live in artificial worlds of illusion that are sanctioned by their peers or by the social pressures to which they choose to conform. Walter Langer, Pamela's tutor, is the only honest person in the play. He is true to himself, has his own strong values, and therefore has established his own self-worth and his identity. He "sticks out like a sore thumb" in the family but is actually envied by them as well.

Louise Harrington is a possessive and pompous person who demands that others live up to her expectations of them. Her living room is "well furnished, and almost aggressively expresses Mrs. Harrington's personality" (9). Shaffer describes her as "a Person of Taste" (9), an unofficial title that she regards as law. She dresses "ostentatiously" while her whole manner "bespeaks a constant preoccupation with style, though without apparent insincerity or affection" (11).

Mrs. Harrington is the consummate role player. She defines herself, her behavior, and the standards for her family by the accepted values of the upper middle class, perhaps even the upper class or aristocracy, to which she aspires to belong. Rather than accept the fact that she is married to a middle-class furniture manufacturer who fashions himself as a plebeian so ably "pulled up by his own bootstraps," Louise instead dreams of herself in the glamour of the upper class. She insists that a vacation home in the country is as essential to her as having a tutor for her daughter and sending her son to Cambridge University. Louise's husband mocks this need to conform: "Apparently, the best people have tutors, and since we're going to be the best people whether we like it or not, we must have a tutor too" (13).

Louise Harrington's insistence that her family must live up to what she believes is a distinctly stratified upper-class code of behavior has ruined her marriage. The major source of tension between Louise and her husband lies in their class differences. Louise cannot accept her husband's "third-rate furniture business"; she despises the fact that he is proud to be from the working class and that he makes no apologies for not having much of a formal education. To Louise, Stanley's background as an orphan who never got past grammar school and later worked his way up through the ranks of a furniture factory represents "shortcomings" (17). Their different interests are a reflection of their backgrounds. Stanley is happy trodding off to the local pub, playing golf, or going hunting. Louise, however, acknowledges, "Heaven knows, I've tried to be interested in his bridge and golf club, and his terrible friends. I just can't do it" (44). Louise insists on discussing plays and poetry; Stanley has no interest in these subjects. Louise immerses herself in French language and culture; Stanley does not understand a word of the language. Louise loves music, particularly classical German; Stanley receives headaches from it.

To escape from the harsh reality of her husband's mediocrity, Louise has created her own illusion, depicting herself as a descendant of French aristocracy. She pleads with Stanley to understand the differences between the two of them:

> It's no good, Stanley. My life was never meant to be like this—limited this way . . . There are times I feel I'm being absolutely choked to death—suffocated under piles of English blankets. Yes, my dear: I'm not English and won't ever be, no matter how hard I try. Can't you ever understand that you married someone who's really a Parisian at heart? (88–89)

In reality, Louise's background was French, but aristocratic it certainly was not. Clive tells Walter that "being French, you know, Mother imagines she's real ormolu in a sitting-room of plaster gilt. She suffers from what I might call a plaster-gilt complex, if you see what I mean. To her the whole world is irredeemably plebeian—especially Father. The rift you may detect between them is the difference between the Salon and the Saloon" (49). The aristocratic airs that Mrs. Harrington assumes are mere illusions, and the only link she has with French aristocracy is through her impoverished

mother who happened to marry an English lawyer. Clive explains the
nature of his mother's aristocratic background:

> The salary was so small that the family would have died of starvation if
> Hélène, my grandmother, hadn't met an English solicitor—on a cycling
> tour of the Loire—married him, and exchanged Brunoy for Bour-
> nemouth. Let us therefore not gasp too excitedly at the loftiness of
> Mother's family tree. Unbeknown to Father, it has, as you see, roots of
> clay. (48)

As an "aristocrat," Louise is nothing more than the mirror image of an
ideal type she tries to imitate. Realizing that she can do nothing to convert
her husband to a more "civilized" lifestyle, Mrs. Harrington tries to mold
the other family members into the image that she has of them. Thus,
Pamela must have a tutor and take French lessons, while Clive must banter
with her in playful French and entice her with the latest news from Cambridge. In short, her son and daughter are being molded into a pattern or
role that she has created for them. Louise is in control of the household, and
she makes sure that Stanley has no say in how it is run. The result is that her
children are beginning to think and act as she does.

Because there is a lack of communication between Louise and Stanley,
Louise has chosen Walter to fill her emotional void.[33] She tries to "adopt"
Walter and make him conform to the high standards she constantly tries to
maintain. Mrs. Harrington sees Walter as a highly cultured tutor, a descendant of Bach and Beethoven. In other words, for Mrs. Harrington, Walter is
a stereotype spouting beautiful poetry and composing fine music—the
epitome of what she would like her family to be. Louise recalls the day that
she first met Walter, and her recollection of the cocktail party during which
they first met has the pathetic tone of a desperate woman living in her own
world of self-created illusion:

> Do you remember—before even I spoke to you I knew you were some-
> thing quite exceptional. I remember thinking: such delicate hands . . .
> and that fair hair [touching it]—it's the hair of a poet. He'll have a soft voice
> that stammers a little from nervousness, and a lovely Viennese ac-
> cent. . . . (45–46)

To Mrs. Harrington, Walter will always speak in a "lovely Viennese accent,"
even though he constantly reminds her that he is German, not Viennese. Of
course, the accent should make no difference to Louise, for she cannot
understand a word of German. Again, what matters to Louise is not
whether she can understand the language, but the idea that it is exotic to
speak a foreign tongue; thus, she tells Clive that "it's not the meaning, it's
the sound that counts, dear. And I'm sure this boy will speak it adorably"
(41).

Louise's attraction to Walter is platonic, yet at the same time, it is sexual as well. Although the sexual implications are often subtle, they exist nevertheless. During my interview with Shaffer, he reinforced the idea that Louise unconsciously is physically attracted to Walter:

> I think that it's very clear that there is a sexual attraction between Louise and Walter. . . . I think that what she sees in Walter is partly a fantasy figure—a handsome Continental figure who is educated, loves music and art, and from that would also come the desire to be taken out by him and probably more. She's not at all pleased when he calls her his mother. I think there is a buried sexuality about this, of course.[34]

Stanley Harrington, much like his wife, has adopted a set of values that were handed down to him, prescribed by a rigid code of roles, norms, values, and mores defined by others. In assuming the role of a rustic with all of the appropriate working-class values that follow, he effectively counters his wife's aristocratic airs that she puts on. Shaffer describes him as "a forceful man in middle age, well built and self-possessed, though there is something deeply insecure about his assertiveness" (12).

The insecurity that Stanley feels is perhaps due to his need to live up to a code of behavior that permits no deviation. Born an orphan, with his mother dying in childbirth, Stanley, whose father was apparently away from home a good deal of the time in service for the Merchant Navy, learned to take care of himself. He was able to earn a decent living and work his way up in the furniture factory without much formal education. Interested in material gains, Stanley expects others to share such interests, including his son Clive, whom he lectures to in no uncertain terms: "You get this through your head once and for all; I'm in business to make money. I give people what they want. I mean ordinary people" (34).

Clive's relationship with his father is tumultuous because Stanley imposes his own values on his son. Clive believes that his father belongs to the "Absolute Power Department" (77) because of the way he characterizes others by how they measure up to his absolute standards. Mr. Harrington wants Clive to be made in the image he has created for his son, so he lectures the young man on the need to be pragmatic: "When you finish at this university which your mother insists you're to go to, you'll have to earn your living. I won't always be here to pay for everything, you know" (16). Stanley mocks Clive's lifestyle and the type of friends with whom Clive associates because they have no obvious utilitarian value: "I mayn't be much in the way of education, but I know this: if you can't stand on your own two feet you don't amount to anything. And not one of that pansy set of spongers you're going round with will ever help you do that" (16). Stanley fears that Clive's association with such friends may ruin his son's career and his chances for advancement: "People still judge a man by the company he keeps. You go around with a lot of drifters and arty boys, and you'll be judged as one of them" (38).

Mr. Harrington's insistence that Clive should measure up to his father's pragmatic and absolute standards destroys any bond between father and son. Shaffer's stage directions tell us that "Clive's nervousness instinctively increases with his [Stanley's] appearance" (12). Stanley quibbles with Clive's matriculation at Cambridge because it is not practical: "Clive, as you know your mother and I didn't see eye-to-eye over sending you to a University. But that's past history now. The point is, what use are you going to make of it?" (36–37). Even worse, Clive wants to study literature in college, a subject that Stanley views as being worthless:

> Stanley. [To Clive.] And this is what you want to study at Cambridge when you get up there next month?
> Clive. Well, more or less.
> Stanley. May I ask why?
> Clive. Well, because . . . well, poetry's its own reward, actually. Like virtue. All Art is, I should think.
> Stanley. And this is the most useful thing you can find to do with your time?
>
> (16)

Stanley rarely cares what Clive thinks, as long as Clive can function in the image that his father believes is appropriate for a young man. Walter speaks the truth when he tells Stanley that Clive "does not wish to be alone with you because always he feels you are—well—judging him. When you look at him, he sees you are thinking—'How useless he is' " (93).

Clive is the protagonist of the play, the middle finger, the center of the action surrounded by the constant tension produced by his parents. Clive resembles the young Peter Shaffer: a "nervous, taut and likable" (11) young man trying to gain confidence in himself at the age of nineteen. As Shaffer did, Clive is attending Cambridge University where he has joined a drama club and would like to study literature, despite the social pressures against it. He has no idea what career to choose (a problem plaguing Shaffer until the success of *Five Finger Exercise*) and feels that he may be "umemployable" (78). Shaffer identifies with Clive, whose search for identity is the focal point of the play.

Clive has no concept of who he is nor does he have a strong sense of identity. Instead, he is only what others tell him to be. He feels as if he is being pulled in two directions by the war that his parents are waging: "The culture war with me as ammunition. 'Let's show him how small he is'— 'Let's show her where she gets off.' *And always through me!*" (106). He speaks with a French accent to please his mother and tells Walter that to keep his father content, he can envision himself walking by his parents' side, "Or, better still, a pace or two behind. 'Clive, to heel, sir. Heel!' Let me introduce myself: 'Spaniel Harrington'" (40). Pamela is correct when she teasingly greets him as the "handsome slave boy" (69), for even Clive admits that in relation to his family, he is nothing more than "Jou-Jou. Toy. More accurately in this case, ornament" (49).

The stifling effect that Clive's parents have on him is represented by a dream with which the young man is plagued. Pamela tells her parents that in this dream Clive is warming himself under nearly ten blankets until his father comes in the room and begins removing the blankets one by one. This is reminiscent of Louise's fear of being choked to death under "piles of English blankets" (88), but it also suggests that Clive's father creates a cold atmosphere or perhaps denies the young man any security of his own. Existentialists may see the dream as a manifestation of a loss of power, in that Clive's fate is being controlled by the actions of others. In essence, Stanley "strips" Clive of any sense of control or security he may have.

Clive would like nothing more than to express his individuality without playing a role for other people. His family treats him as if he were an object, without an identity of his own. Pamela discusses Clive's plight with Walter: "At home, everyone keeps on at him but no one really takes any notice of him. [*Brightly.*] Clive spends his whole time not being listened to" (63). Clive tells his father that the only "right" fellow that he met at Cambridge was an Indian student who demonstrated a thorough understanding of his own independence. Clive tries to explain to his father why it is essential that he establish his own set of values free from the influence of others:

> But *you* don't even know the right way to treat a child. Because a child is private and important and *itself*. Not an extension of you, any more than I am.
> [*He falls quiet, dead quiet—as if explaining something very difficult. His speech slows and his face betrays an almost obsessed sincerity as he sits.*]
> I am myself. Myself. Myself. You think of me only as what I might become. What I might make of myself. But I am myself now—with every breath I take, every blink of the eyelash. (57)

In virtually all of Shaffer's plays, the protagonist, unable to establish an identity for himself, is also sexually sterile.[35] Shaffer depicts Clive as a "nervous," withdrawn individual whose contact with women, as Pamela remarks, is reduced to "not even acquaintanceships" (63). Perhaps this sexual sterility has a bearing on Clive's jealousy of Walter, whom Clive suggests has a desire "to be petted and stroked" (52). Louise is sexually attracted to Walter, and Clive, perhaps unconsciously feeling insecure about his own relationship with women, seeks revenge on Walter by telling Mr. Harrington that he saw Walter kissing Louise's breasts. Walter, however, assures Clive that his problems, perhaps leading to alcoholism, will not improve simply by satisfying sexual conflicts: "Sex by itself is nothing, believe me" (97). Only by establishing his own sense of identity will Clive be able to manage his social and psychological frustrations.

As I mentioned in chapter 2, Shaffer's insecure protagonists often base their existence on a lie to create a false image of themselves or are forced to tell lies that tend to destroy themselves or others. Clive's revelation about Walter's love for Mrs. Harrington is a lie that helps to secure the protagonist's position in the family. It is not unusual for the Shafferian protagonist to try to destroy others through the lie, especially when his secure environment is threatened.[36] When Clive lies to his father about Walter's relationship with Louise, the result is that Walter feels threatened, is asked to leave the house, and eventually tries to commit suicide.[37] As the protagonist develops a strong sense of self-worth and confidence in himself as the creator and controller of his own destiny, the lies will cease.

As John Russell Taylor has noted, Walter is the catalyst of the play.[38] He is the outsider, the "thumb" of the five fingers, yet he plays a crucial role in many of the relationships. Walter is an older brother to Pamela, a potential lover for Louise, and a confidante to Stanley, who must gripe about his predicament to someone other than his wife. Shaffer describes him as "a German youth of twenty-two, secret, warm, precise yet not priggish" (20), a model of ideal behavior who upsets the family's delicate balance.

The key to the play is Walter's relationship with Clive, Shaffer's protagonist. Walter is Clive's "twin," his alter ego who helps Clive to understand how to escape the doldrums of his banal existence. Shaffer acknowledged to me that he admires and has affection for Walter, who is trying to "behave well" in difficult circumstances where others are seeking to use him as a weapon to their best advantage.[39] Walter is a precursor to Atahuallpa, Alan Strang, and Mozart—"primitives" or independent persons who know what they want out of life and who have fashioned their lives for themselves, not for others. Walter has this same type of independent spirit and is not confined by what society thinks of him. At the age of twenty-two, he is able to earn his own living free from his parents and on his own terms in a country that is not his native land. Walter, whose parents live in Mühlbach, Germany, has rejected his country and tells the Harringtons that he has no family. He refuses to speak of his father whom he detests because of the work his parents did in Auschwitz during World War II. In effect, Walter has rejected his family, his country, and his culture (he refuses to teach German even though he could do better at it than with French) so as to live freely without being confined by history and by his cultural heritage.

Walter's presence affects everyone in the household; they unconsciously realize that his independence makes him "different." Pamela says that when she is with him "I always feel like the grubby shirt next to the dazzling white one. He's so fresh! Fresh and beautiful" (74). Clive is also in awe of him, impressed with the idea that he is "such an *excluded* person" (77). Louise, of course, is impressed with his demeanor, his education, and his strong sense of values.

Ashamed of his German heritage, Walter finds England to be "paradise" (46) and would love to rekindle the family spirit that he lost in Germany. He wants a family and friends with whom he can share his life. He is at peace with himself in the Harrington household, and this is why he asks Louise to be a surrogate mother for him. Clive, however, refuses to see Walter's need for a family as demonstrating any sort of independence, and it is not until the end of the play that Clive really begins to understand Walter, the self-made man.

Although Clive is the protagonist of the play, Shaffer seems to identify with Walter and is most sympathetic towards him.[40] Walter is Clive's alter ego, and in trying to dissuade the German tutor from being dependent on the Harrington family, Clive is actually pleading for his own futile existence. Clive views Walter as someone who is "taken in" (50) as an object to be used by others or "taken up! Like a fashion. Or an ornament; a piece of Dresden, a dear little Dresden owl" (50). The Dresden owl refers to Hibou, Louise's nickname for Walter whom she believes resembles an owl because of the way his glasses make him look so erudite. Clive, however, prefers the name "Pou" or "Louse" to characterize Walter's dependence. He warns the tutor that the Harrington family, a tribe of wild cannibals, destroys individuality: "And believe me, love, sooner or later, like any other valuable possession, you will be used. I know this family, let me tell you" (50). Clive criticizes Walter for surrendering his freedom to gain a family: "You've got a crush on our family that's almost obscene. Can't you see how lucky you are to be on your own?" (78–79). Clive is well aware that "the trouble is if you don't spend your life yourself, other people spend it for you. . . ." (78), so it is not unusual for him to question Walter's integrity: "Why have you got to depend all the time? It's so damned weak!" (79).

The difference between Clive and Walter is that the former has no sense of identity and is controlled by others, while the latter is independent and knows what he wants to do with his life. During perhaps the most solemn and significant conversation in the play, Clive asks Walter what his goals are in life. Walter responds assertively: "To live in England. To be happy teaching. One day to marry. To have children, and many English friends . . ." (98). Walter is meeting his goals, created by him and not by family, friends, or society. He is currently teaching, living in England, establishing friendships, and choosing a family with which he feels comfortable. However, when Clive is asked about his purpose in life, he is tentative at first and then assures us that he has needs of his own: "[*Faintly.*] Something—I'm not sure [*Intimately.*] Yes—I think I want . . . to achieve something that only I could do. I want to fall in love with just one person.

To know what it is to bless and be blessed. And to serve a great cause with devotion. [*Appealing.*] I want to be *involved*" (98).

Clive has the potential to establish his own identity like Walter has done, but he needs someone to provide him with the incentive to do so. At the end of the play, Walter has lost his family, his best friend, and his new mother; he is forced to return to Germany because Mr. Harrington will make certain that Walter never receives his naturalization papers and will therefore be denied British citizenship. His suicide attempt can, on the one hand, be construed as a defensive mechanism by someone whose purpose in life has been taken from him. On the other hand, Walter makes a conscious decision to turn on the gas to serve as the catalyst for Clive, unmasking the latent problems of identity with which Clive has been struggling. Before Walter's attempted suicide, he urged Clive to leave his family and live on his own for a while. Walter's "accident" is certainly the "courage" (110) of which Clive speaks—the supreme example of daring independence and existential action that he must learn for himself.

Five Finger Exercise presents a dialectic between two alter egos, one of whom is an independent person, while the other is controlled by family and society. Clive, a sterile individual with the potential to establish a strong identity of his own, learns from his role model, Walter, what courage means. In Shaffer's plays, "courage" refers to adhering to one's own norms and values no matter how different they are from the roles and codified behavior of accepted societal mores and standards. Throughout most of the play, Clive is not yet ready to think and act for himself. He resorts to lying, an act that serves to destroy his alter ego because Clive is jealous of him. However, at the end of the play, before Walter attempts suicide, Clive begins to learn more about himself and those around him through an understanding of the freedom that Walter embraces. Shaffer, as he develops more expertise with regard to form and stage conventions, will make the form of the play correspond to an intuitive communion between the protagonist and his primitive alter ego. *Five Finger Exercise* was an excellent start for him; later on, however, we will see that form will more closely match content, and Shaffer will be able to develop stage conventions that are more interesting than a suicide attempt to assist with the denouement.

5

The Private Ear/The Public Eye:
Not Enough Notes

*T*HE *Private Ear* and *The Public Eye,* two one-act plays, opened in London at the Globe Theatre on 10 May 1962. Both plays were produced by H. M. Tennent and directed by Peter Wood. The cast included Douglas Livingston (Ted), Terry Scully (Bob), Maggie Smith (Doreen, Belinda), Kenneth Williams (Cristoforou), and Richard Pearson (Sidley). Almost all of the reviewers praised the plays while making some sort of reference to which of the plays they believed to be the strongest of the two. Favorable notices came from *The Times, The Illustrated London News, The Spectator, The Christian Science Monitor, Daily Telegraph, Punch, Evening Standard,* and *Daily Express.*[1] W. A. Darlington of the *Daily Telegraph* wrote that "The last *[Eye]* is clever and very funny; but the other will live in one's mind as an exquisite little gem of writing and acting."[2] Milton Shulman agreed with Darlington in that *The Public Eye,* he claimed, is not as successful as *The Private Ear,* yet *Eye* works on stage because of the eccentric Cristoforou, a "fey leprechaun with the combined qualities of Peter Pan, Peter Wimsey and Groucho Marx. . . ."[3] On the other hand, J. C. Trewin of *The Illustrated London News* and Harold Hobson of *The Christian Science Monitor* believed that *Eye* is the better of the two plays.[4] Trewin and Hobson were supported by Bamber Gascoigne who noted that *The Private Ear,* successful but "very slight," did not have the depth of *The Public Eye,* "a brilliantly serious piece of fantasy . . . backed up by many more direct moral precepts, always put with the same lightness."[5] Perhaps Eric Keown summed up most of the critics' favorable responses to the plays with this comment in *Punch:* "In both of them is a vein of pure comedy that is fresh and delightful and in both Mr. Shaffer demonstrates his subtle understanding of human feelings in a way that is suddenly and immensely touching."[6]

Kenneth Tynan's review in *The Observer* was neutral at best.[7] With regard to *The Private Ear,* Tynan lamented that "the tone throughout is sickeningly condescending, like that of certain Noel Coward sketches in the thirties; Mr. Shaffer takes pains to exhibit a mastery of lower-class idiom that he transparently hasn't got."[8] However, Tynan liked The Public Eye much better, admitting that "the second part of the evening finds Mr. Shaffer at large in his own class, and much more at home," and that "Peter Wood's direction, lamentable in the first half, comes to life in the second."[9]

The two noteworthy negative reviews were from Roger Gellert of New Statesman and T. C. Worsley of the Financial Times.[10] Gellert had nothing positive to say about either play, calling them both "deeply flawed."[11] T. C. Worsley was more apologetic, praising the acting ability of the cast and cautioning the reader that the audience enjoyed the plays much more than he did. He claimed that The Private Ear just does not work on stage; although, in his opinion, The Public Eye is better, it also lacks coherence and cohesion.[12]

After their successful run in London, the plays were tried out at the Wilbur Theater in Boston in September 1963, and then debuted in New York at the Morosco Theater on 9 October 1963. Peter Wood now directed a new cast that consisted of Brian Bedford (Bob), Barry Foster (Ted, Cristoforou), Moray Watson (Sidley), and Geraldine McEwan (Doreen, Belinda). Favorable reviews were posted in the Daily News, New York Post, New York Mirror, Time, The Nation, New York World-Telegram, New York Herald Tribune, and Variety.[13] Most of the critics praised Shaffer's wit, his insight into modern social foibles, and his ability to draw interesting characters. The consensus among the majority of the critics was that The Public Eye was the stronger of the two plays.[14]

Howard Taubman's review in The New York Times seems ambivalent.[15] He refers to The Public Eye as "a specimen of an art that has become so rare it might be kept under glass."[16] But he describes The Private Ear as "a trifling ancedote, spun out for an hour" of entertainment that is "commonplace at the core."[17] In a similar vein, John McClain, of the New York Journal American, characterized Ear as a play with "charm and compulsion and humor," while Eye was viewed as a farce that seems to work until Shaffer becomes "philosophical and long-winded."[18] McClain acknowledged that Shaffer "has the gift of a splendid ear for dialogue, an abiding sense of the ridiculous, and an over-powering devotion to his own words," yet he wonders why we have to import these plays when American "craftsmen" can do just as well as the British.[19] The only negative review for both ends of the double bill came from the anonymous critic for Newsweek, who accused Shaffer of "cranking out words unendingly."[20] The review, one paragraph long, stated that both plays were concerned with short circuits in human communication, "a theme that would benefit from a holiday."[21] Praise went to the performers who "superbly pretend that they have something to act."[22]

Although the two plays garnered no major awards, in 1972, almost ten years after their debut in New York, they were turned into films. Shaffer, however, did not write either of the screenplays.

The Private Ear and *The Public Eye* represent an attempt to experiment with dramatic form. For this reason, the plays mark an important step in Shaffer's development as a playwright. In an interview with *The Transatlantic Review,* Shaffer defended the two one-act plays:

> There was some cheap knock-about comedy in it. But the critics who didn't like the double bill, didn't take it for what it was intended. A *jeu d'esprit*. After all this is a privilege of writers. Anouilh has his *pièces roses* and *pièces noires*. In many ways it was a breakthrough for me. . . .[23]

The plays function as mirror images of each other. Both dramas are concerned with the male-female relationship, whether it is exposed in single life *(The Private Ear)* or in marriage *(The Public Eye).* Each play consists of two males and one female in a mixed-up romantic triangle. In both plays, a timid male, insecure in a world of roles others have created for him, is coaxed by his alter ego, his "twin," into developing a more casual relationship with a woman he loves. The result is that the insecure individual learns from his rival how to relate more naturally to himself and to others without forever worrying about his own shortcomings or the expectations that others have of him.

The Private Ear, written in four days, was originally conceived of as a television play.[24] Hugh Beaumont, who was one of London's leading producers and who had staged *Five Finger Exercise,* presented the play to Peter Wood, who suggested that it be performed on stage with another short drama to accompany it. The play is traditional in form, follows the unities, has a cluttered set reminiscent of nineteenth-century realism, and its explicit stage directions seem a bit Shavian. The language, working-class British dialect from the early 1960s, can outdate itself rather quickly.[25] Although these one-act plays did represent a search for new forms of theater, both dramas are still quite conventional in terms of language, style, and *mise-en-scène*.

Bob, nicknamed Tchaik because of his fascination with Tchaikovsky, is the protagonist of *The Private Ear,* and he is the character with whom Shaffer identifies.[26] Bob, the stereotyped young man trying to break free from the control that his environment has on him, is similar to the young Peter Shaffer who was anxious to become a playwright yet was pressured to find more "suitable" employment. Bob would like to detach himself from his bonds to others, yet he is too conditioned to do so. Like Clive, Bob, who is "an awkward young man in his late teens, or early twenties," has no sense of self-awareness; his "whole manner exudes an evident lack of confidence—in himself and in life."[27]

Bob has no identity of his own, a fact that Shaffer underscores by refusing to provide him with a last name, even though we learn the full names of the two minor characters. He is so pathetically dependent on others that he has asked Ted Veasey, his best friend, to "help out with the talk" (20) while they entertain Doreen, a young lady whom Bob recently met at a concert. Bob is dependent on Ted to the point where he can offer no original thoughts of his own and must imitate Ted's vocabulary. "Very chic" (25), Bob says when hanging up Doreen's coat, even though he has just asked Ted what "chic" means. His conversation with Doreen ends up as a series of clichés from Ted's repertoire:

> Alcohol's not really a stimulant at all, you know—it's a depressant. (52)

> That's really raven black, her hair. It's got tints of blue in it. (58)

> Style, you know. It's what they used to call "carriage." (58)

The irony is that the clichés that Bob uses make him look foolish in Doreen's eyes; she realizes that she has heard them before—from Ted, who used some of the same lines earlier in the evening when he was initially trying to impress her.

Shaffer depicts Bob as an insecure individual at ease only when he is with his music. Bob has invited Doreen to spend an evening with him, but it is Ted who makes the plans to assure that the rendezvous is a success. At the start of the play, Ted enters carrying the shopping bag to supply the necessary refreshments and finds Bob absorbed in Mozart. Ted notes that Bob is even having trouble dressing himself: "You're marvelous! The most important night of your life, and you can't even get yourself dressed. All you can do is listen to bloody music" (14). Ted helps his inept friend choose a suitable tie, for the one that Bob had selected stereotyped him as "a twelve pound a week office worker" (15) who lives for the weekends. The evening turns more uncomfortable for Bob as we learn that he is also adept at spilling vases (18), forgetting to buy cocktails for dinner (23), fumbling with cigarette lighters (26), suggesting drinks for Doreen when he has none to give her (28), and finally, trying haplessly to seduce her on the bed (56), an erotic response that nets him a slap in the face.

Bob has no confidence in himself; his identity comes from what other people think or say. Bob is almost incapable of thinking for himself; instead, he tries to imitate Ted, and by doing so, he destroys his self-esteem. Bob, alone with Doreen, "his mind full of how Ted would act under these circumstances" (56), begins seducing the startled young lady without think-ing of what he is doing. Doreen, realizing that Bob is not in control of the situation, begins to show more of an interest in Ted. She leaves Bob's apartment with Ted's address, thereby rejecting Bob in favor of his alter ego, the person whom she sees as being more "responsible" for his own actions.

Bob, like Clive, is faced with a sexually sterile existence to accompany his social aberrations. Ted knows that Bob has met few women, and Doreen is actually the first person that Bob has invited on a date. Bob feels anxious when talking to women and tells Ted that he needs his support during the evening because "Well you know what to say to women. You've had the practice" (20). In essence, Bob's soirée with Doreen, actually the raison d'être of the play, concerns Bob's attempts to communicate with the opposite sex and to break out of his shell by coming to grips with his sterile existence.

As is typically true of Shaffer's sterile protagonists who must lie in order to maintain status quo, Bob tells lies to compensate for his sexual inadequacies. He tries to befriend Doreen by coaxing her to believe that at the concert "you were so wrapped up in listening, so concentrating" (33), although the truth was that Doreen's friend gave her a free ticket "and it seemed silly to waste it . . . Actually it was ever so boring" (44). The big lie, Bob's insistence that Lavinia, who is Ted's girl friend, is in love with him, not only severs his relationship with Doreen, but also destroys any respect she had for him as an independent and truthful person.

The actress who plays Doreen must conjure up a nervous simpleton who has no mind of her own—the perfect match for Bob. Doreen is depicted as an uninspiring, uninformed, nervous working class girl of about twenty whose "reactions are anxious and tight" (24). Without too many thoughts of her own, Doreen can only mimic her father's ideas, to the point where we wish her father had come in her place. As soon as she arrives, she chimes in with, "Unpunctuality's the thief of time, as my dad says" (24), to be followed by, "Like my dad says, 'Money doesn't grow on trees'" (26), or, "He says, if you haven't got drive, you might as well be dead" (32), and finally, "My dad says, 'Drink is the curse of the working classes'" (40). She is hardly the Botticellian vision of Venus that Bob expects to see.

Bob and Doreen are actually made for each other. Like Bob, Doreen is a blue-collar worker, a stenographer who dreams of doing something better with her life yet who is content with doing the same boring routine day in and day out because "there's not much choice" (26). She is unable to express her own opinions about anything and is therefore prone to steal other peoples' ideas and use them as if they were hers. Because of her inadequacies and her inability to be truthful with others, her life has become empty and meaningless. She has lied to Bob by letting him assume that she is a music lover, and, of course, their relationship, based on this lie, will never work. She does not even have the heart to tell Bob, when he pressed her to reveal whether or not her coat was real leopard skin, that it is nylon, not ocelot, a fancy creation of hers.

Ted offers himself as a role model for Bob, who is listless, apathetic, depressed, and uncertain of himself. Bob has asked Ted to help him entertain Doreen because he trusts his friend's "savoir faire" and his experience with women. Ted, an extrovert who is "fitted out gaily by Shaftesbury Avenue to match his own inner confidence and self-approval" (13), is constantly admiring himself as a self-styled Don Juan, continually combing his hair in front of a mirror or trying to be as "chic" as possible. Shaffer described Ted to me:

> He is one of those flip—he's an early model for a Yuppie, in a way—upwardly mobile figures. Bright. Go-getting. I find him rather boring actually. . . . I don't think Ted Veasey's world is as glamorous or as sophisticated as he intended it to be. One day he will probably marry one of those girls and end up as another ordinary husband in one of those suburbs of London.[28]

Bob, however, respects Ted's opinions. He tells Doreen that Ted has "just been promoted to look after a small department of his own. It means quite a bit of responsibility. He's going to go a long way, I think. I mean he's interested and keen—you know" (31). As the evening wears on, Ted does give Bob some advice. After talking with Doreen when Bob is out of the room, Ted discovers what she is really like. He tries to warn Bob that Doreen is an ordinary person, not a Botticelli beauty:

> You know how she feels about you. She thinks you're the most courteous man she's ever met. And so you are, mate. Just don't overdo it, that's all. This is a girl, not a goddess. Just you give her a shove off her pedestal. You'll find she won't exactly resent it. (49)

Ted is much like Louise Harrington in that both are artificial characters who want to impose their values on others. Ted insists on being "chic" and mocks Bob's lifestyle and his obsession for music.[29] Ted, like Louise, seems to think that it is fashionable to use nicknames, adopt a proper French vocabulary, and cultivate a faddish or even an ephemeral tongue. Ted seems to be as harmless as any of Molière's illusory masqueraders, but he is really dangerous because he gives unnecessary advice to others and, in doing so, comes close to destroying the autonomy of the individual.

Bob's conflict is not with Doreen, but with Ted, his alter ego. Bob resents Ted's intrusion into his life, much in the same manner that Clive is offended by Walter's interference in the family. There are a number of instances where Bob hints at the resentment of his mundane existence and the fact that Ted keeps reminding him of his sterile life. He is aware that "I'm just a glorified office boy really. At least that's what Ted keeps on telling me, and I suppose he's right" (31). By admonishing Doreen for "doing the same thing, day in, day out" (26) and spending her whole life "being somebody else's obedient servant, original and two carbons" (53), Bob is also consciously criticizing his own mundane life. Bob does not want to put on airs like his friend Ted and sincerely believes that "things should just happen between people" (21). As the disappointments build up during the evening, Bob turns against his friend and tormentor, first by calling him ignorant (37), and then by violently rejecting his "savoir-faire" (49). The two alter egos clash in front of Doreen with the result that Ted walks out on his "double" so that Bob can fail on his own. Before Ted leaves, Bob explains the source of his frustration with his friend:

> I'm just someone to look down on, aren't I? Teach tricks to. Like a bloody monkey. You're the organ grinder, and I'm the monkey! And that's the way you want people. Well—go home, Ted. Find yourself another monkey! (50)

Throughout the play, Bob has shown that he is more dependent on his stereo, nicknamed Behemoth, than anything else, and only when he is talking about his favorite music is he ever at ease. Like Shaffer, Bob has a fascination for music, and his longest speeches in the play are about stereo speakers, Tchaikovsky, and Benjamin Britten.[30] Yet at the end of the drama, Bob scratches one of his beloved records due to his sexual and social frustrations. This symbolic gesture is a means for him to reduce his dependence on people and objects, particularly his music, Bob's major obsession. The protagonist is reacting against his alter ego, rather than in admiration of him (as will be true of the later plays). The scratching of the record has the same overt effect that Walter's attempted suicide had on Clive: it is a symbolic act that may be the impetus for change within the protagonist. The spectator must conclude that Bob's evening has been enlightening, although "Tchaik" is not yet ready to adapt to change. As Rodney Simard points out, Bob's "brush with the grimy reality that his roommate Ted inhabits sends him back into his own subjective world where he, like the hero of Britten's *Peter Grimes,* can live in isolation and dream of the ideal."[31] Shaffer would probably agree with Simard's assessment. During my interview with him, Shaffer noted that Bob's scratching of the record is a reaction to the purity of the world of art; similarly, "Bob is mocked by this perfect world of lovers where the sweet 'music' seems to be ecstatic and nobody makes a mistake."[32] The play presents this contrast between life and art; things are supposed to happen a certain way, but usually the reality is a far cry from our expectations.

In the later plays, we will see a change in the protagonist as a result of an intuitive means of communicating with his alter ego. Ritualistic theater will work well with this type of spontaneous communication between the role player and his primitive "twin." However, in the early plays, this element of symbolic communication is missing, so the form of the play is appropriate for the content. Again, as Shaffer's style matures, he will begin to find new ways to make the dialectic work on stage.

The Public Eye, like its companion piece, is concerned with the importance that role playing and public image have on our lives. Shaffer's image makers—Ted and Mrs. Harrington—now have a new counterpart: Charles Sidley, a staunch, middle-class gentleman. The sexual and social problems that accrue from role playing are now the basis for Sidley's conflicts with his wife, Belinda. The play examines the trauma that occurs when the image maker, the staid role player, is contrasted with his double or alter ego, an independent rival who creates his own identity to please himself, not others.

Charles Sidley is the prototype of the Shafferian protagonist who must transcend his present monotonous life if he is going to be able to free himself from a controlled, sterile existence. Sidley, a chartered Bloomsbury accountant, "almost finicky in his speech" (63), leads a rigid, carefully controlled life. He is more of a role than a human being and is comparable more to a computer than to an individual who can think and feel for himself. Sidley's "passion for accuracy" or, as he himself puts it, "respect for fact" (64), forces him to treat his wife as if she were some sort of decipherable computerized punch card. His entire life revolves around hiding behind a facade, living up to someone else's arbitrarily imposed standards of excellence, and, naturally, excluding all other models of behavior that do not conform to his highly structured and ideal standards. Belinda continually urges her husband to drop the mask and be himself: "Not your iceberg voice. I can't bear it. 'One would hardly say.' 'I scarcely think.' 'One might hazard, my dear.' All that morning suit language. It's only hiding" (90). Cristoforou, a private detective hired by Sidley to follow Belinda, understands that Sidley is hardly thinking and acting for himself. Instead, he is a composite of roles or what other people, particularly his peers, want him to be. Cristoforou explains to Belinda why her marriage with Sidley is failing: "He's so afraid of being touched by life he hardly exists. He's so scared of looking foolish, he puts up words against it for barriers: Good Taste. Morality. What you *should* do. What you *should* feel. He's walled up on Should like in a tomb" (110–11).

Role playing sometimes leads to the control of others in order for the individual to maintain his secure existence. When Sidley married Belinda, they were in love, and their relationship was shared. Sidley, who found himself slipping into middle age, was attracted by Belinda's youthful enthusiasm. Belinda was intrigued by Sidley's wide range of knowledge and experience in a variety of disciplines. She explains to her husband that "you gave me facts, ideas, reasons for things" (94). What was once a mutually satisfying relationship ended when Sidley began dictating to his wife, refusing to allow her to have any identity of her own.

Sidley, ideal in his role as an accountant who demands perfection, tried to make his wife in his own image. Cristoforou compares Sidley's profession to the priesthood because "people do what you tell them without question" (72). Belinda is treated almost like one of Sidley's clients who must pay homage to the chief priest. Cristoforou explains to Belinda that the need of one person to dominate another in marriage is not so unusual: "Most husbands want to create wives in their own image and resent all changes they haven't caused, all experiences they haven't shared, and—with wives brighter than they are—all new things they can't keep up with" (110).

Sidley is proud that Belinda "surrendered her whole life to me, for remaking" (80). To Sidley, Belinda is an "inferior," a child at heart who has no serious thoughts and ambitions of her own. Belinda's background leads Sidley to this conclusion. She lived the first eighteen years of her life with her parents in Northampton, whose ambition for their daughter was to have her take a job at the library and marry a local boy. Belinda rebelled and ran off to London where she lived for a while with two bohemian artists. Her next partner was Charles Sidley, who saw the urgent need to take this raw talent and sculpt it into an image of his own likeness.

During their first meeting, Sidley plunged right into "the Theory of Natural Selection, the meaning of Id, Ego and Super-Ego . . . Bach's Fugue in C Sharp Minor, Book One, *Well-Tempered Clavier*" (93). Aware that he had married "someone with no sense of her place at all" (81), Sidley admits that he "taught her everything I could" (81). He boasts that he has made his wife in his own image:

> Belinda is the wife of a professional man in a highly organized city in the twentieth century. That is her place. As I have often explained to her, this would undoubtedly be different if she were wedded to a jazz trumpeter in New Orleans, which she seems to think she is. There is no such thing as a perfectly independent person. (82)

Thus, Sidley warns Cristoforou, who has made a sarcastic comment about how Belinda's hat looked like wilted lettuce, that "when you criticize her taste in hats, you are criticizing me" (75). Later, when explaining how he followed Belinda to the statue of Peter Pan in Kensington Gardens, Sidley informs the detective of additional training he has given his wife: "The first week we were married I showed her that statue and explained to her precisely why it was ridiculous. When you criticize her taste in statuary you criticize me" (76). Sidley has apparently conditioned his wife to think and act accordingly; she appears to be what Bob referred to as "a trained monkey" or more like a pet than a human being.

As the consummate role player who stifles independent people such as his wife, Sidley develops sexual and social difficulties. In essence, *The Public Eye,* like *The Private Ear,* is concerned with sexual misunderstandings that develop because the protagonist is living in a microcosm of limited roles, rules, and regulations. The problem comes from within and not, as Sidley believes, because "men of forty shouldn't marry girls of eighteen" (81). There is no more spark in their marriage, and Belinda reminds Sidley of this: "I used to greet you, inside me anyway, forty times a day. Now it's once a fortnight . . . It's all so dead with us now" (95). Sidley had to hire a private detective to spy on his wife because his marriage just was not working any longer.

The social strains again lead to the lie, the Shafferian tool of destruction. Belinda knows that her husband's staid world is artificial. Sidley, supposedly the moral accountant who is beyond reproach in his behavior, seems to spend much of his time cheating on his wife by visiting call girls. He even keeps a copy of the *Ladies Directory* in his desk so as to stay abreast of the whereabouts of noteworthy prostitutes. When Belinda reveals Sidley's hypocrisy to Cristoforou, the accountant is caught in a lie that forces him to cease his masquerade as the defender of morality; in short, Sidley's exposure due to the lie is similar to the unmasking of Bob or Clive, both victims of their own lies.

Belinda wants her freedom and realizes that life with Sidley is a continual struggle to live up to his standards. She is an independent person who is aware of the shortcomings of her husband, yet she makes no attempt to stifle his freedom. She acknowledges that "men should have a change from their wives occasionally" (110), and that includes allowing Sidley to visit Madame Conchita's stable of women.

Belinda's fierce independence is a direct contrast to Sidley's staid, rigid existence, proving that opposites do sometimes attract. She is described as "a pretty young girl of twenty-two, wearing bright unconventional clothes" (87). She occasionally will do whatever comes naturally to her, for she plays no roles and does not have to answer to peers, friends, subordinates, or bosses. When we first see her, she has turned up at Sidley's office unexpectedly on Saturday during the time that is usually allotted for her cooking lesson at Cordon Bleu. Her explanation for the refusal to go gourmet is that "I got tired of learning the right way to hold a saucepan; so I left" (87). Cristoforou explains to her how she differs from her husband: "If you hear a piece of music, you'll either love it or hate it. He won't know what to feel till he knows who it's by. Sick" (111). When Belinda asks for an additional comparison, the detective says, "You're Spirit, Belinda, and he's Letter. You've got passion where all he's got is pronouncement" (111).

Belinda has begun to lose her zest for life because Sidley has tried to destroy this very sense of "spirit" within her. Sidley has been trying to suffocate Belinda very much in the same manner that Clive's parents were trying to stifle his freedom. Sidley believes that Belinda has a strongly defined role to play as the wife of a successful businessman. Her job is to entertain Sidley's friends, get out the port, and nonchalantly leave the room. Belinda, who describes Sidley's "friends" as "a lot of coughing old men with weak bladders and filthy tempers, scared of women and bright red with brandy" (90), resents that she is being taught how to behave. Much in the same manner that Clive was annoyed by his father's constant assessment of him, Belinda sees Sidley as a stern "headmaster" who makes his pupil feel that "I have to defend myself in front of you" (94). Belinda believes that she is being trained and tells Sidley that "this isn't my home. It's my school" (93). Treated as a pet pupil, with the emphasis on "pet," reminiscent of Bob, the trained monkey, Belinda asserts that "I'd forgotten what it was like to be looked at without criticism" (97) and tries to make her husband believe that "you're not my only duty . . . and I'm not yours. You've got to be faithful to all sorts of people. You can't give everything to just one. Just one can't use everything" (91).

Because Sidley treats Belinda as a subordinate, their marriage has been falling apart. Belinda is no longer sexually attracted to her husband and spends a good part of her day trying to release her frustrations by watching perverse horror movies. The rest of the day is spent wandering the streets: "I was trying to think: that's all. Trying to pull myself out of the burrow on my own. I wandered about all over the place, it doesn't matter where" (96). Then one day, she met Julian Cristoforou and established a rapport with him that she never had with her husband.

Cristoforou is the sort of person who is capable of reuniting Belinda and Charles. Belinda has the potential for independent thought, yet her background presupposes any strong will of her own. The private detective provides her with the impetus she needs to revolt against her stifling environment. When she first met Cristoforou as he followed her on her daily meanderings, she intuitively understood that "all I knew was here was someone who approved of me. Who got pleasure out of just being in my company" (98). Belinda, like Cristoforou, is an independent person who appeared at ease with someone who enjoyed her company without trying to dominate her. Although they did not speak to each other, they were still able to communicate intuitively. One day, Cristoforou would follow Belinda, and then the next day she would "shadow" him. When one took the lead, the other would surely follow, each learning from the other's diverse interests. Cristoforou recalls that Belinda prospered from the experience: "I found you aimless in London; I gave you direction. I found you smileless; I gave you joy" (105). Moreover, the benefits were reciprocal, and Cristoforou admits that he learned more about life through Belinda:

For three weeks I walked through London, all alone except for you to point the way. And slowly, in the depths of that long silence, I began to hear a wonderful sound: the rustle of my own emotions growing. . . . We are born living, and yet how ready we are to play possum and fake death. You led me out of the dead land, Belinda—where we hide from new experience because we're afraid to alter. (112)

Cristoforou, who intuitively understands Belinda's independent spirit, acts as her spokesman to devise a scheme to humble his alter ego, Sidley, the staid role player. Sidley married Belinda because he was attracted to her youthful independence in contrast to his own stuffy attitudes. It is perhaps this independent spirit of Cristoforou that threatens Sidley. The rivalry between the two opposing forces, these "twins" that, in the later plays will more aptly reflect the battle between the Apollonian and Dionysian sides of our psyche, becomes intense when Cristoforou pries into the accountant's personal life, thus attempting to disrupt Sidley's private affairs.

In contrast to Sidley's rigid behavior in accordance with roles, rules, and regulations, Cristoforou has a strong identity of his own created by his personal values. Cristoforou is a stock character, the private detective that Shaffer stereotyped in his novels. He is always seen in Shaffer's works as an independent, all-knowing person with a mind of his own, very much the Mr. Verity of modern society. Cristoforou is not a phony but is instead a unique individual open to criticism from himself and others; his "whole air breathes a gentle eccentricity, a nervousness combined with an air of almost meek self-disapprobation and a certain bright detachment" (63). Cristoforou tries to be himself; he refuses to put on airs for others or worry about what others think of him. Sidley's office is not a formal place to him, so it is not unusual for him to visit on Saturdays even though Sidley insists that he be more businesslike and make an appointment on regular work days. Cristoforou is the type of person who eats yoghurt or raisins in Sidley's office because he admits to having a sweet tooth that must be satisfied despite the fact that Sidley's office is not an appropriate place to snack. Role playing is foreign to him, an odd thing for a private detective to reveal. Yet he assures Sidley that "I was everything once. I had twenty-three positions before I was thirty" (65). This probably does not alarm Sidley as much as Cristoforou's admission that "I never fail in jobs, they fail me" (65), an appalling thing to say to a man whose whole life is based on the image that his job reflects to others.

Cristoforou is not someone who hides behind masks or lives in a world of illusion, nor does he need to be recognized by others. He assures Sidley that "last year I became characterless. This year, superfluous" (70). Although the detective is aware that "people do what you tell them without question" (72), he tries his best not to fall within this category; to Cristoforou, this quality is "very rare" (103), but to Sidley, "it's vile" (103). As a man of many eccentricities, Cristoforou is convinced that only he can be the judge of his actions. Even his job precludes that he ignore whatever his employers think of him: "If you give your employer bad news he hates you. If you give him good he thinks his money's been wasted. Either way you can't win" (107–108).

The private detective's extroverted nature, his concern for others, and his strong sense of his own identity are contrasted with Sidley's highly egocentric, selfish behavior coupled with his need to play roles and have others conform to his ideal standards. Cristoforou believes that "alone, I didn't exist; I came alive only against a background of other people's affairs" (104). When he urges Belinda to dry her tears because "they're so excluding" (106), we are reminded of the fear and envy that Clive had of Walter as "an excluded person." Now this fear is transformed into Sidley's apprehension of Cristoforou's threatening extroverted nature. In short, Cristoforou becomes a catalyst from whom Sidley can learn. Antagonism develops as the two alter egos clash, to such an extent that physical violence breaks out.

Cristoforou, in trying to help Belinda, another independent person, devises a plan where Sidley must follow his wife for one month, no matter where she goes, and participate in all of her activities. The game that Cristoforou has devised is designed to break down Sidley's fraudulent world, allowing him to learn more about his wife and about life itself. As Sidley's alter ego, Cristoforou becomes a catalyst for the process of self-discovery, forcing Sidley to accept the idea that as a human being he is more than just a series of roles or an image that he must project to others. Although Cristoforou is not quite the primitive that Shaffer sees in Alan Strang or Atahuallpa, he is certainly their forerunner. As the eccentric who unmasks and humbles the protagonist, Cristoforou provides an initial glimpse of the future Atahuallpa, Alan Strang, Mark Askelon, or Mozart engaged in psychological warfare with a threatening alter ego.

As Shaffer stated, the twin bill was an important breakthrough, allowing him to crystallize and solidify his thematic concerns. In his next play, *The Royal Hunt of the Sun,* his apprenticeship will be complete; the result is a polished union of form, stage techniques, and the same sociological motifs with which he has so thoroughly experimented in these early plays.

6

The Royal Hunt of the Sun:
The Maestro Finds Gold

PETER Shaffer spent six years working on *The Royal Hunt of the Sun*. As early as July 1958, Shaffer was describing the play, already titled, to the media: "This is a large-scale chronicle of the Fall of the Inca Empire in the 16th century. . . . I aim for the immediacy of effect, combined with high theatricality of a Bach Passion."[1] The *New York Herald Tribune* reported that by December 1959, Shaffer had just completed the first draft of the play.[2] Many revisions later, the play was discovered by John Dexter at the National Theatre office after it was rejected by H. M. Tennent as being "unproduceable." In spring 1964, Shaffer and Dexter worked on the epic play for its debut at the Chichester Festival on 6 July.

During its run at Chichester, *Royal Hunt* received mixed notices. The *Evening Standard, The Observer,* and *New Statesman* gave the play favorable reviews.[3] Ronald Bryden of *New Statesman* called the spectacle a "stunning production," praised the acting ability of Robert Stephens (Atahuallpa) and Colin Blakely (Pizarro), and called the play the best work Shaffer had done thus far.[4] Bamber Gascoigne's review in *The Observer* lauded the actors, John Dexter's direction, and costumes designed by Michael Annals: "The fact is that with its ancient armoury of words, costumes, and acting, the theatre can do almost anything—and *The Royal Hunt of the Sun* has each in splendid abundance."[5]

Three publications presented unfavorable reviews: *Financial Times, The Guardian,* and *The Spectator.*[6] Malcolm Rutherford of *The Spectator* saw the play as a parody of the Crucifixion, a drama that "lacks both characters and a language of its own."[7] Benedict Nightingale, writing in *The Guardian,* agreed with Rutherford in acknowledging that *Royal Hunt* was ambitious, perhaps too much so: "Theatrically, the National Theatre's production feels its three and a half hours' length; there are blotches of tedium, digressions, repetition, and a general feeling of muddle. More importantly, there seems to be some essential hollowness."[8] The only neutral review was from Eric Shorter of the *Daily Telegraph.*[9] He praised the performances, the production, and Dexter's direction, but had problems with content: "The result is very strange and rich and quite enjoyable but ultimately unsatisfying."[10]

On 8 December 1964, the National Theatre moved *Royal Hunt* to the Old Vic Theatre in London. Although few changes were made to the script (only one scene was removed from the original version; that scene, Pizarro pleading with Atahuallpa to let his men go free, was performed only on the first night at Chichester and was cut on the second night), the London press this time received the play more warmly. Favorable reviews were written in *The Times, The Sunday Times, Daily Mail, The Sunday Telegraph, Evening Standard,* and *Variety.*[11] Most critics were inundated with the play's spectacle, its broad scope, and its epic proportions. Alan Brien of *The Sunday Telegraph* wrote that "Mr. Shaffer's themes are on a colossal, heroic scale—theology, sociology, psychology, history, politics, morals melted in one giant cauldron. With a 100-piece orchestra, it would make an operatic subject to daunt even Wagner."[12] With its lavish costumes, fine acting, excellent direction, and immaculate stage production, *Royal Hunt* was seen as one of the outstanding post-World War II plays. Bernard Levin, one of London's most highly respected drama critics, did a great deal to enhance Shaffer's reputation when he praised the play in his review for the *Daily Mail*: "This giant drama, seen earlier this year at Chichester, has now moved into the National Theatre's London home, and a third seeing confirms and strengthens my belief that no greater play has been written and produced in our language in my lifetime."[13] Echoing Levin's remarks, *Variety's* review of shows abroad commended Shaffer: "The author's majestic command of language matches the dramatic spectacle, and the religious conflict between the Spaniards and the Incas is shrewdly developed as a vital and integral part of the plot."[14] Myro, *Variety's* reviewer, went on to say that "with this epic play, Peter Shaffer has made one of the great theatrical contributions of our time."[15]

The only major dissenting views came from W. A. Darlington of the *Daily Telegraph* and Penelope Gilliatt of *The Observer.* Darlington had problems following Shaffer's arguments but claimed that fine performances made the play work despite Shaffer's writing.[16] Gilliatt disagreed with her colleague, Bamber Gascoigne, who had enjoyed the play so much at Chichester. Gilliatt instead thought the drama was reduced to the level of a "pageant play" and claimed that there is very little intellectual content in the text.[17]

Buoyed by its success in London, *Royal Hunt* opened at the ANTA Theatre in New York on 26 October 1965. This time John Dexter directed David Carradine as Atahuallpa and Christopher Plummer as Pizarro. Shaffer as usual made some changes for the New York production, the most startling of which was his attempt to shorten what was considered a long second act. Shaffer, receiving some harmful advice that American audiences would not tolerate a second act that was forty minutes longer than the first, removed a segment from act 2 and placed it in act 1: "I thereby ruined the climax of the first act—the massacre—and diminished the intensity of the second. I flattened the play into a conventional shape of two more or less equal acts, when it had first consisted of a long act of character and argument preceded by a shorter gestural prologue. A bad decision on my part, I think."[18] In addition, Shaffer was concerned that if the play were moved to New York, it would lose the sense of wonder and mystery it had for British audiences:

> The sea-change here did not aid my Inca king at all. He appeared on stage, I think, before an audience prepared to make a quite different connection with him than the one made in England by the denizens of Chichester or the Waterloo Road! Cajamarca appeared a very far-off place to the English audience; to Americans, I suspect, it appeared to be not too far from Cheyenne.[19]

Despite Shaffer's fears, the play was warmly received by most critics. Favorable reviews came from *The New York Times, Daily News, The New Yorker, Saturday Review, Newsweek, New York Journal American, New York World-Telegram,* and the *New York Post.*[20] Most critics praised the spectacle's setting and costumes, both by Michael Annals, the mimes arranged by Madame Claude Chagrin, Martin Aronstein's lighting, Marc Wilkinson's sound effects, or John Dexter's direction. Howard Taubman of *The New York Times* commended Shaffer's attempt at experimental drama: "*The Royal Hunt of the Sun* is a brave and daring try to expand the narrow horizons of a theater too often constricted by small minds and limited imaginations."[21] Similarly, Richard Watts, Jr., of the *New York Post,* wrote about Shaffer's synthesis of the arts: "Mr. Shaffer actually never goes very deeply into the conflict of men and civilizations he is writing of, but he has skillful enough dramatic imagination to keep *Royal Hunt of the Sun* steadily arresting, and, aided by the alliance of spectacle and movement, he has provided a play that is dignified, thoughtful and distinguished."[22] John McClain's review in the *New York Journal American* characterized the play as the hit of the 1965 Broadway season: "For size and talent, and for ambitious writing, I don't believe we've had anything to equal Peter Shaffer's *The Royal Hunt of the Sun* in several seasons."[23] Henry Hewes echoed McClain's judgment, calling the play "by far the season's most thrilling, most imaginative, and most beautiful event."[24] Comments such as these initiated the film version of the play, completed in 1968, although without much assistance from Shaffer himself.

Whenever a play of such epic proportions is staged, critics question whether or not the drama has depth or is successful merely because of its pageantry and spectacle. Reviewers for *Commonweal, The Nation, The New*

Republic, and the *New York Herald Tribune* were convinced that the play was more spectacle and "show" than philosophy.[25] Wilfrid Sheed stated, "The production suffers from familiar spectacle problems. It is difficult to take things like the Inca dances seriously because there has been a plethora of these quasi-authentic farragoes inserted recently into routine musicals."[26] He concluded that "essentially this seems to be another of those cases, like *Danton's Death,* where less production would have meant a better play."[27] Harold Clurman also characterized the play as glitter, weak in ideas: "The stage, a raked circular disk, is attractively lit in golden tones and our pleasure (if any) is pictorial. Everything in fact is well arranged though fundamentally conventional—that is, lacking in specific content."[28] Robert Brustein was perhaps more terse in his assessment of form and content when he wrote that "it may be total theatre but it is strictly fractional drama; and being exposed to Peter Shaffer's meditations on religion, love, life, and death for three solid hours is rather like being trapped in a particularly active wind tunnel with no hope of egress."[29]

Some critics also had trouble interpreting the play's religious message. Shaffer has gone on record to express his dislike of how institutions force individuals to play roles. The Church is merely one institution among many that he has criticized: "Take, say, an attack on the Church. It is a waste of energy. Not because I'm afraid to attack the Church, just that I think any form of organised religion is so totally ridiculous."[30] In an interview with *The New York Times,* Shaffer also stated that "I resent deeply all churches. I despise them. No church or shrine or synagogue has ever failed to misuse its power."[31] Yet despite the fact that Shaffer, a Jewish playwright, has made these statements, *Royal Hunt* is only tangentially concerned with any religious issues.[32] Instead, the play focuses on ideas concerning role playing, as well as man's search for immortality or for some meaning in his life.

Although Shaffer's idea of dramatizing the Spanish conquest of Peru makes for splendid theater, it is by no means original. German playwright August von Kotzebuë wrote *Die Spanier in Peru (The Spaniards in Peru)* in 1796, and nineteenth-century French dramatist Gilbert de Pixérécourt penned *Pizarro, ou La Conquête du Pérou* in 1802. One might recall that in *Le théâtre et son double,* Artaud outlined the staging of *La Conquête du Mexique (The Conquest of Mexico),* a spectacle that was to be the first production of his Theatre of Cruelty.[33] Although Artaud had planned to dramatize the relationship between Cortez and Montezuma, it is possible that Shaffer used Artaud's proposal as an outline for his source of information—William Prescott's book, *The Conquest of Peru.*

In an article written for *Plays and Players,* Shaffer described what attracted him to Prescott's book: "You see, I first came on the subject some years back when I had to spend a few weeks in bed, and decided to while away the time reading some big, heavy Victorian book. The book I chose was Prescott's

Conquest of Peru and I was absolutely riveted by it. The whole drama of the confrontation of two totally different ways of life: the Catholic individualism of the invaders and the complete communist society of the Incas."[34] Prescott, a practicing Massachusetts Unitarian, may have stretched history a bit to show the contrast between pagans and Christians and, in particular, the hypocritical values of the Spanish who were supposedly killing in the name of Christ. Nevertheless, Shaffer did borrow liberally from Prescott's historical account. Irena Narell, who has done extensive research on the history of the period, claims that Pizarro never befriended Atahuallpa but only kept him alive because he wanted the gold.[35] Shaffer says that after Atahuallpa's death, Pizarro sat weeping in the streets of Cajamarca. It is not clear what brought Pizarro to tears, so Shaffer invented a story of friendship between the two men.[36] In addition, Shaffer's depiction of Atahuallpa's purity is also fictitious; Narell claims that "he was apparently so intent on saving his own life that he failed to rally his generals and armies against the Spaniards."[37] Shaffer, of course, has exercised his dramatic license; none of these historical inventions should diminish the literary quality of the play.

Anyone familiar with the realistic style of Shaffer's early dramas would find it difficult to recognize him as the author of *The Royal Hunt of the Sun*. After all, bird cries, primitive dances, "savage music," and Inca sign language are far removed from the British tea room. Although *Royal Hunt* is the first of Shaffer's plays to deviate from the well-made play tradition, the content is consistent with the ideas presented in his earlier dramas. The only difference is that in *Royal Hunt,* the conflict between the role player and his alter ego goes beyond a criticism of how *individuals* prevent the blossoming of the human will (how role players define a sense of codified behavior for others to follow), and for the first time, the dialectic includes an attack on institutionalized power. The sexual conflict is still a personal one, but it has now been expanded to include the "rape" of one country by another.

Shaffer's desire to have the stage reflect a "cannibal theater," much like Artaud's Theatre of Cruelty wherein the spectacle purges our latent desires that society restricts, is realized in *Royal Hunt*. The battle of wills between the role player and his alter ego, who is so unstructured and unrestricted that he is literally a primitive, now blossoms on stage. In *Royal Hunt,* Shaffer, for the first time in his career, begins to associate the ritual with the primitive characters found in the play. Pizarro learns that the ceremonies of these primitives are a viable means of structuring one's life, and he begins to envy these liberated individuals to the point where he questions his own inhibited existence. The ritual symbolically communicates the freedom of the primitive, encouraging Pizarro gradually to question his own rigid existence and how it controls his identity.

In the introduction to the play, Shaffer notes that "the Conquistadors deified personal will: the Incas shunned it."[38] A key word here is "deified," a term Shaffer uses to describe how the Western world is codified by fixed rules and regulations that form our individual personalities. Pizarro is governed by what is "right" for Spain, thus merging his "will" with the tenets of organized religion and stratified society. Pizarro, the representative of the King of Spain (Carlos V), must portray the image of a god, to such an extent that he becomes no more than a role, an agent of what Sartre might call "the Other." He is confined by institutions, much in the same manner that Clive of *Five Finger Exercise* is controlled by members of his "family." Pizarro is similar to Clive in that both individuals want to learn more about themselves and have the capability of doing so, yet they need someone to coax them into dropping their masks. Atahuallpa, a primitive who makes his own rules, teaches Pizarro how artificial the Spanish conquistador really is; Pizarro, however, insists on holding on to his godlike role for fear of losing everything.

When Shaffer writes that the Spanish "deified personal will," he implies that they not only are confined by roles, but also seek to impress their will on other people. Maintaining an unexistential position, Pizarro becomes the judge, jury, and executioner of what is "proper conduct," a term that he learns to accept as one with relative value. He is proud to tell Estete, the Royal Veedor and Overseer, that "on this expedition *my* name is the law: there will be no other" (9), although he will later learn that Atahuallpa has no respect for Pizarro's corrupt misuse of power. Pizarro leads the Spanish on their conquest of Peru not only because he wants to find gold, but also for the pleasure of acquiring a few more slaves like Felipillo. As he presents Felipillo to the soldiers, Pizarro promises them that "over there you'll be the masters—that'll be your slave" (5). When Pizarro arrives in Peru, he tells De Soto that "this is my kingdom. In Peru I am absolute. I have choice always" (69); but by playing a god, Pizarro "whom men called the Son of His Own Deeds" (79), destroys the freedom of others.

Pizarro's main interest in the New World is related to his desire to exert his will over an inferior people. In short, he wants to be a god, someone whose immortality will destroy Time. Shaffer, during an interview with *The New York Times,* acknowledged the importance of this theme in the play: "Ultimately, *The Royal Hunt of the Sun* is a play about man's search for immortality."[39]

Pizarro's early life was full of hardships, and now he plans to make up for lost time. Pizarro tells De Soto that "for twenty-two years I drove pigs down this street because my father couldn't own to my mother. Twenty-two years without one single day of hope. When I turned soldier and dragged my arquebus along the roads of Italy, I was so famished I was beyond eating" (7). Pizarro, who frequently refers to his impoverished upbringing as a pig farmer, now seeks glory and immortality to make amends for his lost youth. In the New World, Pizarro confides in De Soto that Peru is like paradise for him, an idyllic place where he can recapture lost time:

> *Pizarro.* Time cheats us all the way. Children, yes—having children goes some steps to defeating it. . . .
> *De Soto.* Did you never think to marry?
> *Pizarro.* With my parentage? The only women who would have had me weren't the sort you married. Spain's a pile of horse-dung . . . When I began to think of a world here, something in me was longing for a new place like a country after rain, washed clear of all the badges and barriers, the pebbles men drop to tell them where they are on a plain that's got no landmarks.
>
> (30–31)

Pizarro knows that at sixty-three years of age, he will soon die without having lived life to the fullest. He warns Atahuallpa about the destructive nature of Time:

> Your skin is singing: "I will never get old." But you will. Time is stalking you, as I did. That gold flesh will cold and blacken . . . Atahuallpa, I'm going to die! And the thought of that dark has for years rotted everything for me, all simple joy in life. All through old age, which is so much longer and more terrible than anything in youth, I've watched the circles of nature with hatred . . . That prison the Priest calls Sin Original, I know as Time. (63)

Pizarro's only interest in conquering Peru is to become an immortal god himself, thus immobilizing Time. He tells De Soto that "if I live this next year I'm going to get me a name that won't ever be forgotten. A name to be sung here for centuries in your ballads, out there under the cork trees where I sat as a boy with bandages for shoes" (7). Pizarro's battle with Time becomes an obsession, and he confesses to Young Martin that "it's the only way to give life meaning! To blast out of time and live forever, *us,* in our own persons. This is the law: die in despair or be a God yourself!" (74). What disturbs Pizarro the most is that "later someone else will conquer Peru and no one will even remember my name" (68), so to avoid this horror, Pizarro justifies his slaughter of the Incas by insisting that he is to "conquer for Christ" (27), a role that qualifies him as a close second to Christ. Pizarro says that he can envision himself as a Christ-like figure in the New World: "But Christ's to be the only one, is that it? What if it's possible, here in a land beyond all maps and scholars, guarded by mountains up to the sky, that there were true Gods on earth, creators of true peace? Think of it! Gods, free of time" (74).

As a self-styled egotistical god, Pizarro realizes that he must continually play the role of a deity if he is to impress Atahuallpa; thus, when the Spanish enter Inca territory, Pizarro tells his troops that "you're not men any longer, you're Gods now. Eternal Gods, each one of you. Two can play this immortality game, my lads. I want to see you move over this land like figures from a Lent Procession. He must see Gods walk on earth. Indifferent! Uncrushable! No death to be afraid of" (23). As the Spanish climb the Andes Mountains, Pizarro encourages their progress, never forgetting his own goals: "You're your own masters, boys. Not peasant [sic] anymore. This is your time. Own it. Live it" (34). The quest that Pizarro is on, the "royal hunt of the sun," actually refers to his search for "the sun," which implies Atahuallpa, or more simply, God.[40]

Pizarro, though, is not beyond salvation and is conscious of his shortcomings. He reveals many of his weaknesses when he talks to Young Martin, whom he treats as a son in need of fatherly advice. In the introduction to the play, Shaffer discusses Pizarro's pessimistic view of life: "Pizarro, like all men, is entangled in his birth. He too is without joy. In his negation he is as anti-life as the bitter Church and the rigid Sun are in their affirmations" (viii). Pizarro, sixty-three years old, is described as "tough, commanding, harsh, wasted, secret" (2), a man who has seen enough of life's brutalities to become bitter and dismayed. In his prologue to the play, Old Martin says, "This story is about ruin" (1); he is speaking not only of the ruin of a civilization but also of the destruction of a human being—Francisco Pizarro. The Spanish commander is sour on life and has lost faith in his peers and in the value of institutions.[41] He is an atheist traveling among priests who truly feel it is their duty to conquer a primitive civilization in order for them to reach Christ, their savior. In addition, his age and maturity weigh heavily upon him, and he realizes that death is a constant reality. His experience has made him a cynic, almost a nihilist, so he has come to the New World to search for the Sun, a source of spiritual renewal or the "fountain of youth" that he needs to rejuvenate himself.

Pizarro, a Shafferian protagonist worthy of redemption, reveals his plight in his fatherly talks with Young Martin. It is likely that Pizarro sees a bit of himself in Young Martin, for the Spanish leader was once preoccupied with codes of chivalry, just as Martin is when he joins Pizarro's expedition. The scars of battle are branded so deeply in Pizarro's skin that honor, glory, and traditions of service have become meaningless to him; he confides in Young Martin, "Soldiers are for killing: that's their reason" (10). Aware that he is the product of useless institutions, Pizarro encourages Young Martin to trust himself, but "don't ever trust me" (17). The Spanish conquistador knows that he uses people and institutions to bolster a favorable, yet false, conception of himself to others. He tells Young Martin that "men cannot just stand as men in the world. It's too big for them and they grow scared. So they build themselves shelters against the bigness, do you see? They call the shelters Court, Army, Church" (10). Pizarro acknowledges that "the world of soldiers is a yard of ungrowable children. They play with ribbons and make up ceremonies just to keep out the rest of the world" (10). Trying to discourage Young Martin from entering a world that restricts the "primitive spirit," Pizarro warns the page that "I've had a life of it boy, and let me tell you it's nothing but a nightmare game, played by brutes to give themselves a reason" (11). It is this type of insight that enables Pizarro to appreciate Atahuallpa's independence and the unadorned simplicity that accompanies it.

In her insightful article on *The Royal Hunt of the Sun, Shrivings,* and *Equus,* Joan F. Dean certainly was accurate when she described Pizarro's personality as "schizophrenic."[42] On the one hand, Pizarro is a role player, a representative of the Spanish Court charged with conquering in the name of state institutions. He is also a glory seeker who is interested in controlling others and immortalizing his name in the annals of history. On the other hand, Pizarro has the potential for change because he is aware of the hypocrisies of the institutions to which he belongs, and he values a code of ethics that challenges the notion that life is based on a prescribed set of formalized and preconceived roles, rules, and regulations.

Although Pizarro bears the brunt of Shaffer's criticism, the soldiers that accompany the Spanish conquistador into Peru are equally guilty of role playing. In the introduction to the play, Shaffer states that he is examining how man "*settles* for a Church or Shrine or Synagogue, how he demands a voice, a law, an oracle, and over and over again puts into the hands of other men the reins of repression and the whip of Sole Interpretation" (vii). Perhaps the key to the play involves the choice betwen Sole Interpretation or Soul Interpretation. As a prophet, the overseer, Estete, warns that "if you serve a king you must kill personal ambition" (16). There is little surprise then when we discover that most of the Spanish soldiers are characterless, a fate reserved for objects rather than human beings.

Although Pizarro mistakenly sees himself as "The Son of His Own Deeds," or Mr. Sole Interpretation, his awareness of a metaphysical *angoisse* or despair makes him different from the soldiers accompanying him to Peru. Hernando De Soto, the second in command, has no sense of awareness of the absurdity of his condition. Shaffer describes him as "an impressive figure in his forties: his whole air breathes an unquestioning loyalty—to his profession, his faith, and to accepted values" (2). He is a product of other peoples' codes of chivalry, and his service to God and to king is unwavering. Similarly, Fray Vincente de Valverde, the Dominican chaplain to the expedition, has a one-track mind: to serve Christ. To him, the pillage of Inca soil is sanctioned by God. Valverde believes that the Incas are merely heathens who will thankfully be saved by the mercy of the Spanish pillagers: "Don't think we are merely going to destroy his people and lift their wealth. We are going to take from them what they don't value, and give them instead the priceless mercy of heaven" (5). Valverde argues that Atahuallpa, a heathen, is not worth saving when Spanish lives, good Christian souls, are at stake. Pizarro's response to him is that of an individual who thinks and questions the system rather than blindly obeying orders: " 'Kill who I bid you kill and I will pardon it.' YOU with your milky fingers forcing in the blade. How dare you priests bless any man who goes slicing into battle? But no. You slice with him. 'Rip!' you scream, 'Tear! blind! in the name of Christ!' Tell me soft Father, if Christ was here now, do you think he would kill my Inca?" (70).

The Spanish soldiers have taken it upon themselves to be the upholders of tradition and the epitome of ethnocentrism. Shaffer notes that "to me, the greatest tragic factor in history is man's apparent need to mark the intensity of his reaction to life by joining a band; . . ." (viii). With this thought in mind, one does not find it difficult to realize that one of Shaffer's major themes is present in Pizarro's futile attempt to castigate his men for their insistence on role playing:

> Ah, the old band. The dear old regiment. Fool! Look, you were born a man. Not a Blue man, or a Green man, but A MAN. You are able to feel a thousand separate loves unordered by fear or solitude. Are you going to trade them all in for Gang-love? Flag-love? Carlos-the-Fifth-love? Jesus-the-Christ-love? (72)

As Atahuallpa suggests, the Spanish are chained, but the Incas are free. Friar de Nizza reiterates Shaffer's thesis when he replies to Atahuallpa's assessment of the Spaniards by stating that "all life is chains. We are chained to food, and fire in the winter. To innocence lost but its memory unlost. And to needing each other" (48).

Martin is the character who best reflects the need to rely on others, and it is he who tells us of the destruction that follows when one blindly obeys the band. Young Martin and Old Martin, played by two different characters on stage, represent the duality, or the schizophrenic nature of Pizarro's personality. Young Martin, a fifteen-year-old page, is much like Pizarro the role player. Old Martin, in his middle fifties, resembles the jaded Pizarro, an individual who has seen too much of life to revere church, state, or any other institution.

Old Martin, the narrator, has witnessed the ruin firsthand and is anxious to tell the story of "the land I helped ruin as a boy" (1). Martin knows full well that the ruin does not merely refer to the collapse of a civilization, but also to the destruction of the individual as well.

Young Martin joined Pizarro's band to serve others, especially his idol, Pizarro: "He was my altar, my bright image of salvation. Francisco Pizarro! Time was when I'd have died for him, or for any worship" (1). Young Martin is the epitome of a worshipper and role player; Diego, when he first introduces the young man to Pizarro, describes him as "a good lad. He knows all his codes of Chivalry by heart. He's aching to be a page, sir" (3). To Pizarro, chivalry is "a closed book" (3), but to the young page, service in the name of king, church, and state will be "glorious" (3). When he first meets Pizarro, Young Martin acts like nothing more than a slave content to bow for his master. Pizarro honestly tells the young man without an identity that "You're a worshipper, Martin. A groveller. You were born with feet but you prefer your knees. It's you who make Bishops—Kings— Generals" (17). Young Martin, the inexperienced idealist, tells Pizarro that "you are all I ever want to be" (17), but Pizarro, aware of the dangers of worshipping false idols and conscious of his own shortcomings, honestly reveals that "I am nothing you could ever want to be, or any man alive" (17). Instead, he understands that Young Martin is living in a fantasy world and has yet to experience the inner machinations of mankind or institutions: "Hope, lovely hope. A sword's no mere bar of metal for him. His world still has sacred objects. How remote . . ." (29).

The situation changes, however, when Young Martin realizes that Pizarro is willing to betray Atahuallpa for the sake of preserving an image. Young Martin, acting as a translator for the Incas, is actually an intermediary who can coexist in both cultures—Inca and Spanish. He begins to see firsthand the hypocrisy of the Spaniards in comparison with the humbled simplicity of the Incas. Feeling that Pizarro has been unfaithful to his promises, Young Martin steps out of his role and speaks to Pizarro in an unrestricted manner. Failing to obtain an adequate reason for Pizarro's betrayal of Atahuallpa, Young Martin admits that "that was my first and last worship too. Devotion never came again" (62) and walks out, refusing to bow to Pizarro, although the Sole Inquisitor reminds the page that the "time was when we couldn't stop you [from bowing]" (62). Old Martin's narrative describes the hypocrisy displayed by those who blindly serve institutions, or even worse, those who serve themselves in the shadow of institutions. With regard to Pizarro, Old Martin candidly acknowledges that "the only wish of my life is that I had never seen him" (2).

As is true in many of Shaffer's dramas, individuals who are insecure enough to rely on role playing or solely on the ideas of others (the band in this instance), exhibit unusual sexual habits. Pizarro, like his Shafferian predecessors, is uncomfortable around women and cannot seem to perform capably when he is with them. He tells De Soto that the only women he felt comfortable with weren't the sort one marries (30–31). As an insecure person, Pizarro bewails that "I used to look after women with hope, but they didn't have much time for me" (31). Pizarro's only sexual relationship with a woman, which he fondly recalls was "the best hour of my life" (31), ended in sorrow.

Feeling secure only with his role and his metier, Pizarro rejected the insecurities and slowly made the transition from heterosexual to bisexual.

There is enough evidence in the play to suggest that Pizarro's affection for Atahuallpa is homosexual in nature, although it is certainly more than that.[43] Pizarro's constant need to touch Atahuallpa, even the urge to bind himself to the Inca leader, is suggestive in nature. The Spanish soldiers fully understand Pizarro's intentions, and De Candia speaks for all of them when he bluntly asks the general if "you think I'm going to die so that you can dance with a darkie?" (72).

Since Pizarro is not the only social deviant in the play, it is unfair to single him out as a sexual aberration. Although Pizarro's dealings with Atahuallpa do not lead to lust, it is fair to assert that the relationship has sexual connotations that are analogous to the Spanish rape of the Incas. Speaking of his former love of women, Pizarro notes that "I loved them with all the juice in me—but oh, the cheat in that tenderness. What is it but a lust to own their beauty, not them, which you never can . . ." (31–32), and it is this "lust" that we witness among Pizarro's men. The first mention of lust among the Spaniards occurs when Felipillo throws himself on an Inca girl, forcing Valverde to wonder, "Is it for this we saved you from Hell? Your old God encouraged lust" (47). The chaplain errs when he assumes that lust is reserved only for primitives, for the Spanish soon assault the Indian porters who are transporting the gold. The "illustrious" conquerors virtually turn into animals and become violent, to the extent that they begin to treat the Incas as sex objects. Shaffer identifies this part of the play as "the Second Gold Procession and The Rape of the Sun" (55), suggesting that the conflict between role players and "primitives" has been made universal through the dramatization of the "rape" of one country by another. Pizarro's sexual conflicts are dramatized on a much broader level to show that nations can even be affected by role playing.

Pizarro is not in the same category as these other "rapists," since he shows signs of ameliorating his condition. The necessary assistance comes from Atahuallpa, the catalyst who unmasks the protagonist as an artificial, insecure person. Pizarro finds that he has much in common with his "twin," Atahuallpa, and the drama soon turns into a psychological battle of wills between a consummate role player and his liberated alter ego. Both men wield a kind of omnipotence over others; as strong, proud individuals, they listen only to what their consciences tell them. Both men are illegitimate; Pizarro acknowledges that "I did not know my mother. She was not my father's wife" (53), and Atahuallpa has had "no wedded mother" (13). Atahuallpa was once a shepherd like his brother, and Pizarro admits that "that was my work long ago. Tending herds" (53). At one point in the play, Atahuallpa goes so far as to call Pizarro his "brother" (60), and when the Spanish conquistador confesses to Atahuallpa that "you see much in my face," the Inca responds with "I see my father" (53). Shaffer himself has stated that Pizarro and Atahuallpa are both "bastards, both usurpers, both unscrupulous men of action, both illiterate—they are mirror images of each other."[44] In addition, both are what Pizarro calls "robber birds"—Pizarro and his men steal gold from the Incas, and Atahuallpa stole the throne from his brother, then killed him.[45] Dr. Jules Glenn has gone so far as to imply that Shaffer may have unconsciously misspelled Atahuallpa, using two *l*'s to indicate twinship.[46] Whatever implications Shaffer may make, it is clear that by the end of the play, both men, tied together by a rope, are literally coexisting with their alter egos.

However similar Pizarro and Atahuallpa are, there are noticeable differences between the two leaders. Pizarro, jaded by life, impotent, pessimistic, and virtually lifeless, has lost faith in church, state, his fellow men (and women), and his profession. He has been deprived of the best part of his life because he has been too busy playing roles and living for others. Atahuallpa, the younger man, is full of life and hardly fears death or has any thoughts about it. His life has meaning; he worships the sun as his god, but at least his values are concrete and allow him to be optimistic and to develop some sort of faith or a reason for existing. Atahuallpa transmits this faith or a sense of worship to Pizarro, presenting the Spanish general with a justification for living.[47] Pizarro is therefore inspired by his younger alter ego's youthful spirit, which Pizarro never developed himself.

Pizarro is striving for omnipotence, so naturally Atahuallpa, a highly respected god in his own kingdom, would be of some interest to the egocentric Spaniard. Pizarro, an atheist who has also lost faith in the cherished values of his society, is intrigued by a living god who truly believes in worship and reverence. Pizarro acknowledges that "he has some meaning for me, this Man-God. An immortal man in whom all his people live completely. He has an answer for time" (44). Shaffer's stage directions specify that whenever Atahuallpa "moves or speaks, it is always with the consciousness of his divine origin, his sacred function and his absolute power" (40–41). As a thirty-three-year-old former shepherd, Atahuallpa seems to be a Christ-like figure.[48] Atahuallpa's Chief insists that the Inca leader "is the Son of the Sun. He needs no wedded mother. He is God" (13). The Chief continues his adulation of Atahuallpa, making the connection between the Inca Sun God and Christ quite clear: "The sun is God. Atahuallpa is his child sent to shine on us for a few years of life. Then he will return to his father's palace and live forever" (13–14). Atahuallpa, wearing "a circlet of plain gold" (37), claims that he is "the vassal of no man . . . the greatest Prince on earth" (37). He reminds the Spanish priests that "a God cannot be killed. See my father. You cannot kill him. He lives for ever [*sic*] and looks over his children every day" (37). Later, the Christ-like figure sings a song about thieves and a finch "nailed on a branch" (52). Ironically enough, the Incas, who refuse to believe in Christ, trust their own god who challenges Pizarro by swearing that "if you kill me tonight I will rise at dawn" (73).[49]

Pizarro is also impressed with Atahuallpa's independence from roles and from the sanctions of others. Atahuallpa's bold assertion that "I need no one" (49) is a terrifying thing to say to a man who is confined by Church, State, and Image. The dialectic that develops between the two men becomes a conflict between free will versus the will of "the band," i.e., acceptable normative standards. Atahuallpa worships the sun, but he is doing it freely, whereas the Spanish worship Carlos V and European tradition as if they were Law.

Atahuallpa, a man who stands alone without the need to rely on the socializing power of institutions, teaches Pizarro the value of the Self, independent of any external control. The Inca's stoical insistence that "proper" conduct is relative from one culture to the next impresses Pizarro to such a degree that he renounces his men and proclaims that "Francisco Pizarro casts off Carlos the Fifth. Go and tell him" (69). Thus, as Shaffer informs us in the introduction to the play, *Royal Hunt* becomes a quest "to separate worship from codification . . ." (viii) or an "attempt to draw a 'free man' surging ahead under his own power" (viii). The result is that Pizarro, like Young Martin, loses faith in roles and in established tradition yet cannot prevent the destruction of free will.[50] The band is always stronger than any individual force that opposes it, so Atahuallpa's death is inevitable.

It is no wonder that Atahuallpa's death demoralizes Pizarro. Although the King of the Sun promised that he would be resurrected, his failure to do so is not the reason why Pizarro becomes so distraught. Atahuallpa supposedly was executed because he was guilty of "usurping the throne and killing his brother; of idolatry and of having more than one wife" (76). But Pizarro understands that Atahuallpa was sentenced because he refused to believe in another religion. In short, the Inca was true to his own values, and his defiance of the band led to his destruction.

To a certain extent, however, the Spanish leader is responsible for the Inca's death because Pizarro, like all of Shaffer's protagonists, lied in order to maintain status quo. As a result, what started out as a harmless "white lie," Pizarro's vow to spare Atahuallpa's life in return for a room full of gold, is blown up to such proportions that it is mistakenly accepted as an affirmation of good faith. Thus, the Inca king's uncompromising spirit—his refusal to denounce his faith even in the face of death—forced the lying Pizarro to realize what type of masqueraders the Spanish really were.

To delineate clearly the differences between Pizarro and Atahuallpa, Shaffer turned to ritualistic theater. In *Five Finger Exercise* and the one-act plays, the protagonists are affected in some way by an alter ego or catalyst. The communication that precipitates a change in the protagonist's behavior is always direct. But in *The Royal Hunt of the Sun,* the ritual helps to distinguish the differences between the freedom of the "primitive" and the restricted status of the role player, thereby providing a more meaningful sort of communication between the two leaders than any direct confrontation could assure. Shaffer, then, is essentially reducing theater to the type of communion so cherished by Artaud. Ritual is frequently a viable means of social communication that can convey a number of social mores. This is exactly how it is used to make a believer out of Pizarro, an individual who ironically is intrinsically interested in "primitive" civilizations and their sense of worship.

In an interview with the *Evening Standard* during the play's initial performances at Chichester, Shaffer discussed his reasons for writing *Royal Hunt:* "What I always wanted to do was to recreate the theatre that relies on imagination. To bring the theatre back to scenes of action and colour, and harness them to an intellectual and spiritual end. I wanted to make the theatre bigger."[51] In the introduction to the play, Shaffer stated that "My hope was always to realise on stage a kind of 'total' theatre, involving not only words but rites, mimes, masks and magics" (x).

This total theatre that Shaffer mentions is similar to what Artaud had in mind for his staging of *The Conquest of Mexico.* In fact, Artaud's intention to contrast the religious views of the West with the pagan worship of the Mexican Indians seems to be a precursor for the ideas presented in *Royal Hunt.* Artaud explained why he chose *The Conquest of Mexico* as an appropriate subject for the modern theater:

> From the historical point of view, *The Conquest of Mexico* poses the question of colonization. It revives in a brutal and implacable way the ever active fatuousness of Europe. It permits her idea of her own superiority to be deflated. It contrasts Christianity with much older religions. It corrects the false conceptions the Occident has somehow formed concerning paganism and certain natural religions, and it underlines with burning emotion the splendor and forever immediate poetry of the old metaphysical sources on which these religions are built.[52]

Artaud intuitively understood that the contrast between the formal, institutionalized culture of Europe and the pagan worship of the Aztecs could best be shown on stage by rites and rituals designed to delineate the differences between the two cultures. Artaud, in his plans for the staging of *The Conquest of Mexico,* seems to have given Shaffer the idea of how to communicate to the audience, in an unconscious way, the Apollonian-Dionysian dialectic: "These images, movements, dances, rites, these fragmented melodies and sudden turns of dialogue will be carefully recorded and described as far as possible with words, especially for the portions of the spectacle not in dialogue, the principle here being to record in codes, as on a musical score, what cannot be described in words."[53] In short, Artaud wanted the form of the play to reflect a rhythmic structure that would duplicate the Aztec rites and rituals.

However similar or different the intentions of Artaud and Shaffer may have been, it is apparent that *Royal Hunt* would have pleased Artaud. Cruelty is graphically presented on stage so as to purge the audience of any sympathy for the devious Spaniards. Pizarro is described as a gruff soldier whose "gestures are blunt and often violent; the expression intense and energetic, capable of fury and cruelty, but also of sudden melancholy and sardonic humor" (2). As Pizarro says early in the play, "Soldiers are for killing: that's their reason" (10), and it is this "killing spirit" that we see manifested in the Spanish drive to conquer Peru. Act 1, so aptly referred to as "The Hunt," is punctuated with discussions concerning lust, slavery, and violence, culminating in the Mime of the Great Massacre, the slaughter of the Incas. Act 2, "The Kill," soon degenerates into the Spanish rape and assault of the Incas, assorted fights among the Spanish soldiers for their share of the gold, and various mob scenes, one of which ends in the violent death of Atahuallpa. During the play, the audience witnesses some rather physical swordplay and hears some direct, coarse language to accompany the violent scenario. By the end of the drama, the audience will have indeed experienced a purging of latent cruelty.

Shaffer's striking vision of total theater in *Royal Hunt* is similar to what Artaud had in mind for his Theatre of Cruelty. Dialogue is frequently replaced by gestures, particularly appropriate in the context of Shaffer's play since sign language is the only means of communication between the Spanish and the Incas. Mime is present in the Indian harvests (19), the ascent of the Andes (25), the massacre of the Incas (38), the dance that Atahuallpa teaches Pizarro (54), and the Gold Procession and "Rape of the Sun" scenes (49, 55). There are twenty-one musical interludes that include everything from Indian laments (39) to a full-scale musical procession into Cajamarca. To accompany the music and dance, there are numerous shrieks and screams (11, 12), savage or violent music (38, 64), harvest songs (52), toil songs (19), menacing chants (67), and tropical bird cries (15, 17, 66, 67) that frighten Pizarro's men throughout their journey. The Mass is recited in conjunction with other blessings to create a rhythmic chanting effect (8, 29, 33, 77, 79). There is also a recurrent humming noise (46, 19) and a frequent display of primitive musical instruments (24, 36, 66) to accompany the ongoing sense of rhythm. In addition, stage lighting is varied to produce what Artaud called "the qualities of particular musical tones" to enhance the rhythmic effects.[54]

Many other stage conventions provide a constant rhythm that helps to unite sound and movement. Especially effective in this regard would be Young Martin's bowing sequence (6), the Inca chants (24), the Valverde-De

Nizza dialogue just before the Mime of the Great Massacre (37), Atahuallpa's commands to bring the gold (45), the call to Ruminagui (67), and Pizarro's last words to Atahuallpa (77). Also, the stichomythic dialogue running throughout the play (11, 14, 24, 33, 77) helps to induce a ritualistic trance, turning the drama into a rite or an elaborate ceremony. When all of these effects are absorbed into one choreographed rhythm, they provide a symbolic sort of communication that is, as Artaud hoped, unconsciously transmitted.

To create a communal type of catharsis, Shaffer turned to masks, as Artaud had suggested. The use of masks turned the play into a ritualistic experience similar to Mass or to the effect achieved by the ancient Greek theater. In an interview with *The Listener,* Shaffer explained the almost sacred function that the masks held for him during the staging of *Royal Hunt:*

> I'll never forget the first time they arrived in the theatre, and a couple of the lads who were playing Inca priest put them on, and the transformation that happened on stage. When there were 16 of them at the end, when they were all assembled round the stage, the temperature in the house rose enormously. And later, when the audience came out of the theatre, they said—how did one get the masks to reflect joy, hope, gloom, and change expression? And what, of course, was happening was not that the masks changed in any way—what was happening was that the changes in the communal imagination and emotion of the audience were being invested in those masks. And when I saw this, I became deeply fascinated because I understood for the first time why the ancient Greek theatre used masks. How they can, when they are very good, take that investment of communal imagination and communal emotion, turn it back to the audience, and reflect it.[55]

The ritual enables Pizarro to realize unconsciously that the Inca's "savage culture" is less restrictive, but not substantially different from some of the Spanish customs. Certain traditional Spanish customs, such as bowing and blessing, correspond to similar functions in the Inca culture, yet the Spanish ceremonies are always more restrictive. When the Spanish soldiers descend to the level of animals while raping and molesting these "primitives," Pizarro can see for himself how "superior" his culture is to that of the Incas. Through a constant barrage of bird cries, toil songs, laments, and chants, Pizarro begins to associate the Inca ritual with the primitive, unrestrained spirit. When Pizarro is asked to imitate Atahuallpa's dance, the Spaniard finds that the ritual is difficult to master. Even though the Spanish ceremonies are similar to the Inca's dance, Pizarro soon understands that Spanish culture is too restrictive, not free to blossom.[56] The Inca rituals are just as "cultured" as the Spanish traditions, and they provide Pizarro with a learning experience that he would never have otherwise obtained. Thus, through the ritual, Pizarro is able to mature, and he learns how artificial his life has been. In coming face to face with an alter ego who, as a primitive, is more at ease with life than he is, Pizarro learns too late that his life has been nothing more than an adherence to the codes and roles created by others. The ritual is important because it codifies Pizarro's transformation or change. Pizarro is certainly affected by the Inca rituals, and for him the ceremonies produce a type of purification similar to a catharsis. It is also hoped that the audience will be able to differentiate between the destructive nature of the Spanish invaders and the soothing quality of the religious ritual, a vibrant force that is intrinsic to the Inca ceremonies.

Atahuallpa conveys this spirituality through rituals, a method of social communication that *shows* Pizarro what worship really means. In this sense, the rituals function as a form of meaningful communication, a learning experience for outsiders. In *Royal Hunt,* the ritual is a method of conjoining two initially separate groups to help form some sort of positive interaction between them. Pizarro learns to identify the "primitive" with sober, honest individuals, and a role player becomes equated with phony masqueraders and image makers. It is the ritual which seems to exemplify the honest intentions of these primitives. In short, the ritual, as well as the play's rhythmic structure, provides unconscious communication of symbolic intent. The ritual demonstrates the differences between the worshippers and the role players, helping the latter to internalize those differences unconsciously.

Although we do not witness a complete rite of passage on stage, the ritualistic social communication is much more effective than the static nonritualistic plays that Shaffer had previously written. The play works on many levels—the unconscious, the sociological, the political, and the psychological. The result is that *The Royal Hunt of the Sun,* a major breakthrough in Shaffer's career, is one of the most powerful combinations of form and content on the modern stage and is a strong representation of the effectiveness of ritualistic drama. Shaffer will later follow up the musical, rhythmic form of *Royal Hunt* with other ritualistic dramas but, alas, not until he has explored other avenues of theatrical experimentation will he return to the style that made one of the great plays of the modern stage so successful.

7
Black Comedy and *The White Liars:*
The Maestro Turns to Farce

In early spring 1965, Kenneth Tynan of the National Theatre asked Shaffer if he had a one-act play to accompany *Miss Julie* for the Chichester Theatre's forthcoming season. Shaffer told him about an idea that he had for a play in which the actors perform in "Chinese darkness"—full light—because of a power failure in a building. When confronted by Laurence Olivier, Shaffer confessed that there really was no play and that he was occupied with other projects. Olivier, however, commissioned Shaffer to get on with the writing, and so Shaffer was faced with a tough deadline to meet. Shortly afterward, Shaffer was trying to compose the play, but he could not get it to work:

> When I was brooding on this and thinking I wish I'd never agreed to do it, someone from the National Theatre rang me up and said: "We've announced your new play and we've got a terrific response at the box office. You must be very pleased." I looked down at my desk at what had been advertised and what the public was apparently responding to so nicely and it was just two pieces of paper, one covered with tomato soup and the other which I had just torn up.[1]

Despite the deadline and Shaffer's inability to get the play going, *Black Comedy* opened with *Miss Julie* on 27 July 1965, at the Chichester Festival. John Dexter directed the play, with a cast that included Derek Jacobi (Brindsley Miller), Maggie Smith (Clea), Albert Finney (Harold Gorringe), and Louise Purnell (Carol Melkett). The reviews were quite good, and no critic panned both the writing and the production. The consensus was that the play was witty, funny, and entertaining, but perhaps a bit too long. In particular, the play was reviewed favorably by *The Times, Punch, Daily Mail, New Statesman, The Manchester Guardian, Evening Standard,* and *The Illustrated London News.*[2]

As usual, the play appeared in New York a little more than a year after its London opening. For the New York premiere, Shaffer wrote *White Lies,* another one-act play originally titled *A Warning Game,* to accompany *Black Comedy.* The debut for the twin bill was 12 February 1967, at the Ethel Barrymore Theatre.[3] John Dexter directed both plays; *White Lies* starred Geraldine Page (Sophie), Donald Madden (Frank), and Michael Crawford (Tom), while *Black Comedy* featured Michael Crawford (Brindsley), Lynn Redgrave (Carol), Donald Madden (Harold), and Geraldine Page (Clea). The New York critics generally reacted positively to both plays, although they had more reservations about them than their London counterparts did. Favorable notices appeared in *Time, Daily News, Wall Street Journal, Saturday Review, The New Yorker, New York World Journal Tribune,* and the *New York Post.*[4] Although Henry Hewes *(Saturday Review),* John McCarten *(The New Yorker),* and the anonymous reviewer in *Time* presented favorable reviews, they did not like *White Lies* and had hardly anything positive to say about the play. Walter Kerr's review in *The New York Times* was neutral.[5] He seemed to enjoy the evening's entertainment, but at the end of the review, he criticized Shaffer: "He knows his craft, he writes for actors, he can indeed be funny. But he is a sort of manufacturer's writer. He fabricates instead of feeling his way, and sometimes he fabricates feeling. The result is that most of his work seems made-up rather than imagined."[6]

The most notable negative reviews were from Harold Clurman of *The Nation* and Mel Gussow of *Newsweek.*[7] Clurman began his review by saying that "*Black Comedy* is altogether void of intellectual significance," but he claimed it was all "very good sport."[8] With this "compliment" fixed in our minds, Clurman went on to say that *Black Comedy* redeems the evening for us because *White Lies* is "trite in the telling, a blank cartridge."[9] He added, "Except for a pleasant surprise in an early scene, *White Lies* is noteworthy only for Geraldine Page's acting of the impecunious fortune-teller, a putative Baroness of foreign origin and accent."[10] Mel Gussow criticized both plays. He wrote that *Black Comedy* is interesting "only for about fifteen minutes—and the play is an hour and six."[11] With regard to *White Lies,* he said that "there are too few surprises in this one, and languorous storytelling sketches."[12] He put the blame squarely on Shaffer's shoulders and not on the performers.

Shaffer was not pleased with *White Lies;* in the preface to his collected works, he stated that "I am afraid that I did not manage to get it quite right. The dramatic pulse was too low, and the work came out a little mechanically."[13] Shaffer therefore rewrote the play as *The White Liars,* which was subsequently revived with *Black Comedy* at London's Lyric Theatre on 21 February 1968. Peter Wood directed James Bolam (Brindsley), Ian McKellen (Harold), and Liz Fraser (Clea) in *Black Comedy.* Ian Mckellen also played Tom in *The White Liars,* and he was given strong support from Dorothy Reynolds as Sophie. This time the reviews were mixed. Shaffer received good press from Jeremy Kingston *(Punch),* Herbert Kretzmer *(Daily Ex-*

press), Rich *(Variety)*, and Peter Lewis *(Daily Mail)*.[14] Kingston particularly praised *The White Liars*, calling Shaffer an "expert in the art of developing a situation so that it brings a roar of laughter one moment and touches the heart the next."[15] Peter Lewis enjoyed both plays and rated Shaffer "our most brilliant theatrical conjuror."[16]

Neutral reviews came from *The Sunday Telegraph, The Manchester Guardian,* and the *Evening Standard*.[17] Milton Shulman of the *Evening Standard* liked *Black Comedy* but thought *The White Liars* was "very thin stuff."[18] Alan Brien of *The Sunday Telegraph* agreed with Shulman, citing *Black Comedy* as "one of the most hilarious displays of pure comic invention ever seen on any stage," while describing *The White Liars* as "a puzzling piece— intelligent, sensitively written, meticulously shaped, almost orchestrated, full of insight and observation, yet somehow for me a cold, unmoving, unconvincing exercise in play-making.[19] Philip Hope-Wallace seemed non-committal but was firm in his belief that *Black Comedy* at the National Theatre was superior to the Lyric Theatre's production.[20]

The three major negative reviews were in *The Times, The Observer,* and *New Statesman*.[21] The consensus among these critics was that *Black Comedy* became a bit too cute as it passed from Broadway back to London and did not match the high standards of the original production. Philip French *(The Observer)* claimed that the proper place for *The White Liars* "would be a thematic television series dealing with the Seven Deadly Sins."[22] Ronald Bryden *(The Observer)* agreed with French, stating that the play is "imperfectly adapted to the stage, with long internal flashbacks conveyed in booming dialogue with piped, offstage voices. . . ."[23] J. R. T., the anonymous reviewer of *The Times,* also panned *The White Liars,* dismissing it as a "frail, wispy little piece" that is "heavy and old-fashioned."[24]

Shaffer, perfectionist that he is, knew that the reviewers had valid reasons for criticizing the play. He was convinced that *The White Liars* still did not work on stage, so he rewrote it again. The third version debuted at London's Shaw Theatre under Paul Giovanni's direction. Shaffer was satisfied with the third writing of the play, and therefore it is that version which will be discussed in this chapter.

Black Comedy was conceived after Shaffer saw a stylized version of the play performed by the Peking Opera in 1955 at the Palace Theatre in London. The Chinese excerpt was from *San Ch'a K'ou (Where Three Roads Meet)*, a farce that thrilled Shaffer and convinced him that the genre was worthy of exploration:

> The sequence they offered was a scene in a lodging house at night where a warrior lays himself down to sleep—it is wordless, this particular scene— and a bandit creeps through the window.
> It is supposed to be pitch darkness, except it is all done in brilliant light, light so ferocious that it almost suggests darkness. The warrior gropes for his

sword and challenges the intruder. They fight with swords so sharp they seemed, if I recall, to cut little bits off the fringes of their clothing. Real swords.

The effect on the audience was extraordinary, because it was wildly funny and wildly dangerous as well, so that they were caught between two emotions of alarm and delight.

Two things struck me. First of all, if high comedy is akin to drama, farce is akin to melodrama. All those great farces of Feydeau are concerned with extremely dramatic situations. Open that door and your marriage is at an end, there's no two ways about it. If you open that drawer, you are ruined. And the other thing that struck me was that I would very much like to use that convention of reverse light and darkness for an English comedy.[25]

Shaffer, trying to be innovative and always seeking to experiment with various forms of drama to find out what will or will not work on stage, turned to farce for the first time in his career.[26] When *Black Comedy* was in Boston for its pre-Broadway run, Shaffer told Samuel Hirsch of *The Boston Herald* his reasons for trying comedy after the success of *Royal Hunt,* a totally different type of play: "I'm fascinated with farce. I'd never done farce before and had always loved the form. I'd seen the plays of Georges Feydeau, the great French farceur, and had always been fond of the well-made play."[27] Shaffer, already adept at total theater, has hinted that comedy, like the well-made play, functions for him as a sort of stabilizing genre in which he can practice tight craftmanship.[28] This is perhaps why he turned to farce after the great demands that *Royal Hunt* made on him; in addition, the one-act play, per se, was ideal to help Shaffer reestablish his foundation in tight dramatic structure after working with a rhythmic and epic style in *Royal Hunt.*

Shaffer no doubt wanted *Black Comedy* to retain the same essential qualities that made the original Chinese play so endearing to him. Shaffer stated that farce "is a form of gestural theatre," and ideally he probably saw the setting as having the primitive, even mystical, qualities of the Balinese theater.[29] Clea sums up Shaffer's feelings about the setting when she says, "it is a very odd room, isn't it? It's like a magic dark room, where everything happens the wrong way round."[30] Shaffer would like the audience to believe that in this magical room we are witnessing a "cannibal theater" in which the participants are reverting "to savages" (120) in an environment where reason is ineffective.

In the dark, one's inner feelings can be easily revealed because the characters on stage can react truthfully to others without having to be concerned with being seen by them. For example, Carol "puts out her tongue" at Harold, secure in the fact that the audience sees the gesture, yet Harold does not. In theory, Shaffer believed that gestures and body movements would make the play work in a stylized fashion.

In addition, the lighting corresponds to Artaud's notions of rhythmic changes that choreograph a play. When Brindsley dashes up to extinguish one of Colonel Melkett's matches, "these strikings and blowings are of course accompanied by swift and violent alterations of the light" (69), producing a hypnotic or rhythmic effect. Although the intent is there, *Black Comedy* never does reach the savagery for which Shaffer had hoped; the play is actually closer to a Chaplinesque farce than to a Balinese mime.

Anyone familiar with Shaffer's work will understand why Brindsley is having what he calls "the worst night of my life!" (59). Not satisfied with his own life, which is albeit a poor sculptor's existence, Brindsley has removed Harold Gorringe's furniture in order to impress both Bamberger, the millionaire art collector, and Carol Melkett's father as well. As soon as Brindsley prays that the evening will be a success, the lights go out right on cue:

> Oh God, let this evening go all right! Let Mr. Bamberger like my sculpture and buy some! Let Carol's monster father like me! And let my neighbor Harold Gorringe never find out that we borrowed his precious furniture behind his back! Amen. (53)

As Shaffer notes in his stage directions, the rest of "the evening is a progress through disintegration" (53).

This disintegration is easy to comprehend when we compare Brindsley, the protagonist, to his predecessors, Clive and Bob. Brindsley, like Clive and Bob, is a sensitive artist who is described as "intelligent and attractive, but nervous and uncertain of himself" (47). The young sculptor seems to have the potential for change because he is creative, witty, spontaneous, and, as described by Shaffer's stage directions, possesses "a free and imaginative mind" (48). Like many of Shaffer's other protagonists, Brindsley realizes the absurdity of role playing and would like to avoid it if possible. He tells Carol that it would be better if he were to strip himself of all pretentious behavior and just be himself when he meets Bamberger: "He's coming to see the work of an unknown sculptor. If you ask me, it would look much better to him if he found me exactly as I really am: a poor artist. It might touch his heart" (50).

Brindsley, however, has brought on his own tragedy during this hectic evening because he has not been true to himself. He insists on playing the role of art connoisseur to impress others; instead of being himself, Brindsley assumes someone else's identity. Like Bob, Brindsley will discover that role playing will turn the evening into a disaster.

Clea is correct to assume that Brindsley will receive his "just desserts" for his efforts to deceive others. Brindsley literally ends up fumbling in the dark when trying to establish a new identity for himself, and Clea so aptly remarks that "you should live in the dark, Brindsley. It's your natural element" (114). Clea, who perhaps needs an *r* on the end of her name to describe her function as a seer in the play, explains the statement she made by summarizing Brindsley's plight: "It means you don't really want to be seen. Why is that, Brindsley? Do you think if someone really saw you, they would never love you?" (114). Brindsley, constantly in need of reinforcement from others to prove that he is important, rejected Clea as a wife because she did not cater to his demands for constant approval. Clea warns Brindsley to stop feeling guilty about this sense of inferiority: "Stop pitying yourself. It's always your vice. I told you when I met you: You could either be a good artist, or a chic fake. You didn't like it, because I refused just to give you applause" (115). Instead, Brindsley turned to Carol Melkett, a silly debutante who adores him, providing him with, as Clea says, "twenty hours of ego-message every day" (115). Brindsley's chic fakery reminds us of Bob's dependence on Ted's vocabulary, two attempts at role playing that will eventually destroy the individual who tries to be something that he is not.

As might be expected in any of Shaffer's dramas, the propensity for image making or role playing will lead to lies, and Brindsley is quite adept in this department; actually, the play itself is based on a lie: Brindsley trying to pass off Harold's furniture as his own. Brindsley lies so frequently to Colonel Melkett that the young sculptor not only fails to impress Carol's father, but also loses any respect that the military man may have had for him. Colonel Melkett swears that "I may not know art, Miller, but I know men. I know a liar in the light, and I know one in the dark" (83). Brindsley's failure to tell Carol that Clea has called, his dubious characterization of Clea as being "just about as cozy as a steel razor blade" (52), and his lie that he has been in love with Clea for only three months instead of four years are enough to ruin his relationships with both women. First, Clea calls him a liar (111), then Carol continues with, "You're lying! . . . You're lying" (112), after Brindsley flatly states, "I'm not. I don't lie" (112). When Harold learns of Brindsley's deceitful trick, Brindsley's disastrous evening is complete, and he is left without a friend *or* a lover. At the end of the play, Brindsley, who desperately tried to lie his way into a new identity, is certainly much worse off than he would have been had he lost favor with Bamberger and Colonel Melkett simply because they did not appreciate his taste in furniture.

As we have noticed in Shaffer's previous plays, the role player's plight is usually intertwined with sexual insecurities and carnal anxieties. Brindsley's relationship with women is strained, even warped, much in the manner that Clive, Bob, Sidley, and Pizarro struggle with their female friends or wives. Brindsley had known Clea for four years before she became disgusted with their relationship and walked out on him. Now Brindsley has tried to become engaged to Carol, but, of course, the marriage plans will never work out. In short, Brindsley, trying to find an identity of his own, obviously has trouble continuing a meaningful relationship with others and is only interested in whomever can give him an "ego-message" (155), whether it is Clea, Carol, or even Harold.

Brindsley's contact with Harold suggests that the former is perhaps bisexual. It is no secret that Harold is homosexual, and we constantly see him groping for Brindsley's affection and love. When Harold returns from vacation, he greets Brindsley by holding hands with him, walking in the room on Brindsley's shoulder, and seeking comfort from his friend: "It's rather cozy in the dark, isn't it?" (67). Harold is glad to see the man he fondly calls "dear" Brindsley (67), but he rejects his friend when he learns that a female rival is in the room. Harold is certainly not at ease with Carol and is particularly angry when he discovers that Brindsley is going to marry her and leave him unattended. Carol remarks that "in five years, I'll feel just like Mrs. Michaelangelo" (86), to which Harold spitefully responds with "There wasn't a Mrs. Michaelangelo, actually . . . He had passionate feelings of a rather different nature" (86).

Although Harold is the confirmed homosexual, his affection for Brindsley proves that the sculptor is more than just a passive accomplice. Harold refers to his affectionate friend as "a very sweet boy" (72) and admits that "I've always assumed there was more than a geographical closeness between us" (85). He shows his affection for Brindsley by kissing his hand (74), and when Brindsley orders Clea up to his bedroom, Harold thinks that he is being addressed and asks, "Do you think this is quite the moment?" (92). It is therefore no surprise that during a game of musical hands in the dark, Harold is the only one to recognize Brindsley's soft touch (113).

Black Comedy continues Shaffer's tirade against role playing. Trying to establish an identity for himself that is based on others' expectations of him, Brindsley becomes a clown fumbling in the dark. By refusing to create his own values, Brindsley merely complicates his sexual and social problems until we witness his disintegration and finally his unmasking on stage.

What makes *Black Comedy* perhaps less effective as metaphysical drama is its form. Shaffer chose farce, and as such, the play works on stage—the audience laughs and is entertained. In comedy, the protagonist may learn a serious lesson, but we are confident that he or she will forever be the buffoon. In short, because *Black Comedy* is farce, there is no need of an alter ego or "twin" to induce some sort of change in the protagonist. In addition, comedy does not produce a catharsis; there is no element of fear, pity, or "cruelty" to be purged. The play works well for what it seeks to accomplish—a comic presentation of sociological ideas—yet fails to satisfy in the same manner that ritualistic theater might.

Black Comedy's perfect companion piece is *The White Liars:* both plays are graphic representations of the dangers of lying, role playing, and image making. Shaffer was not pleased with *White Lies,* the play he wrote to accompany *Black Comedy* in New York. *The White Liars,* a rewritten version of the play, was marred by a tape recording of Vassi's voice that helped to project Sophie's thoughts to the audience. Therefore, Shaffer wrote the play a second time; although it is debateable whether or not the final version of *The White Liars* is an improvement over *White Lies,* it nevertheless is the play with which Shaffer is most pleased and therefore must be considered the definitive edition.[31]

The White Liars is Shaffer's most graphic depiction of an individual's need to establish an identity free from the image and ideas that others have of that person. All of the characters in the play figuratively wear masks and are masquerading as cardboard characters. They each, in turn, lie so regularly that the play becomes a mystery for the spectator to try and unravel the truth. We are back to the early detective novels in which the reader (now the spectator) tries to separate fact from fiction.

Tom, the Shafferian protagonist in *White Lies,* is now a different type of person in *The White Liars.* Tom, similar to Ted in *The Private Ear,* is described as "casual almost to the point of brutality" and is "dressed very 'trendily,' in bright colors."[32] Tom seeks to impress others and feels secure only when he is assured that he is accepted by others. Frank's description of Tom is quite accurate: "He *lives* on worship. It's his food. I mean it quite literally: he can hardly get through a day without two tablespoons of sticky golden worship poured down his throat, preferably by a girl" (160). Tom explains to Sophie that he created a fantasy life for himself in order to play a role that others expected of him. Knowing that his middle-class background (his father is a wealthy accountant from Leeds, and his mother is a would-be aristocrat akin to Louise Harrington) would be a detriment for a career in pop music when working class is considered to be an asset, Tom poses as a poor boy from the North of England. Tom tells Sophie that he chose to play the role: "Well, it's a question of image, really. When I was a kid, in pop music you had to be working class to get anywhere at all. Middle class was right out. Five years ago no one believed you could sing with the authentic voice of the people if you're the son of an accountant—and here we are!" (170). He even adopts a phony accent to go along with his carefully planned charade. Tom, in seeking to impress others, makes the mistake of trying to be something he is not.

Tom is very much like his parents who judge others by the roles that they play. Tom's father, another Stanley Harrington, is embarrassed by his son's artistic ability: "Dad calls me 'Minstrel Boy' whenever I go home, because he finds it embarrassing to have a singer for a son" (170). Tom's mother, modeled on Louise Harrington, pictures her son as a social climber headed for the higher strata of society: "Mother tells her bridge club I'm in London studying music—because *studying* is a more respectable image for her than performing in a cellar" (170). In other words, Tom's parents fail to accept Tom as he really is and instead want to mold him in their image.

When Frank met Tom, the latter had formed his own musical group. Frank, posing as a freelance journalist, approached Tom about doing a story on "The White Liars," Tom's band, for the Sunday papers. Tom consented, and for one month Frank followed Tom everywhere, living with him around the clock. Tom soon realized that Frank, whom Tom later discovered was actually an owner of a boutique, was not a journalist yet wanted to believe in the myth that Tom had created: "He used to sit on the end of my bed with his pencil and notebook, just grooving on it. Bogus journalist interviewing bogus miner! 'You're so lucky,' he'd say: 'so lucky to be born a prole. The working class is the last repository of instinct' " (174). Frank, almost desperate to believe in images to worship, created Tom's life for him, and Tom went along with the fantasy: "I watched him make up my childhood. 'Where were you born?' he'd ask me. Then right away, he'd answer himself. 'Some godawful little cottage in the North, I suppose: no loo, I suppose, no electric light, I suppose.' 'I suppose' meaning 'I want' " (174). Tom therefore told one lie after another to conform to the image that Frank created in this fantasy of his. Tom wanted to be worshipped, to be seen as someone important in other peoples' eyes; thus, he became an identityless person existing only as others depicted him. He explains to Sophie how he fed off of Frank's worship of him: "He gave me a role, that's what he gave! Can't you see that? I'm just acting in a film projected out of their eyes. *I Was a Prisoner on Wet Dream Island!*" (176).

Tom, whom Sophie describes as living "one enormous great *lie* from morning to night" (170), is, like his predecessors Sidley and Brindsley, living a life based on the expectations of others. However, Tom is also similar to Clive, Bob, and Pizarro, in that they are all aware of their shortcomings and are capable of transcending them with the proper assistance. Sophie helps Tom verbalize and conceptualize his role playing, and in doing so, Tom is able to decide for himself how hypocritical he really has been. At the end of the play, he walks out on Frank, leaving his friend with an unperformed concert on his hands. Tom's act is basically an existential one: he makes the decision for himself and begins to take control of his life and to shape his own identity. He is returning to Lichfield where he will not feel as if he has to impersonate someone else to be accepted.

Frank, who is hardly like his name suggests, is quite different than his namesake in *White Lies*. During the first part of *The White Liars,* he appears to be more like Tom was in *White Lies*. Frank is described as "middle class, soft spoken, and gentle; his manner is shy, warm, and immediately likable" (155). Sophie suspects him of trickery after he flips a coin to determine who will win the privilege of seeing the fortune teller and then cheats Tom out of the chance to do so. Virtually everything he tells Sophie is a lie. He swears that Tom is in love with his girlfriend Susan when, in fact, Tom shows no interest in her. Frank also claims to have met Tom when he was a penniless musician singing in an East End pub; taking the young musician under his wing, Frank became his manager and helped create the band, "The White Liars." The truth is that Frank did not treat Tom to free room and board—if anything, it was Frank who received the royal treatment from Tom, an already successful musician with his own band. Frank is not even a journalist; instead, he ran a boutique with his friend Sue until he got fired from the job. In short, as Tom tells Sophie, "From the moment Frank came in here he handed you a pack of lies. One after another" (173).

Sophie mistakenly calls Tom a "taker" or someone who feeds off of others. Unfortunately, she is wrong in her assessment of Tom; he is the "giver" in the play while Frank is the "taker." In order to exist, Frank must take from others. He creates images and roles that he expects others to uphold. He has no sense of self-worth and seeks to worship or idolize those who can conform to the stereotyped vision that he seeks in others. His life is based on a "fix" or an addiction, as Tom puts it, to "the crazy Want . . . for an image to turn him on" (174). Frank is a walking wasteland, an insecure package of lies who lives in his own version of a secure fantasyland. Frank's sexual problems, like Brindsley's, seem quite complex. He has told Sophie that his purpose is to drag Tom away from his girlfriend, Susan. We never actually find out if Susan is indeed his lover—we only know that he works with her daily. At the end of the play, however, Frank reveals the real reason why he fabricated all of these stories and had Sophie trying to scare Tom: "I wanted him to leave her alone! . . . And to stay with me. In—my—bed" (177). Like Shaffer's other confused role makers and role players, Frank seems to be insecure around women and turns to men for comfort and solace. Again, this bisexuality or homosexuality is Shaffer's overt expression of the fate in store for these individuals who fail to achieve a strong sense of identity of their own without the need for images and role models.

Shaffer's female characters are not much to brag about. They are usually given supporting roles in his plays, and not one female functions as a protagonist. The females play minor characters that range from henpecking housewives with rigid aristocratic airs to liberated women with minds of their own. Sophie, however, seems to be Shaffer's only female character who maintains some degree of control over her environment. In fact, during my interview with Shaffer, he confided that he identified more with Sophie than with Frank or Tom.[33]

Tom's relationship with Sue and Frank would undoubtedly have remained strained had Tom not met Sophie, the fortune teller. Sophie Lemberg (née Plotkin) is a sham; everything about her reeks of hypocrisy and deceit. She is living in fantasyland: Grinmouth-on-sea, the "fairyland of the South Coast" where the English visit to forget their cares and immerse themselves in games and other diversions. Sophie is one of these chief diversions who, as a fortune teller, spends her days looking into crystal balls to provide the middle class with hope for the future. The numerous roles that Sophie plays tend to negate her motto that "Lemberg Never Lies," which is painted in gilt letters on her window. As a palmiste, clairvoyante, and "consultant to royalty," Sophie seems to be stretching her value a bit too far.

Sophie Lemberg spends much of her time in her little fantasy world, playing roles to keep others happy. She insists that "I am a Baroness of the Holy Roman Empire. I was born with certain powers" (157). Like Louise Harrington, she is living in the lie that her parents were aristocrats, and of course, Sophie swears that she has inherited that precious royal blood: "Besides, my mother was of Romany blood. It was from her I derive my gift. Her mother had been a noblewoman of that very ancient race . . ." (160). Sophie tells Frank that her father, an amateur musician, played with the Rosé String Quartet, the finest chamber musicians in Austria: "My father knew them intimately. He would invite them each summer to our villa in the country, to play with him. And they would come. 'Sir,' they'd say, it is an honor to play with someone as good as you!" (159). When the Nazis ravaged Europe, her family fled to London where Sophie claimed her father drowned "in middle-class mediocrity" (160) as he sat in Regent's Park every day doing nothing other than reading musical scores. Sophie confidently plays the role that she has created for herself and has begun to believe in her fairy-tale existence. She even tells Frank that her art is sacred because "this hand has held the hand of a royal duchess in intimate spiritual communion. It has held the hand of an Archimandrite—a Prince of the Orthodox Church, who said to me, *bowing* to me, 'Baroness, you are not just a fortune teller: you have the divine gift!' " (162).

Sophie, however, has more in common with Pizarro than with Louise Harrington. Although she is a role player, she understands, yet does not want to admit, that the games she plays are part of her business and that her illusory facade is based on lies. She is aware that her profession is a fake, and even though others see her as a frivolity, she maintains her sense of morality and promises never to cheat them. Unfortunately, her hypocritical lifestyle, like Pizarro's, has made her sour on life. When we first see her, she is living in poverty, has not had a customer in days, and is busying herself with a game of patience. Her environment consists of rotting carpets, broken-down chairs, windows streaked with salt and bird droppings, and rusting iron. Sophie, six weeks behind in her rent, tends to ignore the real world by drowning herself in gin. Grinmouth-on-sea is a microcosm of misery to her: "Not one gleam of sunlight for ten days. Not one soul out walking, jetty to jetty. Nothing but wet sand—rusty iron—plastic bottles all along the shore, and bird shit on the windows" (154). Her fraudulent world has tainted her outlook on life to the point where she calls Grinmouth just a "third-rate holiday resort" and the English Channel "merely a gutter between here and France" (156).

Sophie has had enough both of the lies she tells and of the hypocritical life that she leads; when Frank reveals how he fabricated his story in order to maintain Tom as his bed partner, Sophie is furious at him and lashes out against his phoniness. Sophie decides to help Frank by revealing the truth behind her own fraudulent world. We learn that her father was hardly a baron: "He had no estates, my dear: his estate was a kosher delicatessen in the town of Innsbruck. After Hitler, he worked exactly at the same trade in London. Gherkins in Innsbruck, gherkins in Crawford Street—the Prater Deli: Proprietor Harry Plotkin" (178). Her mother "was not a Romany noblewoman, she was just a gypsy—and not even interesting. Just a quarter-gypsy, not colorful with scarves and lovers—just dull" (178). With regard to her father being a celebrated Austrian musician, Sophie assures Frank that he could play the clarinet quite well, but he only appeared once with the Rosé Quartet, who graciously let Mr. Plotkin play with them for one quarter of an hour during their summer visit to Salzburg.

All of the characters in *The White Liars* play roles and act out their fantasies daily. Sophie and Tom, in particular, are similar in that they lie about their origins: Tom claims that he is poor when, in reality, his family was middle class with even higher aspirations of social mobility. Sophie, on the other hand, came from an impoverished background, yet she wants others to believe that her family had its origins in royalty. Both individuals have learned to live in their fabricated lies and find it difficult to separate fact from fiction.

Both Tom and Sophie are on the verge of being able to break out of their roles, but they need some impetus to do so. Like Pizarro, they are aware of the absurdity of their existence, yet they are too conditioned to change. Sophie and Tom function as twins or alter egos to help each other escape the illusion in their lives. Sophie helps Tom realize that he wanted to be worshipped. His confession is the catharsis that he needs to rationalize his relationship with Frank and Sue. Sophie's role playing, the fact that she poses as a legitimate fortune teller for Tom when she is really a bogus mouthpiece for Frank's lies, has forced her to reexamine her code of ethics. "Lemberg Never Lies," her motto, turns out to be just another "white lie" among her arsenal of fabrications. Tom unmasks her, and at the end of the play, Sophie has a similar catharsis of her own. Now her motto becomes "Plotkin Never Lies," and the audience feels secure that there is some semblance of the truth in this statement.

Sophie and Tom, two alter egos, have assisted each other in coming to grips with reality. The play is the first instance in Shaffer's works where the dialectic between a role player and a catalyst results in both individuals obtaining mutual help. However, the play is again similar to Shaffer's early dramas in that the communication between the two individuals is *direct* and is not intuitively perceived by the audience or by one of the role players.

The White Liars was written to accompany *Black Comedy,* and thematically, it does the job well. Shaffer was confined to a one-act structure, so he was limited in what he could do with the material. Thus, he used what he knew best: sociological themes twisted in a sort of detective story that must be presented and unraveled in an hour or so of theater viewing. *The White Liars* certainly does not diminish Shaffer's importance as a sociologist of the theater, much in the tradition of Ibsen, Shaw, or Albee, yet it does not enhance his reputation as a theatrical innovator. The play is didactic in the sense that the learning experience, if there is one for the audience, is direct. With the completion of *The White Liars,* Shaffer seemed to mature as a playwright. In the later plays, Shaffer continues the formula that was so successful in *The Royal Hunt of the Sun* and uses rites, rituals, and rhythmic patterns to dramatize a change in the protagonist. Let us now examine how the later plays move out of the realm of strictly realistic sociological theater and present a more aesthetic union of form and content.

8

Shrivings: Words, Words, Words

SHAFFER began writing *The Battle of Shrivings* in New York during the student rioting on college campuses across the nation in 1968 and 1969. During Shaffer's sojourns in New York in the late 1960s, he was quite intrigued by the turmoil among America's youths:

> The encounter between Mark and Gideon naturally sprang out of a division of feeling in myself, but it was charged with the violence of this angry city during one of her angriest times, when streets were choked with raging protesters against the Vietnam War, newspapers were filled with the killings at Kent State University, and there drifted through our midst the fantastic army of Flower People, now already turned into ghosts.[1]

As a displaced Englishman in the United States, Shaffer was able to maintain an aloof attitude while observing Wall Street clashes between youngsters and construction workers or students rioting at Columbia University. Shaffer, impressed by the nonaggressive philosophy of some of the dissenters, saw possibilities for a play about the extent that a pacifistic type of humanism could lead to the atrocities that developed from man's inhumanity to man, such as the horror stories that came out of World War II.

The Battle of Shrivings was also inspired by Shaffer's reading about the life of Mahatma Gandhi. At the age of forty, Gandhi informed his wife that, because of his nonviolent stance, he was going to renounce all sexual activity, which he recognized as a source of aggression within himself. Shaffer believed that the idea would be interesting to develop in portraying Gideon as the epitome of nonviolence who has renounced sex as part of his role-playing credo. In addition, British philosopher Bertrand Russell probably was the model that Shaffer used to portray Gideon Petrie as a nonviolent logician adept at sound reasoning.[2]

The Battle of Shrivings opened at the Lyric Theatre in London on 5 February 1970. The play was directed by Peter Hall and produced by H. M. Tennent with a cast that included John Gielgud (Gideon) and Patrick Magee (Mark Askelon) in the lead roles. The critics remained divided in their evaluations of the play, yet there were more significant negative reviews than positive ones.

The play was reviewed favorably in *Punch, Evening Standard,* and *The Manchester Guardian.*[3] Philip Hope-Wallace of *The Manchester Guardian* was perhaps the play's biggest defender, calling it "serious and honourable" theater that contains large parts that "Shaw would not have at all disdained to write."[4] Jeremy Kingston of *Punch* recognized the flaws in the play, yet he described the evening's entertainment as "a work rich in ideas, rich in arresting abuse, rich in scenes that linger in the mind."[5] Frank Marcus, writing in *The Sunday Telegraph,* also had reservations about Shaffer's play, but he was able to recommend it despite its shortcomings.[6] Comparing the play to one of the melodramas of Wilde or Pinero, Marcus believed the content was a bit shallow: "There are seriousness, wit, and clever theatrical carpentry in Mr. Shaffer's play: it is a work of stature. But it does not bear close examination."[7]

Negative reviews of the play were the norm, however, and Shaffer unfortunately received his share of them. The play was panned by *The Times, The Observer, The Christian Science Monitor, The Sunday Times, New Statesman, Daily Telegraph, The Illustrated London News, Financial Times,* and *Variety.*[8] Many of the critics agreed that the play was full of rhetoric but weak in content or in sustaining any sort of viable debate. For example, Harold Hobson of *The Sunday Times* discussed the philosophical merits of the play: "A copious flow of big words for little ideas represents Mr. Shaffer's dramatic programme; and his company, probably the most brilliant in London, is like a bunch of Ancient Pistols banging away at everything within sight."[9] Ronald Bryden of *The Observer* echoed Hobson's remarks: "The idea of combining in one confrontation Bertrand Russell's tragi-comic attempts at befriending T. S. Eliot and D. H. Lawrence is a brilliant one, but Shaffer isn't equipped to cope with its implications."[10] Perhaps the most vociferous criticism came from Benedict Nightingale of *New Statesman* who described the evening's entertainment as "quite the worst play since *Tiny Alice* three weeks ago, and bad in rather the same way: solemn, affected, empty."[11] The public apparently agreed with the critics: *The Battle of Shrivings* ran for slightly less than two months before closing.

Shaffer, admitting that the play "fell somewhere between domesticity and grandeur,"[12] was also a bit shocked by his first major failure on stage. Critics who had previously enjoyed his work now turned against him:

> I was deeply depressed by the failure of this piece and by the derisory quality of the notices which greeted it. The work had meant a great deal to me . . . However, after the pain of dismissal finally abated, I came to acknowledge a certain justness in the verdict—though none at all in the palpable pleasure with which it had been delivered. It seemed to me, on

reflection, that there was a danger in my work of theme dictating event, and that a strong impulse to compose rhetorical dialectic was beginning to freeze my characters into theoretical attitudes.[13]

The rhetorical dialectic, derived from the well-made play tradition and partly from Shaffer's well-equipped Cambridge vocabulary, has been the foundation of Shaffer's dramas ever since the early radio and television plays. Although Shaffer's dialectic works best when supported by Artaudian stage elements or rites and rhythms that are often manifested by musical accompaniment, Shaffer refused to turn *The Battle of Shrivings* into another *Royal Hunt*. Shaffer has been successful on the stage mainly because of his desire to experiment with various dramatic forms. One of Shaffer's goals when writing *The Battle of Shrivings* was to write a philosophical debate without relying on elaborate theatrics, rites, or rituals:

> Other plays of mine had relied for their completion on elaborate stretches of physical action: in this one I wanted the electricity to be sparked almost exclusively from the spoken words—though of course there was a physical set-piece as well in the shape of the Apple Game. My dissatisfaction with the piece, therefore, had nothing to do with its rhetoric, which if anything I wanted to intensify; nor with its verbal duelling, which if anything I wanted to extend. I desired only to make the play more purely *itself.*[14]

Thus, Shaffer, anxious to experiment with a type of drama that once worked well for Ibsen, Brecht, Shaw, and Sartre, was determined to bring sociological debate to the contemporary stage. He rewrote the play completely, making a number of major changes. Shaffer removed from the play the character of Enid Petrie, Gideon's wife, and focused Mark Askelon's attention on Lois Neal, Gideon's secretary: "An assault on a committed girl seemed to me in this situation even more appalling than one on an aggrieved wife. The fact that the girl was also an American clinched the matter for me."[15] The definitive edition, completed in 1971, was finally published in 1974 as *Shrivings.*[16] Later, Shaffer remarked that "I invested more sheer energy into this play than any other. It is really covered with the fingermarks of struggle."[17] As of fall 1987, neither *The Battle of Shrivings* nor any version of the play has been staged in the United States. The revised version (the 1974 edition) has not yet been performed anywhere.

The original play failed to work well on stage, and it has been over a dozen years since the revised version of the play has been published, yet no producer or director has tried to stage it. Shaffer would like to see it staged, perhaps in New York. Presently, Shaffer has only minimal reservations about the project: "I think I'd written it a little too softly. It should be much

tougher. Pacifists can be very tough. I think Gideon is a little too sentimental. Maybe that's not the right word. Perhaps John Gielgud played it in too
soft a manner. It should be very tough, I think."[18]

There are a number of reasons why the play remains a gamble. First, the
play works well in reading but, as a philosophical debate, appears to be too
static for the stage. On paper, the play demonstrates some fine writing and
some beautiful, yet often soporific, poetry that is often lost on a contemporary audience more attuned to the visual than to the aural. Shaffer, with his
keen interest in historical and sociological issues, perhaps was too close to
the play to realize that not everyone in the audience would share his passion
for a debate on ethics that would be suitable for Cambridge University
students. In addition, the complexities of the debate between Mark and
Gideon work well on paper when the reader can leisurely reassess and reread
passages concerning the subtle relationship between the philosopher and his
former student. Unfortunately, most of these subtleties are lost when one
sees the play for the first time and obviously misses many of the religious,
historical, and geographical references that permeate the dialogue. In addition, the play is composed of an intricate and often confusing mélange of
lies piled on top of lies that can only be sorted out by rereading the play over
a number of times, trying to determine when Askelon or Petrie are lying or
when they are merely being facetious. It would be impossible to pick up all
of these nuances when seeing the play for the first time. In short, *Shrivings* is
Shaffer's most illustrious example of closet drama, yet it is a play that has
vast potential for the proper audience.

The second reason that *Shrivings* is unnerving is that Shaffer seems to be a
bit uncertain as to how to make the philosophical dialectic work on stage.
Shaffer has stated that "my intention from the start had always been to stage
a fairly abstract proceeding, and theatrically I am strongly drawn to the cold
which burns. However, it is possible that the proceeding was not abstract
enough, or not cold enough to burn effectively."[19] Indeed, the ritualistic
prayer scenes in which Mark Askelon recites Italian litanies in front of his
deceased wife's shrine bear a close resemblance to the Inca ceremonies of
The Royal Hunt of the Sun. Although he did not admit that *Shrivings* was
intended to be abstract in the sense that it was akin to the theater of the
unconscious, Shaffer emphasized that the play was to be more than an old-
fashioned nineteenth-century debate on sociological issues: "I didn't like the
Ibsenite elements in it. At the last moment, instead of keeping the argument
on the rails, I let the play veer off into one of those confrontation scenes so
beloved of audiences—but now, however, beloved by me."[20] *Shrivings*, a
strange mélange of ritualism, philosophy, history, and sociology, is a dialectic that approaches one of Ibsen's plays from his middle to late period, even
though Shaffer probably intended for it to be closer to a more abstract
play.[21]

On the surface, *Shrivings* focuses on the question of whether or not man changes throughout history. Mark Askelon believes in the Unalterable; his credo is "that we as men cannot alter for the better in any particular that matters. That we are totally and forever unimproveable."[22] In contrast, Gideon Petrie preaches the doctrine of Improveability—that "man is born free to make himself" (65). He tells Mark that "If we know *one thing* about Man, it is that he cannot *stop* altering—that's his condition! He is unique on earth in that he has *no* fixed behaviour patterns!" (64). Shaffer has described the play as a dialectic about man's capability of changing throughout history:

> The play is a debate between a man who insists that life lived rationally, with some attempt to control one's destiny, to conquer the roots of violence and hatred, can slowly produce, for the first time, a real MAN— not something sunk in nature, half-animal, run by adrenalin and instincts. He is opposed by a man who says humans can never change, that that is what the old religious sages meant by Original Sin, that men may shuffle the elements around, seem to change, create the *illusion* of progress, but illusion is all that it is.[23]

Shaffer's fascination with history, one that has remained with him since his college days attending Cambridge University on a scholarship to study history, is certainly apparent in *Shrivings*. To reinforce the debate over whether or not man has changed throughout history, Shaffer sprinkled his play with historical references, some of which are well known while others are relatively obscure. *Shrivings* is filled with images of man from prehistoric times to the 1970s. There are references to the "missing link" (42), "pre-history" (42), the kings of Sassania (61), rulers of Assyria (61), the Byzantine period (64), the Inquisition (33), Torquemada (63), Richard the Third and Lady Anne (80), Metternich (85), John Stuart Mill (104), the "helmeted thugs of Prussia" (85), Chiang Kai-Chek (33), Ghandi (71), the Polish gas chambers of World War II (32), and Vietnam/the invasion of Cambodia (34); as Shaffer so aptly put it, the allusions run from Nineveh to Nuremberg (61). These historical references serve to make the play more of an esoteric closet drama rather than an effective communication device between author and audience.

In addition to these historical references, the play is filled with biblical allusions. The audience must listen closely to pick up the references to Mark, the shepherd "without a flock" (23), "sagging Jesus" (38), "Christ the shepherdess" (38), "Saint Gideon" (50), "Original Sin" (66), and "First Supper" (89).

The names of the characters also reinforce the biblical allusions throughout the play.[24] Gideon was a twelfth-century B.C. judge of Israel and military commander. As Israel's fifth judge (Judg.6–8), he was known for his humility, divine inspiration, tact, and obedience. A man of strong faith, Gideon judged Israel for forty years. His most notable accomplishment was to deliver Israel from the Midianites, a group of nomads (the temptation here is to use the generic term, "philistine") who had penetrated Canaan. In *Shrivings,* Gideon does battle with another "philistine"—Mark Askelon. Mark was a first-century Jew, a son of Mary. He later became an apostle, or more aptly, a disciple of Christ and an attendant of Paul and Barnabas. Yet Mark was guilty of vacillating and was indecisive about his faith (Acts 13:13; 15:38); later, however, he recovered his place in apostolic esteem, eventually becoming a bishop. His body was removed to Venice when he died (St. Mark's Square), serving as a martyr for Christ. Mark's last name is derived from Ashkelon, one of the five leading Philistine cities; Ashkelon was captured by the tribe of Judah during the era of the Judges. Eventually, the descendants of one of the tribes of Israel became known as the Jews of Eastern Europe, the *Askenazim.* Of course, Mark Askelon identifies with his heritage and tells Gideon that "my father was not called Askelon, but Ashkenazy. Israel Ashkenazy, of the ghetto face" (46). Although he has Jewish blood in him, Mark Askelon, like his biblical surname suggests, betrays his heritage and wants nothing to do with organized religion. He was once one of Gideon's apostles, but he turns against his former mentor, all the while hoping to be "saved" by Saint Gideon. David, which is Hebrew for "beloved," is caught between two forces—Gideon, his idol, and Mark, his father—for possession of his soul. David, the young Hebrew youth, fought the Philistines and is now faced with a more modern philistine—Mark Askelon. Although David was a great military officer and eventually became the most successful king Israel ever had, in his early days, he was a page to King Saul. David was a great musician who played the harp to soothe and bemuse the troubled (and often jealous) king. In essence, David is nothing more than an acolyte, a page to Gideon, the Pope of Shrivings, forever whiling away his time literally carving wooden thrones for his patron saint. Yet Mark sees better things for his future "king," which is why he is so upset that David abandoned his education at Cambridge University for a life of obeisance to Gideon.

   Although the audience must listen attentively for often obscure historical and biblical references, as well as for geographical allusions to the Cotswolds (57), to the Apennines, the Alps, and the Dordogne (26), or to the constant chatter about Corfu, behind these obscurities one will find the typical Shafferian dialectic between a role player and his catalyst. The "battle of Shrivings" is waged over the control of two disciples: Lois Neal and David Askelon, both of whom worship Gideon Petrie as some sort of charismatic guru. Mark Askelon, aware of how harmful the master-slave role-playing relationship can be, wages war on Gideon in order to break the peacemonger's hold on his disciples. Shrivings, the "House of Retreat" (13), a place of confession and catharsis, becomes the perfect place for Mark to unmask these insecure people.[25] Mark's weapon is a slight dose of violence, the appropriate tool to unnerve a man dedicated to peace and nonviolence.

Gideon Petrie is the saint of Shrivings, an image that Lois and David are quick to serve. When Mark arrives at Shrivings and is greeted by Lois, she refers to her mentor as a "saint" (24) and later as the "Pope of Reason" (100). It is clear to Mark that Gideon is the role model for others to admire; he is the center of the household, and sarcastically Mark reminds Lois that "what he wants, so want the rest of you" (67). Gideon is so confident of his ability to soothe the wounds of others, stamp them with his brand of humanism, and appease their souls in a gurulike fashion, that he assures Mark that "Now I've found you again I'm not going to let you go until I've mended those damaged wings and sent you soaring up again into the sky of action—your proper element—your *real place!*" (49). Fortunately for Mark Askelon, he has a sense of his own identity and does not need any advice from Gideon.

Gideon has created his own castle: "Shrivings, the Cathedral of Humanism" (30). On the surface, Gideon plays the role of the humanist par excellence. He is addicted to peace and appears to be obsessed with staging nonviolent vigils, fasting in Parliament Square to protest war and violence. His house, a home for wayward transients, is an open invitation of his humanistic universal benevolence. When asked if he would defend Lois from a gun-wielding ruffian, Gideon is certain that he could not, simply because he believes that individuals who breed violence are guilty of promoting it further. To remain loyal to his brand of humanism, Gideon refuses to become violent even when he is threatened by Mark Askelon. Thus, by not casting Mark out of the house after Mark insults Gideon and his two disciples, Lois and David, the peacemaker proves that violence is unnecessary to counter other forms of destructive action.

However, the Gideon Petrie that Mark Askelon sees is quite different from the affectatious President of the World League of Peace that Gideon proposes to be. Gideon actually lectures Lois in much the same manner that Pizarro pleaded with his troops: "You've been given expert courses in all the right subjects. Mangerism, or worship of Family; Flaggism, or worship of Tribe; Thingism, or worship of Money" (41). It would appear that Gideon strongly disapproves of reverence for material goods or for false idols. Lois tells Mark that "we have no maids at Shrivings, sir. Sir Gideon does not approve of servants" (23). Sir Gideon does not need servants when he has two disciples such as David and Lois to cook, clean, type, and sew for him. David even carves a throne for his mentor—a fitting monument to this "humble" saint who boasts that his fast could be more successful if he were to "faint from hunger on the pavement" where "the effect could be sensational" (43). Meanwhile, Gideon literally sits on his throne (41) and innocently warns Lois about the dangers of worshipping false images.

Mark Askelon desperately tries to unmask Gideon and reveal the peacemonger's pretentiousness to Lois and David. Determined to prove that "the Gospel According to Saint Gideon is a lie" (50), Mark, in a battle that begins on what Barbara Lounsberry describes as Good Friday and ends with a resurrection on Sunday,[26] challenges Gideon to a primitive duel. Mark allows himself to be strapped to Gideon's throne in an experiment to see if he can humiliate Gideon to such a degree that the saint of Shrivings will fight violence with violence. Mark is given freedom of speech—a license to say anything he wants to Gideon, Lois, or David. Strapped to the throne, Mark begins to insult Gideon and his automaton-like acolytes. Three apples appear on stage; each represents various degrees of electrical shock that, when touched, make Mark, a willing actor, writhe in pain. Gideon needs only to touch the third apple—the death button—to silence Mark forever. Gideon, a firm believer that man is alterable and that he has progressed from his primitive origins to a more civilized state of nonaggression, adamantly refuses to touch the "death apple." Mark, the jaded pessimist, continues to yell insults in order to prove that man cannot alter and is unimproveable. On the surface, the dialectic is a debate over whether or not man can progress beyond Original Sin; on this level, the play examines issues related to cultural anthropology. On another level, the debate is between a role player and his alter ego, a primitive spirit who is independent in thought and action; in this sense, the play becomes sociology.

Gideon refuses to touch the "death apple" and thereby assumes a nonviolent stance; yet his abstention does nothing to alleviate the tension or to quell Mark's sadistic attack. Gideon is therefore exposed as a shallow and spineless individual who is incapable of taking *any* stand at all, and his weak defense, "I find I am tireder than I thought" (71), makes one wonder if Giddy, a man now true to his unstable namesake, has any values worth defending. Gideon's passivity begins to assume new values for Lois and David. Lois realizes that Gideon is artificial, a shallow individual "making a great Cause out of not caring" (101). She confronts Gideon with his new role: "Do you know what a phoney is? Someone who says Peace because there's no war in him. I don't mean he drove it out—I mean he never had it" (102). Gideon's Gandhi-like vow of renouncing all sexual activity was supposed to have forced his wife, Enid, into marital separation. However, Lois begins to develop a different perspective with regard to their marriage: "No wonder she left you, your wife. No wonder she just got out, poor stupid Enid. She found out what a phoney she was hitched to. What a phoney! (102). Even David, who resents his father's intrusion into this new family that has made him part of the commune, can only pity hapless

Gideon. The saint of Shrivings has had his ego deflated and is reduced to what David describes as "Theories and hopes and vigils and fasts! And *nothing! Lovely nothing!*" (94).

Gideon's hypocrisy is best manifested in his sexual relationships with others. On his forty-fifth birthday, Gideon summoned his wife and announced that he was going to abandon sex, for it was surely "the main source of aggression" (77), nothing more than "a twin act of masturbation, accompanied by murmurs designed to disguise the fact" (77). But Mark sees it otherwise and hypothesizes that Enid did not leave her husband "because of that boring vow of chastity" (71) but simply because "it was the hypocrisy she couldn't take" (71).

All of Shaffer's role players are sexually frustrated individuals, and Gideon Petrie is no exception. Mark reveals that Gideon, the once-happily married patriarch who has no children of his own, is homosexual. Mark swears to Lois that "the only sex Gideon ever really enjoyed was with boys" (71); in short, Mark warns that "Giddy is completely queer, for what that's worth. He never slept with a woman in his life" (81). Mark proceeds to attack Gideon's masculinity, thereby deflating his authoritarian position in the eyes of Lois and David. When Lois tires of watching "the Electrified Man" react to the apples of Original Sin, she urges Giddy to go to bed. Mark, of course, mocks Lois' suggestion: "Ah, that's sweet. 'Why don't we go to bed?' Can you really mean that seriously—to a man you've selected entirely because he can't?" (70). Later in the play, after Mark has had sex with Lois, he chides Gideon, in front of Lois and David, for his sexual inadequacies. Referring to Lois, Mark asks Gideon, "What do you think she wanted from you, eh? Drugs and shrugs, and a pleady kiss once a week. D'you think that satisfies a girl? I know you pot babies. It's all wow and wee-wee, with you, isn't it? You can't get it up to save your stoned lives!" (91).

Homosexual tendencies are much easier to detect when viewing a play than they are in the reading, but the perceptive critic will notice that Gideon frequently puts his arm around David and refers to Mark and his son as "my dear" (e.g., twice on 22, 26, twice on 27, 28, 32, 45, twice on 48, 49, 51, 95).[27] Gideon tries to assuage the charges against him by admitting that "To say I was bi-sexual would have been a ludicrous understatement. I was tri-sexual. Quadri. Quinti. Sexi-sexual, you might say!" (76). He confesses that "throughout my twenties I cheerfully, and indeed gratefully, engaged in repeated encounters with both sexes" (76). Gideon is trying to prove that he had overstimulated sex drives, but Mark is actually revealing just the opposite.

Lois, in particular, gradually begins to accept Mark's account of the facts, not Gideon's. She begins to view Gideon's affections for David as a homosexual encounter rather than as a platonic relationship: "Do you know what a phoney is, Giddy? A person who says the family is obsolete, and all he really wishes is that David Askelon was his own son! . . . It's easy to be chaste when you've got no cock, Giddy" (102). Gideon's sexual inadequacies force Lois to question his sincerity:

> I don't believe your word on anything. Like when you say when you were young, you were attracted to boys and dogs and shit knows what? I tell you, I don't believe a fucking word. *I think you're exactly like me. You can't stand it.* You made that whole thing up just to teach a point. *[English accent]* "Sex Freedom is a jolly good thing!" But I'm willing to bet my ass you never did it at all. (102)

After this tirade, Gideon slaps Lois, a symbolic gesture that reveals the hypocritical nature of this holier-than-thou "peacemaker."

Gideon's illusory life is revealed not merely through his sexual deviations, but also in a Shafferian role player's ability to live a life full of lies. Gideon's daily coexistence with Lois and David is based on a lie: he is untrue to his principles and precarious with his friends. When Gideon accuses Mark of inventing stories about him, Mark shoots back with, "Oh, come now: you can do better than that! You don't have to resort to lies, Gideon. Protect him [David], if you want—but don't lie! It's shocking when *you* do it!" (92). "Shocking" is the only word to describe some of Gideon's intentions. Although he is committed to a cause and has written twenty-five books, Gideon obviously has other reasons for making Shrivings into a retreat for young transients. Gideon's sainthood is exposed as a lie, and it is this hypocrisy that destroys his relationship with his two most loyal supporters, Lois and David.

If Gideon is the omnipotent master, then Lois Neal (Kneel?) is his favorite disciple. Gideon picked up Lois when they met in jail after being arrested during a march in which they participated. For the past two years, Lois has adopted Gideon as a sort of father figure that she never had. She has abandoned her family, her culture, and her religion to serve Gideon.

Although we do not learn much about Lois's family background, we do know that Lois had a strict Catholic upbringing. Reminiscing about her childhood, she is quite selective about the picture that she provides for us: "D'you know the last thing *I'd* see at night when I was a kid? A beautiful plastic Jesus, like the ones they have in taxis to prevent crashes, only bigger. It had these great ruby tears on its face, and I'd have to pray to it before turning out the light: 'Dear Lord, make me a Good Catholic and a Good American. Amen!' " (21). At Shrivings, she is a twenty-five-year-old rebel who cannot wait to greet "the great Mark Askelon" (18) for the first time because of his reputation as a heretic. Lois, who has been in love with Askelon "ever since I read *Wafers of Death* in Doubleday's Bookshop, the first day I arrived in New York" (18), glorifies the poet-scholar because "he wrote about Catholicism like it was a disease" (18). Apparently, drastic changes have occurred in her life since those adolescent years.

Lois is an insecure rebel, a transient who has lost her family and her sense of religion. In addition, she is an outcast of American society, choosing instead to live in England rather than in the violent environment of the American peace movement. Rejecting her family, church, and state, Lois, the rebel who does not know what she wants out of life, has turned to Gideon and David to provide her with another type of "peace."

Lois sees Gideon and David as her new family. Joan F. Dean has noted that Lois has become Gideon's surrogate wife, and although she does not have sex with him (neither Lois nor Gideon want a sexual relationship), she does cook, clean, and type for Gideon in a somewhat old-fashioned marriage.[28] For her favors, Lois receives approval and acceptance into a secure environment. She has no qualms about serving a father figure/mentor, and when David accuses her of being a "disciple" (40), Lois replies, "And proud of it" (40). Mark characterizes her as "Earth Mother—or sorry: Earth Auntie. Unmarried, of course" (70). Mark's remark is particularly appropriate because at Shrivings Lois is able to find a new identity as the Earth Mother who supervises and coordinates the Petrie household. In return, Gideon has dubbed her the Falcon, and she begins to adopt a strong, secure role that previously eluded her.

Mark Askelon is able intuitively to perceive Lois's sense of insecurity behind her role playing. Mark sees Lois as a consummate role player, weak willed and subservient to Gideon: "Who is she, this Illinois idiot, creaming her committed little panties every time you enter the room? [*American accent*] 'Oh, Giddy you're so great! Gee, Giddy, you're so wonderful! You're a fuckin' saint, boy, honest!' . . . Is that what you really want? A sticky little acolyte plunging after a man three times her age, just because he's safe?" (70). Later in the play, Mark, drunk and in bed with Lois, tells her about the dangers of role playing: "Never forgive them. The kneelers! The followers of carriage axels. The motorcade boys. The smart saluters" (85). Lois Neal, as her namesake implies, belongs in a select group of Shafferian role players—alienated characters without a strong sense of identity.

Although she hides behind the mask of "commitment," Lois is actually searching for some sort of stability in her life. She is basically a weak person, impressionable to the extent that she admires Mark Askelon before even meeting him. When she sees Gideon's faltering sense of stability, it is not surprising that she abandons him in favor of Mark, who maintains his own strong feelings about life. Lois is well aware that life is "a great big lie factory, where we've all been made to work every day, printing up labels: Serf. Heretic. Catholic. Communist. Middle-class. And when we're through, we're made to paste them over each other till the original person disappears, and nobody knows who the hell he is any more!" (59). The irony is that Lois fails to understand that she falls into some of the same categories. By the end of the play, after Gideon is exposed as a phony, thereby reducing Lois to a worthless disciple, she echoes her own remarks about role playing by proclaiming to David that "I don't know who I am" (105).

This sense of role playing has turned Lois into a frigid, lifeless individual. Throughout the play, Lois is depicted as a sterile female or what Mark refers to as "forever a Vestal Virgin, waving the flag of Humanity high over your frozen Mount of Venus!" (71). When David, her constant companion, tries to sneak a kiss in on her, "she turns away very coolly" (19), and when he later kisses her abruptly, "she lets herself be kissed, but remains inert" (39). David accuses her of being fearful of even the slightest hint of a sexual relationship with a man, but Lois responds with, "A person is not uptight, my dear, just because she doesn't happen to want that" (39). To Lois, people's sex lives are merely "trivial" (19), and she has always admired Gideon for renouncing all sexual relationships with his wife.

Unfortunately, Lois's aversions to sexual activities are abnormal for a woman of her age. In response to Gideon's claim that he is oversexed, Lois chides her mentor, revealing as much about herself as she does about Gideon: "I think you're exactly like me. You can't stand it!" (102). Lois is sensitive not just about physical sexual activity, but also about the mere mention of sex. Early in the play, Gideon states that Mark's last discussion with his former teacher, eleven years ago, focused on "whether the heart's blood the Furies dropped on Athens in the *Oresteia* was really their menstrual fluid" (20). Shaffer's stage directions reveal that Lois is "a little shocked: trying not to show it" (20). When Mark takes Lois, the virgin, to bed for the first time, it is obvious that the experience turns out to be dismal: "It wasn't exactly the sex act of the era. She's as cold as haddock, you must know that. Deep Freeze Dora, the Tundra Gash!" (91).

Lois and Gideon are probably beyond salvation, but Mark is determined that David, "the chosen one," can be saved. David is different from Lois in that he is able to think for himself when the need warrants. When asked if he would kill the ruffian who might threaten Lois, David says he would break Gideon's almighty code of nonviolence "because I'd rather have Lois alive than somebody I didn't know" (33). David will not hesitate to indulge in a lambchop to break an unreasonable fast or press the "death apple" to quell violence with violence. Mark, seeing his chance to deflate Gideon's power over one of his acolytes, is eager to pursue the game as far as possible, using David as a weapon.

David is bound to Gideon by more than just mutual affection, and like Lois, he views the elderly gentleman as a surrogate father figure. David was sent to England by Mark whose telegrams, stamped with the message, "Regret still not convenient you return. Father," created an inseparable gap between the sage and his offspring. The relationship between David and Mark Askelon is reminiscent of the father-son tension between Clive and Stanley Harrington in *Five Finger Exercise*. Mark, successful in his social life and in his career, views his son as a listless individual who is not working towards any goals; he scorns his son as a "mediocrity," much like Stanley ridiculed Clive. David, who has dropped out of two public schools and Cambridge University within a five-year period, is living on a day-to-day basis as nothing more than Gideon's disciple. When Mark is reunited with his son after a lengthy absence, the young man is busily making furniture for Gideon—an activity that Mark can only construe as a waste of time for someone with so much talent. The confrontation between father and son, with David making "darting glances at his father, but unable to look him fully in the face" (29), is a replay of Stanley Harrington, the successful businessman, admonishing his easily cowed, hapless son, who has yet to prove himself in the business world.

As a result of the tension that David felt at home, he rebelled, rejecting institutions such as family, school, and business. Instead, David chose to live in Gideon's commune, adopting Gideon as his new father. Mark certainly is aware of this and bemoans David's new identity as the Owl, working in tandem with Lois, the Falcon, in Gideon's "stable": "Well, of course, you could hear it—defiance. 'I'm Giddy's boy now. Let's not mistake . . . Son and heir of Shrivings . . .' Sagging Jesus!" (38). David has meticulously garnered his role and is content to spend time serving Gideon, even to the extent of carving a throne for him. Mark can only view it as a wasteful activity for a talented youth who has become a mediocrity: "Who the hell is he? Master carpenter to Gideon Petrie. I sent him to England for *that*—to carve his throne! 'Hail to my new daddy,—Lord of the twenty-five books!' My old daddy only wrote four, and they were just poetry!" (37). At the end of the play, Mark, who has exposed Gideon as a fraud, nevertheless concedes his rights over David and tells him to maintain the symbiotic relationship with the gurulike leader because "you're his son where it matters" (103).

Just as Gideon and Lois were unmasked as phonies with deep-rooted sexual problems to accompany their mediocre and sterile lives, David is also forced to undergo a psychosexual catharsis. Mark begins by claiming that David is illegitimate, an enigma that will always remain unanswered in David's mind, even though Mark later admits that he made up the whole story. But the fact that David is "different" is clearly demonstrated in his homosexual relationship with Gideon. Mark is quick to remind his son that Giulia despised her offspring because "even in her, deep down, was the natural Italian horror of the Unmale" (91). Mark's gruff, "You can't get it up to save your stoned lives!" (91), a comment directed at Gideon as well as David, brings their sterile relationship out into the open. Such a revealing remark helps to clarify David's escapade with Gideon, including his nude romp to Gideon's chamber and the "touching session" that ensues (86). To Mark Askelon, the physical encounters between Gideon and David, such as David innocently toweling off his mentor after a bath, have a perverse animalistic "touch" to them: "Well, there they go, Father and son—hand in hand up the meadow. Touching! The whole hippy dream in one frame: old and young, leaping the generation gap like mountain goats!" (79).

If David and Lois are disciples of Gideon, the role player, then Mark Askelon completes the picture as the mirror image, or Gideon's alter ego. Mark, Gideon's former student, has always been a bit of a gadfly in his quest for truth. Mark's book, *Wafers of Death,* a reassessment of Catholicism, had established the young writer's reputation as someone who was not hesitant to question society's norms and values. Therefore, it is to be expected that when Mark enters Shrivings and is told that all forms of violence are dangerous, he quickly asks, "You mean, the men who freed Belsen were as guilty as the men who made it?" (32). The responses from Lois are so stereotyped that Mark begins to realize how effective Gideon's teachings have been. Mark sees the dangers of one's reliance on rigidly controlled doctrines, particularly if they are blindly accepted by some guru's automatonlike followers.

Through Mark Askelon, Shaffer focuses on one of his favorite themes associated particularly with the later plays: an attack on mediocrity. Shafferian protagonists in these later plays, such as Dysart and Salieri, are obsessed with transcending their static lives in favor of a more "primitive," unrestrained, Dionysian existence. Askelon sees mediocrity depicted deeply within the bowels of Shrivings. In his important speech to the trinity of Christ-like figure and his two apostles, Mark delineates the dangers of mediocrity:

> In 1920 the greatest psychiatrist in Europe analysed the dreams of five hundred patients. From them, he slowly made out—detail by detail—the appalling shape of the Nazi beast. It was there, waiting to spring out of the black cave of the Common Unconscious . . . Out of that deep pit, stinking of orgasm, economical soup, and the halitosis of mediocrity, have risen all the terrors of the earth. (60–61)

Gideon, who has taken weak-willed individuals into his fold, is equated with other despots or gurus who have done the same thing. Askelon mentions the "rulers of Assyria," "the despots of Asia," and the Nazis all in the same breath (61), and it is a fetid breath at that. The sarcasm of Mark's speech is obvious, especially to Gideon: "The pop-eyed Lord of Sassania, primping his silver beard, saying 'Behold perfection! I have no petty thoughts. No haemorrhoids. No moments when I fail to get erection. Long live the King! The King *must* live forever!' "(61). Lois and David, two individuals who choose to follow, like the masses, rather than to think for themselves, are not spared either. Mark, trying desperately to free these two mediocrities from their allegiance to this godlike figure, speaks directly to their plight:

> Who would make such objects? God cannot make anything infallible. Who needs Forever? Who raised these idols from the anonymous dust— hysterical puppets of Ninevah [sic] or Nuremberg? Who linked the wires? Started the sceptre arms flailing, the saluting arms of self-abuse? Who opened their anthem-yelling metal mouths? Who if not I? Him. You. [*Pause*] You walk royal portrait galleries as if you are attending identity parades for murderers. Start looking for yourself there, Miss Neal. You might just begin to understand history better. (61)

Our need to worship perfection or glory in immortals or deities, so despised by Mark Askelon as the "halitosis of mediocrity," is not atypical of mankind. During my interview with Shaffer, he defended Lois's behavior as characteristic of man's need for worship:

> We cannot say that Nuremberg was a creation of wicked men. It was a creation of the people that she [Lois] admired. We created Stalin, just as much as we create Mozart, Napoleon, Hitler. It's a need to feel a kind of glory. . . . It's a need for perfection, too. We want figures who haven't got to pay the mortgage, who haven't got hemorrhoids, who haven't got the anxieties of the average person. . . . We have created such figures. No such figures actually exist in the world. But those statues of pharaohs and impervious beings were created by us—literally made by us with chisels and hammers and then shaped by our desire to see such idolatries. What is Nuremberg but merely an act of identity?[29]

Mark is not the type of person who blindly follows others, nor does he develop theorems or principles to mollify the disorder in other people's lives. He introduces himself as "a shepherd, as my cloak proclaims. I suspect permanently without a flock" (23), a direct reference to Gideon and others like him who see themselves as "Christ the Shepherdess" (38). Mark makes it clear that he is no "sagging Jesus" (38) and castigates Lois for her inability to think and act for herself: "You arrogant little beast, do you imagine I live my life to be approved by *you*?" (60). Thus, the game that Mark devises is designed to change Shrivings from a place of worship to a house of free thinking, an environment where these "acolytes of the unalterable" (62) can come to terms with their own thoughts and feelings. By the end of the play, Mark has achieved the same degree of success that Atahuallpa had over Pizarro. David has regained a father and has begun to think more for himself. Lois, the most hardened supporter of Gideon, becomes convinced that Giddy has ulterior motives for his "house of retreat." She begins to understand that Mark is "not a phoney" (102), and he does not preach a contradictory brand of ethics.

We have had a glimpse of Mark Askelon, the Shafferian protagonist, in many of the earlier works. His description almost matches Mr. Verity, Mr. Fathom, or Pizarro: "In his early fifties, he is the relic of an enormous man. A mass of hair falls from a massive head: eyes stare from an eroded face. He wears a Greek shepherd's cloak with a hood. His voice is still powerful" (23). Lois describes him as "the Grand Old Man, destroyed by suffering" (60), and indeed he has seen enough of life for him to be jaded with mankind. He has a bit of a superiority complex and often feels impatient with the mediocre individuals surrounding him. Mark admits that, in his youth, he was proud of his talents, but he has mellowed since those early days:

> I knew an Encyclopedic Sympathy: there was nobody outside of *me!* I was the arriving lecturer—and the doorman who admits him, cringing. I was the Fabergé Prince . . . I went to parade grounds, brisk in khaki. Returned at night, tired dandruff in an aching bus. I was the arch of the morning—Cream of Corelli—the indigestion of a wasted day! I was a replete, complete Man. (83)

Yet even with such self-esteem and an intuitive understanding of his creative and artistic talents, Mark is aware of the other side of his personality—an inability to enjoy life. Like Clive, Bob, and Pizarro (and later Dysart and Salieri), Mark has trouble relating to other people in a relaxed, natural way. In a cathartic statement at the end of act 2, Askelon reveals his own plight as well as the dilemma faced by Shaffer's other guilt-ridden protagonists:

> Inside me, from my first day on earth, was a cancer. An incapacity for Immediate Life. When I was a boy, the crowd at football matches jumped to its feet, shouting. All I could see was a ball and legs. At student dances, I hopped in silence. They all said: isn't it exciting, the music? I grinned, but heard nothing. (83–84)

Mark wants to know "why was I born without joy. Why do others have it, and not me?" (97–98). As a serious poet and scholar, Mark has no time for frivolous activities; unfortunately, even in his youth, he never experienced the carefree joys of life. Depressed with middle age, Mark realizes that life has cheated him. Youth's fancies are gone, and Mark, committed to the "unalterable," knows that he is condemned to a joyless existence.

Critics have pointed out the similarities between Mark Askelon and Pizarro.[30] Joan F. Dean suggests that both men are faced with a midlife crisis of faith.[31] Askelon and Pizarro are both jaded individuals who begin to learn more about life through a growing awareness and fear of death. They are alienated from others in society and appear bitter about their joyless lives. In addition, as Joan F. Dean and Dennis Klein mention, Pizarro and Askelon have lost faith in social and religious institutions; instead, they have turned to a worship of primitive cultures (Corfu for Askelon and Cajamarca for Pizarro).[32] Furthermore, both men want to be saved by their alter egos: Pizarro learns from Atahuallpa, and Askelon comes to Shrivings for confession or penance; he actually wants to be saved or "shriven" and secretly would like Gideon to reintroduce him to the humanist philosophy that he has long since abandoned.

Although Mark Askelon's main goal during "the battle of Shrivings" is to pull Lois and David away from Gideon's tutelage, thereby freeing them from the dangers of role playing, he does indeed engage in psychological warfare as a sort of catharsis for his pent-up problems. In this sense, Mark is following a long line of "judge-penitents" in dramatic literature. As a moralist who judges others and as a penitent who fails to cure his own psychological woes, Askelon has much in common with Shakespeare's Hamlet, Ibsen's Gregers Werle, O'Neill's Hickey, and Weiss's Jean-Paul Marat. Like Pizarro, Mark has seen the dark side of life and is capable of returning to the humanist philosophy, provided that the patient can be injected with new life and vigor stemming from an appropriate catalyst. Unfortunately, Gideon cannot provide the same type of fresh spiritualism that Atahuallpa stimulated.

Because of his inability to enjoy life, Mark has become a bitter man, callous towards other people and nihilistic in his outlook on life. Alone with Lois, Mark explains his predicament:

I have never lived *Now.* And that 'Never' makes crueller murderers, even than Christ or Country. Look into my eyes. What do you see? The envy? The endless living through others? Jealousy squinting through the glare of commitment? . . . There is where Vietnam starts. Don't sit on pavements to ban armaments: sit, if you must, to ban these eyes. They would kill Gideon, if they could, for his goodness. They would kill David for his instinct. Yes, my own son—as they killed his mother: Giulia. Poor girl, you are looking at a murderer. (84)

Throughout his youth, David, full of life and enthusiasm, was the antithesis of his embittered, sour father. Having had a bit too much brandy, Mark, feeling lofty and capricious, explains to David the relationship to his son:

When you were six, I watched you race your bike through the olive trees. Your mother was standing beside me. Your mouth opened with glee. Hers too. All I got were the mouths opening and shutting. No glee. Just physical movements. I stood there hating you both. Filling up with hate. And you, twisting the handlebars, turned and caught my eye, you shook—and fell off. Giulia screamed and ran to you. I didn't. (97)

David, a perceptive child, saw his father "sticking pins of seconal into his face, saying: 'Let this be the Young! The hateful Young!'" (97). Although Giulia idolized her husband, Mark admits that David saw "the killer in me" (97), and thus the young man had to be sent away to England under the guise of receiving a better education.

Mark is ashamed of the way he has treated his son, but he is even more guilty about the fate of his wife, Giulia. Giulia imagined Mark to be a saint; in her eyes, he was a writer, an educated man who lowered himself to marry a humble Italian girl. Although she was religious, she would hide her prayer book from Mark so as not to irritate him. Mark loved his wife but could not understand why she worshipped him as a saint. One evening, Mark, full of spite for his wife, picked up a girl and made love to her in front of Giulia, his timid, yet faithful companion. Mark describes how the incident eventually led to his wife's death: "It was the next morning she groaned first thing on waking. Very exactly: once. As if she were clearing her throat. [*Pause*] She didn't live three weeks after that. I remember she held the cola bottle night and day. Like a doll to a sick child" (103).

Mark, the judge-penitent, has come to Shrivings to be relieved of all of the guilt that relates to his self-imposed role in the destruction of his family. He has lost his wife, his son, and his mentor—now he hopes that a catharsis will offer him the chance to explain his sense of alienation.

In order to distinguish Mark Askelon from the phonies or role players, Shaffer associates Mark's catharsis with a type of religious rite or ritual. Just as the ritualistic elements of Atahuallpa's culture demonstrated his "primitive" sense of worship in contrast to the well-codified roles of the Spanish, so does Mark's brand of self-styled religion distinguish him from the others at Shrivings. Mark is seen throughout the play as an independent person who thinks and acts for himself, regardless of what society sanctions him to do. We are *told* that Mark adheres to a free-spirited weltanschauung; in addition, the ritualistic catharsis provides the audience with visible proof of Mark's independence as a sort of primitive who creates his own sense of worship complete with a new church, a congregation of one, and a saint worth idolizing. In his prayers to Giulia, Mark becomes a "primitive" (much like Atahuallpa) rejecting all forms of worship and codes except those that are created solely by him.

Mark carries with him an effigy of his wife, whom he refers to as "Santissima, Beatissima Giulia" (36). During stress and when Mark wants to relieve his pent-up guilt feelings, he opens the shrine and speaks directly to his "wife." He retreats to the shrine following his most tense debates with

Gideon: after insulting Gideon and his acolytes at the end of act 1, scene 1 (35–36), after David presses the "death apple" to silence his father (72), and at the end of the play following Gideon's emasculation and subsequent fainting (99). Mark's prayers to Giulia are thus a form of communion and catharsis for him. In a sort of self-created religion, Mark's ceremonial chants function as Mass for this self-proclaimed atheist. Gideon's offhand remark, "I can always rely on you to make a delicious ceremony out of everything" (27), is therefore more accurate than he realizes. This is not some kind of spontaneous and unstructured worship, for Mark, recognizing Giulia as the only saint worth paying homage to, carries the elaborate shrine with him, and at a moment's notice, he is down on his knees before Santa Giulia.

In his prayers to Giulia (36, 38, 44, 72–73, 99–103), Mark, frequently substituting his wife's language—Italian—for the traditional Latin chants, asks for comfort and seeks forgiveness for his sins. His reverence for his wife is so serious that he has formed his own brand of worship, free from outside control. His prayers to Giulia, a ritualistic chant, serve two major purposes. First, the Mass provides order for Mark during times of confusion or tension. Second, the cathartic chanting seems to offer Mark a spiritual cleansing enabling him to engage Gideon in further debate for control of his two disciples.

By the end of the play, Mark is seen as a savage, a grotesque primitive who is enough of a heathen to say and do whatever he likes. The games that he created were certainly effective; Gideon is unmasked as a phony, and Lois and David, both brutally humiliated, are frightened out of their stereotyped existences. But Mark is not merely a primitive heathen who interferes with the lives of others; instead, he is respected for his strong belief in what he accepts as his own brand of truth. Mark does not simply tell others how to order their lives; by basing so much on the significance of a personalized ceremony, he demonstrates to the audience that he is not artificial, like Gideon and his two worshippers.

Shaffer tried to combine a philosophical debate with some of the ritualistic qualities of the Theatre of Cruelty. However, the ceremonial nature of the play, those few scenes where Mark prays to the shrine, do not present a unified and sustained rhythm necessary to make the play work on an archetypal level. *Shrivings* functions on a number of levels, and to this extent, the play goes beyond what Shaffer did with the early dramas. However, it fails to achieve the universal effects of the rhythmic structure of *The Royal Hunt of the Sun, Equus,* or *Amadeus.*[33]

Like all great playwrights, Shaffer is continually experimenting with the form of the play. In *Shrivings,* he tried to let the words dominate other aspects of the *mise-en-scène,* much like the Romantic poets did when they wrote plays. Artaud intuitively understood that a predominance of highly poetic language presented in a formal debate would undermine a sustained rhythmic structure. Shaffer tried to present a balance between the dialectic and the ceremonial elements in the play. Peter Weiss was able to do this effectively in *Marat/Sade,* but he relied much more on mime, song, dance, and choreography to establish the balance. Unfortunately, *Shrivings* degenerates into philosophy at the expense of the few ritualistic scenes that are in the play; as stagecraft suffers and as the language becomes more esoteric, we get more of a "closet drama" effect than we do even in Shaffer's early plays.

In short, *Shrivings* is a play with many merits, and when viewed by a sophisticated audience, it could work quite well as dialectical theater. When viewed by an audience of diverse backgrounds, the play may be misconstrued as either a sociological, historical, or psychological debate. The audience may be unsure if Mark Askelon is debating Gideon for control of his two disciples or because he wants to purge himself of latent psychological problems that have been disturbing him for years. The content of the play is difficult to pin down, even upon close examination of the text. The historical, political, and biblical allusions force the spectator to listen even more closely to catch the significance of some obscure references. In addition, the form of the play also adds to this sense of confusion, forcing the spectator to interpret the importance of isolated ritualistic scenes in what is otherwise a drama of ideas. Shaffer, in effect, tried to do too much. Without significant clarity in form and content, *Shrivings* became an intellectual exercise with an esoteric twist of the theater of the unconscious. *Equus,* Shaffer's next play, is more unified in terms of form, content, and stagecraft—a return to the successful type of production that made *The Royal Hunt of the Sun* the effective play that it was.

9

Equus: The Beat Goes On

EQUUS, one of the most controversial plays of the twentieth century, premiered at the Old Vic in London on 26 July 1973. The production, which starred Alec McCowen as Martin Dysart and Peter Firth as Alan Strang, was stunningly directed by John Dexter and effectively choreographed by Claude Chagrin. Marc Wilkinson's eerie music, Andy Phillips's superb lighting effects, and John Napier's scenic design, including the stylized masks for the horses, made for a breathtaking theatrical event. The New York run began on 24 October 1974, at the Plymouth Theatre. Peter Firth continued in the role of Alan Strang while Anthony Hopkins played opposite him as Dysart; subsequently, Anthony Perkins and Richard Burton succeeded Hopkins in the role of Dysart. *Equus* has been successful throughout the world and has garnered such honors as the Outer Critics' Circle Award, the Los Angeles Drama Critics' Award, the "Tony" Award, and the New York Drama Critics' Circle Award. As a result of the play's success, Shaffer wrote a film screenplay that, in 1977, was adapted by director Sidney Lumet, eventually to become a rather lackluster movie version of the play.[1]

The London reviews of the play were favorable, even though the British, with their traditional love of horses, obviously found Alan Strang's obsession more than a trifle revolting. Positive reviews were written in *The Sunday Times, Daily Telegraph, The Manchester Guardian, Punch, Financial Times, Evening Standard, Variety,* and *New Statesman.*[2] *Variety* praised the play as "philosophical drama, inconclusive per force, but written with sharp intelligence and compassion, often witty and poetic, always challenging the audience to think again about conventional wisdom—about, in truth, alienated existence."[3] The critics particularly lauded John Dexter's direction and John Napier's scenic design, while many reviewers recognized Shaffer's talents for writing powerful scenes that would be a pleasure for our ears as well as for our eyes. Michael Billington described the play as "sensationally good,"[4] containing what Milton Shulman called "stunning dramatic effects."[5] John Barber summed up the critics' positive remarks about the play when he referred to *Equus* as a landmark of the modern theater: "But this remarkable play, with its talk of the dark gods and its plea for an instinctual truth the modern world has lost, must count as one of the National Theatre's bravest and most uncommon achievements."[6]

Equus, however, did receive its share of negative criticism, most of it coming from critics who thought that the dialogue was weak or who were offended by the content of the play. Russell Davies, reviewer for the *New Statesman,* seemed to speak for a number of critics when he wrote, "Visually, then, John Dexter's production was fine; but the argument of the play was worrying."[7] Irving Wardle of *The Times* admitted that "the play instantly fills the theatre with the sense of a potent and ancient force returning to life," but the argument, the text, and the dialogue were found "lacking."[8] Robert Cushman of *The Observer* credited Shaffer for writing "magnificent scenes," turning the play into an effective thriller; however, he had reservations about the play's prose and claimed that *Equus* could not be taken "realistically."[9] The harshest review of the play was credited to Ian Christie of the *Daily Express.* Disgusted with what he called the play's pretentiousness, Christie only had praise for the production, not the writing: "In fact the production, by John Dexter, is so accomplished that it almost blinds you to the fact that you are watching a lot of fearful philosophic claptrap."[10]

In the United States, *Equus* received even more favorable press than it did in London. The play was hailed as a success in *The New York Times, The Nation, The Christian Science Monitor, The New Yorker, Variety, Newsweek, Daily News, Wall Street Journal, Saturday Review,* and *New York Post.*[11] Clive Barnes of *The New York Times* had only positive comments to make, concluding that "this is a very fine and enthralling play. It holds you by the root of drama, and it adds immeasurably to the fresh hopes we have for Broadway's future."[12] Harold Clurman of *The Nation* lauded Shaffer for creating a detective story that is "brilliantly crafted, handsomely written and unusually compelling."[13] Perhaps Edwin Wilson's comments in the *Wall Street Journal* best sum up the positive critical reaction to the drama: "Mr. Shaffer's play is about many things—the Nietzschean conflict between the Dionysian and Apollonian impulses, the problems of normalcy and the attributes of insanity, the need we have to worship a god—and these ideas will be analyzed and criticized for some time to come."[14]

Although there were few negative reviews, the dissenters made their voices heard. T. E. Kalem, writing in *Time,* complained that Shaffer had "blinded the audience to his exaltation of deranged violence as religious passion."[15] Stanley Kauffmann of *The New Republic,* noting that psychiatrists were being maligned, thought that the content was thin and that only the play's theatrical conventions made the drama a success on stage.[16] John Simon of *The Hudson Review* believed that *Equus* was nothing more than a study of pederasty, and he accused Shaffer of stacking the cards against normality with a play that "pullulates with dishonesty."[17]

Equus is a controversial play, and because of its widespread appeal, it has also been criticized almost as much as it has been defended by Shaffer's supporters. Many conservative theatergoers have complained that the obvious sensationalism of the play, particularly the need to portray a young man's obsession with horses, is not suitable for the stage. These critics complain that the blinding of horses is too repulsive an event for any stage and is not an appropriate subject for a play. Yet many of the world's great tragedies deal with murder, patricide, revenge, lust, suicide, and other horrible themes. Incest, for example, is an important motif in tragedies such as *Oedipus the King, Hamlet, Phèdre,* and *'Tis Pity She's a Whore,* as well as modern dramas such as *Ghosts* and *Desire Under the Elms.* In short, *Equus* should not be criticized because of its serious thematic concerns. Even weak-hearted theater patrons should be able to recognize Shaffer's attempts to stylize the grotesque stable scene. When analyzed objectively, *Equus* can be viewed almost as a nonviolent play—certainly one that is much less brutal than the great tragedies of the Western world.

The second major criticism of the play concerns its religious theme. Although the play has been reviewed favorably in many publications that have a religious orientation,[18] some critics insist that, as in *The Royal Hunt of the Sun,* Shaffer is attacking organized religion.[19] In his reaction to the concept of "normal," Dysart, speaking through Shaffer, seems to support worship in any form regardless of whether or not it is organized and codified by society's rules and norms. Yet even the most casual reader will find numerous references that compare Alan's horse-god to Christ. In an interview with *The New York Times,* Shaffer made the connection quite clear: "The boy says to the horse, 'Bear me away,' which is what a lot of religious poets say to their God in their poetry. This particular God is capable of carrying him away."[20] In addition, Shaffer has stated that the blinding of the horses, a scenic image with the power to haunt, has affinities with the "extinction of divinity."[21] Yet the religious motifs are no more the focus of Shaffer's attention in *Equus* than they were in *The Royal Hunt of the Sun;* instead, they are a means to an end. Even the psychological and sexual implications of the play serve only as surface material for the more important underlying issue that Shaffer is trying to explore: the dangers of role playing.

The third concern that critics had was that *Equus* was weak in content and relied mostly on sensationalism and theatrical gimmicks. Hélène L. Baldwin hints that the play is "sexuality sugar-coated with an eroticism" and calls it theater of sensationalism, not Theatre of Cruelty, as Artaud would have it.[22] John Simon agrees that the sensationalism is in the form of homosexuality and sadomasochism; he equates the horse with propagation and insists that phallic imagery is woven throughout the play.[23] Psychiatrist Sanford Gifford calls the play "kitsch" rather than high art because Shaffer, he claims, tries to manipulate the audience both by the violent emotions depicted on stage and by theatrical artifice.[24] James Lee concurs with Gifford and compares the play to the total theater of the 1960s, noting that the drama is full of "muddled logic and tired philosophy" but is effective because of theatrical conventions.[25]

The sensationalism of the play is not contrived. *Equus* does deal quite graphically with psychoanalysis of a young man who has trouble sorting out his religious convictions and sexual inadequacies. The psychosexual and religious motifs are not gratuitous; instead, they are designed to release archetypes latent in the audience similar to what Artaud had in mind for his Theatre of Cruelty (these similarities will be discussed later in this chapter). The "obligatory nude scene" was not written to be "trendy." Shaffer explains that "it's vital to the play, especially that last image of the boy lying under the blanket, stripped of everything. It just works so much better when you've got a stripped human body."[26] In the preface to his collected plays, Shaffer stated that "the final image of an unconscious boy thrown on a wooden bench naked under a blanket, immeasurably lost power if he was clothed. The image of a human sacrifice, which was intended although only lightly stressed, vanished entirely with the assumption of a sweater and jeans."[27] To conclude that the play is "kitsch" because it does not stir fear and pity in the audience (prerequisites for classical tragedy) is to show an ignorance with regard to dramatic form.[28] In addition, the Artaudian stage elements, many of them inventions by John Dexter, enhance the content by creating intuitive communication between characters on stage and the audience, much in the manner of *The Royal Hunt of the Sun.*[29] Such theatrical conventions appear more frequently in contemporary drama, and it is only the naive critic who classifies them as being gratuitous to the modern stage.

The fourth major criticism of the play stems from psychiatrists who claim that Shaffer has distorted and maligned their sacred profession. In a now-famous article written for *The New York Times,* psychiatrist Sanford Gifford led the attack on the play, calling it a "pernicious fallacy."[30] Dr. Gifford was alarmed that theatergoers could take this brand of psychotherapy seriously, because "by weaving together many clinical syndromes, therapeutic methods and psychoanalytic clichés, Shaffer presents us with a fictitious piece of psychopathology."[31] Psychiatrists have a right to be concerned about the play's content because much of *Equus*'s popularity is the result of what Shaffer termed "the long-suppressed resentment of analysts."[32] In an article for *Vogue,* Shaffer wrote, "I think that audiences react to *Equus* the way they do partly because, I suspect, they collectively dislike their analysts immensely and want some way of showing this in public."[33] Gifford and his colleagues probably felt the need to hold on to dissenters who might abandon the long-established "wisdom" of their psychoanalysts. Shaffer is aware of the impact of his play on the New York audience in particular: "In

London the play was performed before audiences of which only a very small percentage had been, or then was, in analysis; in New York it would have been hard to find anybody in the audience, in the first weeks of the run at any rate, who had *not* been or was not so still."[34] Thus, Gifford's assumption is probably sound in that some of the success of the play can be attributed to our secret desire to know more about the private lives of our psychiatrists.

Shaffer has been defensive when critics, particularly psychiatrists, argue that the play is not scientifically accurate and that analysts would never doubt their professional integrity as Dysart does.[35] In his preface, "A Note on the Play," Shaffer acknowledged that when he wrote *Equus*, he "enjoyed the advice and expert comment of a distinguished child psychiatrist. Through him I have tried to keep things real in a more naturalistic sense."[36] The psychiatrist, who asked to remain anonymous, read the completed text and endorsed it emphatically.[37] The play is scientifically valid, for Shaffer is a careful researcher who reads about his subject area thoroughly and explores his research topics with a meticulous obsession for details. Moreover, as Shaffer states in his preface to the play, "psychiatrists are an immensely varied breed, professing immensely varied methods and techniques. Martin Dysart is simply one doctor in one hospital."[38]

Equus is not a critical examination of the psychiatric profession, and Shaffer insists that it is misleading to interpret the play in such a way: "It had never struck me that when I was drawing the part of Dr. Dysart I was making any disturbing comment about psychiatry. Obviously the creation of a doctor of some kind was inevitable if I was going to tell that story at all, but the doctor's part was originally a secondary preoccupation with me."[39] Shaffer asserts that psychiatrists must entertain doubts about their profession all the time, just as many other professionals pose questions about the rewarding values of their own careers.

In June 1975, Shaffer attended a panel discussion on *Equus* with Sanford Gifford, Jules Glenn, and other notable psychiatrists of the Association for Applied Psychoanalysis. Papers that were read concerned critical and psychoanalytical interpretations of the play, with a predominant emphasis on Freudian analysis. Dr. J. Alexis Burland, the last speaker, summed up the set of papers presented. Dr. Burland, who had heard diagnoses of Alan's condition described as a wide range of problems from psychoneurosis with an oedipal-based conflict to schizophrenia, reminded the psychiatrists that *Equus* is a play, not reality.[40] Dysart's dream was consciously invented by Shaffer and is therefore not a dream at all. Alan is not to be psychoanalyzed as a real patient because he is only a fictitious character. In short, psychiatrists have tended to regard *Equus* as actual psychotherapy when, in fact, it is merely a play. Moreover, Shaffer is entitled to poetic license—a fact of which literal-minded individuals should be aware.

Equus was derived from a story that was told to Shaffer by his friend, James Mossman, the celebrated BBC television reporter. Shaffer and Mossman were driving through the English countryside, and as they passed a stable, Mossman recalled the story of a young man who, a number of years earlier, had blinded twenty-six horses. Shaffer remembers Mossman telling him that the youngster "was said to be the son of very 'thou shalt not' parents who were members of some peculiar religious sect. The boy was seduced on the floor of the stable by a girl under the eyes of the horses. They, presumably, in his distorted mind, would go off and tell his father and mother."[41] A few months later, Mossman died, and Shaffer was stuck with a fascinating story that he could not verify. Shaffer spent the next two years trying to interpret Alan Strang's crime and what led up to it, often destroying thirty or forty pages of draft work per day.[42]

Although the only source material for the play comes from Mossman's uncorroborated tale, critics have been quick to note that Shaffer's premise that insanity may be an alternative form of truth, unworthy of being cured by psychoanalysis, can be found in the writings of R. D. Laing.[43] Psychiatrist Jeffrey Berman has noted that the same theme runs throughout Aldous Huxley's *Brave New World* and Anthony Burgess's *A Clockwork Orange*.[44] The strong Apollonian-Dionysian conflict in the play has led Michael Hinden and Doyle W. Walls to Nietzsche's *The Birth of Tragedy* as source material for *Equus*.[45] Barbara Lounsberry has established an elaborate argument that Shaffer's imagery with regard to the sun (Alan's night ride) and the horse is derived from J. E. Cirlot's *A Dictionary of Symbols* and from various interpretations of tarot cards.[46] Biblical imagery in the play comes from the Book of Job and Revelation. Perhaps the most insightful comment on source material comes from John Corbally who described the play as a "why-done-it" along the lines of Agatha Christie's *The Mousetrap*.[47] If Shaffer borrowed from any source, he most certainly returned to his early detective novel writing; instead of unravelling a murder mystery with Mr. Verity or Mr. Fathom at the helm, Dysart assumes the role of a detective to find the rationale behind Alan's unusual behavior.

Equus, like *The Royal Hunt of the Sun,* is Shaffer's attempt to unite an existential and sexual search for identity with a ritualistic representation of spiritual freedom. In an interview with Peter Adam, Shaffer revealed that *Equus* was fundamentally concerned with "the envy of one man who hasn't experienced emotion, and the worship transcendentally of somebody whom he believes has."[48] Dysart, insecure in his role playing, begins to learn from his patient, the primitive catalyst, Alan Strang. Through Alan, the psychiatrist becomes more aware that he must evade roles and adhere to his own values instead. Alan reveals the hypocrisy in Dysart's life as the primitive's brand of worship becomes more real to the psychiatrist than does his own preference for the "Normal." Dysart's new sense of consciousness will provide him with the first step in pursuing an identity that he will have created for himself, not for others.

Most of the play revolves around an exploration of Alan Strang's struggle for identity. The young man is caught between a religious mother and a father who is an atheist. Both parents push Alan in opposite directions as they demand that he become what *they* want him to be. Rejecting those values that he can only deem contradictory, Alan begins to explore various ways to establish an identity that will have its own intrinsic and rewarding value to him.

Frank Strang oppresses Alan more than anyone else does. He refuses to allow Alan to watch television and instead, directs his son into the "proper" norms of society—working in a certain electrical shop of which Mr. Strang approves. Frank Strang exerts an iron hand over Alan's lifestyle; the seventeen-year-old even adopts his father's vocabulary. Frank's favorite expression, "if you receive my meaning," is mockingly repeated by Alan (61), but even in more serious moments, Alan resorts to his father's terminology. This is most clearly shown by Alan's use of the word "swiz," a name he calls Dysart (43), or as Frank would have it, something that relieves you of "your intelligence and your concentration" (32).

Frank Strang, as his first name implies, is quite candid when it comes to stamping his strong image on others. Cut in the same mold as his precursor, Stanley Harrington, Frank is the epitome of the old-guard socialist who has become successful on his own. He is a practical sort of man who preaches a work ethic and values his business acumen. According to Frank, religion has no practical value and is reduced to Marx's cliché, the "opium of the people" (34). Thus, Frank "doesn't set much store by Sundays" (35) and prefers working for profit rather than wasting his time in church. Frank reasons that the Bible will never make one rich; instead, it is "just bad sex" (40). Shaffer, however, exposes Frank's hypocritical nature (an ironic use of his namesake) when later in the play we learn that he spends much of his time secretly visiting pornographic movie theaters to enjoy the "bad sex" that he so disdains.

Alan's father relieves the boy of the few pleasurable moments in his life, and as a prying Grand Inquisitor, the printer more than stamps his impression on his son and takes away his freedom. Alan, with his love for old westerns, is forced to sneak over to a neighbor's house to watch them on television because his father considers "the tube" to be "a dangerous drug" (32). In addition, Mr. Strang discovers Alan's first sexual affair and then makes his son feel guilty about it. Frank also pulled Alan off a horse that he was riding on the beach, an incident that becomes a traumatic experience because Alan's sexual and spiritual freedom was disturbed. This disruption of Alan's freedom is made clear when we come to understand that this incident helped to form Alan's "strange" personality. The result of Mr.

Strang's actions is that Alan fears his father, whom he associates with a godlike tyrant creating laws and rules for others to obey. It is no wonder that Alan feels insecure around Dysart, the epitome of the Grand Inquisitor resembling Frank Strang: "On and on, sitting there! Nosey Parker! That's all you are! Bloody Nosey Parker! Just like Dad. On and on and bloody on! Tell me, tell me, tell me! . . . Answer this, Answer that. Never Stop!—" (67).

Equus contains an unusual number of images related to eyes, and much of this eye imagery focuses on Frank Strang's role as a godlike figure for his son. Alan, who compares himself to Christ, the son of God, associates himself with Equus, the son of the horse-god. During the scene of self-mutilation where Alan flagellates himself with a wooden coat hanger, he does so in his bedroom in front of the photograph of the "horse with the huge eyes" (58). As he admonishes himself as "Equus, my only begotten son," Alan is unconsciously berating himself in front of his father, the horse-god. For Alan, Frank Strang has assumed the identity of the horse-god, and his eyes reflect God's judgment. Alan always feels so insecure around his father that he "lies under the blanket" when his father enters the acting square (37).

There are numerous references in the play to eyes, and these images serve to reinforce in Alan the stern, judgmental attitude of his father and Alan's subsequent blinding of the horses. Dora Strang used to repeat to Alan over and over again that " 'God sees you, Alan. God's got eyes everywhere—' " (56). She tells Dysart that she allowed Alan to sneak out of the house to watch television in spite of Frank's protests because "what the eye does not see, the heart does not grieve over" (37). When Alan is knocked off the horse at the beach, Frank calls the animal dangerous: "Look at his eyes. They're rolling" (48), but the horseman makes the connection clear when he says, "So are yours!" (48). At the age of six, Alan may not have intuitively made the comparison between the eyes of his godlike father and the eyes of his horse-god. However, he later becomes fascinated both with the horses' eyes in the photograph hanging in his bedroom and with Nugget's eyes, which he spends a great deal of time staring into (103). In addition, when Dysart asks Alan to name his favorite British monarch, Alan chooses King John because "he put out the eyes of that smarty little—" (34), a reference to John's order to have Hubert de Burgh burn out the eyes of Arthur of Bretagne, the king's nephew.

On the night that Alan blinded the six horses, he spent the early part of the evening at a pornographic theater with Jill Mason.[49] Guilt dominates the scene as Alan focuses his attention on the eyes of the pornographers: "All around me they were all looking. All the men—staring up like they were in church" (105–106). When Frank enters, Alan's first reaction is, "Oh God" (106), perhaps an unconscious reference to his father as the omnipotent individual who sees through all of the evil going on behind his back.[50]

Outside, while waiting an unbearably long time for a bus that would not come, Alan can only think of his father's eyes, "staring, straight ahead" (107). Later during the same evening, Alan accompanies Jill to the stables. When Alan abreacts, he tells Dysart that he stared into her eyes, and she reciprocated, saying, "I love your eyes" (112). By the time the two of them arrived at the stables, the eye imagery was well ingrained in Alan's consciousness. Dysart, already aware that Alan links eyes with his father's godlike control over his son, has only to say the right words to achieve catharsis: "The Lord thy God is a Jealous God. He sees you. He sees you forever and ever, Alan. He sees you! . . . *He sees you!*" (121). Alan's response solidifies the association between father and god: "Eyes! . . . White eyes—never closed! Eyes like flames—coming—coming! . . . God seest! God seest! . . . NO . . ." (121). Alan, hoping to erase the guilt he has over his "romp in the hay" with Jill and evade his father's godlike aura that sees all evil, blinds the horses, thereby abandoning the tight "reins" of his father's authority.

It was Frank Strang's idea to have Alan work in an electrical shop rather than with him as a printer's apprentice because Frank believed that his son did not have "the aptitude," and "printing's a failing trade" (61). Alan's job in the electrical shop does little to provide the confused lad with the spiritual freedom that he seeks. Instead, the young man becomes mesmerized by commercialism. When the customers enter the shop, they ask him, "Are you a dealer for *Hoover*?" (62) or demand "the heat retaining *Pifco*" (62). Alan's response is always, "Sorry" (62), and, as was true in his relationship with his father, Alan is made to feel guilty and is forced to succumb to the whims and wishes of others. Since this commercialization is a direct antithesis to Alan's freedom, it is not difficult to imagine that when Alan's liberty is destroyed by Dr. Dysart, the young man will return to his particular socialization process and therefore become no more than a series of television advertisements. Thus, it is not unbelievable for this restless primitive to regress to the state of repeating Doublemint gum jingles or other such advertisements.

Because Alan is in awe of his father and even fears him, much of his early childhood training is the result of his strong association with his mother. Alan's knowledge about sex and the Bible is based on the type of education Dora Strang, an ex-school teacher, wanted her son to receive. Mrs. Strang tells Dysart that in teaching Alan about life, "I told him the biological facts. But I also told him what I believed. That sex is not *just* a biological matter, but spiritual as well" (40). Alan accepted his mother's religious values simply because his personality in the formative years was being shaped by the training he received from his parents.

Beginning with the ideas he learned from his mother, Alan searches for his identity—a quest that becomes a spiritual communion with a personal god. When he was twelve, Alan had in his bedroom a picture of Christ on his way to Calvary. Dora Strang acknowledges that "the Christ was loaded down with chains, and the centurions were really laying on the stripes" (51). In a rage, Alan's father, who had previously insisted that "it's the Bible that's responsible for all this" (39), ripped the picture from the wall; Alan then replaced the beaten Christ with a picture of a horse with the eyes staring straight ahead. Alan identified with Christ, not as a redeemer or as one who is resurrected, but as an individual who suffers and is beaten. The young primitive believed that the world was replete with oppression and felt that he was literally being strapped down with chains. Alan was most impressed with the idea that Christ was omnipotent and could transcend his slavery, thus controlling his own fate in the midst of external forces. Alan therefore wanted to become one with Christ in order to obtain complete control of his existence.[51]

The spiritual quest is further complicated when Alan views the horse as his new god. Mrs. Strang used to tell Alan "that when Christian cavalry first appeared in the New World, the pagans thought horse and rider was one person" (36). Alan is fascinated by the idea, especially when his mother reveals that the pagans "thought it must be a god" (36). The story unconsciously reminds Alan of Christ, since the religious idea of "becoming one" is associated with the Holy Trinity.[52] In short, Alan mistakenly compares cavalry with Calvary and identifies the concept of "becoming one" with Christ. Alan's vision of horses stems partly from his mother's reading of the horse imagery in the Book of Job. That particular biblical passage describes the horse as an animal with "strength" and a "neck of thunder" (36), capable of pounding the ground "with fierceness and rage" (36). To Alan, Equus, which Dora explains to Alan is the Latin word for "horse," represents omnipotence galloping freely in the field of "Ha! Ha!" (36).

Alan internalizes the stories and tries to imitate Christ by uniting with Equus, the horse-god, thus becoming master and slave at the same time. One evening, when Alan was fifteen, Frank Strang noticed his son chanting prayers to his newly created god, then kneeling in reverence. After the biblical "begats" and Alan's resurrection as "Equus, my only begotten son" (58), Alan takes out a string and coat hanger and begins to beat himself. The important point here is that the thrashing is self-imposed. Alan has taken on the sins of the world for himself and masochistically enjoys the idea that he is able to control this oppression. For the first time in his life, the thrashing is not external, and Alan is now pleased to have this new power that he can control.[53]

Alan's spiritual quest to obtain a union with the horse-god continues throughout the play; it is most noticeable in reference to Alan's ride on the beach. Alan relates the experience to Dysart:

Alan. "It never comes out. They have me in chains."
Dysart. Like Jesus?
Alan. Yes!
Dysart. Only his name isn't Jesus, is it?
Alan. No.
Dysart. What is it?
Alan. No one knows but him and me.
Dysart. You can tell me, Alan. Name him.
Alan. Equus.

(76)

Alan associates the horse's bit and bridle with Christ's chains, as the young man views himself as one who is bridled and suffers "for the sins of the world" (76). More importantly, the horse conveys a sense of godlike omnipotence for Alan: "All that power going any way you wanted" (55). Alan, recalling the ecstasy of that initial ride on the horse at the beach when he was only six years old, respects the power of the horse-god and expresses a desire to become a horse-rider—a cowboy: "I wish I was a cowboy. They're free. They just swing up and then it's miles of grass . . . I bet all cowboys are *orphans!*" (56). This freedom seems to be a latent reference to Alan's family life. For Alan, an orphan represents freedom from societal, particularly familial, restraints and is someone who, by his very nature, must be in control of his own life.

Later, Alan gets a job in the stables, the Temple or "His Holy of Holies" (76). Upon seeing the stable for the first time, Alan "starts almost involuntarily to kneel on the floor in reverence" (64). Alan begins to take the horses out at night, for he can be with his personal god only when he is alone. In an effort to "become one" with the horse, Alan obeys "Straw Law": ride—or fall. He explains to Dysart that "Straw Law" means, "He was born in the straw, and this is the law" (77), an obvious reference to the horse-god as a Christ-like figure.

The ritualistic exorcism that ends act 1, Alan's midnight ride on Nugget, is a visual representation of Alan's spiritual and existential relationship with the horse-god. The scene begins with symbolic communication between Alan and Nugget: "Alan first ritually puts the bit into his own mouth, then crosses, and transfers it into Nugget's" (79). In the nude, Alan begins the ride but not before he bridles himself with the Manbit, his "sacred stick" which unites horse and rider (81). Alan, still unconsciously viewing the horse as Christ, gives Nugget a piece of sugar as "His Last Supper" (82). Alan leads the horse out of the stable, riding Nugget without a saddle so as to achieve a flesh-to-flesh union between horse and rider. The scene presents Alan astride Nugget, riding in the sacred field of Ha-Ha. We see the primitive's fantasies come to life as he identifies with his god:

My mane, stiff in the wind!
My flanks! My hooves!
Mane on my legs, on my flanks, like whips!
Raw!
Raw!
I'm raw! Raw!
Feel me on you! *On* you! *On* you! *On* you!
I want to be *in* you.
I want to BE you forever and ever!—

(84–85)

In a ceremonial chant, Alan calls out to "Equus the Godslave, Faithful and True" (83) and mimes a symbolic ride on his god, reminiscent of Christ's ride on the white horse in Revelation.[54] As Alan whips the horse, he cries out against his enemies, representing the commercialism of his father's world: "The Hosts of Hoover. The Hosts of Philco. The Hosts of Pifco. The House of Remington and all its tribe!" (84). These commercial industries are inessential to Alan's spiritual quest for an identity.[55] In addition, Alan castigates "the Hosts of Jodhpur. The Hosts of Bowler and Gymkhana. All those who show him off for their vanity" (84). Thus, Alan's midnight ride is also a break with his mother's values—principles that confine the young man to a role or codified behavior defined by others. Alan associates the word "hosts" with the Godhead, for these are the forces that destroy the Self and reduce his longed-for omnipotent spirit to nothing more than the state of being "sorry." As the horse-god at the end of act 1, Alan, like Christ, tramples his enemies. Alan "becomes one" with himself, and Shaffer reinforces this concept by ending act 1 with Alan's appropriate cry, "AMEN!" (85).

Underlying Alan's existential search for an identity is the fact that Alan is also experiencing a type of sexual awakening.[56] Mrs. Strang has assured Alan that sex has spiritual value, but it is obvious that Alan has had very little contact with any physical sexual activity. When Alan begins to identify with Equus, the horse-god, the relationship becomes sexual. During Alan's ride on the horse at the beach, it is evident that even at age six, the experience is remembered chiefly as sexual titillation. Shaffer aptly names the horse Trojan, a fitting reference to the sexual comfort the "ride" is about to give Alan. The horseman carries a riding crop, and the punishment doled out reminds us of Alan's masochistic flagellation with his own coat hanger. While Alan is on horseback, the dialogue becomes sexually oriented:

Tight now. And grip with our knees. All right?
All set? . . . Come on, then, Trojan. Let's go! (46)

Alan, when speaking of that wonderful ride, recalls that "It was *sexy*" (55) and is particularly aware of the sexual experience as a means of control: "The fellow held me tight, and let me turn the horse which way I wanted. All that power going any way you wanted . . . His sides were all warm, and the smell . . ." (55). Thus, when Mr. Strang pulls Alan from the mare, he seems in a sense to be interfering with Alan's sexual pleasure: "I could have bashed him" (55), Alan states, while telling Dysart of the incident.

The implications of Alan's sexual union with the horse are seen throughout the play. John Simon notes that the horse is frequently associated with propagation, and certainly the image of "riding" has sexual connotations.[57] During Alan's ride on Nugget, the ritualistic ceremony that ends act 1, the spiritual becomes entwined with the sexual. Alan's "I'm stiff! Stiff in the wind!" (84) is phallic, as could be "Knives in his skin! Little knives—all inside my legs" (83). The chanting of "I want to be *in* you" (85) and "Make us One Person!" (85) are obviously references to intercourse. Since Alan and Equus are one person, master-slave, or horse-rider, the sexual relationship is actually masturbatory. Alan's experience with the horse on the beach is frightening to him because the only image he can vividly recall is the cream dropping from the horse's mouth. Because this experience with horses is sexual as well as spiritual, Alan is particularly terrified at the unconscious sexual implications that the dripping cream has for him.

Working at the stables, Alan develops a sexual rapport with Nugget. Alan is so ashamed of his sexual activities that he refuses to ride Nugget when others are nearby. He takes Nugget out only in the secrecy of the evening and then, completely in the nude, he "rides" the horse. Alan's only piece of equipment is a Manbit, a stick that he places in his mouth to prevent ejaculation or, as Alan puts it, "So's it won't happen too quick" (81).[58] Alan then proceeds to whip Nugget, an act that exemplifies his newly gained power, possibly brought to life by the riding crop in the horseman's hand as he was whipping Trojan on the beach.

Alan refuses to see the horse as anything but a free and uncontrolled spirit, and his mother's insistence on putting bowler hats and jodhpurs on the horse suggests the repression of the powerful union of man and god, which represents an existential sense of Being for Alan. At the end of act 1, in his invocation against the foes of Equus, Alan cites "the Hosts of Jodhpur. The Hosts of Bowler and Gymkhana" (84). The idea that Mrs. Strang wants to "clothe" or mask the horse interferes with Alan's sexual gratification: "The horse isn't dressed. It's the most naked thing you ever saw! More than a dog or a cat or anything. Even the most broken down old nag has got its *life*! To put a bowler on it is *filthy!*" (56). This particular view that Mrs. Strang has toward horses is reminiscent of Frank Strang's refusal to let Alan ride freely and enjoy the sexual pleasure it gives him. Such sexual repression seems to force Alan to turn inward for his carnal desires.

One night, Jill Mason leads Alan into sexual experiences with another person. She begins the long evening by telling Alan that "I love horses' eyes. The way you can see yourself in them" (103). Then she follows up with, "D'you find them sexy?" (103). Alan covers his true feelings by insisting that Jill is "daft" for asking such questions. Not realizing that Alan can have sex only with his personal god, Jill escorts him on a date. They enter a pornographic movie theater, and Alan immediately associates the sexually oriented locale with a spiritual environment: "All the men—staring up like they were in church. Like they were a sort of congregation" (105–106).

Jill tries to introduce Alan to what is considered to be the "normal" conception of sex. Alan begins to understand this when he sees his father in the porno theater, then thinks to himself: "They're not just Dads—they're people with pricks!. . . And Dad—he's just not Dad either. He's a man with a prick, too. You know, I'd never thought about it" (110). But Mr. Strang maintains that he was in the theater for business reasons only and instead castigates Alan for being there. Thus, Alan's father unconsciously represses the development of any mature sexual knowledge on Alan's part. This is confirmed when Alan returns to the stables with Jill and refuses to have intercourse with her. Alan is frigid because Equus, Alan's conscience, appearing in the form of his father's watchful eyes, is bothering him. When Alan removes his clothes, the nudity associated with his "mount" is too much for him to bear. In short, Alan suppresses the horse-god, an embodiment of his own superego that is guilty about sex.[59] In a rage, Alan blinds the horses, thus striking out at his own sexual insecurities.

Mr. and Mrs. Strang have tried to raise Alan according to conflicting philosophies, so it is no wonder that Alan has developed sexual and spiritual anxieties that culminated in psychiatric treatment. Yet Alan is actually a character with a strong sense of self-awareness. By refusing to live by the superficial norms and values of others, Alan is envied as a person who creates his own identity. As critic Doyle W. Walls has noted, "At least it is a myth that says yes to the present rather than placing its hope in time to come, as the mother's Christianity and the father's socialism trust."[60]

A number of critics have noted the parallels between Alan Strang and Atahuallpa.[61] Both of these characters are primitives who reject the codes and norms of others in favor of their personal brand of worship. Alan and Atahuallpa choose to worship the horse and the sun, respectively, rather than adhere to more disciplined forms of homage. Alan and Atahuallpa, both younger than their respective admirers, Dysart and Pizarro, are actually close to God, whereas the older men seem to be unable to worship freely.[62] Shaffer indicates that establishing one's own brand of worship can be disastrous. Alan and Atahuallpa are destroyed by external forces that seek to teach these primitives that it is more important to conform to the norm than it is to seek your own personal identity—even if it means destroying vital myths and replacing them with a sterile existence.

Alan may find that these "normal" individuals deem it necessary for him to seek psychiatric help, yet he cannot justify the hypocritical values that these people share. Alan sees his father as a role player whose strict moral values mask the fact that he is busy attending pornographic movies. Frank Strang's precursor seems to be Charles Sidley, the staid businessman who adopts the mores expected of him but secretly visits call girls in his spare time. Alan realizes that his father lives in lies: "I kept thinking—all those airs he put on! . . . 'Receive my meaning. Improve your mind!' . . . All those nights he said he'd be in late. 'Keep my supper hot, Dora!' 'Your poor father: he works so hard!' . . . Bugger! Old bugger! . . . Filthy old bugger!" (109). Mrs. Strang fills Alan's head with religious stories that become less acceptable when the young man sees that his parents contradict their own values. Everyone tries to be what they are not, but only Alan strives to understand and control his own life, free from the influence of others. Dysart understands that Alan has created his own sense of worship: "He can hardly read. He knows no physics or engineering to make the world real for him. No paintings to show him how others have enjoyed it. No music except television jingles. No history except tales from a desperate mother. No friends. Not one kid to give him a joke, or make him know himself more moderately. He's a modern citizen for whom society doesn't exist" (93). Alan has rejected the sense of "vitality" that modern society offers; instead, he has created his own brand of worship, and he has constructed his own value system within this mythical code of ethics.

Even though much of the play concerns Alan's rehabilitation, the astute student of Shaffer's works will recognize Dysart as the protagonist of the play. Much of the drama deals with the education that Dr. Dysart receives from his patient. Dysart learns that Alan has created his own form of worship, while the psychiatrist is still searching for some semblance of a personal identity. Through his association with Alan, Dysart begins to understand the inability of modern society, a vapid band of role players, to invigorate our inner drives and impulses.

Dysart, the God of the Normal, is, in essence, a role player who lives up to immutable codes and regulations. He is fond of the fact that "the Normal is the indispensable, murderous God of Health, and I am his Priest" (74), a position that enables him to control others and socialize them so that they can conform to society's expectations. Moreover, Dysart views psychiatry not just as a useful therapeutic tool, but also as a profession that gratifies his strong ego. When asked by Hesther Salomon whether or not he knows that he has done a fine job working with children, Dysart responds with an egotistical, "Yes, but do the children?" (30).[63] Almost in the next breath he proudly admits that "I feel the job is unworthy to fill me" (30).

Dysart tries to believe that he is living a worthwhile life, but the truth is that illusions and lies control his existence. Dysart describes a typical evening at home as nothing more than sitting by the fireplace, watching his wife knit clothes for orphans. Meanwhile, Dysart, frustrated with his lackluster job and with his wife's predictable middle-class attitude, takes refuge in his own illusion—ancient Greek culture. Thumbing through his art books on ancient Greece, Dysart finds a world of adventure, wonder, ecstasy, and excitement to replace his midlife crisis. Dysart can never evade the real world; every time he confronts his wife Margaret with his lofty visions, she brings him back to reality. For example, when Dysart passes her a picture of Cretan acrobats, she can only remark that "the Highland Games, now there's *norrmal [sic] sport!*" (71). In short, in both his work and home environments, Dysart is forever a prisoner and constant defender of the "Normal."

Dysart knows full well that his carefully regulated bourgeois existence prevents him from ever touching the bowels of Greek civilization, his true love. Each year Dysart trudges off to seek the primitive ancient Greek culture for which he longs. In a sarcastic manner, Dysart explains to Hesther how he surrenders to his primitive gods: "I tell everyone Margaret's the puritan, I'm the pagan. Some pagan! Such wild returns I make to the womb of civilization. Three weeks a year in the Peleponnese, every bed booked in advance, every meal paid for by vouchers, cautious jaunts in hired Fiats, suitcase crammed with Kao-Pectate! Such a fantastic surrender to the primitive" (95). Meanwhile, Alan, creating his own sense of worship—which is what Dysart would love to do—is being treated for insanity. Thus, it is not unusual for the psychiatrist to lose a certain amount of respect for a profession that seems more like a sham where, as he tells Alan, "Everything I do is a trick or a catch" (98).

Dysart, the role player, realizes that his structured life is accompanied by sexual problems. In this sense, he is no different than his predecessors—Clive Harrington, Charles Sidley, Brindsley Miller, Francisco Pizarro, and Gideon Petrie. The psychiatrist is fooling everyone when he suggests that he cannot have children because his wife is a puritan. Alan hits a bit too close to home when he states that Dysart never has sex with his wife: "I bet you don't. I bet you never touch her. Come on, tell me. You've got no kids, have you? Is that because you don't fuck?" (69). Actually, there is little contact between Dysart and his wife, whom the psychiatrist has not kissed in six years. They spend their evenings in the same room, but she is absorbed in her knitting while he sees visions of Doric temples. This lack of contact between the dentist and the psychiatrist—two professionals who ironically enough spend most of their time caring for others—on the surface appears to be a sterile relationship. Dysart acknowledges that beneath the surface, the marriage suffers from his own sterility: "I imply that we can't have children: but actually, it's only me. I had myself tested behind her back. The lowest sperm count you could find" (95).

While treating Alan, Dysart begins to understand more about himself and comes to realize what freedom really means. Alan gradually exposes Dysart, but it is clear that Dysart, like Pizarro, unconsciously wants to benefit from a cathartic stripping away of pretensions of which these two men are aware but cannot control. Dysart claims that he can learn from Alan because his patient is a free spirit, not a phony who lives by roles imposed on him by society. Alan controls his own fate; as Dysart says, his free will reflects "his pain. His own. He made it" (94). The doctor laments to Hesther that Alan "has known a passion more ferocious than I have felt in any second of my life. And let me tell you something: I envy it" (94). The psychiatrist can only dream of primitive cultures and their sacred rites and rituals; Alan lives them.[64] Again, Shaffer, the Cambridge University graduate who does know quite a bit about history, art, music, and Western civilization—ideas of which Alan is ignorant—reflects his envy of free-spirited youths through the eyes of a middle-class protagonist who is jaded and a bit pessimistic about opportunities that have been lost in life.[65]

Dysart's contact with Alan has changed the psychiatrist, who is now more conscious of his artificial existence and how his life contrasts with Alan's "primitive" sense of worship. Dysart begins to compete with Alan, his alter ego, and the resulting battle of wills becomes a struggle between a Dionysian youth (Alan) and the Apollonian man (Dysart). Dysart consciously identifies with his "twin" or alter ego, Alan, the horse-god:

You see, I'm wearing that horse's head myself. That's the feeling. All reined up in old language and old assumptions, straining to jump clean-hoofed on to a whole new track of being I only suspect is there. I can't see it, because my educated, average head is being held at the wrong angle. I can't jump because the bit forbids it, and my own basic force—my horsepower, if you like—is too little. (22)

Psychiatrist Jules Glenn has done extensive research on the similarities between Dysart and Alan.[66] Glenn views Alan and Dysart as "twins" who share a love-hate relationship with each other.[67] Dysart admits that he envies Alan; in other words, he longs to possess Alan's sense of freedom, yet he resents Alan for possessing what he cannot have. Glenn explains Dysart's feelings to us:

There is much for an adult to envy in a teenager. Youth has life ahead while the adult's is closer to the end. The adolescent is nearing his peak, while the grown-up's powers are waning. The adolescent is often taller, stronger, sexually more driven, more imaginative, more confident, feeling capable of all, omnipotential. He will soon replace his father. Who would not wish for these powers? The adult has decided he cannot accomplish all, cannot be the Renaissance man, and has committed himself to limited accomplishment. Longing for a past time when all was possible, he may well envy youth. [68]

During the play, Dysart gradually identifies with Alan, and as the drama progresses, he becomes more like his alter ego. Both Alan and Dysart are fascinated by myths; Dysart is immersed in his art books on Greek civilization and dreams of mythology while Alan lives his myths. Both individuals have sadomasochistic tendencies: Alan blinds horses, stabbing at his conscience, and Dysart dreams of carving up children, expressing doubts about his profession as a psychiatrist. Dysart's last lines in the play relate to this identification with Alan's neuroses: "I stand in the dark with a pick in my hand, striking at heads!" (125). In addition, the psychiatrist and his patient have sexual problems and are frigid around women. Together, Dysart and Alan function as a unit to solve their sexual and social difficulties.

As an aging dreamer, Dysart bemoans Paradise Lost and sees the future in Alan. Dennis Klein reminds us that Dysart is sterile and has no offspring, so perhaps Alan is the son for which he is looking. [69] At the same time, Alan is searching for a father to advise and guide him; Dysart becomes the father that Frank Strang could never be for Alan. [70] As the play progresses, the two alter egos grow more alike and begin to understand each other's needs. Alan tries to make the relationship more equal by having Dysart answer questions, forcing the psychiatrist to act as the patient. In turn, Alan, the patient, has acted largely as a confessor for Dysart, thus allowing the psychiatrist to abreact to his deeply rooted psychological problems.

Dysart's contact with Alan has changed the psychiatrist to the extent that he now suffers nightmares. Dysart has been disturbed by an explicit dream in which he acts as a priest in ancient Greece who officiates at the sacrifice of small children. Wearing the mask of King Agamemnon, Dysart asserts that "it's obvious to me that I'm tops as chief priest. It's this unique talent for carving that has got me where I am" (29). Unfortunately, the "chief priest" has begun to have doubts about his work. In his dream, Dysart admits that "I've started to fell distinctly nauseous. And with each victim, it's getting worse" (29). At the end of the dream, the mask slips, the knife is torn out of his hands, and then he awakens.

As a psychiatrist, Dysart has "tampered" with many children, but his face has remained hidden behind the role he must play. While treating Alan, he begins to identify with King Agamemnon, who lived under the curse of the House of Atreus and sacrificed his daughter, Iphigenia, to conquer Troy. [71] Dysart sees himself as the cursed priest destroying the suffering patients brought before him. Images within the dream relating to knives and "pop-eyed masks" force Dysart anxiously and unconsciously to recall Alan's blinding of the horses with the sharp pick. In short, the psychiatrist has committed the ultimate crime of his profession: he has felt guilty about treating his patient. As the mask in the dream slips, green sweat runs down the doctor's face—a sign that nausea is the result of this guilt. Dysart, whose profession is based on *The Interpretation of Dreams,* fully understands why treating Alan will have serious repercussions for both individuals.

Gradually, Dysart begins to understand that Alan's brand of worship is not so abnormal, and a thousand local gods can be revered just as easily as one. Alan may not worship the proper gods, but at least he chooses his own fate, much like Dysart, who candidly acknowledges that "I shrank my *own* life. No one can do it for you. I settled for being pallid and provincial, out of my own eternal timidity" (95). Dysart has chosen to uphold the "Normal," but his contact with Alan has forced him to have doubts about his role. However, Dysart is superior to Shaffer's early role players in that, like Pizarro, he can recognize his own flaws. He tells Alan of his dislike for the role he must play, but the student of Shaffer's work will recognize the author speaking: "The Normal is the good smile in a child's eyes—all right. It is also the dead stare in a million adults. It both sustains and kills—like a God. It is the Ordinary made beautiful: it is also the Average made lethal" (74). Dysart discovers that his life has held very little meaning for him, but his experience with Alan has forced him to question his existence and ask, "What am I doing here? I don't mean clinically doing or socially doing—I mean *fundamentally!*" (88). The conversion is complete when Dysart remarks that "actually, I'd like to leave this room and never see it again in my life" (100). Dysart wants to switch from his role of God of the Normal to a God unto Himself, existential-style. Therefore, when Alan tells Dysart that gods do not die, the doctor responds with, "Yes, they do" (100). The reference here has a double meaning. Dysart has already told Hesther that "life is only comprehensible through a thousand local Gods. And not just the old dead ones with names like Zeus—no, but living Geniuses of Place and Person!" (71). In other words, because of the multiplicity of the many varied forms of worship, man has dared to be different. Dysart also would like to be different by destroying his reverence for the "Normal" and substituting it with a more viable form of worship. In addition, as Shaffer explained to me during my interview with him, Dysart's response to Alan's suggestion that gods do not die is an assurance that the doctor plans to destroy Alan's sense of worship, or the deity within him.[72]

However, as the psychiatrist's name implies, the doctor's old personality "dies hard," simply because it is not easy for him to free himself from the role.[73] Dysart, like his predecessor, Pizarro, a member of the band, a product of profession, institution, and society, will destroy the worship of the primitive.[74] The masters, Pizarro and Dysart, will annihilate the primitive and the spirit of free will in order to maintain the status quo. Thus, it is not unusual to hear Dysart promise to shape Alan as a Disciple of the Normal, at the expense of the teenager's freedom: "I'll erase the welts cut into his mind by flying manes. When that's done, I'll set him on a nice mini-scooter and send him puttering off into the Normal world where animals are treated *properly*: made extinct, or put into servitude, or tethered all their lives in dim light, just to feed it!'' (124).

Shaffer seems to be saying that the band, society, and the institutions into which individuals must be properly assimilated destroy free will and worship. To "cure" Alan, Dysart must erase the young man's sense of mythology and replace it with a form of worship that society accepts as "normal." The essence of Shaffer's argument then is sociological; *Equus* is a treatise on the failure of modern society to provide appropriate channels for the blossoming of individuals. Shaffer laments the fact that the codes, rules, and mores of modern society help foster the attitude that the average be made desirable or the ordinary be made beautiful. In short, individuals who do not play roles—the primitives—will be destroyed by societal forces beyond their control in order to channel their mythological sense of worship into more socially acceptable attitudes and beliefs.

No matter what one may think of the content of the drama, it is the form of the play that makes *Equus* an effective work of art. Shaffer tried to model the play on the ancient ritualistic Greek dramas. As C. J. Gianakaris has noted, the setting, a square that "resembles a railed boxing ring" (13), is modeled on the *theatron* of classical Greek drama.[75] The set, virtually a bare stage with benches, can easily be converted into any desired locale. In the Greek theater, there was a close intermingling of audience and performers, and the audience, because of its intimate familiarity with the subject matter, was never far removed from the center of the action. Shaffer tries to achieve the same sort of effect in *Equus* as part of the audience is seated in rows of bleachers surrounding the action of the play. When the actors "on stage" do not directly take part in a "scene," they go off to the sides, in effect, intermingling with the audience. In addition, Dysart acts as a narrator to further implicate the audience into the action of the play.

Equus contains many of the key elements found in classical Greek tragedy. There is a chorus "made by all the actors sitting round upstage, and composed of humming, thumping, and stamping" (18) to herald the presence of Equus the horse-god. The actors portraying the horses wear masks that ideally produce "an exact and ceremonial effect" (17) similar to the Greek rituals. They play is performed as one continuous action, and although Shaffer does designate thirty-five breaks in the drama, there are no scenes per se. Dennis Klein has discovered that *Equus* is structured much like a classical Greek tragedy, with Dysart's opening monologue as the prologue, the therapy sessions as the episode, and Dysart's closing sermon as the exode, all accompanied by a choral effect.[76] Moreover, much of the dialogue is stichomythia, particularly appropriate for nonnaturalistic theater.

Although Shaffer modeled *Equus* along the lines of classical Greek theater, the play is not a tragedy. *Equus* does not follow the unities: flashbacks interrupt any unity of time, and the diverse settings would be foreign to

Greek tragedy. Dysart is obviously the protagonist, but is he a tragic figure? As a psychiatrist, he has no claims to nobility. He never mentions any wish to ascend to the pinnacle of his career à la Willy Loman, so there is no great fall from the heights. The audience is purged of the emotions of pity and fear, but it is Alan's abreaction that leads to the purification, not anything Dysart says or does. The abreaction cannot be a catharsis, which must come from Dysart. The psychiatrist recognizes his dilemma: he is a role player who establishes an identity through socially sanctioned channels. At the outset of the play, Dysart recognizes his shortcomings—his first speech of the play, the very first words uttered on stage, reflect his understanding of his "flaw." Dysart's insight therefore destroys any chance of peripeteia. In addition, Neil Timm has pointed out that although Dysart learns from his interaction with Alan, no new social order is created at the end of the drama.[77] There is no evidence in the play to suggest that Dysart will abandon his profession or that he will do anything different in his practice of psychiatry.

Equus works well on stage because it is effective Theatre of Cruelty as Artaud suggested it should be performed. Dysart, the rational Apollonian man, is interested in studying primitive cultures; he would like nothing better than to live among them. Alan, a primitive, reflects the Dionysian spirit incapable of adjusting to the roles and norms of modern society. The rituals presented on stage become the vital link in the chain that both binds the doctor with his patient and assists in reversing the learning process that normally occurs between the two. While observing Alan's ritualistic behavior, Dysart achieves symbolic communication from Alan's anthropomorphic sense of worship, and by doing so, he matures and begins to reach a new level of understanding. Most importantly, the ritualistic nature of the play serves to communicate intuitively to the audience the Apollonian-Dionysian struggle on stage.

Artaud, himself a frequent patient in mental asylums, viewed theater as a therapeutic cure for psychopathological disorders. In *Le théâtre et son double,* Artaud discussed theater as a therapeutic tool: "I propose to bring back into the theater this elementary magical idea, taken up by modern psychoanalysis, which consists in effecting a patient's cure by making him assume the apparent and exterior attitudes of the desired condition."[78] Alan's treatment, an exorcism that is therapeutic for the audience as well, is the perfect theme for Artaud's Theatre of Cruelty. Furthermore, the dramatization of such a horrible crime as the blinding of six horses is the visceral, grotesque, and unnerving type of thematic nexus that will purge the audience's unconscious drives and impulses. Artaud again enlightens us with regard to the importance of shocking the spectators out of their mundane existence:

After sound and light there is action, and the dynamism of action: here the theater, far from copying life, puts itself whenever possible in communication with pure forces. And whether you accept them or deny them, there is nevertheless a way of speaking which gives the name of "forces" to whatever brings to birth images of energy in the unconscious, and gratuitous crime on the surface.

A violent and concentrated action is a kind of lyricism: it summons up supernatural images, a bloodstream of images, a bleeding spurt of images in the poet's head and in the spectator's as well.[79]

Equus reflects the type of ritualistic drama that Artaud had in mind for his Theatre of Cruelty. Shaffer abides by Artaud's wish to abolish the stage and use a single space in which the audience can interact with the actors. The chorus provides a uniform rhythm, a constant pulsating effect in which the humming, thumping, and stamping produce vibratory sensations that work through the skin as well as on our minds. Noises, cries, and groans weave throughout the production, creating a constant rhythmic structure that covertly affects our inner drives, impulses, and archetypes. Particularly effective are the tape-recorded cries of "Ek" in Alan's nightmare (scene 8), the Equus Noise before and during Alan's ride on Trojan (scene 10), the constant humming of trade names that accompanies Alan's litany against commercialism (scene 15), the choric effect during Alan's first visit to Dalton's stables (scene 16), the reverberations of "TELL ME" as Alan reacts to Dysart's inquisition (scene 16), Dysart's hypnotism of Alan, captured by a loud metallic sound on tape (scene 19), the Equus Noise accompanying Alan's ride on Nugget (scene 20), the warning noises during Jill's seduction in the stable (scene 32), and the haunting vibratory effects, culminating in screaming and stamping of the horses' hooves as Alan blinds the horses (scene 34).

In his stage directions, Shaffer explicitly stated how the horses were to be portrayed. He wanted to create a stylized effect whereby mime, gesture, and movement would bring the horses to life:

> Animal effect must be created entirely mimetically, through the use of legs, knees, neck, face, and the turn of the head which can move the mask above it through all the gestures of equine wariness and pride. Great care must also be taken that the masks are put on before the audience with very precise timing—the actors watching each other, so that the masking has an exact and ceremonial effect. (17)

Shaffer's image of the horse recalls Artaud's excitement over Jean-Louis Barrault's mime, *Autour d'une mère,* performed in 1934–35 as an adaptation of William Faulkner's *As I Lay Dying.* Artaud describes Barrault's mime of the centaur-horse with awe and mystery:

> It is here, in this sacred atmosphere, that Jean-Louis Barrault improvises the movements of a wild horse, and that one is suddenly amazed to see him turn into a horse.

His spectacle demonstrates the irresistible expressiveness of gesture; it victoriously proves the importance of gesture and of movement in space. He restores to theatrical perspective the importance it should never have lost. He fills the stage with emotion and life.[80]

Shaffer and John Dexter believed, like Artaud, that the horse could convey an archetypal effect that would evoke terror more than the spoken word.[81] In his interview with *The New York Times,* Shaffer assessed the effects of gesture, mime, and sound as they related to the unconscious effects that the horses had on the audience:

The effect of these metal hooves bashing on the wood of the stage is quite extraordinary. In the last scenes of the play, they acquire their own terror, almost as though you were inside the boy's head. People have asked me how we amplified the sound. We didn't. It's the accumulated weight of the play that does it.[82]

Artaud insisted that mannikins and masks should be used to enhance the concrete imagery in any play, but "all objects requiring a stereotyped physical representation will be discarded or disguised."[83] Shaffer chose silver wire and leather masks to represent the horses' heads, yet the actors' own heads are not concealed. Shaffer, as Artaud suggested, warned that "any literalism which could suggest the cosy familiarity of a domestic animal—or worse, a pantomime horse—should be avoided" (17).

After viewing the Balinese dancers, Artaud was convinced that mime, gesture, and physical movements could provide a play with a rhythmic structure that could function in conjunction with language. In *Equus,* Shaffer uses mime to enhance the carefully calculated rhythm of the play. Mime helps to decrease the impact of the language, making the images more intuitive than intellectual. In particular, Alan's self-imposed thrashing (59), Alan's first experience with the grooming of the horses in the stable (65–66), and the opening of the stable door during the seduction scene (115), all provide the audience with nonverbal communication directly related to sexual drives and impulses.

Shaffer uses ritualistic drama to provide symbolic communication between Dysart, the protagonist, and his alter ego, Alan. In tragedy, the catharsis evokes a sense of pity and terror, but much of the "talking out" stage is verbal. Ritualistic theater goes beyond the verbal level to provide symbolic communication between the actors and the audience through a release of our latent drives and instincts. Such ritualistic communication is presented in primarily two scenes: Alan's ride on Nugget at the end of act 1 and the seduction scene that concludes the play.

Alan's ride on Nugget begins with the rhythmic humming of the chorus as Alan mimes leading Nugget out of his sacred stable. Alan reverently kneels to the horse as he puts on "sandals of majesty," kissing them devoutly. The ceremonious nature of the scene continues as Alan "first ritually puts the bit into his own mouth, then crosses, and transfers it into Nugget's" (79). Alan then strips of all clothes and adornments before his god and becomes one with the animal as he rides Nugget without a saddle. The anthropomorphic ceremony continues as Alan offers Equus the talisman, the sacred Manbit. A symbolic piece of sugar, "his Last Supper" (82), is offered to Nugget as Alan kneels before his godslave and says, "Take my sins. Eat them for my sake" (82). Alan mounts Nugget, then he "whispers his God's name ceremonially" (82). The horse-rider, Alan, begins a ritualistic chanting of a genealogical litany. As the audience is assaulted with the Equus noise and a rhythmic incantation against the foes of the godhead, the set begins to rotate. The increased speed of the turntable, the change of lighting, and the rhythmic dialogue all serve to create a terror that cuts directly through the skin to the bone. The Equus noise increases until Alan becomes one with his god. The "amen" concludes the religious ceremony.

The sexual connotations of the scene also relate to our inner urges, instincts, and impulses. Alan mimes stripping off his clothes so that he can ride Nugget in the nude. As was previously mentioned, Alan puts the Manbit in his mouth, "So's it won't happen too quick" (81), a reference to ejaculation. Then Alan engages in a type of masturbatory foreplay, touching Nugget all over his body. Alan "mounts" the horse and engages in a "ride" at night when no one can see him. During the sexual seduction of the horse, Alan fills his litany with such phallic references as "knives in his skin" (83) and "Stiff in the wind" (84). Obviously, Alan's "Feel me on you! *On* you! *On* you! *On* you! (85) and "Make us One Person!" (85) have strong sexual implications.

Speaking of the ride at the end of act 1, Shaffer noted that "I found it very difficult to write. I experimented with onomatopoeia, with keeping the frenzy verbal, but there must be a moment when the visceral takes over."[84] Shaffer's efforts to create total theater—a complex interplay of language, mime, lighting, gesture, movement and intonation—to affect our unconscious libidinal urges proves that ritualistic drama can be as effective as classical tragedy in producing this sense of terror in the audience.

Equally impressive as ritualistic drama is Alan's attempted seduction of Jill in the stables. Again, the scene begins when the chorus initiates a faint hum and the actors "ceremonially put on their masks" (113). The setting is like a temple, or as Alan puts it, "the Holy of Holies" for his sacred god. As Alan and Jill remove their clothes, the dialogue that describes the seduction becomes increasingly rhythmic, uniting the ritual with the sex act:

Alan. I put it in her!
Dysart. Yes?
Alan. I put it in her.
Dysart. You did?

Alan. Yes!
Dysart. Was it easy?
Alan. Yes.
Dysart. Describe it.
Alan. I told you.
Dysart. More exactly.
Alan. I put it in her!
Dysart. Did you?
Alan. All the way!
Dysart. Did you, Alan?
Alan. All the way. I shoved it. I put it in her all the way.
Dysart. Did you?
Alan. Yes!
Dysart. Did you?
Alan. Yes! . . . Yes!

(117)

Alan, embarrassed by his unsuccessful sexual encounter, kneels on the stable floor to ask forgiveness of his god. The scene in which Alan blinds the horses develops into an Artaudian mélange of savage cries, slashing hooves, and rhythmic gestures superseded by the horses themselves: "archetypal images—judging, punishing, pitiless" (122). The climax of the sexual ritual occurs when Dysart tries to comfort Alan but can only soothe the young man by urging him to breathe "In . . . Out . . . In . . . Out . . . That's it . . . In. *Out . . . In : . . Out . . .*" (122), creating a rhythm which suggests that the sexual ceremony is over.

Through the use of ritualistic theater, Dysart, as well as the audience, is able to appreciate the freedom expressed in primitives such as Alan Strang. Shaffer uses total theater as a means to distinguish Alan's primitive existence from a more socialized means of worship. Theatre of Cruelty enables Shaffer to portray social communication between two people without having to resort either to a didactic or a naturalistic form of writing. The ritualistic elements of the play tie together the sexual, sociological, and psychological motifs effectively. Without this sort of "unconscious communication," Shaffer would be prone to preaching; the result might be a carbon copy of one of Ibsen's nineteenth-century plays—effective theater but not innovative. Instead, *Equus,* through a graceful fusion of form, content, and stage conventions, forces us to be our own psychiatrists exploring the real motives behind our "normal" existence.

10

Amadeus: Just the Right Notes

AMADEUS, the quintessence of Shaffer's ability to unite a sociological perspective with what Artaud might refer to as a calculated rhythm governing a play, had been ringing in Shaffer's ears for many years. In an interview with *The New York Times,* sixteen years before *Amadeus* opened in London, Shaffer was bantering around the idea of a charade based on the Faust theme.[1] The next indication we have of Shaffer's preoccupation with the theme is in 1970 when Sydney Edwards, interviewing Shaffer for the *Evening Standard,* informed us that Shaffer's next play would be based on the Faust legend.[2] Approximately one year later, Shaffer reiterated his interest in having the protagonist bargain with God when, in an April 1971 interview with Glenn Loney of *After Dark,* Shaffer admitted that "I'd like to do a play about the Faustian bargain, using lysergic technique to express, at some point, an expanded consciousness."[3] Then, in 1973, after the premiere of *Equus,* Shaffer was still insisting that the project would be a part of his theatrical *oeuvre.* He told Christopher Ford of *The Manchester Guardian* that "I'd like to do a play on the Faust legend. Peter Brook said to me once that that's the one legend that's dead for the twentieth century. I think it's the most alive. It's a question of what you give for what, and I don't mean money."[4] Shaffer's dreams of staging a version of the Faust legend, expressed as early as 1963, would be realized in 1979—five plays and numerous revisions later—with the premiere of *Amadeus* in London.

Shaffer, who claims to have spent three years reading all of the available literature on Mozart, began writing the play in 1977. Shaffer admits that the arduous work made him feel like Sisyphus: "I spent virtually a whole year attempting a different opening scene every week. It was an exceedingly hard task to find the center of the work—to reduce a mass of historical material to anything remotely coherent and yet dramatic—and at times I really believed I would never achieve it."[5] After years of agony, Shaffer was able to enjoy the fruits of his labor as *Amadeus* opened under Peter Hall's direction at the Olivier Theatre on 2 November 1979. With an able cast consisting of Paul Scofield (Salieri), Simon Callow (Mozart), and Felicity Kendal (Constanze), *Amadeus,* glistening with John Bury's scintillating scenic design and Harrison Birtwistle's direction of Mozart's music, charmed London audiences. After a successful run of eighteen months, the play was transferred to Her Majesty's Theatre, opening on 2 July 1981. Peter Hall now directed Frank Finlay as Salieri and Richard O'Callaghan as Mozart. The American premiere was in Washington, D.C., in November 1980, prior to the New York debut on 17 December at the Broadhurst Theatre. The original British production team opened in New York with a cast that included Ian McKellen (Salieri), Tim Curry, later succeeded by Peter Firth (Mozart), and Amy Irving (Constanze). In New York, Americans greeted the play with the same type of enthusiasm displayed by London audiences. *Amadeus* went on to win five Tony Awards, including one for Best Drama, as well as the prestigious *Evening Standard* drama award. Successful productions of the play were soon mounted in Paris, Berlin, Warsaw, Vienna, and Sydney, Australia, with the play being the number one box-office attraction in West Germany, Switzerland, and Austria during the 1981–82 seasons. On 1 February 1982, Shaffer, encouraged by the reception the play had received worldwide, including translations into twenty-two languages, began working with director Milos Forman on the film version of *Amadeus*. Released in 1984, *Amadeus* (the film) was later to receive an Academy Award for Best Screenplay and during 1985 and the early part of 1986, was quite successful in the videocassette market.[6] In addition, on 23 January 1983, the revised 1981 version of the play was broadcast on BBC Radio 3 by the original 1979 National Theatre cast under direction by Peter Hall.

British critics seemed to have been divided as to the initial reception of the play in 1979. *Amadeus* was reviewed favorably in *The Guardian, The Observer,* and *Variety,* but Steve Grant of *The Observer* and Michael Billington of *The Guardian* had reservations about the play's overall impact.[7] Billington enjoyed the first half of the play but expressed doubts about act 2 in which Salieri and Mozart were reduced to god-destroyer and god: "The presentation, in short, is immaculate. But having wisely decided that Salieri was a spiritual, rather than a literal poisoner, I just wished Shaffer had not tried to elevate the play into a majestic homily on the death of a god."[8] Steve Grant, after criticizing the play as "grossly unhistorical" and chastizing Shaffer for burdening Mozart with a crude vocabulary, admits that *Amadeus* "is also a marvellously engrossing and often amusing costume thriller, a feast for the eye and the ear, a vehicle for immense acting performances and a pretty fair introduction to the musical genius, if not the personal charms of W. A. Mozart."[9] Echoing Grant's assessment of the play was John Barber of the *Daily Telegraph* who enjoyed the performance and Peter Hall's direction but was annoyed at Mozart's depiction as "a vain, rude, cackling buffoon."[10]

Other London critics found Shaffer's historical treatment to be implausible, thereby coloring their attitudes toward the play itself. Unfavorable reviews were printed in the *Financial Times, The Sunday Times,* and *New*

Statesman.[11] For example, Benedict Nightingale, writing in *New Statesman,* claimed that Shaffer's presentation of Mozart did not focus exclusively enough on the musician's best talents: "One trouble is that his [Shaffer's] appreciation of the composer is too vague, generally and mindlessly rhapsodic, akin to one of those soaring but unevenly informative travelogues about the beauties of Rome or the wonders of Peking."[12] James Fenton of *The Sunday Times,* in a scathing indictment of the play, maintained that the acting and Peter Hall's production were not enough to override Shaffer's "appalling" depiction of Mozart: "He talks foul; and it is difficult to object to the way Mozart talks without seeming to object to foul language in the theatre."[13] B. A. Young of the *Financial Times* was able to recognize that Shaffer's portrayal of Mozart was through Salieri's eyes, yet he reprehended Shaffer for presenting Mozart's genius in the form of "coprophilous language" and a "high-pitched giggle that I can't take."[14]

American audiences and critics, in particular, received the play more favorably than did British reviewers. Shaffer drew praise from the *Daily News, The New York Times, The New Yorker, Variety, Wall Street Journal, New York Post, Time,* and *The Christian Science Monitor.*[15] Frank Rich of *The New York Times* was impressed by Peter Hall's production, the high-quality acting, and Shaffer's prose.[16] Hobe of *Variety* described *Amadeus* as "artfully written, superbly acted, handsomely produced and thoroughly engrossing, though emotionally arid."[17] However, no critic had more complimentary words for the play than Clive Barnes of the *New York Post:* "This is a play of the most infinite diversions, a play to savor, enjoy, laugh at and yet one that leaves the most agreeable aftertaste of thought to it. The memories of its frozen vignettes, and passionate ideas, will last years after the journey home. And that is what true theater is all about."[18]

Although most reviews of *Amadeus* in New York were favorable, Shaffer drew his share of criticism from such publications as *Saturday Review, The Christian Century, New York, The Nation, The New Republic,* and *Women's Wear Daily.*[19] The negative responses of the critics were typical of reviewers who in the past had praised Peter Hall's direction and John Bury's scenic design, all the while citing Shaffer as one whose sense of "theatrics" disguises a play that is weak in content. Stanley Kauffmann of *Saturday Review* noted that "the production sparkles" but concluded that "once again Shaffer has had the acumen to discern a large-scale possibility, and once again he has reduced it with gimmicks."[20] Janet Karsten Larson of *The Christian Century* also noted that "gimmicks and slapstick keep a play going that has nowhere to go."[21] Robert Brustein's comments in *The New Republic* were no less vicious:

> . . . *Amadeus* is no more the important play it has been proclaimed than *Rosencrantz and Guildenstern Are Dead* is *Waiting for Godot.* Like Tom Stoppard, Peter Shaffer manufactures smart impersonations—in this case

an over-inflated costume drama masquerading as a tragedy. Shaffer, in fact, like Stoppard, reminds me of Beaumont and Fletcher in the way he disguises with technical dazzle and smooth surfaces the absence of real artistic depths.[22]

John Simon's review in *New York* suggested that Shaffer was using striking production effects, sexual titillation, and Mozart's reputation to appeal to a middle-class audience.[23] Howard Kissel of *Women's Wear Daily*, also concerned with Shaffer's portrayal of Mozart as a "ninny" whose idiotic laugh was like that of "Bugs Bunny," was impressed by the spectacle but refused to succumb to "English accents, fancy costumes, and elementary Freudianism."[24]

Critics mainly complained of Shaffer's notorious ability to malign subject matter. They argued that Shaffer: (1) distorted Mozart's personality, caricaturing him as a silly, coarse, and foul-mouthed individual; (2) altered historical material for his own purposes; and (3) created a Mozart-Salieri feud when actually there is no evidence to suggest that Salieri poisoned his rival. Let us examine each argument in detail in order to dispel such complaints about the play, which were usually written both in haste and without proper rationale.

Shaffer's depiction of Mozart has obviously unnerved a number of critics. For example, John Barber of the *Daily Telegraph* allowed Mozart's vocabulary to color his opinion of the play.[25] Steve Grant, critiquing the play for *The Observer*, accused Shaffer of demeaning the stature of such a great musical genius: "For example, on the basis of a few naughty missives, he lumbers Mozart with a scatological vocabulary which makes the final book of *Gulliver's Travels* seem like a monument to potty training."[26] Potty training must have also been on the mind of Janet Karsten Larson who castigated Shaffer because "Mozart is portrayed as a spoiled prodigy fixated at the anal stage of sexual craving."[27] Is the subject of the play Mozart or Little Hans?

Critics were particularly appalled that Shaffer could dare reduce the Enlightenment—an age of Lockean democracy resting on good sense, reason, and moderation—to a bawdy caricature of life at court. Mozart, the child genius who epitomized the Age of Reason, could never be seen otherwise in the eyes of critics who often assumed cultural and ethnic ties with the Great Tradition. Note, however, that these same critics took little notice of Shaffer's portrayal of Pizarro in *The Royal Hunt of the Sun:* obviously, the Great Tradition does not have its roots in Spanish culture.

Unfortunately, the critics did not do their homework. Shaffer's depiction of Mozart is historically accurate. In a PBS television interview, Shaffer discussed Mozart's immaturity:

[Mozart] was dragged all over Europe. . . . He was shown off. He became a show-off. He had always been rewarded with snuff boxes . . .

and pats on the head. . . . And he had a thoroughly lovely childhood. Then it became more and more difficult as he got on. And, I think, in the end, he ended up as a kind of child inside . . . wondering where it had all gone—where it had all gone wrong.[28]

In his article on *Amadeus* written for *Saturday Review,* Roland Gelatt quotes Caroline Pichler's work on the eighteenth century and cites intimate knowledge of Mozart, the man:

> Mozart, and Haydn, whom I [Pichler] knew well, were persons who displayed in their contact with others absolutely no other extraordinary intellectual capacity and almost no intellectual training, or scientific or higher education. Everyday character, silly jokes, and in the case of the former [Mozart] an irresponsible way of life were all that they displayed to their fellow man.[29]

An examination of the literature on Mozart clearly reveals that the child prodigy maintained his childlike characteristics throughout his life. Mozart's closest friend, his sister Nannerl, noted that "outside of music he was, and remained nearly always, a child."[30] Alfred Einstein, one of Mozart's most conscientious biographers, characterized Mozart as the man we see in Shaffer's play:

> Until the end of his life Mozart preserved his capacity for enjoying word-distortions, childish nicknames, exuberant nonsense, and humorous obscenity—a trait of South-German gaiety which has never been understood and will never be understood in the less uninhibited regions of the Main. . . . He was a child and always remained one; childishness is sometimes necessary to a creator for purposes of relaxation, and to conceal his deeper self.[31]

In a letter dated 16 February 1778, Leopold, Mozart's father, repudiated his son for his childlike conduct:

> My son! You are hot-tempered and impulsive in all your ways! Since your childhood and boyhood your whole character has changed. As a child and a boy you were serious rather than childish and when you sat at the clavier or were otherwise intent on music, no one dared to have the slightest jest with you. . . . But now, as far as I can see, you are much too ready to retort in a bantering tone to the first challenge—and that, of course, is the first step towards undue familiarity, which anyone who wants to preserve his self-respect will try to avoid in this world.[32]

Indeed, a close examination of Mozart's letters reveals a continuous penchant for childlike activities. Although Mozart's foolishness is seen throughout his correspondence, it is particularly apparent in letters 79a, 166a, 179a, 236, 249a, 293, 561, and 613. For example, letter 236, addressed to "Dearest Coz Fuzz," Mozart's cousin, Maria Anna Thekla (whom Mozart referred to as his "Bäsle"), begins with these lines: "I have received reprieved your dear letter, telling selling me that my uncle carbuncle, my aunt can't and you too are very well hell. Thank God, we too are in excellent health wealth. Today the letter sent from my papa Ha! Ha! dropped safely into my claws paws."[33] Shaffer has read Mozart all too well and has used the letter in act 1, scene 5, where Mozart and Constanze are playing cat and mouse in the library of Baroness Waldstädten:

> *Mozart.* I'm going to pounce-bounce! I'm going to scrunch-munch! I'm
>   going to chew-poo my little mouse-wouse! I'm going to tear her to bits
>   with my paws-claws![34]

In a letter written to choirmaster Stoll at Baden, Mozart begins with this "charming ditty":

> Stoll, my dear
> You're a little bit queer
> And an ass, I fear.
> You've been swilling some beer!
> The minor, I hear,
> Is what tickles your ear![35]

Even Mozart's letters to his wife, written at an age when he was supposedly more mature, reflect this foolishness, which Mozart consciously accepted:

> Dearest little wife, if only I had a letter from you! If I were to tell you all the things I do with your dear portrait, I think that you would often laugh. For instance, when I take it out of its case, I say, "Good-day Stanzerl!—Good-day, little rascal, pussy-pussy, little turned-up nose, little bagetelle, Schluck und Druck," and when I put it away again, I let it slip in very slowly, saying all the time "Nu—Nu—Nu—Nu—!" with the peculiar *emphasis* which this word so full of meaning demands, and then just at the last, quickly, "Good night, little mouse, sleep well." Well, I suppose I have been writing something very foolish (to the world at all events); but to us who love each other so dearly, it is not foolish at all.[36]

Mozart's nonsense language, interspersed throughout the play, derives from much of his correspondence. For example, in letter 249a, written to his father, Mozart signs off with, "I can't write anything sensible today, as I am rails off the quite. Papa be annoyed not must. I that just like today feel. I help it cannot. Warefell. I gish you nood-wight, Sound sleeply. Next time I'll sensible more writely."[37] Letter 236 concludes with "as always, your little old piggy wiggy" and is signed "Wolfgang Amadé Rosy Posy," with a postscript of, "My greetings bleatings to all my good friends sends. Addio, booby looby."[38] Other notorious frivolities in the play, such as the measuring of Constanze's calves in act 1, scene 10, and Mozart's word game with "Trazom," or "Mozart" spelled backwards, can be found in letters 448 and 180a, respectively.[39]

Critics who accuse Shaffer of filling Mozart's mouth with obscenities have not examined the letters very closely. Mozart's correspondence is filled with scatological diction, especially letters 80a, 91a, 102a, 214b, 224, 232a, 236, 242, 254, 346, 363, 493, 496, 499, and 564.[40] Four-letter words abound in the correspondence, and as Emily Anderson, the editor of the letters, states, Mozart seemed to be unaware that any audience would be unsuitable for his foul mouth:

> A study of the whole correspondence, however, shows clearly that it was not only when writing to his *"Bäsle"* that Mozart indulged in this particular kind of coarseness, but that on occasion he did so when writing to his mother and to his sister; and that certainly his mother and very probably the whole family and indeed many of their Salzburg friends were given to these indelicate jests.[41]

Shaffer has ironically reproduced history on stage, but critics refuse to acknowledge that Mozart, the darling of the bourgeoisie, could be so offensive. Shaffer is actually interested in recreating history, allowing the public to view the real—and unexpurgated—Mozart on stage. For years, historians had a distorted view of Mozart's personality because Georg Nikolaus von Nissen, Constanze's second husband, eliminated or altered Mozart's scatological vocabulary when he helped Constanze write the famous musician's biography. As Einstein notes, Nissen's work, the first major biographical study of Mozart, was filled with "omissions, suppressions, and even misrepresentations."[42] In her introduction to *The Letters of Mozart and His Family,* Emily Anderson explains that before she published the definitive, unexpurgated collection of Mozart's letters, critics had a biased view of what the musical genius must represent: "Even in Germany an excessive prudishness or possibly a certain unwillingness to admit that the writer, formerly regarded as the Raphael or the Watteau of music, should have been capable of expressing himself with such grossness, has hitherto prevented their [the letters] publication *in toto.*"[43] Today's theater critics would be less shocked at Mozart's crudities if they knew more about eighteenth-century society. Einstein, an authority on the period, informs us that "it must not be forgotten that in the eighteenth century all human and animal functions took place more publicly than in our more civilized and hygienic days, and that unembarrassed reference to matters of an intimate nature was not confined to the lower or middle classes."[44]

The second major objection to the play concerns Shaffer's treatment of historical material. Critics have accused Shaffer of distorting history for his own purposes. First, no play can be considered to be historically accurate because the use of dialogue precludes veracity and authenticity. Unless the playwright transcribes conversations verbatim, the dialogue will always be somewhat speculative, even if the author is aiming for truth. For example, even Renaissance history plays are largely fictitious because the dialogue would have to be based on the author's biased views of history. Although the plot of a play may be derived from historical records, the language is created and therefore "colored" by the playwright. Second, the issue of whether or not the artist has an obligation to present facts accurately is moot because poetic license allows the playwright to color history for aesthetic purposes.

Shaffer rarely chose to exert his poetic license on the material and tried to maintain historical accuracy. During his three years of preliminary work on the play, Shaffer read everything he could about Mozart.[45] The result is that the play comes very close to reproducing the major historical events, although Shaffer asserts that "neither play nor picture [film] represents a documentary life of Mozart, but both borrow deliberately and delightedly from the conventions of his operas."[46]

The play contains two major deviations from historical accounts. The first alteration Shaffer made concerns Salieri's coercion of Mozart to betray the rituals of the Freemasons. Shaffer recognizes the discrepancy:

> I have of course taken certain liberties with this part of the story. I have no reason to believe that the Masons actually repudiated Mozart, or that Baron Van Swieten announced that he would never speak to him again. Nevertheless, Masonic anger over *The Magic Flute* constitutes one of the most persistent rumors attached to the Mozartian legend; and the worthy Baron actually did pay for a third-class funeral when he could have easily afforded much better, for the composer he had patronized, which does suggest some deep offense which Mozart had given him. Indeed, one totally absurd story, which never quite dies out, actually implicates the Masons in causing Mozart's early death! (x)

Shaffer also took some liberties with the ominous figure who commissioned Mozart to write the Requiem Mass. Mozart's health was failing at the time, and therefore he surmised that the messenger was sent by God, who was urging Mozart to write his own mass.[47] In an article written in *The Observer,* Shaffer explained the historical facts and how he created the Messenger of Death in accordance with the events of 1791:

> The factual truth is that the patron was a certain Count Walsegg who, incredibly, hoped to pass the Requiem off as his own work. Who his messenger was has never been finally established. One version declares that he was the Count's cadaverous steward; another that he was the son of the mayor of Vienna, secretly assisting the Count's absurd plan. The lack of exact knowledge on this point has encouraged me in my play *Amadeus,*

under the full prompting of dramatic licence, to offer my own candidate for this alarming role.[48]

The last complaint about Shaffer's treatment of historical matters is that the author prejudices a case against Salieri and creates a feud between Mozart and the First Kapellmeister where none actually existed. Shaffer is accused of depicting Salieri as someone who is fanatically envious of Mozart, when supposedly no such fanaticism existed. What attracted Shaffer to the intrigues of Salieri against Mozart was the mystery surrounding Mozart's death in 1791:

> There is a tradition that a terrible storm raged in Vienna the day Mozart was buried, and that because of it his mourners never reached the graveyard. Well, I came across an article by someone who had looked up the weather records for 1791 and had discovered that the day of Mozart's burial wasn't at all stormy. This started me on a train of speculation. Why had the mourners consistently stuck to their story about the bogus storm? Was it a conspiracy? Had they all decided on a convenient excuse for denying knowledge of just where Mozart's grave was located so that nobody would be able to carry out an exhumation and postmortem? If so, whom were they protecting? Could it have been Antonio Salieri, who would much later claim to have poisoned Mozart? I thought I detected the kernel of a drama here, and I made a few notes.[49]

Shaffer, the former writer of detective novels, now had a real mystery to unravel. Although Shaffer spent years reading about Mozart, the material on Salieri was virtually nonexistent. There was no biography on Salieri written in English, so Shaffer had to read in Italian with a dictionary beside him to help with the translation. After critically examining most of the historical records, Shaffer concluded that "I am positive that Salieri intrigued against Mozart"; although he acknowledged that Salieri may have poisoned Mozart's mind, there is no evidence to suggest that the court composer literally poisoned Mozart.[50]

There is, however, plenty of evidence to suggest that Salieri deviously tried to sabotage Mozart's musical compositions. Salieri is mentioned in ten of Mozart's letters, and most of these references are casual and of little importance.[51] When Salieri's name first appears in the letters, Anderson interjects with a footnote stating, "He was on most cordial terms with Haydn and Beethoven, but appears to have intrigued against Mozart."[52] In nearly half of the references to Salieri, Mozart speaks of him with contempt and scorn, continually suggesting that Salieri was vilifying his reputation. For example, when Mozart sought appointment as music master to the Princess of Wurtemberg, he wrote to his father that "Salieri is not capable of teaching her the clavier! All he can do is to try to injure me in this matter by recommending someone else, which quite possibly he is doing!"[53] Mozart refers to "Salieri's plots" (letter 572), and Leopold, writing to his daughter about *Le Nozze di Figaro (The Marriage of Figaro),* swears that "Salieri and all his supporters will again try to move heaven and earth to down his opera."[54] In yet another letter, Mozart speaks with contempt of Salieri, who tried to sabotage Mozart's insertion of an aria to be sung by Valentin Adamberger in July 1783 as part of the opera *Il curioso indiscreto* by Pasquale Anfossi.[55] Music historians have recognized the animosity between the two rivals and have matter of factly recorded it in the various biographies on Mozart.

Assuming that one recognizes the intense rivalry between the two composers, is there any evidence to suggest that Salieri conspired to murder Mozart? Music critic Donal Henahan claims that Shaffer was unfairly indicting Salieri when Franz Xaver Süssmayr, Mozart's last pupil as well as his assistant, is a more appropriate candidate for the dubious honor. Süssmayr even had a motive for destroying his mentor because he was believed to have been Constanze's lover. Henahan sarcastically implied that Shaffer should write another play: "Süssmayr, you know, was a pupil of Salieri's before joining the Mozart family circle. Who knows what dark fantasies could be spun out of that?"[56]

Unfortunately, the "fantasies" are closer to fact than to fiction. Mozart told Constanze during his illness in 1791 that he believed someone was trying to poison him. Medical authorities of the period have ruled out poisoning as the cause of death. Posthumous diagnoses have attributed Mozart's death to Bright's disease, rheumatic fever, consumption, goitre, brain inflammation, and dropsy, but Harold C. Schonberg, noted music historian and author of *The Lives of the Great Composers,* says that the most plausible cause of Mozart's death was uremia (kidney failure).[57] Nevertheless, in the 1790s, rumors persisted that Salieri had poisoned Mozart, perhaps fed by Salieri's conspicuous presence at the gravesite—the only member of the court to attend Mozart's funeral.[58]

In 1823, thirty-two years after Mozart's death, Salieri confessed to the murder of Mozart. Yet in a discussion with his former student, pianist-composer Ignaz Moscheles, Salieri swore that he had nothing to do with Mozart's death.[59] However, in 1823, Salieri attempted suicide, although his motivations for doing so are unknown. Is it possible that Salieri had guilty feelings about Mozart's death? If not, why did he bring the issue up thirty-two years later? In the 1820s, rumors were again sprouting about Salieri's role in Mozart's death, but most authorities ignored Salieri's confession as the rantings of a senile old man. Two years later, in 1825, Salieri was dead— forever doomed to specious notoriety.

Critics who argue that the Mozart-Salieri feud exists only in the dark recesses of Shaffer's imagination fail to recognize the presence of it in literary history. In 1830, five years after Salieri's death, Alexander Pushkin wrote

Mozart and Salieri, a two-scene play offering reasons for Mozart's death. Originally titled *Envy,* the play explores the jealousy that led the once-pious Salieri to poison Mozart because the latter's genius reduced Salieri's work to trivialities. In 1897, Rimsky-Korsakov turned Pushkin's play into a one-act opera with the same title. Even the biographical literature of the nineteenth century presupposes Shaffer's dialectical warfare. In one of the first major biographies written about Mozart, Alexander Ulibischev, in a melodramatic tone typical of the middle of the nineteenth century, recognizes Salieri's envious disposition:

> Salieri had read the score of *Don Giovanni,* and you know that the works one reads with the greatest attention are those of one's enemies. With what admiration and despair it must have filled the heart of an artist who was even more ambitious of glory than of mere reknown! What must he have felt in his inmost soul! And what serpents must have again crawled and hissed in the wreath of laurel that was placed over his head![60]

The dialectic in *Amadeus* is readily discernible. Salieri, an established mediocrity, exists in a world of roles, rules, and codified behavior patterns. On the other hand, Mozart, Salieri's rival, is a free-spirited individual, a genius who creates his own conduct of behavior and establishes his own mores. The two alter egos clash as they engage in an Apollonian-Dionysian battle for the court's recognition and favor. The audience is asked to judge Salieri's confession and to determine whether or not he will be immortal as a result of his machinations against Mozart. We will make our decisions based on Salieri's actions and on the complex interplay of Mozart's and Salieri's music that permeates the play.

Mozart intrudes in a steadfastly rigid society of role players who refuse to change with the times. Shaffer depicts the court of Joseph II as an artificial world of appearances where individuals flaunt their "plumes and sequins" but certainly not their imaginative capabilities. The court is stilted, rigid, insular, conservative, and opposed to change from the outside. Conformity is a virtue that is encouraged by the mediocrities who are in power to perpetuate their fiefdom.

Emperor Joseph II oversees an illusory society of "fêtes and fireworks" designed to mask a world filled with political scheming and maneuvering for positions and power. The Venticelli, Shafferian representatives of popular opinion during the Enlightenment, think, talk, and act alike—much like the other puppets who inhabit the mundane world of the court. Count Johann Kilian Von Strack is described as nothing more than "a court official to his collarbone" (12), and gullible Count Franz Orsini-Rosenberg, upholder of tradition, is reduced to being "benevolent of all things Italian" (12). Even Baron Van Swieten, once one of Mozart's patrons, is a stick-in-the-mud who has "yet to find *anything* funny" (13) and is nicknamed "Lord

Fugue" for his conservative taste in music. Indeed, it is Count Rosenberg who strongly condemned Mozart's use of a pasha's harem for the setting of *The Abduction from the Seraglio*. He is so much of a court lackey that he insists on removing a ballet from *Figaro*—a dance that is essential to the overall continuity of the opera—simply because Joseph II has forbidden ballet in operas. Later, Baron Van Swieten is the one who objects to *Figaro* because its plebeian subject matter was not suitable for opera, which, according to Van Swieten, "is here to ennoble us . . . It is an aggrandizing art!" (56). As Mozart, the outsider, invades the secure, mediocre world of the court, his sense of genius becomes a threat to these role players. Mozart, who refuses to succumb to the illusory, artificial world of his superiors, is casually dismissed by those who refuse to change. Salieri, Rosenberg, and the other members of court merely echo the Emperor's norms and values: Mozart's music has "too many notes."[61]

Entering this artificial microcosm is Mozart who, although he is not a threat to anyone, including Salieri, is perceived as an outsider who does not comfortably fit in with eighteenth-century society. Unlike Salieri, Mozart, because he is a genius, need not (and perhaps cannot) play by the rules of the court. For example, Mozart's opera, *The Abduction from the Seraglio,* is set in a bordello, much to the horror of Count Orsini-Rosenberg who chastizes Mozart for his inappropriate choice. Baron Van Swieten cannot imagine why Mozart would want to set a Beaumarchais play, "rubbish" in his words, to music. When Mozart is told that *Figaro* is unsuitable for staging because opera must "ennoble" the court, Mozart responds with, "You're all up on perches, but it doesn't hide your arseholes! You don't give a shit about gods and heroes! If you are honest—each one of you—which of you isn't more at home with his hairdresser than Hercules?" (57). Again, it is Mozart's sublimity in contrast to the court's mediocrity that makes the Freemasons vilify *The Magic Flute* as a betrayal of sacred norms and values. In short, Mozart's music was antithetical to the principles of the Enlightenment. Although Mozart's music appealed to the masses, the court found it reprehensible; each concert was played a few times, then forgotten. Thus, as the play progresses, Mozart moves further away from the court as his destruction is, as Werner Huber and Hubert Zapf have noted, "marked by poverty, alcoholism, begging, and finally, a pauper's funeral."[62]

Mozart's personality is also in sharp contrast to the orderliness and restraint of the court. Mozart tries to be himself, even if this means being rude, flamboyant, boastful, arrogant, vain, and immature. He represents the "natural" man who is not confined by societal rules and sanctions. His "unforgettable giggle—piercing and infantile" (16) often breaks up the solemnity of the world of nobility with which he is forced to interact. Rather than succumb to the values predetermined for him by others, Mozart creates his own rules by which to play. Mozart does not avoid sexual games with Constanze even while they are in the formal setting of Baroness Waldstädten's library. During the play, Mozart is often seen creating word games or clowning with Constanze, unlike Salieri, who takes his role seriously. Mozart's scatological language may be gauche in court circles, but it is appropriate for his purposes. This "obscene child," as Salieri calls him, much closer to a wild animal than to a court composer, is more "natural" and more at ease with life than Salieri could ever be, and the latter envies Mozart for just this reason.

Mozart also handles sex in a more "natural" way than anyone else at court. Mozart's open, unrestrained, animalistic, even primitive attitude toward sex is offensive to Salieri and to members of the nobility. Indeed, when the audience first sees Mozart (act 1, scene 5), he is stalking Constanze, behaving more like an animal than a refined musician. The audience, initially feeling ill at ease with Mozart's coarse language and vulgar gestures, intuitively perceives that Mozart is alienated from eighteenth-century mores. As the scene wears on, sexuality and animality merge in Mozart's explicit language: "pounce-bounce," "chew-poo," "paws-claws," "fangs-wangs," and "puss-wuss" (16). Mozart not only engages in sadomasochistic acts, but also brings up references to oral and anal sex, forcing Salieri to continually refer to his rival as "the Creature." Although his crudities abound throughout the play, Mozart is not ashamed of his animallike behavior and feels comfortable with himself, even though others are uneasy about his casual rapport with women. This nonchalant attitude toward women is reflected in Mozart's spontaneous marriage proposal to Constanze in the midst of their game playing. Constanze even explains to Mozart that she is aware that he has "had every pupil who ever came" to him (36). Mozart, not troubled by psychological problems that would have an adverse effect on his sex life, is certainly not sterile, and soon after his marriage to Constanze, they have a child. Mozart's sexual behavior is crude and animalistic, yet the natural release of his primitive drives prevents him from echoing the sterility found in the role players who surround him.

In his refusal to be influenced by roles and codified behavior that he does not wish to accept as his own, Mozart can be classified with Shaffer's other outcasts, particularly Atahuallpa and Alan Strang.[63] Atahuallpa, Alan, and Amadeus—three characters whose names begin with "A," as Jules Glenn might say, "perhaps unconsciously for 'Anthony' "—function as strong-willed young foils for their rivals who are middle-class role players. Atahuallpa, Alan, and Mozart are closer to God than are their respective alter egos: Pizarro, Dysart, and Salieri. Atahuallpa is the son of a god; Alan worships his own god and even becomes one with the horse-god, while Mozart is seen as "God's flute," an individual who receives his musical inspiration through God. As Mozart's middle name implies, he is "beloved of God." Atahuallpa, Alan, and Mozart are privileged individuals; because they are independent persons who refuse to be reduced to mediocrities governed by artificial codes and by rules that stifle their freedom, these Dionysian spirits have preserved an individuality that is envied by their sterile alter egos.

Although the title of the play suggests that the focus is on Mozart, the protagonist actually is Salieri, much like *Equus* where the misleading title leads one to believe that Shaffer is more interested in Alan Strang than Dysart. Shaffer made substantive changes in the London version of *Amadeus* to de-emphasize Mozart's immaturity while reinforcing Salieri's wicked plotting.[64] Greybig, Salieri's servant, who spoke disparagingly of Mozart, was removed from the New York edition, the definitive version of the play. The elimination of Greybig put the emphasis on Salieri, who now is the sole perpetrator of Mozart's decline. Shaffer's rewrite increased the sympathy for Mozart and more closely tied Salieri to criminal activity. Shaffer, in his preface to the revised version of the play, explains the changes:

> One of the faults which I believed existed in the London version was simply that Salieri had too little to do with Mozart's ruin. In the second act he was too often reduced to prowling hungrily around the outside of the composer's apartment, watching his decline without sufficiently con-tributing to it. Dramatically speaking, Salieri seemed to me to be too much the observer of the calamities he should have been causing. Now, in this new version, he seems to me to stand where he properly belongs—at the wicked center of the action. (ix–x)[65]

Salieri, like his predecessor, Pizarro, seeks fame and fortune, even if the quest invites destruction of individuals along the way. As he confesses to the audience, Salieri reveals to us that "I wanted *Fame*. Not to deceive you, I wanted to blaze like a comet across the firmament of Europe!" (7). As a child, Salieri, believing in his own unique view of God as the stern tradesman of the Old Testament, went to church as if he were playing "dialing for dollars." Praying to "an old candle-smoked God in a mulberry robe, staring at the world with dealer's eyes" (8), Salieri decided to enter into a Faust-like pact with the Almighty. At the age of sixteen, upon leaving Legnago, never to return, Salieri struck a bargain with God: "*Signore,* let me be a composer! Grant me sufficient fame to enjoy it. In return, I will live with virtue. I will strive to better the lot of my fellows. And I will honor You with much music all the days of my life!" (8).

Salieri's egotism carries him to fame and fortune much like Pizarro's obsession with immortality took him to Cajamarca in search of gold. Before he met Mozart, Salieri seemed to have been quite pleased with his bargaining ability, for he was a well-respected composer throughout Aus-tria, and he was faithful to God's precepts. Salieri was not a troublemaker at court, was a good teacher and had many students, was presumed to be chaste, and revered the power of God. Although he had many opportunities to seduce his students and even admitted his love for his prize pupil, Katherina Cavalieri, Salieri confides in the audience that "because of my vow to God I was entirely faithful to my wife. I had never laid a finger upon the girl [Cavalieri]—except occasionally to depress her diaphragm in the way of teaching her to sing" (10). As Salieri's name begins to spread throughout Europe, his quest for affluence becomes obsessive, and like Pizarro, he begins to surround himself with golden treasures (54). As "the stage turns to gold" (55) in act 2, scene 4, Salieri basks over his once-successful pact with God: "My own taste was for plain things—but I *denied* it! The successful lived with gold, and so would I! . . . I grew confident. I grew resplendent. I gave salons and soirées, and worshiped the season round at the altar of sophistication!" (55).

Throughout the play, Salieri's egotistical drive for fame and fortune coincides with his gluttonous attitude toward sweets. Salieri's gluttony is continually reinforced by his constant eating of confections. In the first scene of the play, Salieri confesses to his epicureanism:

> It's a little repellent, I admit, but actually, the first sin I have to confess to you is gluttony. Sticky gluttony at that. Infantine, *Italian* gluttony! The truth is that all my life I have never been able to conquer a lust for the sweetmeats of Northern Italy, where I was born. From the ages of three to seventy-three, my entire career has been conducted to the taste of almonds sprinkled with sifted sugar. (7)

Indeed, Salieri's gluttony is highly pronounced during his most insecure moments: his first meeting with Mozart (15), his attempted seduction of Constanze (41), his challenge to God at the end of act 1 (48), his refusal to secure Mozart a position at court even though Constanze offered her body to him in return for the favor (51), and his apprehension over the possible success of *Figaro* (78). Salieri's conspicuous consumption of such delights as Veronese biscuits, Milanese macaroons, and *crema al mascarpone* throughout the play serves to reinforce his insatiable appetite for the "sweet life" of ego gratification. In effect, Salieri's hunger for life's eternal pleasures never seems to be resolved.

Salieri's pact with God appears sacred until Mozart arrives in Vienna in 1781. Immediately, Salieri feels threatened by his alter ego—a genius revealed in the personification of an uncouth, "obscene child." Before 1781, Salieri basked in the glory of the court and was rewarded for it:

> We took unremarkable men—usual bankers, run-of-the-mill priests, ordinary soldiers and statesmen and wives—and sacramentalized their mediocrity. We smoothed their noons with strings *divisi!* We pierced their nights with *chitarrini!* We gave them processions for their strutting, sere-

nades for their rutting, high horns for their hunting, and drums for their wars! (10–11)

Even as a child, Salieri knew that "music is God's art" (7), and his agreement with God secured his right to be the purveyor of such art. Mozart's entrance in 1781 interfered with Salieri's intimacy with God. Salieri clearly associates Mozart's music with genius; it is only through God that Mozart could have acquired such talent. Salieri's pact with God appears to be ludicrous; as a pious, God-fearing man who has vowed to live a chaste and honorable life, he now witnesses God's inspiration being passed to someone who is "spiteful, sniggering, conceited, infantine" (47). In the eyes of Salieri, Mozart, coarse, vulgar, unchaste with women, and too vain and pretentious for the humble behavior of court society, has succeeded in reducing the significance of Salieri's bargain with God. Salieri, in turn, vows to strike at God through his divine agent, Mozart:

> So be it! From this time we are enemies, You and I! I'll not accept it from You—*do you hear?* . . . They say God is not mocked. I tell You, *Man* is not mocked! . . . *I* am not mocked! They say the spirit bloweth where it listeth: I tell You NO! It must list to virtue or not blow at all! [*Yelling*] *Dio ingiusto*—You are the Enemy! I name Thee now—*Nemico Eterno!* And this I swear: To my last breath I shall *block* You on earth, as far as I am able! (47)

Mozart, Salieri's alter ego, functions as a catalyst for the depraved protagonist. As a result of Mozart's presence in Vienna, Salieri breaks his pact with God and becomes a ruthless person bent on seducing Mozart's wife, reducing Mozart to a dependent, childlike state, and physically destroying him by starving out and mentally abusing the composer. Ironically, Mozart's music has no effect on Salieri's reputation from 1781 to 1791. Mozart's music, exquisitely crafted and pure in form, was not in vogue during the latter part of the eighteenth century. Salieri's music, however, flourished despite Mozart's innovations. In short, Mozart's sense of genius had absolutely nothing whatever to do with Salieri's success or failure in musical circles. As the Enlightenment ended (after Mozart's death), musical tastes changed during the Romantic era, elevating Mozart's status while reducing Salieri's importance as an innovative composer. As C. J. Gianakaris points out, Salieri composed no important works after 1804.[66] Meanwhile, Mozart's reputation soared, and he began to be revered as a musical genius of infinite talent.

Although Salieri seeks to destroy Mozart to vent his anger on God, the court composer is also driven by envy of his alter ego. In contrast to Mozart, the iconoclast whose genius towers over the banality surrounding him, Salieri, the mediocrity, subsists in role playing.[67] Salieri embellishes his role as the court's lackey—he would love nothing better than to be the Emperor's eternal footman or sublime toady. He later succeeds Giuseppe Bonno as First Royal Kapellmeister because he has been a team player loyal to church and state. Salieri confesses to the audience that "we musicians of the eighteenth century were no better than servants: the willing slaves of the well-to-do. This is quite true. It is also quite false. Yes, we were servants. But we were learned servants! And we used our learning to celebrate men's average lives" (10). Constanze, no great philosopher herself, even has enough insight as to reduce Salieri to one who is "acting a pretty obvious role" (44). Salieri, of course, recognizes his own mediocrity (46), and the play becomes a justification for his raison d'être. His last line in the play, "Mediocrities everywhere—now and to come—I absolve you all. Amen!" (96), is an attempt to include the audience in his impoverishment. The stage directions tell us, "He extends his arms upward and outward to embrace the assembled audience in a wide gesture of benediction—finally folding his arms high across his own breast in a gesture of self-sanctification" (96–97). In short, the mimetic and the verbal are united in the last image of the play to reinforce Salieri's mediocrity in the minds of the audience.[68]

This sterile existence is demonstrated through Salieri's sex life, or lack thereof. The insipid nature of his life at court parallels his sterile relationship with women; not only does his music lack spark or vitality, his sex life is bland as well. Mozart compares Salieri's lifeless music with the court composer's sexual inadequacies: "Have you heard his music? That's the sound of someone who *can't get it up!*" (37). Like Dysart's relationship with Margaret, Salieri finds his marriage with Teresa to be lackluster, devoid of passion or spirit. He sarcastically moans that "I required only one quality in a domestic companion—lack of fire. And in that omission Teresa was conspicuous" (10). Throughout the play, Salieri describes his wife as *"La Statua"* (42), literally "a very upright lady" (42), "respectable" (9), and in the stage directions, she is referred to as "more statuesque than ever" (65). Salieri, loyal to his sterile wife, feels starved for companionship or contact with women. Perhaps his insatiable infatuation with sweets is a manifestation of abortive sexual desires. He admits that his best pupil, Katherina Cavalieri, excites him, yet his fidelity to his wife coupled with his sexual inadequacies only serve to frustrate him further: "I was very much in love with Katherina—or at least in lust. But because of my vow to God I was entirely faithful to my wife . . . My ambition burned with an unquenchable flame" (10).

Salieri's desire to seduce Constanze stems as much from his sexual frustrations and sterile existence as it does from his envy of Mozart. Of course, Salieri views Constanze's seduction as a means of stripping Mozart of his possessions, but it also represents Salieri's attempt to relieve his sexual anxieties: "Part of me—much of me—wanted it, badly. *Badly.* Yes, badly was the word!'' (40). During act 1, scene 11, Salieri bribes Constanze: he urges her to trade sex for his assurance of Mozart's acquisition of the position as tutor to Princess Elizabeth. As Constanze begrudgingly obliges, Salieri tempts her with "Nipples of Venus," a sweet concoction of Roman chestnuts in brandied sugar, again uniting Salieri's sexual appetite with his lust for sweets. Salieri then demands a kiss from her, but after the second caress, he tries to embrace her. As she attempts to leave, Salieri pleads with her to pity him because "I've no cunning. I live on ink and sweetmeats. I never see women at all . . ." (43). However, when Constanze returns to Salieri's apartment in act 2, scene 1, she reconsiders his bribe and invites him to seduce her. Salieri, frigid like Pizarro and Dysart, could not make the most of the moment. He ashamedly admits to the audience that "I regret that my invention in love, as in art, has always been limited" (51). Fortunately for Salieri, his sexual deprivation does not go unabated. The next day, upon giving Katherina Cavalieri her lesson, she received the exact same treatment that was given to Constanze—seduction with Nipples of Venus and kisses—culminating in the abandonment of Salieri's vow of sexual virtue to his wife. Salieri, continually deprived of sex, turns his relationship with his pupil into a lustful affair. Eventually, Cavalieri became Salieri's mistress, and for years they carried on a relationship in secret, unbeknownst to Teresa.

Salieri's desire for fame and immortality has warped his perspective on life. His selfish need to gain favor with the court in order to maintain his status has cost him his freedom. His life is passionless, sterile, and empty because his structured existence is so confining that it prevents individual growth. Constantly hiding behind a role, Salieri develops an identity to fit what others want him to be rather than what he could have been. As Janet Karsten Larson so aptly notes, the audience can never discover the real Salieri because he is constantly hiding behind a mask.[69] He plays at being the consummate court musician, although in reality he is a mediocre composer. He adopts an artificial air of fidelity with regard to his marriage, but in reality, he cheats on his wife behind her back. His relationship with Mozart resembles the Othello-Iago comraderie—friendship exists on the surface, but resentment is the reality behind the illusion. Thus, the masked figure of *Don Giovanni* is quite apropos to Salieri's machinations: it is merely another mask to wear in the series of roles that Salieri, the Court Lackey, chooses to adopt.

Salieri realizes his own mediocrity through Mozart's music. Salieri's pact with God was considered sacrosanct until Mozart exposed the court composer's insecurities. Through Mozart's talents, Salieri recognized a sense of genius that was foreign to the mediocre world to which he was accustomed. He tells the audience that "we were both ordinary men, he and I. Yet from the ordinary he created Legends—and I from Legends created only the ordinary!" (70). And so although Salieri vows to destroy Mozart in order to nullify God's power through Mozart, his magic flute, in reality, the court composer's desire for fame and immortality becomes negligible as he intuitively understands that Mozart's Absolute Music will—and should—exist for eternity. Thus, Salieri's quarrel with God becomes moot; it cannot be divorced from Salieri's envy of Mozart—a passion that controls all of Salieri's Iago-like deceptions, as well as his overt tirade against God's omnipotence.

Salieri envies Mozart for two reasons. First, like Dysart and Pizarro, his predecessors, Salieri latently craves the youthful spirit of his alter ego. In 1781, Salieri, at age thirty-one, was six years older than Mozart—yet he felt that the younger musician had accomplished more in his career than had the established and supposedly more "successful" mentor. Mozart's "primitive" spirit had captured Salieri's fancy, and although he is often abhorred by Mozart's perversity and infantilism, Salieri secretly identifies with the younger man's freedom and his enjoyment of life. Like Charles Sidley, Salieri is controlled by institutions and suppresses his ego, and quite possibly his sense of creativity, in order to succumb to the mediocre society that controls his life. Mozart, on the other hand, creates beautiful music because his youth and vitality enable him to experiment in a way that Salieri cannot. Huber and Zapf have noted the contrast between Salieri's "world of marionettes" and Mozart's autonomous existence: "In the end, what comes across in the composite portrayal with its satirical depiction of society is Shaffer's characteristic general sympathy for the individual outsider as opposed to the social conformist: an underlying preference for emotional rather than functional values, for 'passionate' life rather than institutional order."[70] Moreover, Salieri's lack of sexual prowess is perhaps a corollary of the older man's inability to "perform" to the best of his ability. As Michael Gillespie has suggested, Salieri, the aging composer, sees his younger rival as having the vitality and youthful enthusiasm that has long since dissipated for the older man.[71] Salieri, seasoned by time and jaded by the vagaries of divinity, compares himself to Adam (46) who was banished from Paradise and suffers from Original Sin—which, in Salieri's view, is akin to lost youth and a loss of man's primitive qualities that could provide some excitement in our lives.

The second reason why Salieri envies Mozart relates to the idea that Salieri considers Mozart to be God's instrument and is awarded God's benevolence in a way that Salieri, who believes that he has earned God's respect and therefore should be adequately accommodated, is not. In the "Introduction to the Film Edition" of *Amadeus,* Shaffer writes, "To me there is something pure about Salieri's pursuit of an eternal Absolute through music, just as there is something irredeemably impure about his simultaneous pursuit of eternal fame."[72] As Salieri begins to realize that Mozart, a foul-mouthed rascal with manners foreign to court mores, is the voice of the eternal Absolute through his music, Salieri's envy becomes obsessive. In short, Salieri sees Mozart as the vehicle to undermine and ridicule a world that he had formerly defended and trusted.

The result of Salieri's envy is a dialectic between a role player and his primitive alter ego, a Dionysian-Apollonian clash between two distinctly different individuals. Salieri, the product of roles, rules, and norms, maintains a love-hate relationship with his alter ego, an innovator who creates his own conduct of behavior. Salieri reveals to Mozart that "we are both poisoned, Amadeus. I with you: you with me" (88). As Huber and Zapf suggest, the contrast is between two protagonists: Salieri, who is dominated by a strong superego that manifests itself in his attempt at controlling and ordering his life according to well-defined precepts, and Mozart, who is often guided by an id that releases a scatological vocabulary and an unrestrained spirit.[73] The differences between the two individuals are continually seen throughout the play. For example, Mozart's language is colloquial and natural while Salieri's is lofty and often excessively formal. Mozart has no sexual inadequacies while Salieri suffers from a sterile marriage, is ill at ease around women, and must cheat on his wife. As Huber and Zapf note, the culmination of these differences can be found in the types of music each man produces: "In a way, Salieri and Mozart come to personify two different modes of opera-writing and everything that these stand for: Italian versus German, the heroic (mythological matter) versus the everyday, tragedy versus comedy, grand opera versus *Singspiel*."[74]

This love-hate relationship that Salieri has for Mozart is probably the stimulus for Salieri's willingness to play a surrogate father for his rival after Leopold dies. As a father figure to Mozart, Salieri can abate his envy by actually getting a chance virtually to become one with his idol. Salieri's "wide gesture of paternal benevolence" (69) toward the crestfallen Mozart can be perceived as a means of literally touching the genius that he can never actually become. At the same time, Salieri, posing both as a surrogate father and as a masked father figure haunting Mozart, fulfills his desire to destroy his alter ego. When Salieri, hiding behind the masked figure that plagued Mozart, reveals himself at the end of the play, the audience realizes that Mozart has regressed to a childlike state at the hands of a stern, reprimanding father. Mozart is reduced to a childish voice crying for "Papa": "Take me, Papa. Take me. Put down your arms and I'll hop into them. Just as we used to do it! . . . Hop-hop-hop-hop-UP! *[He jumps up onto the table. Salieri watches in horror.]* Hold me close to you, Papa. Let's sing our little kissing song together. Do you remember?" (89). Just as Salieri becomes senile at the end of the play, Mozart, in contrast, becomes infantile. Nevertheless, Salieri has managed to take his revenge on Mozart: "Behold my vow fulfilled. The profoundest voice in the world reduced to a nursery tune" (89).

There is, however, a distinct difference between Salieri and the other Shafferian role players who preceded him. Although Pizarro strove for fame, fortune, and immortality, his passion for Atahuallpa made him aware of his shortcomings, and he gradually changed and became more receptive to his id throughout the play. Dysart was also aware of Alan Strang's passion for life, and although he tried to maintain Alan's vital sense of worship, his métier redirected his obligations to society, not to the individual. Unlike Pizarro and Dysart, Salieri shows little sympathy for preserving Mozart's unique individuality. Instead, Salieri is seen as an evil character determined to destroy the primitive Dionysian forces. Indeed, when the audience first sees Salieri on stage, he appears old and grotesque, wrapped in a shawl, which he sheds, reptilianlike—reminiscent of Stoppard's Henry Carr—to become the much younger man. The stage directions coincide with Salieri's evil, snakelike behavior, again recalling references to Original Sin:

> *Savage whispers fill the theater. We can distinguish nothing at first from this snakelike hissing save the word* Salieri! *repeated here, there and everywhere around the theater. Also, the barely distinguishable word* Assassin!
>
> *The whispers overlap and increase in volume, slashing the air with wicked intensity.* (1)

We see Salieri's evil perpetrated at every turn; he tries to destroy Mozart, demean him in the eyes of the Emperor, steal his wife, starve him out, and reduce him to a childlike state. He is content that "for the rest of time whenever men say Mozart with love, they will say Salieri with loathing!" (94). Salieri is not positively affected by his alter ego; instead, he insists that he will be remembered, if not in fame, then in infamy.

Salieri seems to forget that evil has a way of coming full circle, often working against those who initiate it. His plight becomes ironic—instead of achieving fame and immortality, Salieri is even denied his chance of being a household word in infamy. As Mozart's reputation declined during the Enlightenment, Salieri's music flourished. But the fame was insignificant to Salieri because he realized, through an intuitive appreciation of Mozart's music, that his search for the Absolute in art could never be fulfilled by such a mediocre artist. In 1823, Salieri, reminding the audience of the events of 1781 to 1791, acknowledges that "I was to be bricked up in fame! Embalmed by fame! Buried in fame—but for work I knew to be *absolutely worthless!* This was my sentence: I must endure thirty years of being called 'Distinguished' by people incapable of distinguishing!" (93). During the Romantic era, Mozart's music gained wider acceptance while Salieri became a forgotten man. Thus, Salieri's claim to fame, ludicrous by his own admission, soon dissipated. His confession of guilt with regard to his well-conceived machinations against Mozart and his responsibility for Mozart's death were taken to be the ravings of a deranged man, a "rambling of the mind believed in truth by no one but the deluded old man himself" (96). Even his suicide attempt is a failure. In short, the cards are stacked against Salieri even more than they are against Shaffer's other role players, for Salieri, envious of his primitive alter ego, decides to use his envy for evil purposes. Thus, Salieri, whom Shaffer himself has described as "a man of virtue,"[75] becomes consumed by envy precipitated by a search for an Absolute, eventually tempting him to teach God his lessons.

Throughout the play, Shaffer uses a constant rhythmic structure to accentuate the differences between Salieri, the role-playing mediocrity, and Mozart, his primitive, unrestrained alter ego. In *Amadeus,* the audience is forced to make important judgments about Salieri's guilt or innocence. Perhaps never before in any of Shaffer's plays has the audience been so intrinsically involved with the protagonist's fate. As Salieri acts as confessor or judge-penitent, the spectator is asked to decide whether or not he will be held responsible for the events surrounding Mozart's destruction and whether or not he will be worthy of immortality. As Rodney Simard points out, the spectator knows Mozart only through Salieri's eyes and must make his own judgment based on Salieri's honesty:

> The entire world of the drama, hinged upon external, historical reality, is within the mind of Salieri and is thus subjective; his perceptions are what are at issue in this play, for at this point, even Salieri does not know if he killed Mozart. Ultimately, the reader must assign responsibility and guilt in the absence of a god who rewards and punishes.[76]

Through a continuous rhythmic framework that unconsciously affects the audience as they watch the play, the spectator intuitively associates Mozart, and particularly his music, with the pure, unrestrained harmony of the primitive in contrast to the excessive verbiage consciously transmitted through Salieri, who represents artifice at every turn.

The structure of the play reflects the constant tension between Salieri, who is closely associated with the stagnant, artificial world of the court, and Mozart, the composer of grand operas. The audience will intuitively determine the differences between the art and artifice of Mozart and Salieri, respectively, not only through the dialogue but also through a constant musical/rhythmic structure that clearly delineates mediocrity from genius. As the play progresses, the audience associates Salieri's formal language with banal music, while Mozart's primitive, repetitive language becomes linked with sublime musical genius that is repulsive to Emperor Joseph II and his court lackeys. (Salieri, of course, recognizes Mozart's music as being Absolute, yet his mediocrity prevents him from duplicating it.) In his longest speech of the play, Mozart, speaking for Shaffer, reveals the role of a good "composer" or playwright: "That's our *job,* we composers: to combine the inner minds of him and him and him, and her and her—the thoughts of chambermaids and Court Composers—and turn the audience into God" (57–58). The play becomes a veritable concert of pulsating rhythms enabling the audience to determine, in an archetypal way, the differences between Mozart and Salieri.

Music, in particular, reinforces many of these rhythms throughout the play. Responding to Donal Henahan's critique of the play, Shaffer, in a letter to *The New York Times,* stated that he wanted to "triumphantly blazon Sound as the central obsession of the fable, even in a visual medium [film]."[77] Shaffer has stated that he conceived of the structure of the play as an opera: "Here was an opening chorus, the whispers of the populace. Here, with the entrance of the two gossipy courtiers, was a duet. Here is a trio, and later a quintet. Salieri's monologues are big arias. The play has the savor, the smell and taste, of an opera."[78] Indeed, in the acknowledgments in the New York edition of the play, Shaffer refers to *Amadeus* as "black opera" (xiii). In short, Shaffer carefully wrote a play in which musical interludes serve to reinforce speeches that are often musical in structure.[79]

Salieri, obsessed with finding an Absolute in music, consciously involves the audience in his quest—and this is his undoing, for the audience, through the music, identifies Salieri as the mediocrity and Mozart, "God's flute," as the voice of talent. Mozart's music allows the audience to feel Salieri's pain: as we hear the sublime music—"God's art" as Salieri describes it—penetrate throughout the theater, we intuitively understand Salieri's misery in terms that no words can adequately convey. Salieri's music, described by Mozart as "tonic and dominant, tonic and dominant, from here to resurrection" (32), most memorably conveyed in the banal March of Welcome for Mozart, is unfavorably compared to Mozart's music during the play. Salieri's attempt at music is lauded at court—birds of a feather do flock together. In contrast, Mozart's music is deemed vulgar, sensual, or too complex for a society that can better respond to "fêtes and fireworks." However, through the interplay of concert arias, solemn adagios (K. 361), the triumphant flourishes and chords of arpeggios (the march from *The Marriage of Figaro*), the complex modulations of *The Abduction from the Seraglio,* serenades of exquisite beauty and grace (the Twenty-ninth Symphony), innovative rondos (Piano Concerto in A Major, K. 448), the timeless profundity of *The Magic Flute,* the sinister archetypal sounds of *Don Giovanni,* and the exquisite, carefully crafted terzettos of *Così fan tutte,* the audience develops its own intrinsic appreciation of Mozart's sense of genius. Salieri's lofty language becomes associated with staccato rhythms (21), "recitativo secco" (6), or "snakelike hissing" (1) and "savage whispers" (1), while Mozart, the "obscene child" the primitive "Creature" as Salieri calls him, is shown to be innovative, interesting, and sophisticated through his music.

The distinction between the sterile middle-class role player and his alter ego is made clear through Mozart's music. In *The Royal Hunt of the Sun* and *Equus,* various rites and rituals distinguished the catalysts or primitives from their rivals. In *Amadeus,* music becomes a substitute for the Artaudian elements in the earlier plays that transmitted a sense of unconscious communication between the two alter egos or between the audience and the primitive as protagonist. As Barbara Lounsberry has noted, ". . . Shaffer has found in Mozart's music an evocative and aural symbol of divinity equivalent to the sun and horse images of the earlier plays."[80] This "symbol of divinity," if not perceived unconsciously by the audience, is continually reinforced throughout the drama because Salieri's search for an Absolute in music is channelled through God; yet Mozart, the primitive, is actually much closer to God than Salieri will ever be. What begins as a sociological drama becomes metaphysical through the music interspersed throughout the play.

Although music is the dominant means for creating a constant harmony or rhythm in the play, Shaffer also has used a number of Artaudian devices to reinforce a musiclike, continuous movement to unite the various scenes or "episodes" of the drama. For example, in the stage directions to the play, Shaffer tells us that "changes of time and place are indicated throughout by changes of light. In reading the text, it must be remembered that the action is wholly continuous" (xvi). In other words, as Artaud suggested, changes in lighting should play an intrinsic part in creating a constant rhythm throughout the play. The continuous musical action is manifested by actors who flow in and out of the set, changing the props. Shaffer says that such a fluid movement of the actors "will aid the play to be acted throughout in its proper manner: with the sprung line, gracefulness and energy for which Mozart is so especially celebrated" (xvi).

To ensure that the play maintains a constant rhythmic structure, Shaffer included the two Venticelli, "purveyors of fact, rumor and gossip" (1). As fine-tuned instruments, they present a refrain for the overall operatic structure of the play. In act 1, scene 1, their rapid speech "has the air of a fast and dreadful overture" (2), and indeed they do introduce or reinforce various motifs throughout Shaffer's musical "score." Their repetitive refrains, such as "I don't believe it" (2) or "Sir" (11), as well as their stichomythic dialogue, create a constant reverberating effect that can only reinforce the savage whispers and cries, the snakelike hissing, and the long, echoing booms that punctuate the scenario.

In addition, Mozart's own dialogue reflects the emphasis on onomatopoeia and metronomic rhythm so prevalent in musical scores. As Huber and Zapf have discovered, "Sound and rhythm in general are important throughout the play, especially in the characterization of Mozart: for instance, in both his artistic word-play and—as a sort of noisy, irritating counterpoint to his music—his piercing giggle."[81] During their cat-and-mouse game, Mozart and Constanze seem to talk or "sing" in nursery rhyme patterns:

> *Mozart.* And you're squeaky-peeky. And Stanzi-manzi. And Bini-gini!
> *[She surrenders.]*
> *Constanze.* Wolfi-polfi!
> *Mozart.* Poopy-peepee! *[They giggle.]*
> *Constanze.* Now don't be stupid.
> *Mozart [Insistent: like a child].* Come on—do it . . . Let's do it. "Poppy."
> *[They play a private game, gradually doing it faster, on their knees.]*
> *Constanze.* Poppy.
> *Mozart. [Changing it].* Pappy.
> *Constanze. [Copying].* Pappy.
> *Mozart.* Pappa.
> *Constanze.* Pappa.
> *Mozart.* Pappa-pappa!
> *Constanze.* Pappa-pappa!
> *Mozart.* Pappa-pappa-pappa-pappa!
> *Constanze.* Pappa-pappa-pappa-pappa! *[They rub noses.]*
> *Together.* Pappa-pappa-pappa-pappa! Pappa-pappa-pappa-pappa!
>
> (80)

Later, at the end of the play, Mozart is reduced to reciting the same type of nursery rhyme:

> *Mozart.* Oh God! . . . Oh God! . . . Oh God!
>
> . . . .
>
> *Mozart. [Crying out at the top of his lungs].* PAPAAAAA! . . . . *[In a childish voice]* Papa! *[Silence]* Papa . . . Papa . . . *[He extends his arms; imploringly. He speaks as a very young boy.]* Take me, Papa. Take me. Put down your arms and I'll hop into them. Just as we used to do it! . . . Hop-hop-hop-hop-UP!
>
> (88–89)

Perhaps an explanation for the worldwide success of *Amadeus* is that it works on so many levels—sociological, psychological, metaphysical, aural, and visual. Through Mozart's music and through the various stage innovations suggested by Artaud, Shaffer has created a play that is universal in scope, capable of being appreciated by diverse audiences. As in *The Royal Hunt of the Sun* and *Equus,* there is a sort of symbolic communication between the protagonist and his alter ego, and that unconscious empathy is transferred to the audience as well. The constant interplay between conscious and unconscious experience, history and fiction, art and life, actor and audience, all integrated by a continuous rhythmic structure, serve to make *Amadeus* the profound artistic achievement that it has proven to be.

11
Conclusion

In assessing all of Peter Shaffer's *oeuvre,* one discovers a complex interplay of sociological, metaphysical, philosophical, and psychological motifs. Critics have focused primarily on Shaffer's messages concerning the need for passion in modern society, the importance of worship, and the necessity to create some sense of meaning in our sterile, vapid lives. Yet, upon close examination, these motifs can only be found in Shaffer's major plays; the astute critic would have difficulty in applying such themes to Shaffer's early and minor works.

There is, however, one theme that dominates all of Shaffer's works, from the early detective novels to *Amadeus.* Shaffer is predominantly concerned with the dangers of role playing—the reasons why individuals refuse to be true to themselves and allow their passions to be controlled by other people or institutions. In Shaffer's plays, role playing is synonymous with hypocrisy, lies, and deceit, often leading to a socially and sexually sterile existence. By not establishing his or her sense of identity, the role player often retreats behind the secure world of established norms and values. Although the role player finds safety in positive sanctions for his normative behavior, his existence is actually a facade, which only serves to perpetrate mediocrity. The raison d'être of the play then becomes a means to unravel the truth behind a world full of lies and misconceptions.

Shaffer's protagonists can be classified into four distinct groups of individuals. This classification system is useful in determining an overall appreciation of Shaffer's multifarious microcosm.

The first group (Group A) consists of role players who live in an artificial world of illusion and hypocrisy. Its members include the citizens of Amnestie, Stanley and Louise Harrington, Ted Veasey, Charles Sidley, Brindsley Miller, Frank, and Gideon Petrie. This group of individuals is quite content with its mediocrity; in fact, many of them would like to impose their values on others, assuming that what is normative behavior for them must be universally accepted. These people are often staid, formal, shallow, artificial, and dependent on what others may think of them. They are frequently afraid of being themselves and exist merely to impress others.

197

PETER SHAFFER

On Shaffer's totem pole, they are hopelessly mired at the bottom.

The second group (Group B) is the role players who would like to supersede their illusory and mediocre existences but are too conditioned by their controlled environments to break free. This group includes Clive Harrington, Bob, Tom, and Sophie Lemberg, née Plotkin. Each of these characters is aware of his or her shortcomings but cannot transcend them. The result of their dependence is that they resort to lies and lead sexually sterile lives. Although they are frustrated individuals, their sense of awareness with regard to their illusory and shallow existences separates them from members of Group A.

Group C—Francisco Pizarro, Martin Dysart, and Antonio Salieri—include the role players who willfully seek to transcend their mediocre existences. These three individuals, wiser and a bit more jaded or pessimistic about life than the members of Group B, are not only frustrated with their sterile lives, but also understand the means to fulfillment in life. Pizarro, Dysart, and Salieri are products of institutionalized behavior and are therefore accustomed to adhering more to the whims of others than to their own instincts and impulses. Yet they each consciously seek fame and immortality: they want to be closer to God rather than to the mediocrities surrounding them. In contrast to members of Group B, they are aware not only of their illusory and meaningless lives, but also of the need to free themselves from roles in order to regain "Paradise Lost" (the elixir of youth). Members of Group C understand the need to establish one's own sense of values, particularly if one wants to be closer to God's favor.

The last group (Group D) consists of individuals who have established their own sense of identity free from the influence of other persons or institutions. They include Mr. Verity/Mr. Fathom, Walter, Julian Cristoforou, Atahuallpa, Mark Askelon, Alan Strang, and Wolfgang Amadeus Mozart. Members of this group are self-made men true to their own values and beliefs; they refuse to be judged by anyone else, especially not by the mediocrities with whom they must interact. Because these characters are at ease with themselves and do not put on airs for others, they possess a youthful, often eccentric, spirit to be imitated and admired. They are frequently considered "primitives" by others around them; yet because they can create their own brand of worship and refuse to be told how to think and act, they become virtually omnipotent and assume a godlike aura. Members of this group are existentialists who have created their own sense of identity; they rest at the top of Shaffer's totem-pole hierarchy.

The list below will clarify these various groups so that one can distinguish them at a glance:

Group A: Citizens of Amnestie, Stanley and Louise Harrington, Ted Veasey, Charles Sidley, Brindsley Miller, Frank, and Gideon Petrie

Group B: Clive Harrington, Bob, Tom, Sophie Lemberg

Group C: Francisco Pizarro, Martin Dysart, Antonio Salieri

Group D: Mr. Verity/Mr. Fathom, Walter, Julian Cristoforou, Atahuallpa, Mark Askelon, Alan Strang, Wolfgang Amadeus Mozart

Using this list, one can learn more about Shaffer's dialectic, which establishes the structure of each play. (See table below.)

No dialectic: *Black Comedy*
Group A vs. Group A: ———
Group A vs. Group B: *The Private Ear*
Group A vs. Group C: ———
Group A vs. Group D: The novels, *The Public Eye, Shrivings*
Group B vs. Group B: *The White Liars*
Group B vs. Group C: ———
Group B vs. Group D: *Five Finger Exercise*
Group C vs. Group D: *The Royal Hunt of the Sun, Equus, Amadeus*
Group D vs. Group D: ———

For example, in *Black Comedy,* there is no dialectic—the play is simply a study of role playing and its consequences. Also, we can discover that there is never a dialectic between members of Group A and Group A, Group A and Group C, Group B and Group C, or Group D and Group D. *The Private Ear* is the only play that presents a conflict between a member of Group A (Ted) and his counterpart in Group B (Bob). A character from Group A is contrasted with his alter ego in Group D in the novels, *The Public Eye,* and *Shrivings. The White Liars* represents a situation where two members of Group B (Tom and Sophie) clash, whereas *Five Finger Exercise* is the only instance in which the dialectic is between an individual from Group B (Clive) and one from Group D (Walter). Finally, the conflict between alter egos from Group C and Group D is expressed in *The Royal Hunt of the Sun, Equus,* and *Amadeus.*

The dialectic almost always presents conflicts that are sociological, except in one category: Group C versus Group D. Most of the conflicts are sociological wars of identity with some loved one at stake. In other words, the tug-of-war between the two alter egos is waged over either a girl friend *(The Private Ear),* wife *(The Public Eye),* mother *(Five Finger Exercise),* acolytes *(Shrivings),* or mutual lover *(The White Liars).* Yet the conflict between Group C and Group D is substantially different than Shaffer's sociological dialectics because *The Royal Hunt of the Sun, Equus,* and

Amadeus deal with metaphysical issues. The two alters ego wage warfare to decide God's favor.

In *The Royal Hunt of the Sun,* God must judge history and side either with the Spanish rapists or with Atahuallpa and his sun worshippers. In *Equus,* the choice is between Normality and horse worship. *Amadeus* poses the question of whether God favors his "magic flute" or the epitome of mediocrity. In only these three plays, the audience assumes a godlike role to make judgments with regard to the dialectic—Shaffer makes it clear that the audience plays a much more intrinsic role in *The Royal Hunt of the Sun, Equus,* and *Amadeus* because a narrator is provided to draw the audience intimately into the Apollonian-Dionysian struggle.

Shaffer's three most intriguing plays—*The Royal Hunt of the Sun, Equus,* and *Amadeus*—have achieved worldwide success because they work on various levels—the metaphysical as well as the sociological and psychological. To elevate the audience to a godlike role of omnipotence, Shaffer has used a carefully controlled rhythmic structure and other ritualistic aspects of Theatre of Cruelty. The spectator is asked to play God and differentiate mediocrity from genius, the latter reflected in rites, rituals, and rhythms associated with the "primitive" we see on stage. In short, Shaffer used this rhythmic structure sparingly but effectively, personifying his most elaborate thematic and stylistic approaches to the theater.

This study has shown Peter Shaffer to be a consummate playwright. In terms of *mise-en-scène,* few critics would argue with Shaffer's ability to dazzle audiences with elaborate scenic designs, period pieces that offer splendid costuming possibilities, epic theater, and scintillating musical interludes. Like O'Neill, Shaffer is a master of dialogue and dialects, capturing the essence of lower-class cockney as well as formal rhetoric; the power of his language has attracted some of Britain's greatest actors and actresses to deliver the lines that he has written. In addition, Shaffer, like Ibsen, Strindberg, O'Neill, Brecht, and Albee, his innovative predecessors in the theater, has successfully experimented with form. His willingness to write realistic or social drama, one-act plays, farce, epic theater, grand opera, ritualistic drama, and philosophical theater reflects his flexibility and his need to constantly alter the form of the play to match its content.

Although some critics have accused Shaffer of writing plays that are shallow in content, this study has shown that his plays are quite intricate and complex. Many themes and motifs weave in and out of his canon: the dangers of role playing, the need for worship, the importance of establishing one's own identity, the nature of Time and how it affects "Paradise Lost," as well as the conflict between reality and a life of illusion, fantasy, or masquerade. Shaffer's theater is also broad in scope, spanning metaphysics, philosophy, sociology, psychology, and anthropology. The plays are rich in ideas and defy any type of casual, buttoned-down examination.

Shaffer plans to continue writing plays; it will be interesting to see which avenues he chooses to explore after *Yonadab*. For now, suffice it to say that in terms of unity of form, content, and *mise-en-scène,* Shaffer is one of the most creative playwrights of the modern stage and has already established an important role in theatrical history.

Notes

Introduction

1. James Vinson, ed., *Contemporary Dramatists* (New York: St. Martin's Press, 1982), 709.

2. Most critics have not analyzed Shaffer's works seriously. Often, there is no attempt to assess the play at hand in relationship to other works in Shaffer's canon. If critics would make such an assessment, they would discover that all of Shaffer's plays revolve around the same basic conflict between a role player and his astute, yet primitive, alter ego. Instead, *The Royal Hunt of the Sun* is mistakenly perceived by some critics as a critique on Resurrection, *Equus* is seen as a diatribe on psychiatry, and *Amadeus* is distorted history that belittles Mozart, the middle-class stereotype of genius. For an insightful summary of the pretentious attitude that critics have toward Shaffer, see Michael Hinden, "Trying to Like Shaffer," *Comparative Drama* 19, no. 1 (1985): 14–29.

3. Tom Buckley, " 'Write Me,' Said the Play to Peter Shaffer," *The New York Times Magazine*, 13 April 1975, 32.

4. Jules Glenn seems to be pursuing this theme in all of Shaffer's plays. See "Alan Strang as Adolescent: A Discussion of Peter Shaffer's *Equus*," *International Journal of Psychoanalytic Psychotherapy* 5 (1976): 473–87; "Anthony and Peter Shaffer's Plays: The Influence of Twinship on Creativity," *American Imago* 31 (Fall 1974): 270–92; "Twins in Disguise: A Psychoanalytic Essay on *Sleuth* and *The Royal Hunt of the Sun*," *Psychoanalytic Quarterly* 43, no. 2 (1974): 288–302; "Twins in Disguise. 2. Content, Form and Style in Plays by Anthony and Peter Shaffer," *The International Review of Psycho-Analysis* 1, no. 3 (1974): 373–81; and "Twins in the Theater: A Study of Plays by Anthony and Peter Shaffer," in *Blood Brothers: Siblings as Writers*, ed. Norman Kiell (New York: International Universities Press, 1983), 277–99.

5. Of particular note with regard to *Equus* would be James W. Hamilton's article, "*Equus* and the Creative Process," *Journal of the Philadelphia Association for Psychoanalysis* 6 (1979): 53–64.

6. Buckley, " 'Write me,' " 32.

7. Don Ross, "Peter Shaffer is an Enemy of 'Togetherness,' " *New York Herald Tribune*, 3 January 1960, sec. 4, p. 3.

8. Buckley, " 'Write Me,' " 32.

9. Glenn Loney, "Which Twin Has the Tony?" *After Dark*, April 1971, 21.

10. Barbara Gelb, ". . . And Its Author," *The New York Times*, 14 November 1965, sec. 2, p. 4.

11. Roland Gelatt, "Mostly. *Amadeus*," *Horizon*, September 1984, 50.

12. Gelb, ". . . And Its Author," sec. 2, p. 4.

13. Brian Connell, "The Two Sides of Theatre's Agonised Perfectionist," *The Times*, 28 April 1980, 7.

14. Ibid.

15. Gelatt, "Mostly *Amadeus*," 50.

16. These are *The Woman in the Wardrobe* (1951), *How Doth the Little Crocodile?* (1952), and *Withered Murder* (1955). During my interview with Shaffer in New York City on 19 April 1986, he told me that the first novel was actually started before he went to Cambridge University. He wrote the first novel himself; for the latter two novels, Anthony devised the plots, and Peter did the writing.

17. Connell, "The Two Sides," 7. This search for identity in which an individual is torn between his own drives on the one hand and normative behavior sanctioned by society on the other, will be the dominant theme in virtually all of Shaffer's plays.

18. Gelatt, "Mostly *Amadeus*," 50–51.

19. Gelb, ". . . And Its Author," sec. 2, p. 4.

20. Ibid.

21. Ibid.

22. Buckley, " 'Write Me,' " 34.

23. Gelatt, "Mostly *Amadeus*," 51.

24. Connell, "The Two Sides," 7.

25. Roland Gelatt, "Peter Shaffer's *Amadeus:* A Controversial Hit," *Saturday Review,* November 1980, 13.

26. Gelatt, "Mostly *Amadeus*," 51.

27. Peter Shaffer, interview with author, New York City, 19 April 1986.

28. Dennis Klein, *Peter Shaffer* (Boston: G. K. Hall, 1979), 24.

29. Connell, "The Two Sides," 7.

30. Peter Shaffer, "Labels Aren't for Playwrights," *Theatre Arts,* February 1960, 20.

31. Gelatt, "Mostly *Amadeus*," 51.

32. Shaffer, "Labels Aren't for Playwrights," 20.

33. Connell, "The Two Sides," 7.

34. Peter Shaffer, interview with author, New York City, 19 April 1986.

35. Peter Shaffer, "Preface," *The Collected Plays of Peter Shaffer* (New York: Harmony Books, 1982), ix.

36. The final version of the film screenplay was improvised by Brook. See Barry Pree, "Peter Shaffer," *The Transatlantic Review* 14 (Autumn 1963): 65.

37. Shaffer, "Preface," x.

38. When I say that the play is "no longer extant," it simply means that the text is not available in any library, bookstore, publishing firm, or in any performer's hands. We may not conclude that one of the actors or technicians who had been working on the play in 1963 never secured a copy of the pantomime for himself or herself. It is beyond the scope of this research to contact any of the original cast members to determine if a text of the play exists. Peter Shaffer told me that he has no copy of his own.

39. Shaffer, "Preface," x.

40. Earlier in the year (1963), Shaffer had participated with Peter Hall, Peter Brook, Charles Marowitz, and Michel St. Denis in a reading of Artaud's works and letters followed by a roundtable discussion on the Theatre of Cruelty. See "Artaud for Artaud's Sake," *Encore* 11 (January–June 1964): 20–31.

41. Shaffer, "Preface," xi.

42. Ibid., xii.

43. Klein, *Peter Shaffer,* 69.

44. Shaffer, "Preface," xiii.

45. Ibid.

46. Peter Shaffer, *Shrivings* (London: André Deutsch, 1974), 10–11.

47. George Oppenheimer, "A Playwright's Critique," *Newsday* (Long Island), 6 November 1965, 37W.

48. Shaffer, *Shrivings,* 9.

49. Shaffer, "Preface," xiv.

50. Ibid., xiii.

51. Ibid., xv.

52. Ibid., xvi.

53. Ibid.

54. Peter Shaffer, *Amadeus* (New York: Harper & Row, 1981), ix.

55. For a more detailed account of this collaboration, see Harlan Jacobson, "As Many Notes as Required," *Film Comment,* September/October 1984, 50, 53–55; Peter Shaffer, "Making the Screen Speak," *Film Comment,* September/October 1984, 51, 56–57; and C. J. Gianakaris, "Drama into Film: The Shaffer Situation," *Modern Drama* 28, no. 1 (1985): 83–98.

Chapter 1. Peter Shaffer: Sociologist of the Theater

1. Peter Shaffer, "Preface," *The Collected Plays of Peter Shaffer* (New York: Harmony Books, 1982), viii.

2. Ibid.

3. Tom Buckley, " 'Write Me,' Said the Play to Peter Shaffer," *The New York Times Magazine,* 13 April 1975, 38.

4. Peter Shaffer, "Labels Aren't for Playwrights," *Theatre Arts,* February 1960, 20.

5. Shaffer admits that playwriting and particularly the overwhelming acceptance of his plays by the public has given him a stronger sense of identity over the years: "As time passed, however, I seem to have come to a much firmer idea of myself. I think this happens through work. Work is inevitably a statement—therefore a commitment. Almost nothing is more exposing than writing a play and having people sit down and look at it. Their approval—say, their laughter at a joke you've thought of, or their applause at the end of a speech—offers a confirmation that you exist as you." See Buckley, " 'Write Me,' " 40.

6. Shaffer did not choose the image of a chameleon arbitrarily. He mentions chameleons in relationship to his own personality on at least one other occasion. See Buckley, " 'Write Me,' " 40.

7. Brian Connell, "The Two Sides of Theatre's Agonised Perfectionist," *The Times,* 28 April 1980, 7.

8. See Jules Glenn, "Anthony and Peter Shaffer's Plays: The Influence of Twinship on Creativity," *American Imago* 31 (Fall 1974): 271.

9. For another summary of twinship studies in Shaffer's plays, see James W. Hamilton, "*Equus* and the Creative Process," *Journal of the Philadelphia Association for Psychoanalysis* 6 (1979): 59.

10. Anthony Shaffer is also a successful playwright and the author of *Sleuth, Murderer,* and *Frenzy.*

11. James Hamilton has argued that Peter Shaffer's experience concerning the failure of *The Battle of Shrivings* coupled with Anthony's success with *Sleuth* in the early 1970s fueled Peter to do a better job on his next play, which turned out to be *Equus.* See Hamilton, "Creative Process," 61.

12. Jules Glenn, "Twins in Disguise. 2. Content, Form and Style in Plays by Anthony and Peter Shaffer," *The International Review of Psycho-Analysis* 1, no. 3 (1974): 376.

13. Shaffer, of course, has read a number of these psychoanalytical studies of his works, but he admits that he has not experienced the intense rivalry with Anthony that some of these critics have seen. (See Buckley, " 'Write Me,' " 32.) With regard to Shaffer's own thoughts on the subject, he says: "The thing one discovers quite quickly about twins is that they're like any other siblings. They don't necessarily have the same likes and dislikes. Tony adores sports; I detest them. And I have a deep passion for music, which he does not share at all to the same extent." (See Roland Gelatt, "Mostly *Amadeus,*" *Horizon,* September 1984, 50.)

14. During my interview with Shaffer, he had some very harsh words for Dr. Glenn and his colleague, Dr. Sanford Gifford. Apparently, both men have overstepped their boundaries in prying into the personal lives of Peter and Anthony Shaffer.

15. Michael Gillespie, "Peter Shaffer: 'To Make Whatever God There Is,' " *Claudel Studies* 9, no. 2 (1982): 61.

16. The term "Paradise Lost" was suggested by Gillespie in his article (ibid., p. 62); his insight is so pertinent that I prefer to use his own wording here.

17. Shaffer has, on occasion, made a reference to role playing and conformity in relationship to sterility. See, for example, his comment during a roundtable discussion with Peter Brook, Peter Hall, Charles Marowitz, and Michel St. Denis: "Artaud for Artaud's Sake," *Encore* 11 (January–June 1964): 24.

18. For example, see Barbara Gelb, ". . . And Its Author," *The New York Times,* 14 November 1965, sec. 2, p. 2; and Barry Pree, "Peter Shaffer," *The Transatlantic Review* 14 (Autumn 1963): 64.

19. Renee Winegarten, "The Anglo-Jewish Dramatist in Search of His Soul," *Midstream* 12 (October 1966): 50.

20. For a more detailed discussion of the importance of marriage and family in Shaffer's plays, see Joan F. Dean, "The Family as Microcosm in Shaffer's Plays," *Ball State University Forum* 23, no. 1 (1982): 30–34.

Chapter 2. Form Follows Function

1. Peter Shaffer, "Preface," *The Collected Plays of Peter Shaffer* (New York: Harmony Books, 1982), viii.

2. John Russell Taylor, *Peter Shaffer,* Writers and Their Work Series, no. 244 (Harlow, Essex: Longman Group, 1974), 12.

3. Shaffer has stated this on a number of occasions. See Roland Gelatt, "Mostly *Amadeus,*" *Horizon,* September 1984, 52; and Peter Adam, "Peter Shaffer on Faith, Farce and Masks," *The Listener,* 14 October 1976, 477.

4. Philip Oakes, "Philip Oakes Talks to Peter Shaffer," *The Sunday Times,* 29 July 1973, 33. Shaffer does indeed work better when he is prodded by directors or faced with deadlines. John Dexter discussed how much Shaffer procrastinated with the writing of *Equus* and came up with silly excuses for not finishing the play. When Shaffer told Dexter that he was hesitant to continue writing for fear of not being able to find a boy with the qualities needed to play Alan, Dexter exploded with, "You can always cast a play. It will just take a long, long look. That's the silliest reason I've ever heard for not putting your fingers on the typewriter. Get on with it!" See Tom Buckley, " 'Write Me,' Said the Play to Peter Shaffer," *The New York Times Magazine,* 13 April 1975, 28.

5. See Michael Hinden, "When Playwrights Talk to God: Peter Shaffer and the Legacy of O'Neill," *Comparative Drama* 16, no. 1 (1982): 49–63.

6. Peter Shaffer, interview with author, New York City, 19 April 1986.

7. Of course, Brecht's theater works better in theory than it does in practice. Many of his greatest scenes are highly emotional—witness Kattrin's drumming on

the roof and her subsequent death at the end of *Mother Courage* and Gruscha's test of the chalk circle in *The Caucasian Chalk Circle*.

8. See C. J. Gianakaris, "Theatre of the Mind in Miller, Osborne and Shaffer," *Renascence* 30, no. 1 (1977): 33.

9. Brian Connell, "The Two Sides of Theatre's Agonised Perfectionist," *The Times,* 28 April 1980, 7.

10. Buckley, " 'Write Me,' " 38.

11. George Oppenheimer, "A Playwright's Critique," *Newsday* (Long Island), 6 November 1965, 37W.

12. Adam, "Faith, Farce and Masks," 476–77.

13. Peter Shaffer, interview with author, New York City, 19 April 1986.

14. Adam, "Faith, Farce and Masks," 477.

15. Buckley, " 'Write Me,' " 20.

16. Glenn Loney, "Which Twin Has the Tony?" *After Dark,* April 1971, 22.

17. See R. B. Marriott, "Peter Shaffer Calls for Magic and Mystery," *Stage and Television Today,* 31 July 1958, 8; Peter Shaffer, "The Cannibal Theater," *The Atlantic Monthly,* October 1969, 49, 50; "Peter Shaffer's Personal Dialogue," *The New York Times,* 6 October 1963, sec. 2, p. 3; "Artaud for Artaud's Sake," *Encore* 11 (January–June 1964): 25; and Gelatt, 52.

18. Marriott, "Magic and Mystery," 8.

19. Peter Shaffer, " 'To See the Soul of a Man,' " *The New York Times,* 24 October 1965, sec. 2, p. 3.

20. Oakes, "Philip Oakes," 33.

21. Shaffer, "The Cannibal Theater," 49.

22. Ibid.

23. Ibid.

24. Ibid.

25. Ibid.

26. Rodney Simard, *Postmodern Drama: Contemporary Playwrights in America and Britain* (Lanham, Md.: University Press of America, 1984), 103.

27. Antonin Artaud, *The Theater and Its Double,* trans. Mary Caroline Richards (New York: Grove Press, 1958), 28. "Une vraie pièce de théâtre bouscule le repos des sens, libère l'inconscient comprimé, pousse à une sorte de révolte virtuelle . . ." (Antonin Artaud, *Le théâtre et son double* [Paris: Gallimard, 1964], 39).

28. Artaud, *The Theater,* 92. "Le théâtre ne pourra redevenir lui-même, c'est-à-dire constituer un moyen d'illusion vraie, qu'en fournissant au spectateur des précipités véridiques de rêves, où son goût du crime, ses obsessions érotiques, sa sauvagerie, ses chimères, son sens utopique de la vie et des choses, son cannibalisme même, se debondent, sur un plan non pas supposé et illusoire, mais intérieur" (Artaud, *Le théâtre,* 139).

29. Artaud, *The Theater,* 101. "Du point de vue de l'esprit cruauté signifie rigueur, application et décision implacable, détermination irréversible, absolue" (Artaud, *Le théâtre,* 154).

30. Artaud, *The Theater,* 102. "C'est à tort qu'on donne au mot de cruauté un sens de sanglante rigueur, de recherche gratuite et désintéressée du mal physique. . . . Il y a dans la cruauté qu'on exerce une sorte de déterminisme supérieur auquel le bourreau suppliciateur est soumis lui-même, et qu'il doit être le cas échéant *déterminé* à supporter. La cruauté est avant tout lucide, c'est une sorte de direction rigide, la soumission à la nécessité" (Artaud, *Le théâtre,* 154).

31. Antonin Artaud, *Selected Writings,* ed. Susan Sontag and trans. Helen Weaver (New York: Farrar, Strauss and Giroux, 1976), 156–57. "Le spectateur qui vient chez nous sait qu'il vient s'offrir à une opération véritable, où non seulement son esprit

mais ses sens et sa chair sont en jeu. Il ira désormais au théâtre comme il va chez le chirugien ou chez le dentiste. Dans le même état d'esprit, avec la pensée évidemment qu'il n'en mourra pas, mais que c'est grave, et qu'il ne sortira pas de là-dedans intact. Si nous n'étions pas persuadés, de l'atteindre le plus gravement possible, nous nous estimerions inferieurs à notre tâche la plus absolue. Il doit être bien persuadé que nous sommes capables de la faire crier" (Antonin Artaud, *Oeuvres complètes,* vol. 2 [Paris: Gallimard, 1961], 7).

32. Artaud, of course, had a selfish reason for devising this type of theater. Throughout his life, Artaud claimed that he was possessed by demons (he even worshipped Satan at one point only later to become obsessed with Christ and with the Bible). For Artaud, theater was therapeutic—a means of purging his soul of vices, similar to the way that psychodrama is used as a cathartic tool for patients confined to mental asylums. Artaud, in and out of such asylums for most of his life, apparently found his own form of self-induced therapy.

33. For a more thorough discussion of Artaud's Theatre of Cruelty, see Albert Bermel, *Artaud's Theatre of Cruelty* (New York: Taplinger Publishing Co., 1977); Martin Esslin, *Antonin Artaud* (London: J. Calder, 1976); Bettina Knapp, *Antonin Artaud: Man of Vision* (New York: David Lewis, 1969); and Eric Sellin, *The Dramatic Concepts of Antonin Artaud* (Chicago: University of Chicago Press, 1968).

34. Artaud, *The Theater,* 30. "Si le théâtre essentiel est comme la peste, ce n'est pas parce qu'il est contagieux, mais parce que comme la peste il est la révélation, la mise en avant, la poussée vers l'extérieur d'un fond de cruauté latente par lequel se localisent sur un individu ou sur un peuple toutes les possibilités perverses de l'esprit" (Artaud, *Le théâtre,* 42).

35. Artaud, *The Theater,* 60. "Ses réalisations sont taillées en pleine matière, en pleine vie, en pleine réalité. Il y a en elles quelque chose du cérémonial d'un rite religieux, en ce sens qu'elles extirpent de l'esprit de qui les regarde toute idée de simulation, d'imitation derisoire de la réalité. . . . Les pensées auxquelles elle vise, les états d'esprit qu'elle cherche à créer, les solutions mystiques qu'elle propose sont émus, soulevés, atteints sans retard ni ambages. Tout cela semble un exorcisme pour faire AFFLUER nos démons" (Artaud, *Le théâtre,* 90–91).

36. Artaud, *The Theater,* 116. "Créer des Mythes voilà la véritable objet du théâtre, traduire la vie sous son aspect universel, immense, et extraire de cette vie des image où nous aimerions à nous retrouver" (Artaud, *Le théâtre,* 176–77).

37. Artaud, *The Theater,* 124. "Le chevauchement des images et des mouvements aboutira, par des collusions d'objets, de silences, de cris et de rhythmes, à la création d'un véritable langage physique à base de signes et non plus de mots" (Artaud, *Le théâtre,* 188).

38. For an extended analysis of Artaud's use of hieroglyphs and symbols, as well as for a discussion of the ritualistic sources of such signs, see Sellin's book on Artaud, *The Dramatic Concepts of Antonin Artaud.*

39. E. T. Kirby, *Total Theatre* (New York: E. P. Dutton and Co., 1969), xiii.

40. Artaud, *The Theater,* 39. "Cette poésie très difficile et complexe revêt de multiples aspects: elle revêt d'abord ceux de tous les moyens d'expression utilisables sur une scène, comme musique, danse, plastique, pantomime, mimique, gesticulation, intonations, architecture, éclairage et décor" (Artaud, *Le théâtre,* 55–56).

41. Artaud, *The Theater,* 37. ". . . la scène est un lieu physique et concret qui demande qu'on le remplisse, et qu'on lui fasse parler son langage concret" (Artaud, *Le théâtre,* 53).

42. Artaud, *The Theater,* 37. "Je dis que ce langage concret, destiné aux sens et indépendant de la parole, doit satisfaire d'abord les sens, qu'il y a une poésie pour les sens comme il y en a une pour langage, et que ce langage physique et concret auquel

je fais allusion n'est vraiment théâtral que dans la mesure où les pensées qu'il exprime échappent au langage articulé" (Artaud, *Le théâtre*, 53–55).

43. Artaud, *Selected Writings*, 347–48. "Non que la parole y soit méprisée, mais celle-ci est prise à l'état concret, pour sa valeur vibratoire, sonore, elle provoque le geste est le geste la provoque; et celui-ci a cessé d'être conditionné par elle. Et c'est ainsi qu'une sorte de nouvelle poésie dans l'espace apparaît" (Antonin Artaud, *Oeuvres complètes*, vol. 8 [Paris: Gallimard, 1971], 349–50).

44. Unfortunately, Artaud's theories do not necessarily conform to what we see in his plays. In *The Cenci,* for example, words are used much more in the denotative sense to communicate ideas rather than just for their vibratory or incantatory effects.

45. Artaud, *The Theater*, 72. "Il ne s'agit pas de supprimer la parole au théâtre mais de lui faire changer sa destination, et surtout de réduire sa place, de la considérer comme autre chose qu'un moyen de conduire des caractères humains à leurs fins extérieures, puisqu'il ne s'agit jamais au théâtre que de la façon dont les sentiments et les passions s'opposent les uns aux autres et d'hommes à homme dans la vie" (Artaud, *Le théâtre*, 109).

46. Artaud, *The Theater*, 94. "Il ne s'agit pas de supprimer la parole articulée, mais de donner aux mots à peu près l'importance qu'ils ont dans les rêves" (Artaud, *Le théâtre*, 142).

47. Subsequent chapters will discuss the Artaudian elements in each play in detail.

48. "*Equus:* Playwright Peter Shaffer Interprets its Ritual," *Vogue,* February 1975, 192.

49. Shaffer, " 'To See the Soul of a Man,' " sec. 2, p. 3.

50. Phyllis Funke, "A Playwright in a Hurry," *The Courier-Journal* (Louisville), 7 November 1965, sec. F, p. 1.

51. Roland Gelatt, "Peter Shaffer's *Amadeus:* A Controversial Hit," *Saturday Review,* November 1980, 12.

52. For example, see Peter Shaffer, "What We Owe Britten," *The Sunday Times,* 18 November 1973, 35.

53. Peter Shaffer, "One Family Split Four Ways," *Life,* 21 March 1960, 97.

54. Peter Shaffer, interview with author, New York City, 19 April 1986.

55. Peter Shaffer, "Paying Homage to Mozart," *The New York Times Magazine,* 2 September 1984, 22.

56. For a more thorough treatment of the role of music in *Amadeus,* see C. J. Gianakaris, "Drama into Film: The Shaffer Situation," *Modern Drama* 28, no. 1 (1985): 83–98.

57. In a harsh attack on *Equus,* Hélène L. Baldwin claimed that Shaffer used Artaudian elements in the play yet failed to stress myth or to make the play the universal rite for which Artaud strived. Echoing other critics, Baldwin accused Shaffer of titillating the audience with sexuality spiced with cruelty. Of course, there is the almost obligatory comment that John Dexter made the play work, and the Artaudian elements were derived from his imaginative sense of stage direction. She concluded that Artaud would have rejected *Equus* as unworthy of his Theatre of Cruelty. Unfortunately, she failed to take into account that Artaud would probably reject virtually all of modern drama, with the exception of a few plays by LeRoi Jones (Amiri Baraka), Kenneth Brown, Peter Weiss, and Jean Genet, as unworthy candidates for his Theatre of Cruelty; he would also have to reject some of his own plays, including *The Cenci,* because he had trouble making them work on stage and, at the same time, conform to the rigorous standards he created. See Hélène L. Baldwin, "*Equus:* Theater of Cruelty or Theater of Sensationalism?" *Philological Papers* (West Virginia University) 25 (1978): 118–27.

58. "Artaud for Artaud's Sake," 25.
59. Ibid.

Chapter 3. The Early/Unpublished Works: Minor Chords

1. During my interview with Shaffer (19 April 1986), he explained to me why he used a pseudonym for the detective novels: "I had a sense that I wasn't going to continue as a detective writer. I didn't particularly think that it was a good idea . . . I just felt that I would rather reserve whatever writing I did of a more serious nature for my own name."

2. Peter Shaffer, *The Woman in the Wardrobe* (London: Evans Brothers, 1951), 13. All subsequent citations are from this edition and are included within parentheses in the text.

3. Peter and Anthony Shaffer, *How Doth the Little Crocodile?* (New York: Macmillan, 1957), 153. All subsequent citations are from this edition and are included within parentheses in the text.

4. On the last page of *How Doth the Little Crocodile?,* Shaffer good-naturedly ridicules his first novel. Sir Rupert, a member of the Beverley Club, is trying to entice Fathom to tackle another murder case:

"There was also an unidentified woman tied up in the wardrobe."

"Woman in the wardrobe!" snorted Fathom contemptuously, settling himself again for sleep. "It sounds like a cheap novelette. You people really must try to preserve some standards." (185)

5. Peter and Anthony Shaffer, *Withered Murder* (New York: Macmillan, 1956), 8. All subsequent citations are from this edition and are included within parentheses in the text.

6. Don Ross, "Peter Shaffer is an Enemy of 'Togetherness,'" *New York Herald Tribune,* 3 January 1960, sec. 4, p. 3.

7. "TV: Cloak and Dagger," *The New York Times,* 28 January 1958, 55.

8. Peter Shaffer, interview with author, New York City, 19 April 1986.

9. Dennis Klein, *Peter Shaffer* (Boston: G. K. Hall, 1979), 26–27.

10. Peter Shaffer, "But My Dear," in *That Was the Week That Was,* ed. David Frost and Ned Sherrin (London: W. H. Allen, 1963), 50. All subsequent citations are from this edition and are included within parentheses in the text.

11. Peter Shaffer, "The President of France," in *That Was the Week That Was,* ed. David Frost and Ned Sherrin (London: W. H. Allen, 1963), 95. All subsequent citations are from this edition and are included within parentheses in the text.

12. "Pantomime by Stealth," *The Times,* 20 December 1963, 5.

13. See "Pantomime by Stealth," 5; Philip Hope-Wallace, "Joan Littlewood Panto," *The Guardian,* 20 December 1963, 7; W. A. Darlington, "Cinderella Goes to the Moon by Rocket," *The Daily Telegraph and Morning Post,* 20 December 1963, 13; T. C. Worsley, *"Merry Roosters' Panto,"* *Financial Times,* 20 December 1963, 20; Milton Shulman, "Cinderella is Fine—For Grown-Ups," *Evening Standard,* 20 December 1963, 4; and Herbert Kretzmer, "A Dim Little Blonde With No Magic," *Daily Express,* 20 December 1963, 4.

14. Peter Shaffer, interview with author, New York, 19 April 1986.

Chapter 4. *Five Finger Exercise:* The Sweet Music Begins

1. Peter Shaffer, "Labels Aren't for Playwrights," *Theatre Arts,* February 1960, 20.

2. See "Children vs. Parents: Subtle Play at the Comedy," *The Times*, 17 July 1958, 4; Harold Hobson, "Irma Translated," *The Sunday Times*, 20 July 1958, 9; Milton Shulman, "Mr. Culver Gets the Treatment," *Evening Standard*, 17 July 1958, 10; Alan Brien, "Eating People Is Wrong," *The Spectator*, 25 July 1958, 133–34; Patrick Gibbs, "Fine Acting in Striking Play," *Daily Telegraph*, 17 July 1958, 10; T. C. Worsley, "Give Me a Good Play," *New Statesman*, 26 July 1958, 112–13; and Rich, "Shows Abroad," *Variety*, 23 July 1958, 58.

3. Philip Hope-Wallace, *"Five Finger Exercise,"* *The Manchester Guardian*, 17 July 1958, 5.

4. W. L. Webb, "Committed to Nothing But the Theatre," *The Manchester Guardian*, 27 August 1959, 4.

5. Shulman, "Mr. Culver," 10.

6. Ian Dallas, "The Naturalists," *Encore* 10 (September 1958): 28.

7. Gibbs, "Fine Acting," 10.

8. Kenneth Tynan, "Fathers and Sons," *The Observer*, 20 July 1958, 13.

9. Kenneth Tynan, "Roses and Thorns," *The New Yorker*, 12 December 1959, 100–102..

10. There was a brief trial run in Washington, D.C. before the play appeared on Broadway.

11. All of Shaffer's plays have opened first in London and then in New York. Shaffer frequently rewrites the British version of the play to make it more suitable for American audiences. At times, the changes in the revised play are slight, a mere substitution of an obscure British reference for a more comprehensible American expression. However, Shaffer is frequently not satisfied with the London version of the play, and therefore he often makes substantial changes in the American edition. Thus, it is important to remember that when one reads criticism on Shaffer, particularly an English critic's review, one should realize that the reviewer may have seen a slightly different variation of the play.

Shaffer, who spends much of his time on both sides of the Atlantic, insists that American audiences will have a difficult time understanding many British customs and idiomatic expressions. He has stated that "for better or worse, I am an English writer with English rhythms, and I wouldn't trust myself to do American dialogue." (See Peter Buckley, "Out to Lunch," *Vanity Fair*, May 1986, 136.) For a more detailed discussion of Shaffer's views on revising British plays for an American audience, see "Scripts in Trans-Atlantic Crossings May Suffer Two Kinds of Changes," *Dramatists Guild Quarterly* (Spring 1980), 29.

12. For a discussion of changes in the New York production, see Stuart W. Little, "Briton Wrote New Scene to Open His Play in New York," *New York Herald Tribune*, 8 December 1959, 21.

13. See Brooks Atkinson, "The Theater: *Five Finger Exercise,*" *The New York Times*, 3 December 1959, in *New York Theater Critics' Reviews—1959*, 210; Richard Watts, Jr., "A Powerful Play From England," *New York Post*, 3 December 1959, in *New York Theater Critics' Reviews—1959*, 208; John McClain, "Top Drawer Import With Sterling Cast," *New York Journal American*, 3 December 1959, in *New York Theater Critics' Reviews—1959*, 207; Robert Coleman, *"Five Finger Exercise* Thrilling,"* *Daily Mirror*, 3 December 1959, in *New York Theater Critics' Reviews—1959*, 210; Frank Aston, *"Five Finger Exercise* Subtle and Substantial," *New York World-Telegram*, 3 December 1959, in *New York Theater Critics' Reviews—1959*, 208; Walter Kerr, *"Five Finger Exercise,"* *New York Herald Tribune*, 3 December 1959, in *New York Theater Critics' Reviews—1959*, 209; Gore Vidal, "Strangers at Breakfast," *The Reporter*, 7 January 1960, 37; Tom Driver, "Drama Wanted: Fresh Air," *Christian Century*, 6 January 1960, 15–16; Harold Clurman, "Theater," *The Nation*, 19 De-

cember 1959, 475–76; Tynan, "Roses and Thorns," 100–102; Hobe, "Shows on Broadway," *Variety,* 9 December 1959, 70; Jack Balch, "The Openings," *Theatre Arts,* February 1960, 14–16; and "New Plays on Broadway," *Time,* 14 December 1959, 77.

14. Watts, Jr., "Powerful Play," 208.

15. Atkinson, *"Five Finger Exercise,"* 210.

16. Hobe, "Shows on Broadway," 70.

17. Clurman, "Theatre," 476.

18. John Chapman, *"Five Finger Exercise* a Doodle," *Daily News,* 3 December 1959, in *New York Theater Critics' Reviews—1959,* 209.

19. Ibid.

20. Ibid.

21. Don Ross, "Peter Shaffer is an Enemy of 'Togetherness,'" *New York Herald Tribune,* 3 January 1960, sec. 4, p. 3.

22. See Tom Buckley, "'Write Me,' Said the Play to Peter Shaffer," *The New York Times Magazine,* 13 April 1975, 37.

23. Barry Pree, "Peter Shaffer," *The Transatlantic Review* 14 (Autumn 1963): 64–65.

24. Frederick Brisson, "Preface," *Five Finger Exercise* (New York: Harcourt, Brace and Co., 1958), 6. All subsequent citations are from this edition and are included within parentheses in the text.

25. R. B. Marriott, "Peter Shaffer Calls for Magic and Mystery," *Stage and Television Today,* 31 July 1958, 8.

26. At times in the play, we seem to grasp, through Clive's explicit language, a sense of the battle between the primitive and his rational alter ego. Clive, however, speaks quite openly only when he is drunk—Shaffer's rationale for allowing this sort of language to enter the British tea room. Like Albee, at least in this play, Shaffer presents savagery on stage only when it is the result of intoxication. Later, when Shaffer learns more about his craft, this sort of cannibalistic theater, the battle between the Apollonian and the Dionysian, becomes more natural for him to write without relying on the effects of alcohol.

27. Joan F. Dean, "The Family as Microcosm in Shaffer's Plays," *Ball State University Forum* 23, no. 1 (1982): 30.

28. Ross, "Enemy of 'Togetherness,'" sec. 4, p. 3.

29. Peter Shaffer, "Preface," *The Collected Plays of Peter Shaffer* (New York: Harmony Books, 1982), vii.

30. Peter Shaffer, interview with author, New York City, 19 April 1986.

31. For example, see Ross, "Enemy of 'Togetherness,'" sec. 4, p. 3.

32. Joseph A. Loftus, "Playwright's Moral Exercise," *The New York Times,* 29 November 1959, sec. 2, p. 1.

33. The relationship between Walter and Louise is discussed in detail in Dennis Klein's book on Shaffer. See Dennis Klein, *Peter Shaffer* (Boston: G. K. Hall, 1979), 37–49.

34. Peter Shaffer, interview with author, New York City, 19 April 1986.

35. In his essay on the early plays of Peter Shaffer, Charles A. Pennell claimed that Clive's latent homosexuality is the focal point of the play, the impetus for conflicts between Clive and Walter. There is no evidence in the play that Clive has any homosexual tendencies, although it is possible to mistake his "come away with me" speech to Walter in act 2, scene 2, in a sexually connotative way. See Charles A. Pennell, "The Plays of Peter Shaffer: Experiment in Convention," *Kansas Quarterly* 3, no. 2 (1971): 100–109.

36. Most memorable would be the dishonesty in the Pizarro-Atahuallpa rela-

tionship and the bond shared by Mozart and Salieri.

37. Does Walter succeed in his suicide attempt? The stage directions tell us that he is still alive at the end of the play, and Clive assures Pamela that Walter only "fell down and hurt himself" (110). Walter briefly regains consciousness and explains that "mir fehlt nichts" (109), so we must assume that he is unharmed.

38. See John Russell Taylor, *The Angry Theater* (New York: Hill and Wang, 1969), 274. Also see Klein, *Peter Shaffer*, 37, for a similar discussion about Walter's role in the play.

39. Peter Shaffer, interview with author, New York City, 19 April 1986.

40. This has also been noted by Wayne Paul Lawson, "The Dramatic Hunt: A Critical Evaluation of Peter Shaffer's Plays," Ph.D. diss., Ohio State University, 1974, 62.

Chapter 5. *The Private Ear/The Public Eye:* Not Enough Notes

1. See "Variations on a Triangle," *The Times,* 11 May 1962, 12; J. C. Trewin, "Eyes and Ears," *The Illustrated London News,* 26 May 1962, 860; Bamber Gascoigne, "Touched by Pleasure," *The Spectator,* 18 May 1962, 653; Harold Hobson, "*Blitz* Costly, Wholesome, Stupendous . . . And Out of Date," *The Christian Science Monitor,* 12 May 1962, 4; W. A. Darlington, "Making up for Lost Time," *Daily Telegraph,* 11 May 1962, 16; Eric Keown, "At the Play," *Punch,* 16 May 1962, 767–68; Milton Shulman, "Mr. Shaffer—First Sex-War Reporter," *Evening Standard,* 11 May 1962, 21; and Herbert Kretzmer, "More Sparkle From Off-Beat Mr. Shaffer," *Daily Express,* 12 May 1962, 7.

2. Darlington, "Lost Time," 16.

3. Shulman, "Sex-War Reporter," 21.

4. Trewin, "Eyes and Ears," 860; and "*Blitz* Costly," Hobson, 4.

5. Gascoigne, "Touched by Pleasure," 653.

6. Keown, "At the Play," 768.

7. Kenneth Tynan, "London Can Keep It," *The Observer,* 13 May 1962, 25.

8. Ibid.

9. Ibid.

10. See Roger Gellert, "Encircling Gloom," *New Statesman,* 18 May 1962, 732; and T. C. Worsley, "*The Private Ear: The Public Eye,*" *Financial Times,* 11 May 1962, 26.

11. Gellert, "Encircling Gloom," 732.

12. Worsley, "*Private Ear,*" 26.

13. See John Chapman, "*Private Ear* and *Public Eye* Are Irresistible English Comedies," *Daily News,* 10 October 1963, in *New York Theater Critics' Reviews—1963,* 249; Richard Watts, Jr., "Two Delightful London Comedies," *New York Post,* 10 October 1963, in *New York Theater Critics' Reviews—1963,* 251; Robert Coleman, "*Eye-Ear* Delightful Imports," *New York Mirror,* 10 October 1963, in *New York Theater Critics' Reviews—1963,* 248; "Love Antic and Frantic," *Time,* 18 October 1963, 76, 78; Harold Clurman, "Theater," *The Nation,* 9 November 1963, 305–306; Norman Nadel, "Emotions Gently Laid Bare in Shaffer's *Eye* and *Ear,*" *New York World-Telegram,* 10 October 1963, in *New York Theater Critics' Reviews—1963,* 248; Walter Kerr, "*Private Ear* and *Public Eye,*" *New York Herald Tribune,* 10 October 1963, in *New York Theater Critics' Reviews—1963,* 249; and Hobe, "Shows on Broadway," *Variety,* 16 October 1963, 54.

14. Of those critics who expressed a preference for either play, *The Public Eye* was preferred by Harold Clurman *(The Nation),* Norman Nadel *(New York World-Telegram),* Richard Watts, Jr. *(New York Post),* the anonymous reviewer in *Time,* and

Howard Taubman, "The Theater: 2 Comedies by Shaffer," *The New York Times,* 10 October 1963, in *New York Theater Critics' Reviews—1963,* 251. John McClain, "An Import—But Why?" *New York Journal American,* 10 October 1963, in *New York Theater Critics' Reviews—1963,* 250, preferred *The Private Ear.*

15. Taubman, "Comedies," 251.
16. Ibid.
17. Ibid.
18. McClain, "Import," 250.
19. Ibid.
20. "*The Private Ear* and *The Public Eye,*" *Newsweek,* 21 October 1963, 104.
21. Ibid.
22. Ibid.
23. Barry Pree, "Peter Shaffer," *The Transatlantic Review* 14 (Autumn 1963): 63.
24. Ibid.
25. It almost seems as if Shaffer's intentions were to belie the critics who claimed that he was an Establishment playwright incapable of handling working-class dialect.
26. Shaffer admitted this in the interview with Barry Pree of *The Transatlantic Review.* See Pree, "Peter Shaffer," 63.
27. Peter Shaffer, *The Private Ear and The Public Eye* (New York: Stein and Day, 1964), 13. All subsequent citations from both plays are from this edition and are included within parentheses in the text.
28. Peter Shaffer, interview with author, New York City, 19 April 1986.
29. Characters who do not have an ear for music or who are hostile to music are not dear to Shaffer's heart. The tendency to dislike music (Mr. Harrington, Ted, Emperor Joseph II, etc.) is a clear-cut indication of Shaffer's attitude towards them.
30. London audiences received a good laugh when Bob says that his favorite musician is Benjamin Britten. In "What We Owe Britten," *The Times,* 18 November 1973, 35, Shaffer explains that his infatuation with Britten began in 1945 during a summer evening in which he had heard a performance of *Peter Grimes* on the radio. In *The Times* article, Shaffer wrote that from 1945 to 1973, he saw the opera over twenty times: "Nothing I have seen in the spoken theatre has ever affected me more powerfully than this piece." Dennis Klein, in his book on Shaffer, suggests that *Peter Grimes* is particularly appropriate for the situation described in *The Private Ear* because it is the story of an alienated individual in love with an ideal woman. Peter, a social misfit, refuses the help of his friend, just as Bob rejects Ted's assistance. See Dennis Klein, *Peter Shaffer* (Boston: G. K. Hall, 1979), 61.
31. Rodney Simard, *Postmodern Drama: Contemporary Playwrights in America and Britain* (Lanham, Md.: University Press of America, 1984), 106.
32. Peter Shaffer, interview with author, New York City, 19 April 1986.

Chapter 6. *The Royal Hunt of the Sun:* **The Maestro Finds Gold**

1. R. B. Marriott, "Peter Shaffer Calls for Magic and Mystery," *Stage and Television Today,* 31 July 1958, 8.
2. Stuart W. Little, "Briton Wrote New Scene to Open His Play in New York," *New York Herald Tribune,* 8 December 1959, 21.
3. See Milton Shulman, Review of *The Royal Hunt of the Sun, Evening Standard,* 8 July 1964, 4; Bamber Gascoigne, "All the Riches of the Incas," *The Observer,* 12 July 1964, 24; and Ronald Bryden, "Ruin and Gold," *New Statesman,* 17 July 1964, 95–96.
4. Bryden, "Ruin and Gold," 96.

5. Gascoigne, "Riches of the Incas," 24.

6. See B. A. Young, *"The Royal Hunt of the Sun," Financial Times*, 8 July 1964, 24; Benedict Nightingale, *"The Royal Hunt of the Sun* at Chichester," *The Guardian*, 8 July 1964, 7; and Malcolm Rutherford, "The Christ That Died," *The Spectator*, 17 July 1964, 82, 84.

7. Rutherford, "The Christ That Died," 82.

8. Nightingale, "Chichester," 7.

9. Eric Shorter, "Exotic Epic Play by Peter Shaffer," *Daily Telegraph*, 8 July 1964, 16.

10. Ibid.

11. See "Stage Challenge to Production," *The Times*, 9 December 1964, 9; Harold Hobson, "In Search of Bliss," *The Sunday Times*, 13 December 1964, 25; Bernard Levin, "Yes, It's the Greatest Play in My Lifetime," *Daily Mail*, 10 December 1964, 18; Alan Brien, "Silent Epic—With Words," *The Sunday Telegraph*, 13 December 1964, 12; Milton Shulman, "A Search for Faith in a Feast of Spectacle," *Evening Standard*, 9 December 1964, 14; and Myro, "Shows Abroad," *Variety*, 16 December 1964, 64.

12. Brien, "Silent Epic," 12.

13. Levin, "Greatest Play," 18. Of course, what is important about Mr. Levin's comments is that it is unusual for any critic to make such a definitive statement about any play. His remark about *Royal Hunt* being the greatest play in our lifetime has been paraphrased by numerous critics and has been used as effective promotional material for the play.

14. Myro, "Shows Abroad," 64.

15. Ibid.

16. W. A. Darlington, "Conquistador in Search of a Faith," *Daily Telegraph*, 9 December 1964, 18.

17. Penelope Gilliatt, "A Huge Stride Backwards—With the Inca," *The Observer*, 13 December 1964, 24.

18. Peter Shaffer, "Scripts in Trans-Atlantic Crossings May Suffer Two Kinds of Changes," *Dramatists Guild Quarterly*, Spring 1980, 31.

19. Ibid., 30.

20. See Howard Taubman, "The Theater: Pizarro, Gold and Ruin," *The New York Times*, 27 October 1965, in *New York Theater Critics' Reviews—1965*, 296; John Chapman, *"The Royal Hunt of the Sun* Fills the ANTA Theater with Beauty," *Daily News*, 27 October 1965, in *New York Theater Critics' Reviews—1965*, 295; John McCarten, "Gods Against God," *The New Yorker*, 6 November 1965, 115–16; Henry Hewes, "Inca Doings," *Saturday Review*, 13 November 1965, 71; "Hunting Heaven," *Newsweek*, 8 November 1965, 96; John McClain, "Size, Style and Talent," *New York Journal American*, 27 October 1965, in *New York Theater Critics' Reviews—1965*, 293; Norman Nadel, *"Royal Hunt* a Shimmering Sunburst of Talent," *New York World-Telegram*, 27 October 1965, in *New York Theater Critics' Reviews—1965*, 294; and Richard Watts, Jr., "With Pizarro in Inca Peru," *New York Post*, 27 October 1965, in *New York Theater Critics' Reviews—1965*, 295.

21. Taubman, "Pizarro," 296.

22. Watts, Jr., "In Inca Peru," 295.

23. McClain, "Size, Style and Talent," 293.

24. Hewes, "Inca Doings," 71.

25. See Wilfrid Sheed, "Conquest," *Commonweal*, 19 November 1965, 215; Harold Clurman, "Marking Time," *The Nation*, 22 November 1965, 397–98; Robert Brustein, "Familiar Peru, Exotic Brooklyn," *The New Republic*, 27 November 1965, 45–46; and Walter Kerr, Untitled review of *The Royal Hunt of the Sun, New York*

Herald Tribune, 27 October 1965, in *New York Theater Critics' Reviews—1965,* 294–95.

26. Sheed, "Conquest," 215.
27. Ibid.
28. Clurman, "Marking Time," 397.
29. Brustein, "Familiar Peru," 45.
30. Barry Pree, "Peter Shaffer," *The Transatlantic Review* 14 (Autumn 1963): 64.
31. Barbara Gelb, ". . . And Its Author," *The New York Times,* 14 November 1965, sec. 2, p. 2.
32. Some critics insist that the religious themes overshadow all of Shaffer's other intentions. Harold Hobson's review in *The Sunday Times* claimed that the play was about the possibilities of resurrection (p. 3). Malcolm Rutherford, writing in *The Spectator,* believed *Royal Hunt* was a parody of the Crucifixion (p. 82), while Jeremy Kingston's review in *Punch* depicted the dialectical arguments against Christianity as a major weakness of the play. See "Theatre," *Punch,* 15 July 1964, 99.
33. Antonin Artaud, *The Theater and Its Double,* trans. Mary Caroline Richards (New York: Grove Press, 1958), 126. Artaud's influence on *Royal Hunt* will be discussed in greater depth later in this chapter. For a more detailed comparison between Artaud's plan and Shaffer's play, see Peter L. Podol, "Contradictions and Dualities in Artaud and Artaudian Theater: *The Conquest of Mexico* and the Conquest of Peru," *Modern Drama* 26, no. 4 (1983): 518–27.
34. Peter Shaffer, "In Search of a God," *Plays and Players,* October 1964, 22.
35. See Howard Taubman, "About a 'Royal Hunt,'" *The New York Times,* 14 November 1965, sec. 2, p. 1.
36. Gelb, ". . . And Its Author," sec. 2, p. 2.
37. Ibid.
38. Peter Shaffer, *The Royal Hunt of the Sun* (New York: Stein and Day, 1965), vii. All subsequent citations are from this edition and are included within parentheses in the text.
39. Peter Shaffer, " 'To See the Soul of a Man,' " *The New York Times,* 24 October 1965, sec. 2, p. 3.
40. Shaffer discussed the theme of his play in an interview with John Russell Taylor. See "Shaffer and the Incas," *Plays and Players,* April 1964, 12.
41. Karl-Heinz Westarp has noted that Shaffer, using Pizarro as his spokesman, is a demythologizer rather than a myth maker. See "Myth in Peter Shaffer's *The Royal Hunt of the Sun* and in Arthur Kopit's *Indians,*" *English Studies* 65 (April 1984): 120–28.
42. See Joan F Dean, "Peter Shaffer's Recurrent Character Type," *Modern Drama* 21, no. 3 (1978): 299–300. The article provides significant insight into Pizarro's personality and compares him with Mark Askelon and Martin Dysart.
43. The gesture of affection between Pizarro and Atahuallpa at the end of 2.5 can be construed as a homosexual one: "Tentatively Pizarro extends his hand to him. Atahuallpa takes it and rises. Quietly they go off together" (55). The binding of the two men in 2.10 seems to be a gesture that is sexual as well as social in nature.
44. Taylor, "Shaffer and the Incas," 12.
45. Atahuallpa was told by his father to kill his brother, the shepherd, who was "fit only to tend herds" (53), whereas Atahuallpa was rightfully born to tend his nation. One is reminded of the twinship studies conducted by Dr. Jules Glenn. The implication is that this deep-rooted rivalry between twins is present in Shaffer's major plays. Dr. Glenn indicates that "Shaffer" (actually Schäfer) is the German word for shepherd. (See Jules Glenn, "Twins in Disguise: A Psychoanalytical Essay on *Sleuth* and *The Royal Hunt of the Sun,*" *Psychoanalytic Quarterly* 43, no. 2 [1974]:

296.) Glenn claims that the Peter/Anthony dialectic is manifested in the sibling rivalry of Atahuallpa and his brother. If we assume that Pizarro is also a brother to Atahuallpa, with Shaffer, of course, identifying with Pizarro, the protagonist, this dialogue becomes much more interesting:

> *Pizarro.* You see much in my face.
> *Atahuallpa.* I see my father.
> *Pizarro.* You do me honour, lad.
> *Atahuallpa.* Speak true. If in your home your brother was King, but fit only for herds, would you take his crown?
> *Pizarro.* If I could.
> *Atahuallpa.* And then you would kill him.
> *Pizarro.* No.

(53)

Pizarro would not kill his brother (he tries everything in his power to keep Atahuallpa alive despite the wishes of the Spanish soldiers), yet he cannot trust Atahuallpa, for he had his own brother killed and might do the same to Pizarro, his surrogate brother. Glenn sees this unconscious love-hate relationship (Peter/Anthony) manifested in the Pizarro/Atahuallpa brotherhood.

46. Glenn, "Psychoanalytic Essay," 296.

47. The contrast between Pizarro's lost faith and Atahuallpa's sense of worship has been explored by a number of critics. For example, see Dean, "Recurrent Character Type," 297–305; Michael Gillespie, "Peter Shaffer: 'To Make Whatever God There Is,'" *Claudel Studies* 9, no. 2 (1982): 61–70; Dennis Klein, "*Amadeus:* The Third Part of Peter Shaffer's Dramatic Trilogy," *Modern Language Studies* 13 (1983): 31–38; Dennis Klein, *Peter Shaffer* (Boston: G. K. Hall, 1979), 91–92; Barbara Lounsberry, "'God-Hunting': The Chaos of Worship in Peter Shaffer's *Equus* and *Royal Hunt of the Sun*," *Modern Drama* 21, no. 1 (1978): 13–28; and James R. Stacy, "The Sun and the Horse: Peter Shaffer's Search for Worship," *Educational Theatre Journal* 28, no. 3 (1976): 325–37.

48. Dennis Klein also makes this comparison in his book on Shaffer, as does Barbara Lounsberry in her article on *Equus* and *Royal Hunt.* See Klein, *Peter Shaffer,* 93, and Lounsberry, "'God-Hunting,'" 18–19.

49. Barbara Lounsberry argues that Pizarro also has Christ-like attributes and therefore has an intrinsic interest in his godlike counterpart. She describes Pizarro's expedition as a "Second Coming" of Christ, entering Peru with a wound in his side. He spends six weeks in the forests (approximately forty days) before traveling to Cajamarca, which she equates with Jerusalem. Lounsberry notes that "Pizarro tells his men to move over the land as if they were 'figures from a Lent Procession' (p. 23), and indeed the road is lined with eucalyptus trees (p. 27)." See Lounsberry, "'God-Hunting,'" 19.

50. This point is admirably noted by Stacy, 335–37.

51. "Peter Shaffer Restores the Spectacle," *Evening Standard,* 8 July 1964, 6.

52. Artaud, 126. "Au point de vue historique, *la Conquête du Mexique* pose la question de la colonisation. Elle fait revivre de façon brutale, implacable, sanglante, la fatuité toujours vivace de l'Europe. Elle permet de dégonfler l'idée qu'elle a de sa propre supériorité. Elle oppose le Christianisme à des religions beaucoup plus vieilles. Elle fait justice des fausses conceptions que l'Occident a pu avoir du paganisme et de certaines religions naturelles et elle souligne d'une manière pathétique, brûlante, la splendeur et la poésie toujours actuelle du vieux fonds métaphysique sur lequel ces religions sont bâties" (Antonin Artaud, *Le théâtre et son double* [Paris: Gallimard, 1964], 192).

53. Artaud, 128. "Ces images, ces mouvements, ces danses, ces rites, ces musiques, ces mélodies tronquées, ces dialogues qui tournent court, seront soigneusement notés et décrits autant qu'il se peut avec des mots et principalement dans les parties non dialoguées du spectacle, le principe étant d'arriver à noter ou à chiffrer, comme sur une partition musicale, ce qui ne se décrit pas avec des mots" (Artaud, *Le théâtre*, 194).

54. Artaud, 95. "des qualités des tons particulières . . ." (Artaud, *Le théâtre*, 145).

55. Peter Adam, "Peter Shaffer on Faith, Farce and Masks," *The Listener*, 14 October 1976, 477.

56. Shaffer probably chose to dramatize the conquest of the Incas because Spanish culture is so traditional and is rigidly regulated and codified by a strong sense of religion; it therefore makes quite a contrast with the freedom reflected by the Inca spirit. Artaud also believed that such a contrast between the two cultures would make for an interesting play.

Chapter 7. *Black Comedy* and *The White Liars:*
The Maestro Turns to Farce

1. Brian Connell, "The Two Sides of Theatre's Agonised Perfectionist," *The Times*, 28 April 1980, 7.

2. See "Total Darkness Lit by Brilliant Gags," *The Times*, 28 July 1965, 14; David Frost, "Theatre," *Punch*, 4 August 1965, 174–75; Bernard Levin, "Out of the Darkness, a Blind Farce," *Daily Mail*, 29 July 1965, 12; Ronald Bryden, "No-Man's Land," *New Statesman*, 6 August 1965, 194–95; Philip Hope-Wallace, "*Black Comedy* and *Miss Julie* at Chichester," *The Manchester Guardian*, 28 July 1965, 7; Milton Shulman, "It's a Mad, Mad Romp . . . ," *Evening Standard*, 28 July 1965, 4; and J. C. Trewin, "When the Light is Dark Enough at Chichester," *The Illustrated London News*, 7 August 1965, 36.

3. The play had a two-week trial run in Boston during January before its New York debut.

4. See "Dancing in the Dark," *Time*, 17 February 1967, 70; John Chapman, "Peter Shaffer's Black Comedies: A Splendid Theatrical Evening," *Daily News*, 13 February 1967, in *New York Theater Critics' Reviews—1967*, 371; Richard P. Cooke, "Shaffer Strikes Again," *Wall Street Journal*, 14 February 1967, in *New York Theater Critics' Reviews—1967*, 372; Henry Hewes, "When You're Having More Than One," *Saturday Review*, 25 February 1967, 59; John McCarten, "Chinese Kookie," *The New Yorker*, 25 February 1967, 91; Norman Nadel, "Hilarity Never Stops for *Black Comedy*," *New York World Journal Tribune*, 13 February 1967, in *New York Theater Critics' Reviews—1967*, 373; and Richard Watts, Jr., "Comedy of Light in Darkness," *New York Post*, 13 February 1967, in *New York Theater Critics' Reviews—1967*, 372.

5. Walter Kerr, "Theater: Vaudeville Variations on Chinese Theme," *The New York Times*, 13 February 1967, in *New York Theatre Critics' Reviews—1967*, 372.

6. Ibid., 374.

7. See Harold Clurman, "Theatre," *The Nation*, 27 February 1967, 285–86, and Mel Gussow, "Shedding No Light," *Newsweek*, 20 February 1967, 102–103.

8. Clurman, "Theatre," 286.

9. Ibid.

10. Ibid.

11. Gussow, "Shedding No Light," 102.

12. Ibid., 103.

13. Peter Shaffer, "Preface," *The Collected Plays of Peter Shaffer* (New York: Harmony Books, 1982), xiii.

14. See Jeremy Kingston, "Theatre," *Punch,* 28 February 1968, 319; Herbert Kretzmer, "Fortune Telling? My Own Forecast is a Hit," *Daily Express,* 22 February 1968, 3; Rich, "Show Abroad," *Variety,* 13 March 1968, 75; and Peter Lewis, "Black or White, It's Mostly Magic," *Daily Mail,* 23 February 1968, 12.

15. Kingston, "Theatre," 319.

16. Lewis, "Black or White," 12.

17. See Alan Brien, "Middle-Aged Absurdity," *The Sunday Telegraph,* 25 February 1968, 14; Philip Hope-Wallace, "Peter Shaffer Double Bill at the Lyric Theatre," *The Manchester Guardian,* 22 February 1968, 6; and Milton Shulman, "Dark Laughter . . . ," *Evening Standard,* 22 February 1968, 4.

18. Shulman, "Dark Laughter," 4.

19. Brien, "Absurdity," 14.

20. Hope-Wallace, "Double Bill," 20.

21. See J. R. T., "New Players Encouraged to Ape," *The Times,* 22 February 1968, 13; Ronald Bryden, "Red-nosed Revival," *The Observer,* 25 February 1968, 26; and Philip French, "Surprise, Surprise," *New Statesman,* 1 March 1968, 279.

22. French, "Surprise," 279.

23. Bryden, "Red-nosed Revival," 26.

24. J. R. T., "New Players," 13.

25. Connell, "Agonised Perfectionist," 7.

26. During my interview with Shaffer, he mentioned that it is important to write comedy from time to time because it tests the playwright's talents. Laughter is the acid test to determine whether or not the playwright is reaching his audience. In addition, Shaffer said that when the audience laughs in the appropriate places, it gives the playwright a feeling that he "belongs to the human race," reducing his sense of alienation from others.

27. Samuel Hirsch, "English Playwright Finds New York is His Real Home," *The Boston Herald,* 11 January 1967, C33.

28. See Connell, "Agonised Perfectionist," 7. In this article, Shaffer refers to the Apollonian-Dionysian conflict in his plays and also within him. He feels that comedy and the well-made play (the Apollonian) is a well-balanced contrast to his hidden desires—i.e., total theater (the Dionysian).

29. Connell, "Agonised Perfectionist," 7.

30. Peter Shaffer, *Black Comedy and White Lies* (New York: Stein and Day, 1967), 111. All subsequent citations are from this edition and are included within parentheses in the text.

31. Although *White Lies* was produced on Broadway, it should be treated as a draft of the play. Shaffer felt that the play needed to be polished up a bit more, so he virtually rewrote it. Shaffer's revisions do not merely involve changing a few words.

The first rewrite, the version of the play that was staged at the Lyric Theatre in London, was highlighted by a tape recording that "represents whatever is happening inside Sophie's head at the moment it is heard; either present thought, or recollection." See "Note on the Tape," *The White Liars and Black Comedy* (New York: Samuel French, 1968), 4. In addition, Shaffer sensed that putting Vassi's voice on tape to talk with Sophie, his former lover, added little to the play. He insisted on a second rewrite, which is now the definitive version of the play.

There are a number of differences between *White Lies* and the final version of *The White Liars;* some of them are major changes, and others are minor ones.

In *White Lies,* Frank is an aggressive rake, a confident, cocky, even threatening individual similar to Ted in *The Private Ear.* In *The White Liars,* he is much more subdued, polite, and less cocky or threatening. In the latter play, Tom appears to be the more outspoken, aggressive, and extroverted individual.

In *White Lies,* Frank was devious and vicious; he asked Sophie to devise a story in which Tom would be caught in bed with Frank's girlfriend, Helen. As the story unfolds, a mysterious figure in a corduroy jacket (supposedly Frank) enters and sets the bed on fire, turning Tom and Helen into ashes. In *The White Liars,* there is no mention of a "burning bed"; instead, Sophie actually helps Frank with the story and makes up her own denouement, thereby making Frank look less deceitful. In the original play, Sophie agreed to help Frank because she was being bribed, whereas in the rewritten version, she sides with Frank because she sees Tom as a "taker" while she and Frank are "givers." In other words, Tom is erroneously classified as a "working-class thug" who takes from others, and Sophie despises these types of individuals.

In *White Lies,* Sophie took a liking to Tom almost immediately because he reminded her of Vassili, Sophie's lover. In *The White Liars,* however, Tom and Sophie are hardly compatible at first, and it is actually Tom who unmasks the fortune teller as the liar. Tom decides on his own to drop the mask and tell the truth about his past—Sophie hardly plays a part in Tom's decision.

Perhaps the most important change in the play relates to Tom's motives for lying about his past. In the earlier play, Tom lied about his working-class background to gain acceptance into the world of pop music where a middle-class background was a detriment. When he learned that Helen (now Susan in *The White Liars*) doted on the image that he had created for himself, Tom decided to stick with the phony story. In *The White Liars,* Tom already had a successful band when he first met Frank, who, posing as a journalist, approached Tom so that he could do a story on Tom's pop music group. As Frank asked Tom questions about his background, Tom knew that Frank, actually the owner of a boutique and a bogus journalist, idolized the myth of the working-class musician. So Tom, in order to keep Frank's myth alive, became what Frank wanted him to be.

The only other major changes in the play involve Sophie. In *White Lies,* she had a parakeet and engaged in a running dialogue with Vassili's portrait. In the latter play, the parakeet is gone, and Vassili is now replaced with a photo of Sophie's father.

There are certainly many other changes, but they appear to be relatively minor ones.

32. Peter Shaffer, *The White Liars* in *The Collected Plays of Peter Shaffer* (New York: Harmony Books, 1982), 155. All subsequent citations are from this edition and are included within parentheses in the text.

33. Peter Shaffer, interview with author, New York City, 19 April 1986.

Chapter 8. *Shrivings:* Words, Words, Words

1. Peter Shaffer, "A Note on the Play: 1974," in *Shrivings* (London: André Deutsch, 1974), 9.

2. During my interview with Shaffer (19 April 1986), he confirmed the fact that Bertrand Russell was one of the models for Gideon Petrie. Critics were able to make the connection because Russell died on 2 February 1970, three days before the play opened in London.

3. See Jeremy Kingston, "At the Theatre," *Punch,* 11 February 1970, 236; Milton Shulman, "Arguments Without Soul," *Evening Standard,* 6 February 1970, 24; and Philip Hope-Wallace, "*Battle of Shrivings* at the Lyric Theatre," *The Manchester Guardian,* 6 February 1970, 8.

4. Hope-Wallace, "Lyric Theatre," 8.

5. Kingston, "At the Theatre," 236.

6. Frank Marcus, "Poet v. Philosopher," *The Sunday Telegraph,* 8 February 1970, 14.

7. Ibid.

8. See Irving Wardle, "Philosopher of Peace," *The Times,* 6 February 1970, 13; Ronald Bryden, "Echoes of Russell," *The Observer,* 8 February 1970, 31; Harold Hobson, "Gielgud, Shaffer, and Hall—Had a Great Fall," *The Christian Science Monitor,* 13 February 1970, 6; Harold Hobson, "All Too Black and White," *The Sunday Times,* 8 February 1970, 53; Benedict Nightingale, "Some Immortal Business," *New Statesman,* 13 February 1970, 227; Eric Shorter, "Gielgud and Magee as Mouthpieces of Ideas," *Daily Telegraph,* 6 February 1970, 16; J. C. Trewin, "Noisy Weekend," *The Illustrated London News,* 21 February 1970, 26; B. A. Young, "The Battle of Shrivings," *Financial Times,* 6 February 1970, 3; and Bail, "Show Abroad," *Variety,* 11 February 1970, 61.

9. Hobson, "All Too Black and White," 53.

10. Bryden, "Echoes of Russell," 31.

11. Nightingale, "Immortal Business," 227.

12. Shaffer, "A Note on the Play: 1974," 7.

13. Peter Shaffer, "Preface," *The Collected Plays of Peter Shaffer* (New York: Harmony Books, 1982), xiv.

14. Shaffer, "A Note on the Play: 1974," 7–8.

15. Ibid., 9.

16. The earlier version of the play has never been printed and was not included in the collected edition of Shaffer's dramas. Shaffer has no plans to print the play.

17. Shaffer, "Preface," xiii.

18. Peter Shaffer, interview with author, New York City, 19 April 1986.

19. Shaffer, "A Note on the Play: 1974," 7.

20. Glenn Loney, "Which Twin Has the Tony?" *After Dark,* April 1971, 22.

21. During his discussion of *Shrivings* in an interview with *After Dark* (April 1971), Shaffer revealed why profound philosophical questions are difficult to state in the form of dialectical theater. Shaffer noted that theater is more than just a debate between two parties: one side must have an advantage, otherwise the audience will feel cheated or confused. What is interesting here is that Shaffer chose *Marat/Sade* as his example of a dialectic that works on stage (Loney, "Which Twin?" 22). Yet *Marat/Sade* works well not just because one party (Sade) has the edge in the debate; the play is effective because Peter Weiss was able to combine Artaudian elements with a philosophical debate that even Brecht would have appreciated. Unfortunately, *Shrivings* fails to unite ritualistic theater with the Ibsenite elements.

22. Peter Shaffer, *Shrivings* (London: André Deutsch, 1974), 50. All subsequent citations are from this edition and are included within parentheses in the text.

23. Loney, "Which Twin?" 22.

24. For a more thorough discussion of the religious nomenclature in the play, see Dennis Klein, "Literary Onomastics in Peter Shaffer's *Shrivings* and *Equus,*" *Literary Onomastics Studies* 7(1980):127–38.

25. In his introduction to the play, Shaffer tells us that in the Middle Ages, Shrivings was a House of Retreat (13). Wayne Paul Lawson was the first person to note that Shrivings, by its Latin and Old English origins, means penance or confession. See "The Dramatic Hunt: A Critical Evaluation of Peter Shaffer's Plays," Ph.D. diss., Ohio State University, 1974, 120.

26. See Barbara Lounsberry, "Peter Shaffer's *Amadeus* and *Shrivings:* God-Hunting Continued," *Theatre Annual* 39 (1984):26.

27. The reader must keep in mind that "my dear" can also be an expression of endearment, and the British sometimes use it in such a manner. Some of Shaffer's

other characters use this expression, although not as often as Gideon does. In addition, one should recall that Shaffer parodied homosexual connotations of "dear" in his one-scene satire, "But My Dear," written for *That Was the Week That Was.*

28. See Joan F Dean, "The Family as Microcosm in Peter Shaffer's Plays," *Ball State University Forum* 23, no. 1(1982):33.

29. Peter Shaffer, interview with author, New York City, 19 April 1986.

30. See Joan F Dean, "Peter Shaffer's Recurrent Character Type," *Modern Drama* 21, no. 3 (1978):297–305; Dennis Klein, *Peter Shaffer* (Boston: G. K. Hall, 1979), 104; and Lounsberry, "God-Hunting Continued," 25.

31. Dean, "Recurrent Character Type," 297.

32. Ibid., 297–98; and Klein, *Peter Shaffer,* 104.

33. Rites and rhythmic structures, so important in unconsciously developing communication between the audience and the protagonist, perhaps are not as essential in *Shrivings* as in the other three plays mentioned. For example, in *The Royal Hunt of the Sun, Equus,* and *Amadeus,* a narrator is used to address the audience directly, yet no such narrator exists in *Shrivings,* forcing one to question Shaffer's intentions of involving the audience directly in the performance.

Chapter 9. *Equus:* The Beat Goes On

1. The film was not a box-office success, despite excellent performances by Richard Burton, Peter Firth, and Joan Plowright. During a Special Session, "Assessing Peter Shaffer's Stage Mastery," held at the Modern Language Association (MLA) Convention on 29 December 1983, Shaffer expressed disappointment in the movie, noting that the stylized presentation of the play was lost in director Sidney Lumet's literal application of the screenplay to the film. Furthermore, in letters and tapes to C.J. Gianakaris, Shaffer also discussed his displeasure with the film version of *Equus:* "I wrote the script originally. Not that it did me much good, because the script I wrote was not really shot. I think . . . I did much more imaginative work than was shot. . . . I don't want to attack anybody particular. Sidney Lumet did a very competent job. And he included me in all the time. What depressed me about the film is that it didn't have any of the images I wanted to see in it. I was very disappointed in the visual side of it." See C.J. Gianakaris, "Drama into Film: "The Shaffer Situation," *Modern Drama* 28, no. 1 (1985):87.

2. See Harold Hobson, "Shaffer Gallops to Glory and Explains What Makes Him Run," *The Sunday Times,* 29 July 1973, 33; John Barber, "Fascinating Play on an Obsession," *Daily Telegraph,* 27 July 1973, 13; Michael Billington, "*Equus* at the Old Vic," *The Manchester Guardian,* 27 July 1973, 12; Jeremy Kingston, "Theatre," *Punch,* 8 August 1973, 188; B. A. Young, *"Equus,"* Financial Times, 27 July 1973, 3: Milton Shulman, "Milton Shulman at the Old Vic," *Evening Standard,* 27 July 1973, 28–29; Pit, "Shows Abroad," *Variety,* 8 August 1973, 44; and Russell Davies, "Horses for Courses," *New Statesman,* 3 August 1973, 165–66.

3. Pit, "Shows Abroad," 44.

4. Billington, "At the Old Vic," 12.

5. Shulman, "Milton Shulman," 29.

6. Barber, "Fascinating Play," 13.

7. Davies, "Horses for Courses," 165.

8. Irving Wardle, "Shaffer's Variation on a Theme," *The Times,* 27 July 1973, 15.

9. Robert Cushman, "Horsemanship at the National," *The Observer,* 29 July 1973, 30.

10. Ian Christie, "Not a lot of Horse-Sense," *Daily Express,* 27 July 1973, 10.

11. See Clive Barnes, "*Equus* a New Success on Broadway," *The New York Times,*

25 October 1974, in *New York Theater Critics' Reviews—1974*, 204–205; John Beaufort, "Brilliant British Import," *The Christian Science Monitor*, 4 November 1974, in *New York Theater Critics' Reviews—1974*, 202; Harold Clurman, "Theatre," *The Nation*, 16 November 1974, 506–507; Brendan Gill, "Unhorsed," *The New Yorker*, 4 November 1974, 123–24; Hobe, "Show on Broadway," *Variety*, 30 October 1974, 88, 90; Jack Kroll, "Horse Power," *Newsweek*, 4 November 1974, 60; Douglas Watt, "*Equus* is a Smashing Psychodrama," *Daily News*, 25 October 1974, in *New York Theater Critics' Reviews—1974*, 201–202; Edwin Wilson, "Conflicting Elements in a Human Soul," *Wall Street Journal*, 28 October 1974, in *New York Theater Critics' Reviews—1974*, 203; Henry Hewes, "The Crime of Dispassion," *Saturday Review*, 25 January 1975, 54; Martin Gottfried, "Shaffer's *Equus* at the Plymouth," *New York Post*, 25 October 1974, in *New York Theater Critics' Reviews—1974*, 206.

12. Barnes, "New Success," 205.

13. Clurman, "Theatre," 506.

14. Wilson, "Conflicting Elements," 203.

15. T. E. Kalem, "Freudian Exorcism," *Time*, 4 November 1974, 119.

16. Stanley Kauffmann, "*Equus*," *The New Republic*, 7 December 1974, 33.

17. John Simon, "Hippodrama at the Psychodrome," *The Hudson Review* 28, no. 1 (1975):105.

18. *Equus* has done quite well with regard to reviews written in publications with a religious orientation. For example, see Dean Ebner, "The Double Crisis of Sexuality and Worship in Peter Shaffer's *Equus*," *Christianity and Literature* 31, no. 2 (1982):29–47; Samuel Terrien, "*Equus*: Human Conflicts and the Trinity," *Christian Century*, 18 May 1977, 472–76; Frederick Sontag, "God's Eyes Everywhere," *Christian Century*, 17 December 1975, 1162, 1164; and Harold Hobson, "A Triumph at London's National Theater [sic]," *The Christian Science Monitor*, 10 August 1973, 14.

19. Those critics who have implied that the play is either an attack on church doctrine or a defense of unrestricted worship or madness include John Corbally, "The *Equus* Ethic," *New Laurel Review* 7, no. 2 (1977):53–58; Jack Richardson, "The English Invasion," *Commentary*, February 1975, 76–78; and William Lynch, "What's Wrong With *Equus*? Ask Euripides," *America*, 13 December 1975, 419–22.

20. Mel Gussow, "Shaffer Details a Mind's Journey in *Equus*," *The New York Times*, 24 October 1974, 50.

21. Peter Shaffer, "Figure of Death," *The Observer*, 4 November 1979, 37.

22. Baldwin characterizes *Equus* as a soap opera that titillates the audience with "sexuality spiced with cruelty." See "*Equus*: Theater of Cruelty or Theater of Sensationalism?" *Philological Papers* (West Virginia University) 25 (1978):118–27.

23. Simon, "Hippodrama," 99–102.

24. Sanford Gifford, "Pop Psychoanalysis, *Kitsch*, and the 'As If' Theater: Further Notes on Peter Shaffer's *Equus*," *International Journal of Psychoanalytic Psychotherapy* 5 (1976):463–71.

25. James Lee, "*Equus*, Round Three," *Exchange* 2 (Spring 1976):66.

26. Tom Buckley, "'Write Me,' Said the Play to Peter Shaffer," *The New York Times Magazine*, 13 April 1975, 30.

27. Peter Shaffer, "Preface," *The Collected Plays of Peter Shaffer* (New York: Harmony Books, 1982), xv.

28. Psychiatrists such as Sanford Gifford have compared the play to tragedy and have concluded that there is little empathy for the characters and not much audience participation; thus, fear and pity cannot be purged. Gifford assumes that because the play is not a tragedy, it cannot be effective theater. This is an obvious example of the faulty logic that can accrue when psychiatrists attempt to become theater critics. Interestingly enough, almost all of the psychiatrists who have written on the play

deal with content; they neglect form, style, diction, stagecraft, setting, costuming, lighting, music, and movement, simply because they do not have the expertise to discuss these often vital components of a play. *Equus,* of course, ironically succeeds as drama because of the effective interweaving of these theatrical components, which psychiatrists unfortunately ignore.

29. John Dexter actually decided on the performers doing the final scene in the nude. Furthermore, Dexter was responsible for the bare set, the lighting effects, the use of bleachers for spectators, as well as for the stylized set of masks for the horse-actors.

30. Sanford Gifford, "Psychoanalyst Says Nay to *Equus,*" *The New York Times,* 15 December 1974, sec. 2, p. 5.

31. Ibid., 1.

32. Shaffer, "Preface," xvi.

33. "*Equus:* Playwright Peter Shaffer Interprets Its Ritual," *Vogue,* February 1975, 192.

34. Peter Shaffer, "Scripts in Trans-Atlantic Crossings May Suffer Two Kinds of Changes," *Dramatists Guild Quarterly,* Spring 1980, 30.

35. The critics who maintain this belief include Kauffmann (*"Equus,"* 33) and Simon ("Hippodrama," 101).

36. Peter Shaffer, *Equus* (New York: Avon Books, 1974), 11. All subsequent citations are from this edition and are included within parentheses in the text.

37. Buckley, " 'Write Me,' " 30.

38. Shaffer, *Equus,* 11–12.

39. Shaffer, "Scripts in Trans-Atlantic Crossings," 30.

40. J. Alexis Burland, "Discussion of Papers on *Equus,*" *International Journal of Psychoanalytic Psychotherapy* 5 (1976): 501–502.

41. Buckley, " 'Write Me,' " 20.

42. Gussow, "Mind's Journey," 50.

43. The first critic to point this out was John Russell Taylor, *Peter Shaffer,* Writers and Their Work Series, no. 244 (Harlow, Essex: Longman Group, 1974), 27. Other critics who have noted the similarities beween *Equus* and Laing's work include Dennis Klein, *Peter Shaffer* (Boston: G. K. Hall, 1979), 128, and Gifford, "Psychoanalyst Says Nay to *Equus,*" 5.

44. Jeffrey Berman, "*Equus:* After Such Little Forgiveness, What Knowledge?" *The Psychoanalytic Review* 66, no. 2 (1979): 408.

45. See Michael Hinden, "When Playwrights Talk to God: Peter Shaffer and the Legacy of O'Neill," *Comparative Drama* 16, no. 1 (1982): 55, and Doyle W. Walls, "*Equus:* Shaffer, Nietzsche, and the Neuroses of Health," *Modern Drama* 27, no. 3 (1984): 314–15. Walls states, however, that the link between Shaffer and Nietzsche is "tenuous," although Hinden is more certain of the parallels.

46. Barbara Lounsberry, " 'God-Hunting': The Chaos of Worship in Peter Shaffer's *Equus* and *Royal Hunt of the Sun,*" *Modern Drama* 21, no. 2 (1978): 13–28, especially 22–27.

47. Corbally, "The *Equus* Ethic," 53.

48. Peter Adam, "Peter Shaffer on Faith, Farce and Masks," *The Listener,* 14 October 1976, 476.

49. Shaffer, realizing that the original story of the blinding of twenty-six horses was too unwieldy for the stage, changed the number to six. The number seems to have a significant part in the play. In J. E. Cirlot's *A Dictionary of Symbols,* 2d ed., trans. Jack Sage (London: Routledge and Kegan Paul, 1974), 233, Cirlot explains that the Greeks (the culture that Dysart worships) viewed six as the number associated with hermaphrodites. It is also known as the symbol of ambivalence, equilibrium

(the scales), and virginity. The number both applies to Dysart, the sterile role player, and to Alan, the virgin. When taken together, the Alan Strang–Martin Dysart "twinship" can be construed as the balance of the scales—each needs the other and feeds off of his alter ego. The number six seems to pervade the whole play. Both characters interact with each other and with five different characters in the play (Frank and Dora Strang, Jill Mason, Harry Dalton, and Hesther Salomon). Dysart, who has not kissed his wife in six years (95), is distraught over his sterile life. Alan, who eventually blinds six horses, had his first sexual experience with a horse at age six on the beach. Six years later, at age twelve, Alan takes the picture in his room of the beaten Christ and replaces it with a photograph of a horse staring straight ahead. About six years later, at age seventeen, Alan has begun to identify with Equus as a sort of sexual partner. In addition, the three episodes, each taking place in six-year intervals, suggest the mark of the devil: 666. Shaffer downplays the use of this number, but he allows Dora to sermonize about the Beast: "But if you knew God, Doctor, you would know about the Devil. You'd know the Devil isn't made by what mummy says and daddy says. The Devil's *there*. . . . I only knew he was my little Alan, and then the Devil came" (91).

50. I am indebted to Jeffrey Berman for this insightful comment. His analysis of eye imagery in the play led me to some useful information about Alan's relationship to his father. See Berman, "Such Little Forgiveness," 417–18.

51. Shaffer, who has referred to his admiration for Jung, is probably using a Jungian idea here. In *Aion: Researches into the Phenomenology of the Self,* trans. R. F. C. Hull (Princeton: Princeton University Press, 1959), Jung claims that "Christ exemplifies the archetype of the Self. He represents a totality of divine or heavenly kind, a glorified man, a Son of God *sine macula peccati,* unspotted by sin" (37). In his chapter, "A Psychological Approach to the Trinity," in *Psychology and Religion: West and East,* trans. R. F. C. Hull (Princeton,: Princeton University Press, 1955), Jung states that "through the Christ-symbol, man can get to know the real meaning of his suffering: He is on the way towards realizing his wholeness. As a result of integration of conscious and unconscious, his ego enters the 'divine' realm, where it participates in 'God suffering' " (157).

52. Jung writes about wholeness in the Trinity (*Aion,* 224) and in Christ (*Aion,* 41). The idea was suggested by James R. Stacy, "The Sun and the Horse: Peter Shaffer's Search for Worship," *Educational Theatre Journal* 28, no. 3 (1976): 332.

53. There are no references in the play to suggest that Alan was physically thrashed by his parents. However, it is interesting to note that Alan's genealogical litany includes "Spankus," and it is exactly in the *middle,* the center of this order: Prince; Prance; Prankus; Flankus; Spankus; Spunkus the Great; Legwus; Neckwus; Fleckwus, the King of Spit; and Equus (58).

54. Alan's ride on the horse is reminiscent of Revelation 19:11–15. Alan calls out to "Equus the Godslave, Faithful and True" (83). The passage in the King James Bible (Revelation 19:11) is as follows: "And I saw heaven opened, and behold a white horse; and he that sat upon him *was* called Faithful and True, and in righteousness he doth judge and make war."

Alan's Manbit, the sacred bit for his mouth, the "sharp chain" that Dysart acknowledges is in his own mouth, is from Revelation 19:15: "And out of his mouth goeth a sharp sword, that with it he should smite the nations; and he shall rule them with a rod of iron; and he treadeth the winepress of the fierceness and wrath of Almighty God." See *The New Layman's Parallel Bible* (Grand Rapids, Mi.: Zondervan Bible Publishers, 1981), 3184.

55. A number of critics have pointed this out, including Ebner, "Double Crisis," 36; Lounsberry, " 'God-Hunting,' " 22; and Walls, "Neuroses of Health," 319.

56. Psychiatrists (and some literary critics) examining the play have been quick to

point out that Alan has an Oedipus complex. Dr. Julius L. Stamm believes that Alan's love for horses is a displacement of oedipal desires, much like Freud's famous patient, "Little Hans." He equates Jill Mason (an older woman) with Alan's mother and hypothesizes that Alan's blinding of the horses is a reaction against the father figure watching over the son having sexual relations with his mother. See Julius L. Stamm, "Peter Shaffer's *Equus*—A Psychoanalytic Exploration," *International Journal of Psychoanalytic Psychotherapy* 5 (1976): 455–57. Dr. Jules Glenn also believes that Alan was actually destroying his father's eyes in the stable because Alan was having "tabooed oedipal gratification" with Jill. See Jules Glenn, "Alan Strang as an Adolescent: A Discussion of Peter Shaffer's *Equus*," *International Journal of Psychoanalytic Psychotherapy* 5 (1976): 480, and Glenn, "Twins in the Theater: A Study of Plays by Peter and Anthony Shaffer," in *Blood Brothers: Siblings as Writers*, ed. Norman Kiell (New York: International Universities Press, 1983), 290. In the latter article, Glenn states that after Alan blinds the horses, he turns the pick on his own eyes, blinding himself like Oedipus.

Psychiatrists, by their very nature, find Freudian implications even in our daily activities. Alan, as has already been discussed, fears his father's authoritarianism. However, there is no evidence in the play that Alan has any sexual attraction for his mother. Jill Mason is slightly older than Alan, but she in no way can be equated with Alan's mother. For additional insight into psychoanalytic interpretations of the play, see Margaret A. Emelson, "A Horse of a Different Color: A Critique of Peter Shaffer's *Equus*," *Journal of Evolutionary Psychology* 1, no. 2 (1980): 75–80.

57. Simon, "Hippodrama," 99.

58. Simon even suggests that the "bite" of "Manbit" refers to the French homonym for "penis" (ibid., 101).

59. The idea was originally noted by Taylor, *Peter Shaffer*, 30.

60. Walls, "Neuroses of Health," 316.

61. See Joan F. Dean, "Peter Shaffer's Recurrent Character Type," *Modern Drama* 21, no. 3 (1978): 297–305; Michael Gillespie, "Peter Shaffer: 'To Make Whatever God There Is,'" *Claudel Studies* 9, no. 2 (1982): 61–70; Klein, *Peter Shaffer*, 124; Lounsberry, "'God-Hunting,'" 13–28; and Stacy, "Search for Worship," 325–37.

62. This is Gillespie's thesis in his article. See "Whatever God There Is," 61–63.

63. Hesther Salomon's role in the play is to provide the audience with the necessary background material and to act as a sounding board for Dysart's frustrations. Dennis Klein notes that her first name is derived from the biblical Queen Esther who prudently saved the Hebrews from destruction, while Salomon is a take-off on King Solomon, Israel's wisest king. (See Klein, *Peter Shaffer*, 128.) In the play, she is the strong voice of reason, urging Dysart to continue his work for the good of humanity. Barbara Lounsberry has aptly compared Hesther to De Soto, and although Hesther is an admirable and "noble" character, Lounsberry also finds her to be "enigmatic." (See Lounsberry, "'God-Hunting,'" 27.) De Soto was certainly a Shafferian role player, yet his nobility extended only as far as his lineage. Dean Ebner's analysis of Hesther as an advocate of social norms is perhaps more appropriate. (See Ebner, "Double Crisis," 32.) In this sense, Hesther Salomon could easily be mistaken for De Soto.

64. This point has been made by Russell Vandenbroucke, "*Equus*: Modern Myth in the Making," *Drama and Theater* 12, no. 2 (1975): 131.

65. For a more detailed discussion of the concept of "Paradise Lost" in *The Royal Hunt of the Sun, Equus,* and *Amadeus,* see Gillespie, "Whatever God There Is," 61–70.

66. See Glenn's articles, "Alan Strang as an Adolescent," 473–87; "Anthony and Peter Shaffer's Plays: The Influence of Twinship on Creativity," *American Imago* 31 (Fall 1974): 270–92; and "Twins in the Theater," 277–99.

67. Again, the idea that Shaffer was a twin himself competing with brother

Anthony for love and affection is Glenn's starting point. Glenn claims that the twins are literally joined in the prenatal stage, and each brother later seeks a union with his alter ego. Glenn transfers this rivalry to the Alan Strang–Martin Dysart relationship. Even psychiatrist James W. Hamilton has gone so far as to suggest that *Shrivings,* Shaffer's previous play, was a failure while *Sleuth,* written in the same year, was successful; the competition between the two playwrights, Hamilton claims, forced Peter to write a successful play *(Equus)* the next time out. Hamilton makes the connection between Alan Strang and Anthony Shaffer quite clear when he notes that they both have the same initials (it is assumed that Peter identifies with Dysart). See James W. Hamilton, "*Equus* and the Creative Process," *Journal of the Philadelphia Association for Psychoanalysis* 6 (1979): 53–64.

68. Glenn, "Alan Strang as an Adolescent," 484.

69. Klein, *Peter Shaffer,* 124.

70. Glenn believes that Alan unconsciously wishes for a "twin" to whom he can relate. Alan, Glenn asserts, is preoccupied with doubles: the two "u's" in "Equus," the Doublemint gum jingle (which was, in the London production, a catchy tune for Double Diamond Beer, a popular brew in the United Kingdom), horses' eyes, etc. See Glenn, "Alan Strang as an Adolescent," 478; "Anthony and Peter Shaffer's Plays," 276; and "Twins in the Theater," 292. In addition, according to Glenn, Alan's obsession to make horse and rider one person ("Two shall be one") is related to Shaffer's unconscious drive for twinship.

71. For a more detailed psychiatric interpretation of Dysart's dream, see Berman, "Such Little Forgiveness," 410–15, and Stamm, "Psychoanalytic Exploration," 454–55.

72. Peter Shaffer, interview with author, New York City, 19 April 1986.

73. There have been a number of interpretations of Dysart's name. James W. Hamilton believes that the doctor's name relates to his symbolic dream in which the psychiatrist destroys a heart—"dies heart" (Hamilton, "Creative Process," 59). Doyle W. Walls states that Dysart's name "reveals that one quality needed to remedy his existenital problem is art; however, he finds that he lacks the spiritual power of art, that power which generates creation" (Walls, "Neuroses of Health," 320). Michael Hinden suggests that Shaffer chose the name to reflect dysfunction of the healing art (Hinden, "Legacy of O'Neill," 54). Dennis Klein seems to agree with Hinden, explaining that "dys" is the Greek prefix for "difficulty," so appropriate for Dysart who has difficulty performing his art (Klein, *Peter Shaffer,* 128).

74. The relationship between Pizarro and Dysart has been explored by a number of critics. John M. Clum, "Religion and Five Contemporary Plays: The Quest for God in a Godless World," *South Atlantic Quarterly* 77, no. 4 (1978): 418–32, has compared the two characters (429) as have Klein (*Peter Shaffer,* 124) and Gillespie ("Whatever God There Is," 61–65). Joan F. Dean notes that Dysart and Pizarro are each associated with an ancient culture, are trapped by the reverence for the Normal and the Civilized, respectively, and are positively affected by younger alter egos who do not share the older men's pessimism about modern society ("Recurrent Character Type," 297–305). James R. Stacy's article is also an extensive study of the two characters. He mentions that Alan and Atahuallpa worship the horse and the sun, respectively, just as primitives once did. Pizarro and Dysart, both impotent and lifeless, cannot find worship in modern society. Although they long to worship like their alter egos, Pizarro and Dysart allow the band to control their lives, thus destroying the free will of the primitives ("Search for Worship," 325–37). Finally, Barbara Lounsberry depicts Pizarro and Dysart as men in despair, in contrast to Atahuallpa and Alan, younger men who try to be gods. Unfortunately, the idealism of Atahuallpa and Alan is tarnished when faced with the representatives of the "real" world—Pizarro and Dysart (" 'God-Hunting,' " 13–28).

75. See C. J. Gianakaris, "Theatre of the Mind in Miller, Osborne and Shaffer," *Renascence* 30, no. 1 (1977): 39.

76. Klein, *Peter Shaffer,* 136.

77. See Neil Timm, "*Equus* as a Modern Tragedy," *Philological Papers* (West Virginia University) 25 (1978): 133.

78. Antonin Artaud, *The Theater and Its Double,* trans. Mary Caroline Richards (New York: Grove Press, 1958), 80. "Je propose d'en revenir au théâtre à cette idée élémentaire magique, reprise par la psychanalyse moderne, qui consiste pour obtenir la guérison d'un malade à lui faire prendre l'attitude extérieure de l'état auquel on voudrait le ramener" (Antonin Artaud, *Le théâtre et son double* [Paris: Gallimard, 1964], 122).

79. Artaud, *The Theater,* 82. "Après le son et la lumière il y a l'action, et le dynamisme de l'action: c'est ici que le théâtre loin de copier la vie se met en communication s'il le peut avec des forces pures. Et qu'on les accept ou qu'on les nie, il y a tout de même une façon de parler qui appelle forces ce qui fait naître dans l'inconscient des images énergiques, et a l'extérieure le crime gratuit.

Une action violente et ramassée est une similitude de lyrisme: elle appelle des images surnaturelles, un sang d'images, et un jet sanglant d'images aussi bien dans la tête du poète que dans celle du spectateur" (Artaud, *Le théâtre,* 125).

80. Artaud, *The Theater,* 145. "C'est là, dans cette atmosphère sacrée, que Jean-Louis Barrault improvise les mouvements d'un cheval sauvage, et qu'on a tout à coup la surprise de le voir devenu cheval.

Son spectacle prouve l'action irrésistible du geste, il démontre victorieusement l'importance du geste et du mouvement dans l'espace. Il redonne à la perspective théâtrale l'importance qu'elle n'aurait pas dû perdre. Il fait de la scène enfin un lieu pathétique et vivant" (Artaud, *Le théâtre,* 214).

81. During my interview with Shaffer, he recalled having dinner in France with Jean-Louis Barrault, who made the comparison between *Equus* and the centaur-horse. Unfortunately, Shaffer admitted that his French is a bit weak, and he therefore could not pick up the specific references to which Barrault was referring.

82. Buckley, " 'Write Me,' " 26.

83. Artaud, *The Theater,* 97. ". . . des choses qui exigent d'habitude leur figuration objective seront escamotées ou dissimulées" (Artaud, *Le théâtre,* 148).

84. Gussow, "Mind's Journey," 50.

Chapter 10. *Amadeus:* Just the Right Notes

1. "Peter Shaffer's Personal 'Dialogue,' " *The New York Times,* 6 October 1963, sec. 2, p. 3.

2. Sydney Edwards, "What the Riots Did to Peter Shaffer," *Evening Standard,* 9 January 1970, 20.

3. Glenn Loney, "Which Twin Has the Tony?" *After Dark,* April 1971, 22.

4. Christopher Ford, "High Horse," *The Manchester Guardian,* 6 August 1973, 8.

5. Peter Shaffer, "Preface," *The Collected Plays of Peter Shaffer* (New York: Harmony Books, 1982), xvi.

6. An examination of the film version of the play is beyond the scope of this book, which is primarily concerned with Shaffer's theater. One must keep in mind that there are major differences between the theatrical and film versions of *Amadeus.* More people have probably seen *Amadeus* in movie theaters and on videocassettes than in the theater. Therefore, one must be careful not to confuse the stage version with a substantially different screenplay for the cinema.

In the "Introduction to the Film Edition" of *Amadeus,* Shaffer stated his reservations about working in the film medium. Because of the negative experiences

Shaffer has had in seeing his previous plays turn into lackluster screenplays (which Shaffer often did not write), he was reluctant to collaborate with Milos Forman on the project. In addition, Shaffer, with an ear for a rhythmic structure that may work only on stage, feared a medium that was increasingly becoming more visual at the expense of the verbal: "The cinema is a worrying medium for the stage playwright to work in. Its unverbal essence offers difficulties to anyone living largely by the spoken word." See Peter Shaffer, "Introduction to the Film Edition," *Amadeus* (New York: Signet, 1984), xiii.

How does Shaffer feel about the film version of the play? During my interview with Shaffer, he compared the film to the play: "I love the play *Amadeus,* certainly the American version. I'm very fond of it. But the film I can't claim to be that fond of. It's surprising that one has had universal success with the film. And yet, I think there are coarsenesses in it which I deplore. I sometimes wish it was nearer to the play—more complex and more elegant than it is. The American version of the play is a better piece of work. I think it's more interesting. I think it's truer. The writing in the film is a bit ordinary. There's only one thing I really like very much in the film, which is the dictation scene. It's not as good as the climax in the stage version—the eating of the Requiem. I think the scene of the dictating of the Requiem to a ravenous Salieri is not entirely probable, but it does have a kind of mythic element which I rather like. It's cheeky and outrageous, but in some ways, it has a rather dramatic suitability. And I love the idea of writing a film script for a popular film which consists of about ten pages of nothing but musical direction. I like that very much since most of the young people who see the film have no idea that music was written down at all, let alone how Mozart wrote it. What is interesting is that the cinema, as anyone will tell you over and over again, is a visual medium, concerned largely with visual things. Not so. The climax of *Amadeus* was about music and notes. Just two guys, one lying in bed and the other writing at the end of the desk. And yet, I don't think that could have been staged in the theater."

For information concerning the film production, see Harlan Jacobson, "As Many Notes as Required," *Film Comment,* September/October 1984, 50, 53–55, and Peter Shaffer, "Making the Screen Speak," *Film Comment,* September/October 1984, 51, 56–57. In the latter article, Shaffer mentions that he took more liberties with the historical material in the film version, particularly with regard to Salieri's night-long vigil with Mozart. For an excellent analysis of *Amadeus* as film, see C.J. Gianakaris, "Drama into Film: The Shaffer Situation," *Modern Drama* 28, no. 1 (1985):83–98. The article is intriguing in that it explains Shaffer's painstaking efforts to learn a new medium of art. Working closely with director Milos Forman, Shaffer, starting on 1 February 1982, spent four months—five days a week, twelve hours a day—in a Connecticut farmhouse rewriting the play for the cinema. Shaffer told Gianakaris that the work was tedious, but he hoped to learn more about film: "I just trust that it [the *Amadeus* project] is all for the best! At least I'm learning a little about thinking cinematically. If that is ultimately important I don't mind" (89).

Michiko Kakutani's article, "How *Amadeus* was Translated From Play to Film," *The New York Times,* 16 September 1984, sec. 2, pp. 1, 20, discusses the changes made from play to film. Because of the visual impact of cinematography, long speeches that were in the play have been eliminated from the film version. For example, Salieri's long monologue to God in which he becomes judge-penitent and dragon-slayer at the end of act 1 is now replaced by a visual image—tossing a crucifix into a fire. Salieri no longer confesses to the audience but now tries to absolve himself in front of a priest. Kakutani notes that another important change from play to film is that the latter focuses on Mozart rather than on Salieri. By depicting Mozart as a well-rounded, often complex, individual and also by deemphasizing his scatological language that strongly dominated his stage personality, Shaffer has created a more empathetic character who now dominates the dialectic. For additional details, see also Henry Kamm, "Milos Forman Takes His Cameras and *Amadeus* to Prague," *The New York Times,* 29 May 1983, sec. 2, pp. 1, 15.

7. See Michael Billington, "Divining for a Theme," *The Guardian,* 5 November 1979, 11; Steve Grant, "Much Ado About Mozart," *The Observer,* 11 November 1979, 16; and Pit, "Shows Abroad," *Variety,* 14 November 1979, 90, 92.

8. Billington, "Divining," 11.

9. Grant, "Much Ado," 16.

10. John Barber, "Mozart Depicted as a Popinjay," *Daily Telegraph,* 5 November 1979, 15.

11. See B. A. Young, *"Amadeus,"* *Financial Times,* 5 November 1979, 15; James Fenton, "Can We Worship This Mozart?" *The Sunday Times,* 23 December 1979, 43; and Benedict Nightingale, "Obscene Child," *New Statesman,* 9 November 1979, 735.

12. Nightingale, "Obscene Child," 735.

13. Fenton, "Can We Worship," 43.

14. Young, *"Amadeus,"* 15.

15. See Douglas Watt, *"Amadeus* Questions the Gift of Genius," *Daily News,* 18 December 1980, in *New York Theater Critics' Reviews—1980,* 68; Frank Rich, "The Theater: *Amadeus* by Peter Shaffer," *The New York Times,* 18 December 1980, in *New York Theater Critics' Reviews—1980,* 64; Brendan Gill, "Bargaining With God," *The New Yorker,* 29 December 1980, 54; Hobe, "Shows on Broadway," *Variety,* 24 December 1980, 62; Edwin Wilson, "Peter Shaffer's Astigmatic View of God," *Wall Street Journal,* 19 December 1980, 25; Clive Barnes, *"Amadeus:* A Total Triumph!" *New York Post,* 18 December 1980, in *New York Theater Critics' Reviews—1980,* 65; T.E. Kalem, "Blood Feud," *Time,* 29 December 1980, 57; and John Beaufort, "Mozart Murdered? Unlikely, but It Makes for an Unusual Play," *The Christian Science Monitor,* 22 December 1980, in *New York Theater Critics' Reviews—1980,* 66.

16. Rich, "The Theatre," 64.

17. Hobe, "On Broadway," 62.

18. Barnes, 65.

19. See Stanley Kauffmann, "Shaffer's Flat Notes," *Saturday Review,* February 1981, 78–79; Janet Karsten Larson, *"Amadeus:* Shaffer's Hollow Men," *The Christian Century,* 20 May 1981, 578–83; John Simon, " 'Amadequus,' Or Shaffer Rides Again," *New York,* 29 December 1980/5 January 1981, 62–63; Stephen Harvey, *"Amadeus,"* *The Nation,* 17 January 1981, 59–60; Robert Brustein, "The Triumph of Mediocrity," *The New Republic,* 17 January 1981, 23–24; and Howard Kissel, *"Amadeus,"* *Women's Wear Daily,* 19 December 1980, in *New York Theater Critics' Reviews—1980,* 66–67.

20. Kauffmann, "Flat Notes," 78.

21. Larson, "Hollow Men," 580.

22. Brustein, "Mediocrity," 232.

23. Simon, " 'Amadequus,' " 62.

24. Kissel, *"Amadeus,"* 67.

25. Barber, "Mozart As Popinjay," 15.

26. Grant, "Much Ado," 16.

27. Larson, "Hollow Men," 581.

28. C.J. Gianakaris, "Shaffer's Revisions in *Amadeus,"* *Theatre Journal* 35, no. 1 (1983):96.

29. Roland Gelatt, "Peter Shaffer's *Amadeus:* A Controversial Hit," *Saturday Review,* November 1980, 11.

30. C.J. Gianakaris, "Fair Play?" *Opera News,* 27 February 1982, 36.

31. Alfred Einstein, *Mozart: His Character, His Work,* trans. Arthur Mendel and Nathan Broder (London: Oxford University Press, 1945), 29.

32. Emily Anderson, *The Letters of Mozart and His Family,* vol. 1 (London: Macmillan, 1966), 483.

33. Ibid., 358.

34. Peter Shaffer, *Amadeus* (New York: Harper & Row, 1981), 16. All subsequent citations are from this edition and are included within parentheses in the text.

35. Emily Anderson, *The Letters of Mozart and His Family,* vol. 2 (London: Macmillan, 1966), 965.

36. Ibid., 922.

37. Anderson, *Letters,* vol. 1, 392.

38. Ibid., 360.

39. In Anderson, *Letters,* vol. 2, 802 (letter 448), Mozart expresses his annoyance at Constanze for allowing a young gallant to measure her legs. In letter 180a, written to Nannerl, Mozart signs his name "Gnagflow Trazom" and later uses "Trazom" in a letter to his father. See Anderson, vol. 1, 240, 316.

40. See Anderson, *Letters,* vol. 1, 115, 134, 148, 292, 325, 351, 358, 372, and 403; vol. 2, 643, 672, 853, 856, 860, and 927.

41. Ibid., vol. 1, xiii. Even in his letters to Leopold, a strict, conservative, and authoritarian father, Mozart shows little restraint with his language (see letters 214b, 224, 232a, 363, 493, 496, and 499). Mozart even had the gall to criticize Archbishop Hieronymus Colloredo before and after the archbishop dismissed Mozart from his service. Mozart refers to the archbishop as the "arch-booby" (letter 396) and on 12 July 1783, writes to his father that "I suppose I need not repeat that I care very little for Salzburg and not at all for the Archbishop, that I shit on both of them and that it would never enter my head voluntarily to make a journey thither, were it not that you and my sister lived there" (letter 496).

42. Einstein, *Mozart,* 76.

43. Anderson, *Letters,* vol. 1, xiii.

44. Einstein, *Mozart,* 28.

45. There are a number of excellent biographies on Mozart. In addition to Einstein's book, see Eric Blom, *Mozart* (London: J.M. Dent and Sons, 1956); Otto Erich Deutsch, *Mozart: A Documentary Biography,* trans. Eric Blom, Peter Branscombe, and Jeremy Noble (Stanford: Stanford University Press, 1965); Wolfgang Hildesheimer, *Mozart,* trans. Marion Faber (New York: Vintage Books, 1983); Otto Jahn, *The Life of Mozart,* 3 vols., trans. Pauline D. Townsend (New York: Edwin F Kalmas, 1970); Friedrich Kerst, *Mozart: The Man and the Artist Revealed in His Own Words,* trans. Henry Edward Krehbiel (New York: Dover Publishers, 1965); Michael Levey, *The Life and Death of Mozart* (New York: Stein and Day, 1971); Henry Raynor, *Mozart* (London: Macmillan, 1978); Stanley Sadie, *Mozart* (New York: Grossman Publishers, 1970); and W.J. Turner, *Mozart: The Man & His Works* (New York: Tudor Publishing Co., 1938).

46. Peter Shaffer, "Paying Homage to Mozart," *The New York Times Magazine,* 2 September 1984, 38.

47. In the London production, the masked figure was Salieri's servant, Greybig, dispatched by the court composer to drive Mozart insane. For the definitive version of the play—the New York production—Shaffer eliminated Greybig, leaving Salieri as the Messenger of Death, thereby more directly involving him in Mozart's destruction.

48. Peter Shaffer, "Figure of Death," *The Observer,* 4 November 1979, 37.

49. Gelatt, "Controversial Hit," 13.

50. Harold C. Schonberg, "Mozart's World: From London to Broadway," *The New York Times,* 14 December 1980, sec. 2, p. 35.

51. Actually, Anderson notes Salieri's name nine times in her index, not including footnoted information and Leopold's correspondence. The indexer missed the reference to Salieri in letter 494, p. 854.

52. Anderson, *Letters,* vol. 2, 693.

53. Ibid., 818.

54. Ibid., 897.

55. Ibid., 854.

56. Donal Henahan, "Never Mind Salieri, Süssmayr Did It," *The New York Times,* 23 September 1984, sec. 2, p. 21. In a letter to *The New York Times,* Shaffer responded to Henahan, insisting that there will be no further versions of the play. See Peter Shaffer, "Salieri Really Was the Only Choice," *The New York Times,* 14 October 1984, sec. 2, p. 8.

57. Harold C. Schonberg, "Mozart As 'A Silly Little Man,'" *The New York Times,* 2 March 1980, sec. 2, p. 27.

58. Others in attendance were Baron Van Swieten, Süssmayr, at least two Viennese musicians, and Mozart's two brothers-in-law. Constanze did not attend.

59. For more details about Salieri's confession, see Schonberg, "Mozart's World," 1, 35, and Harold C. Schonberg, "The Villain of *Amadeus* in Real Life," *The New York Times,* 1 February 1981, sec. 2, pp. 1, 17.

60. Schonberg, "Mozart As 'A Silly Little Man,'" 21. Interestingly enough, Ulibschev's words echo the first lines in *Amadeus: "Savage whispers fill the theater. We can distinguish nothing at first from this snakelike hissing save the world Salieri! repeated here, there and everywhere around the theater"* (1).

61. This phrase actually appears in a letter that Leopold wrote to Mozart on 7 December 1780 (letter 371). Leopold recalled a meeting with violinst Karl Michael, Ritter von Esser, whom Mozart, playing in Mainz eighteen years earlier at the age of seven, "criticized by telling him that *he played well, but that he added too many notes and that he ought to play music as it was written.*" See Anderson, *Letters,* vol. 2, 683.

62. See Werner Huber and Hubert Zapf's important article, "On the Structure of Peter Shaffer's *Amadeus,*" *Modern Drama* 27, no. 3 (1984):307.

63. A number of critics have compared Mozart to Alan Strang. See Michael Gillespie, "Peter Shaffer: 'To Make Whatever God There Is,'" *Claudel Studies* 9, no. 2 (1982):61–70; Jules Glenn, "Twins in the Theater: A Study of Plays by Peter and Anthony Shaffer," in *Blood Brothers: Siblings As Writers,* ed. Norman Kiell (New York: International Universities Press, 1983), 277–99; Michael Hinden, "Trying to Like Shaffer," *Comparative Drama* 19, no. 1 (1985): 14–29; Huber and Zapf, 299–313; Dennis Klein, "*Amadeus:* The Third Part of Peter Shaffer's Dramatic Trilogy," *Modern Language Studies* 13, no. 1 (1983):31–38; and Barbara Lounsberry, "Peter Shaffer's *Amadeus* and *Shrivings:* God-Hunting Continued," *Theatre Annual* 39 (1984): 15–33.

64. For a thorough discussion of Shaffer's revisions of *Amadeus,* see Gianakaris, "Shaffer's Revisions," 88–101. Gianakaris notes that Shaffer has never revised a play so extensively, which is unusual because *Amadeus* was quite successful in London. Many of these changes were made during the play's trial run in Washington, D.C., before the New York premiere.

65. Indeed, in the list of characters, presented in their order of importance in the play, Salieri's name is seen first; Mozart is listed second.

66. C.J. Gianakaris, "A Playwright Looks at Mozart: Peter Shaffer's *Amadeus,*" *Comparative Drama* 15, no. 1 (Spring 1981):51.

67. Frank X. Mikels and James Rurak claim that Salieri's mediocrity is the result

of his rebellion against God. See "Finishing Salieri: Another Act to *Amadeus*," *Soundings* 67, no. 1 (1984): 51. This religious interpretation of the play seems contrived. Salieri's pact with God does not establish his mediocrity; instead, a more existential approach, through Salieri's *actions,* would establish his character traits in a more convincing manner.

68. This image has become the "logo" for *Amadeus* and was depicted on the original playbill and on the cover of the Harper & Row edition of the play. The menacing person in black is actually Salieri dressed as the Masked Figure who haunts and beckons Mozart. At the same time, then, the Masked Figure is Salieri beckoning the audience to come to terms with its own mediocrity (role playing)—Shaffer's central theme throughout virtually all of his works.

69. Larson, "Hollow Men," 580.

70. Huber and Zapf, "Structure of *Amadeus*," 307.

71. Gillespie, "Whatever God There Is," 63–64.

72. Shaffer, "Introduction to the Film Edition," xvii.

73. Huber and Zapf, "Structure of *Amadeus*," 305–306.

74. Ibid., 304.

75. Shaffer made the comment in an interview with David Gillard on the eve of the radio presentation of *Amadeus* in London. See "Deadly Rivals," *Radio Times,* 22–28 January 1983, 4.

76. Rodney Simard, *Postmodern Drama: Contemporary Playwrights in America and Britain* (Lanham, Md.: University Press of America, 1984), 113.

77. Peter Shaffer, "Salieri Really Was the Only Choice," sec. 2, p. 8.

78. Schonberg, "Mozart's World," 35.

79. In my interview with Shaffer, he acknowledged that "the speeches are musical. But they're not Mozartian rhythms. However, there is a slight aria in which the beginning of the play, it has been pointed out to me, resembles slightly the overture of *The Marriage of Figaro* . . . I think the beginning of the play is musical in its set of balances."

80. Lounsberry, "God-Hunting Continued," 21.

81. Huber and Zapf, "Structure of *Amadeus*," 310.

Bibliography

Only the sources that have actually been used to compile the information in this book are listed here.

Works by Peter Shaffer

Amadeus. New York: Harper & Row, 1981.

Black Comedy and *White Lies.* New York: Stein and Day, 1967.

"But My Dear." In *That Was the Week That Was,* edited by David Frost and Ned Sherrin. London: W. H. Allen, 1963.

"The Cannibal Theater." *The Atlantic Monthly,* October 1960, 48–50.

Equus. New York: Avon Books, 1974.

"Figure of Death." *The Observer,* 4 November 1979, 37.

Five Finger Exercise. New York: Harcourt, Brace and Co., 1958.

How Doth the Little Crocodile?, with Anthony Shaffer. New York: Macmillan, 1957.

"In Search of a God." *Plays and Players,* October 1964, 22.

"Introduction to the Film Edition." *Amadeus.* New York: Signet, 1984.

"Labels Aren't for Playwrights." *Theatre Arts,* February 1960, 20–21.

"Making the Screen Speak." *Film Comment,* September/October 1984, 51, 56–57.

"Paying Homage to Mozart." *The New York Times Magazine,* 2 September 1984, 22–23, 27, 35, 38.

"Preface." *The Collected Plays of Peter Shaffer.* New York: Harmony Books, 1982.

"The President of France." In *That Was the Week That Was,* edited by David Frost and Ned Sherrin. London: W. H. Allen, 1963.

The Private Ear and *The Public Eye.* New York: Stein and Day, 1964.

The Royal Hunt of the Sun. New York: Stein and Day, 1965.

"Salieri Really Was the Only Choice." *The New York Times,* 14 October 1984, sec. 2, p. 8.

"Scripts in Trans-Atlantic Crossings May Suffer Two Kinds of Changes." *Dramatists Guild Quarterly,* Spring 1980, 29–33.

Shrivings. London: André Deutsch, 1974.

" 'To See the Soul of a Man.' " *The New York Times,* 24 October 1965, sec. 2, p. 3.

"What We Owe Britten." *The Sunday Times,* 18 November 1973, 35.

The White Liars and *Black Comedy.* New York: Samuel French, 1968.

Withered Murder, with Anthony Shaffer. New York: Macmillan, 1956.

The Woman in the Wardrobe. London: Evans Brothers, 1951.

Secondary Sources

Adam, Peter. "Peter Shaffer on Faith, Farce and Masks." *The Listener,* 14 October 1976, 476–77.

Anderson, Emily. *The Letters of Mozart and His Family.* 2 vols. London: Macmillan, 1966.

Artaud, Antonin. *Oeuvres complètes.* Vol. 2. Paris: Gallimard, 1961.

———. *Oeuvres complètes.* Vol. 8. Paris: Gallimard, 1971.

———. *Selected Writings.* Edited by Susan Sontag and translated by Helen Weaver. New York: Farrar, Straus and Giroux, 1976.

———. *The Theater and Its Double.* Translated by Mary Caroline Richards. New York: Grove Press, 1958.

———. *Le théâtre et son double.* Paris: Gallimard, 1964.

"Artaud for Artaud's Sake." *Encore* 11 (January–June 1964): 20–31.

Aston, Frank. "*Five Finger Exercise* Subtle and Substantial." *New York World-Telegram,* 3 December 1959, in *New York Theater Critics' Reviews—1959,* 208.

Atkinson, Brooks. "The Theater: *Five Finger Exercise.*" *The New York Times,* 3 December 1959, in *New York Theater Critics' Reviews—1959,* 210.

Bail. "Show Abraod." *Variety,* 11 February 1970, 61.

Balch, Jack. "The Openings." *Theatre Arts* 44, no. 2 (1960): 14–16.

Baldwin, Hélène L. "*Equus:* Theater of Cruelty or Theater of Sensationalism?" *Philological Papers* (West Virginia University) 25 (1978): 118–27.

Barber, John. "Fascinating Play on an Obsession." *Daily Telegraph,* 27 July 1973, 13.

———. "Mozart Depicted As a Popinjay." *Daily Telegraph,* 5 November 1979, 15.

Barnes, Clive. "*Amadeus:* A Total Triumph." *New York Post,* 18 December 1980, in *New York Theater Critics' Reviews—1980,* 65.

———. "*Equus* as a New Success on Broadway." The New York Times, 25 October 1974, in *New York Theater Critics' Reviews—1974,* 204–5.

Beaufort, John. "Brilliant British Import." *The Christian Science Monitor,* 4 November 1974, in *New York Theater Critics' Reviews—1974,* 202.

———. "Mozart Murdered? Unlikely, But It Makes for an Unusual Play." The *Christian Science Monitor,* 22 December 1980, in *New York Theater Critics' Reviews—1980,* 66.

Berman, Jeffrey. "*Equus:* After Such Little Forgiveness, What Knowledge?" *The Psychoanalytic Review* 66, no. 3 (1979): 406–22.

Bermel, Albert. *Artaud's Theatre of Cruelty.* New York: Taplinger Publishing Co., 1977.

Billington, Michael. "Divining for a Theme." *The Guardian,* 5 November 1979, 11.

———. "*Equus* at the Old Vic." *The Manchester Guardian,* 27 July 1973, 12.

———. "A Voyeur of Divinity." *Manchester Guardian Weekly,* 22 December 1985, 5.

Blom, Eric. *Mozart.* London: J. M. Dent and Sons, 1956.

Brien, Alan. "Eating People Is Wrong." *The Spectator,* 25 July 1958, 133–34.

———. "Middle-Aged Absurdity." *The Sunday Telegraph,* 25 February 1968, 14.

———. "Silent Epic—With Words." *The Sunday Telegraph,* 13 December 1964, 12.

Brisson, Frederick. "Preface." *Five Finger Exercise.* New York: Harcourt, Brace and Co., 1958.

Brustein, Robert. "Familiar Peru, Exotic Brooklyn." *The New Republic,* 27 November 1965, 45–46.

———. *The Third Theater.* New York: Alfred A. Knopf, 1969.

———. "The Triumph of Mediocrity." *The New Republic,* 17 January 1981, 23–24.

Bryden, Ronald. "Echoes of Russell." *The Observer,* 8 February 1970, 31.

———. "No-Man's Land." *New Statesman,* 6 August 1965, 194–95.

———. "Red-nosed Revival." *The Observer,* 25 February 1968, 26.

———. "Ruin and Gold." *New Statesman,* 17 July 1964, 95–96.

Buckley, Peter. "Out to Lunch." *Vanity Fair,* May 1986, 136.

Buckley, Tom. " 'Write Me,' Said the Play to Peter Shaffer." *The New York Times Magazine,* April 13, 1975, 20–21, 25–26, 28, 30, 32, 34, 37–38, 40.

Burland, J. Alexis. "Discussion of Papers on *Equus.*" *International Journal of Psychoanalytic Psychotherapy* 5 (1976): 501–5.

Cerny, Lothar. "Peter Shaffer—*Equus.*" In *Englische Literatur der Gegenwart, 1971–75,* edited by Rainer Lengeler, 157–70. Dusseldorf: August Bagel Verlag, 1977.

Chapman, John. "*Five Finger Exercise* a Doodle." *Daily News,* 3 December 1959, in *New York Theater Critics' Reviews—1959,* 209.

———. "Peter Shaffer's Black Comedies a Splendid Theatrical Evening." *Daily News,* 13 February 1967, in *New York Theater Critics' Reviews—1967,* 371.

———. "*Private Ear* and *Public Eye* Are Irresistible English Comedies." *Daily News,* 10 October 1963, in *New York Theater Critics' Reviews—1963,* 249.

———. "*The Royal Hunt of the Sun* Fills the ANTA Theater With Beauty." *Daily News,* 27 October 1965, in *New York Theater Critics' Reviews—1965,* 296.

"Children vs. Parents: Subtle Play at the Comedy." *The Times,* 17 July 1958, 4.

Christie, Ian. "Not a Lot of Horse Sense." *Daily Express,* 27 July 1973, 10.

Cirlot, J. E. *A Dictionary of Symbols,* 2d ed. Translated by Jack Sage. London: Routledge and Kegan Paul, 1974.

Clum, John M. "Religion and Five Contemporary Plays: The Quest for God in a Godless World." *The South Atlantic Quarterly* 77, no. 4 (1978): 418–32.

Clurman, Harold. "Theater." *The Nation,* 19 December 1959, 475–76.

———. "Theater." *The Nation,* 9 November 1963, 305–6.

———. "Theater." *The Nation,* 22 November 1965, 397–98.

———. "Theater." *The Nation,* 27 February 1967, 285–86.

———. "Theater." *The Nation,* 16 November 1974, 506–7.

Cohen, Marshall. "Theater 66." *Partisan Review* 33, no. 2 (1966): 269–76.

Cohn, Ruby. *Currents in Contemporary Drama.* Bloomington: Indiana University Press, 1969.

Coleman, Robert. "*Eye-Ear* Delightful Imports." *New York Mirror,* 10 October 1963, in *New York Theater Critics' Reviews—1963,* 248.

———. "*Five Finger Exercise* Thrilling." *Daily Mirror,* 3 December 1959, in *New York Theater Critics' Reviews—1959,* 210.

Connell, Brian. "Peter Shaffer: The Two Sides of Theatre's Agonised Perfectionist." *The Times,* 28 April 1980, 7.

Cooke, Richard P. "Shaffer Strikes Again." *Wall Street Journal,* 14 February 1967, in *New York Theater Critics' Reviews—1967,* 372.

Corbally, John. "The *Equus* Ethic." *New Laurel Review* 7, no. 2 (1977): 53–58.

Costick, Julian F. *Antonin Artaud*. Boston: G. K. Hall, 1978.

Crowell's Handbook of Contemporary Drama. New York: Thomas Y. Crowell, 1971.

Cushman, Robert. "Horsemanship at the National." *The Observer*, 29 July 1973, 30.

Dallas, Ian. "The Naturalists." *Encore* 10 (September 1958): 24–28.

"Dancing in the Dark." *Time*, 17 February 1967, 70.

Darlington, W. A. "Cinderella Goes to the Moon by Rocket." *Daily Telegraph and Morning Post*, 20 December 1963, 13.

———. "Conquistador in Search of a Faith." *Daily Telegraph*, 9 December 1964, 18.

———. "Making up for Lost Time." *Daily Telegraph*, 11 May 1962, 16.

Davenport, Marcia. *Mozart*. New York: Charles Scribner's Sons, 1956.

Davies, Russell. "Horses for Courses." *New Statesman*, 3 August 1973, 165–66.

Dean, Joan F. "The Family As Microcosm in Shaffer's Plays." *Ball State University Forum* 23, no. 1 (1982): 30–34.

———. "Peter Shaffer's Recurrent Character Type." *Modern Drama* 21, no. 3 (1978): 297–305.

Deford, Frank. "Peter Shaffer's *Equus* Celebrates the Horse As an Awesome Pagan Idol." *Sports Illustrated*, 3 March 1975, 9.

Deutsch, Otto Erich. *Mozart: A Documentary Biography*. Translated by Eric Blom, Peter Branscombe, and Jeremy Noble. Stanford: Stanford University Press, 1965.

Driver, Tom. "Drama Wanted: Fresh Air." *Christian Century*, 6 January 1960, 15–16.

Ebner, Dean. "The Double Crisis of Sexuality and Worship in Shaffer's *Equus*." *Christianity and Literature* 31, no. 2 (1982): 29–47.

Edwards, Sydney. "What the Riots Did to Peter Shaffer." *Evening Standard*, 9 January 1970, 20–21.

Einstein, Alfred. *Mozart: His Character, His Work*. Translated by Arthur Mendel and Nathan Broder. London: Oxford University Press, 1945.

Emelson, Margaret A. "A Horse of a Different Color: A Critique of Peter Shaffer's *Equus*." *Journal of Evolutionary Psychology* 1, no. 2 (1980): 75–80.

"*Equus*: Playwright Peter Shaffer Interprets Its Ritual." *Vogue*, February 1975, 136–37, 192.

Esslin, Martin. *Antonin Artaud*. London: J. Calder, 1976.

Fenton, James. "Can We Worship This Mozart?" *The Sunday Times*, 23 December 1979, 43.

Flood, Jerry. "God's Flute." *Opera News*, 31 January 1981, 18.

Ford, Christopher. "High Horse." *The Manchester Guardian*, 6 August 1973, 8.

French, Philip. "Surprise, Surprise." *New Statesman*, 1 March 1968, 279.

Frost, David. "Theatre." *Punch*, 4 August 1965, 174–75.

Funke, Phyllis. "A Playwright in a Hurry." *The Courier-Journal* (Louisville), 7 November 1965, sec. F, p. 1.

Gascoigne, Bamber. "All the Riches of the Incas." *The Observer*, 12 July 1964, 24.

———. "Touched by Pleasure." *The Spectator*, 18 May 1962, 653.

Gassner, John. *Dramatic Soundings*. New York: Crown Publishers, 1968.

Gelatt, Roland. "Mostly *Amadeus*." *Horizon*, September 1984, 49–52.

———. "Peter Shaffer's *Amadeus*: A Controversial Hit." *Saturday Review*, November 1980, 11–14.

Gelb, Barbara. ". . . . And Its Author." *The New York Times,* 14 November 1965, sec. 2, pp. 1–2, 4.

Gellert, Roger. "Encircling Gloom." *New Statesman,* 18 May 1962, 732.

Gianakaris, C. J. "Drama into Film: The Shaffer Situation." *Modern Drama* 28, no. 1 (1985): 83–98.

——. "Fair Play?" *Opera News,* 27 February 1982, 18, 36.

——. "A Playwright Looks at Mozart: Peter Shaffer's *Amadeus.*" *Comparative Drama* 15, no. 1 (1981): 37–53.

——. "Shaffer's Revisions in *Amadeus.*" *Theatre Journal* 35, no. 1 (1983): 88–101.

——. "Theatre of the Mind in Miller, Osborne and Shaffer." *Renascence* 30, no. 1 (1977): 33–42.

Gibbs, Patrick. "Fine Acting in Striking Play." *Daily Telegraph,* 17 July 1958, 10.

Gifford, Sanford. "Pop Psychoanalysis, *Kitsch* and the 'As If' Theater: Further Notes on Peter Shaffer's *Equus.*" *International Journal of Psychoanalytic Psychotherapy* 5 (1976): 463–71.

——. "Psychoanalyst Says Nay to *Equus.*" *The New York Times,* December 15, 1976, sec. 2, pp. 1,5.

Gill, Brendan. "Bargaining With God." *The New Yorker,* 29 December 1980, 54.

——. "Unhorsed." *The New Yorker,* 4 November 1974, 123–24.

Gillard, David. "Deadly Rivals." *Radio Times,* 22–28 January 1983, 4.

Gillespie, Michael. "Peter Shaffer: 'To Make Whatever God There Is.'" *Claudel Studies* 9, no. 2 (1982): 61–70.

Gilliatt, Penelope. "A Huge Stride Backwards—With the Inca." *The Observer,* 13 December 1964, 24.

Glenn, Jules. "Alan Strang as an Adolescent: A Discussion of Peter Shaffer's *Equus.*" *International Journal of Psychoanalytic Psychotherapy* 5 (1976): 473–87.

——. "Anthony and Peter Shaffer's Plays: The Influence of Twinship on Creativity." *American Imago* 31 (Fall 1974): 270–92.

——. "Twins in Disguise: A Psychoanalytic Essay on *Sleuth* and *The Royal Hunt of the Sun.*" *Psychoanalytic Quarterly* 43, no. 2 (1974): 288–302.

——. "Twins in Disguise. 2. Content, Form and Style in Plays by Anthony and Peter Shaffer." *The International Review of Psycho-Analysis* 1, no. 3 (1974): 373–81.

——. "Twins in the Theater: A Study of Plays by Peter and Anthony Shaffer." In *Blood Brothers: Siblings as Writers,* edited by Norman Kiell, 277–99. New York: International Universities Press, 1983.

Gottfried, Martin. "Shaffer's *Equus* at the Plymouth." *New York Post,* 25 October 1974, in *New York Theater Critics' Reviews—1974,* 206.

Grant, Steve. "Much Ado About Mozart." *The Observer,* 11 November 1979, 16.

Gussow, Mel. "Shaffer Details a Mind's Journey in *Equus.*" *The New York Times,* 24 October 1974, 50.

——. "Shedding No Light." *Newsweek,* 20 February 1967, 102–3.

Hamilton, James W. "*Equus* and the Creative Process." *Journal of the Philadelphia Association for Psychoanalysis* 6 (1979): 53–64.

Harvey, Stephen. "*Amadeus.*" *The Nation,* 17 January 1981, 59–60.

Hayman, Ronald. "John Dexter: Walking the Tightrope of Theatrical Statement." *The Times,* 28 July 1973, 9.

Henahan, Donal. "Never Mind Salieri, Süssmayr Did It." *The New York Times,* 23 September 1984, sec. 2, pp. 1, 21.

Hewes, Henry. "The Crimes of Dispassion." *Saturday Review,* 25 January 1975, 54.

———. "Inca Doings." *Saturday Review,* 13 November 1965, 71.

———. "When You're Having More Than One." *Saturday Review,* 25 February 1967, 91.

Hildesheimer, Wolfgang. *Mozart.* Translated by Marion Faber. New York: Vintage Books, 1983.

Hinden, Michael. "Trying to Like Shaffer." *Comparative Drama* 19, no. 1 (1985): 14–29.

———. "When Playwrights Talk to God: Peter Shaffer and the Legacy of O'Neill." *Comparative Drama* 16, no. 1 (1982): 49–63.

Hirsch, Samuel. "English Playwright Finds New York is His Real Home." *The Boston Herald,* 11 January 1967, C33.

Hobe. "Show on Broadway." *Variety,* 30 October 1974, 88, 90.

———. "Shows on Broadway." *Variety,* 9 December 1959, 70.

———. "Shows on Broadway." *Variety,* 16 October 1963, 54.

———. "Shows on Broadway." *Variety,* 24 December 1980, 62.

Hobson, Harold. "All Too Black and White." *The Sunday Times,* 8 February 1970, 53.

———. "*Blitz* Costly, Wholesome, Stupendous . . . And Out-of-Date." *The Christian Science Monitor,* 12 May 1962, 4.

———. "Gielgud, Shaffer, and Hall—Had a Great Fall." *The Christian Science Monitor,* 13 February 1970, 6.

———. "In Search of Bliss." *The Sunday Times,* 13 December 1964, 25.

———. "Irma Translated." *The Sunday Times,* 20 July 1958, 9.

———. "Shaffer Gallops to Glory and Explains What Makes Him Run." *The Sunday Times,* 29 July 1973, 33.

———. "A Triumph at London's National Theater [*sic*]." *The Christian Science Monitor,* 10 August 1973, 14.

Hope-Wallace, Philip. "*Battle of Shrivings* at the Lyric Theatre." *The Manchester Guardian,* 6 February 1970, 8.

———. "*Black Comedy* and *Miss Julie* at Chichester." *The Manchester Guardian,* 28 July 1965, 7.

———. "*Five Finger Exercise.*" *The Manchester Guardian,* 17 July 1958, 5.

———. "Joan Littlewood Panto at Wyndham's." *The Guardian,* 20 December 1963, 7.

———. "Peter Shaffer Double Bill at the Lyric Theatre." *The Manchester Guardian,* 22 February 1968, 6.

Huber, Werner and Hubert Zapf. "On the Structure of Peter Shaffer's *Amadeus.*" *Modern Drama* 27, no. 3 (1984): 299–313.

Hughes, Catharine. "The Best Play in Town." *America,* 24 January 1981, 62.

Hughes, Elinor. "The Brains Behind *The Eye* and *Ear.*" *The Boston Sunday Herald,* 29 September 1963, sec. 4, p. 3.

"Hunting Heaven." *Newsweek,* 8 November 1965, 96.

Jacobson, Dan. *The Rape of Tamar.* New York: Macmillan, 1970.

Jacobson, Harlan. "As Many Notes as Required." *Film Comment,* September/October 1984, 50, 53–55.

Jahn, Otto. *The Life of Mozart.* 3 vols. Translated by Pauline D. Townsend. New York: Edwin F. Kalmas, 1970.

Joffee, Linda. "New Peter Shaffer Play Profound But Lacks Punch." *The Christian Science Monitor,* 18 March 1986, 29–30.

Jones, Anne Hudson. "Thomas Szasz' Myths of Mental Illness and Peter Shaffer's *Equus.*" In *Proceedings of Asclepius at Syracuse: Thomas Szasz Libertarian Humanist.* Compiled by M. E. Grenander. Albany, N.Y.: Institute for Humanistic Studies, State University of New York, 1980, 282–90.

Jung, Carl Gustav. *Aion: Researches into the Phenomenology of the Self.* Translated by R. F. C. Hull. Princeton: Princeton University Press, 1959.

———. *Psychology and Religion: West and East.* Translated by R. F. C. Hull. Princeton: Princeton University Press, 1955.

Kakutani, Michiko. "How *Amadeus* Was Translated From Play to Film." *The New York Times,* 16 September 1984, sec. 2, pp. 1, 20.

Kalem, T. E. "Blood Feud." *Time,* 29 December 1980, 57.

———. "Freudian Exorcism." *Time,* 4 November 1974, 119–20.

Kamm, Henry. "Milos Forman Takes His Cameras and *Amadeus* to Prague." *The New York Times,* 29 May 1983, sec. 2, pp. 1, 15.

Kauffmann, Stanley. *"Equus." The New Republic,* 7 December 1974, 18, 33.

———. "Shaffer's Flat Notes." *Saturday Review,* February 1981, 78–79.

Keown, Eric. "At the Play." *Punch,* 16 May 1962, 767–68.

Kerr, Walter. *"Five Finger Exercise." New York Herald Tribune,* 3 December 1959, in *New York Theater Critics' Reviews—1959,* 209.

———. *"Private Ear and Public Eye." New York Herald Tribune,* 10 October 1963, in *New York Theater Critics' Reviews—1963,* 249.

———. "Theater: Vaudeville Variations on Chinese Theme." *The New York Times,* 13 February 1967, in *New York Theater Critics' Reviews—1967,* 373–74.

———. Untitled review of *The Royal Hunt of the Sun. New York Herald Tribune,* 27 October 1965, in *New York Theater Critics' Reviews—1965,* 294–95.

Kerst, Friedrich. *Mozart: The Man and the Artist Revealed in His Own Words.* Translated by Henry Edward Krehbel. New York: Dover Publishers, 1965.

Kingston, Jeremy. "At the Theatre." *Punch,* 11 February 1970, 236.

———. "Theatre." *Punch,* 15 July 1964, 99.

———. "Theatre." *Punch,* 8 August 1973, 188.

Kirby, E. T. *Total Theatre.* New York: E. P. Dutton, 1969.

Kissel, Howard. *"Amadeus." Women's Wear Daily,* 19 December 1980, in *New York Theater Critics' Reviews—1980,* 66–67.

———. *"Equus." Women's Wear Daily,* 18 October 1974, in *New York Theater Critics' Reviews—1974,* 203–4.

Klein, Dennis A. *"Amadeus:* The Third Part of Peter Shaffer's Dramatic Trilogy." *Modern Language Studies* 13, no. 1 (1983): 31–38.

———. "Literary Onomastics in Peter Shaffer's *Shrivings* and *Equus.*" *Literary Onomastics Studies* 7 (1980): 127–38.

———. *Peter Shaffer.* Boston: G. K. Hall, 1979.

Knapp, Bettina. *Antonin Artaud: Man of Vision.* New York: David Lewis, 1969.

Kretzmer, Herbert. "A Dim Little Blonde With No Magic." *Daily Express*, 20 December 1963, 4.

———. "Fortune Telling? My Own Forecast Is a Hit!" *Daily Express*, 22 February 1968, 3.

———. "More Sparkle From Off-Beat Mr. Shaffer." *Daily Express*, 12 May 1962, 7.

Kroll, Jack. "Four from the London Stage." *Newsweek*, 13 January 1986, 64–65.

———. "Horse Power." *Newsweek*, 4 November 1974, 60.

———. "Mozart and His Nemesis." *Newsweek*, 29 December 1980, 58.

Lambert, J. W. "Plays in Performance." *Drama* 111 (Winter 1973): 14–37.

Larson, Janet Karsten. "*Amadeus*: Shaffer's Hollow Men." *The Christian Century*, 20 May 1981, 578–83.

Lawson, Wayne Paul. "The Dramatic Hunt: A Critical Evaluation of Peter Shaffer's Plays." Ph.D. diss., Ohio State University, 1974.

Lee, James. "*Equus*, Round Three." *Exchange* 2 (Spring 1976): 49–59.

Leggett, Paul. "Theology Opens on Broadway." *Christianity Today*, 11 December 1981, 68–69.

Levey, Michael. *The Life and Death of Mozart*. New York: Stein and Day, 1971.

Levin, Bernard. "Out of the Darkness, a Blind Farce." *Daily Mail*, 29 July 1965, 12.

———. "Yes, It's the Greatest Play in My Lifetime." *Daily Mail*, 10 December 1964, 18.

Lewis, Allan. *The Contemporary Theater*. New York: Crown Publishers, 1971.

Lewis, Peter. "Black or White, It's Mostly Magic." *Daily Mail*, 23 February 1968, 12.

Little, Stuart W. "Briton Wrote New Scene to Open His Play in New York." *New York Herald Tribune*, 8 December 1959, 21.

Loftus, Joseph A. "Playwright's Moral Exercise." *The New York Times*, 29 November 1959, sec. 2, pp. 1, 3.

Loney, Glenn. "Recreating *Amadeus*: An American Team Recreates John Bury's Design." *Theater Crafts*, March 1981, 10–15.

———. "Which Twin Has the Tony?" *After Dark*, April 1971, 21–23.

Lounsberry, Barbara. " 'God-Hunting': The Chaos of Worship in Peter Shaffer's *Equus* and *Royal Hunt of the Sun*." *Modern Drama* 21, no. 1 (1978): 13–28.

———. "Peter Shaffer's *Amadeus* and *Shrivings*: God-Hunting Continued." *Theatre Annual* 39 (1984): 15–33.

"Love Antic and Frantic." *Time*, 18 October 1963, 76, 78.

Lumley, Frederick. *New Trends in Twentieth Century Drama*. New York: Oxford University Press, 1967.

Lynch, William. "What's Wrong With *Equus*? Ask Euripides." *America*, 13 December 1975, 419–22.

McCarten, John. "Gods Against God." *The New Yorker*, 6 November 1965, 115–16.

McClain, John. "An Import—But Why?" *New York Journal American*, 10 October 1963, in *New York Theater Critics' Reviews—1963*, 250.

———. "Size, Style and Talent." *New York Journal American*, 27 October 1965, in *New York Theater Critics' Reviews—1965*, 293.

———. "Top Drawer Import With Sterling Cast." *New York Journal American*, 3 December 1959, in *New York Theater Critics' Reviews—1959*, 207.

Marcus, Frank. "Poet v. Philosopher." *The Sunday Telegraph,* 8 February 1970, 14.

Marriott, R. B. "Peter Shaffer Calls for Magic and Mystery." *Stage and Television Today,* 31 July 1958, 8.

Mikels, Frank X., and James Rurak. "Finishing Salieri: Another Act to *Amadeus.*" *Soundings* 67, no. 1 (1984): 42–54.

Myro. "Shows Abroad." *Variety,* 16 December 1964, 64.

Nadel, Norman. "Emotions Gently Laid Bare in Shaffer's *Eye* and *Ear.*" *New York World-Telegram,* 10 October 1963, in *New York Theater Critics' Reviews—1963,* 248–49.

———. "Hilarity Never Stops for *Black Comedy.*" *World Journal Tribune,* 13 February 1967, in *New York Theater Critics' Reviews—1967,* 373.

———. "*Royal Hunt* a Shimmering Sunburst of Talent." *New York World-Telegram,* 27 October 1965, in *New York Theater Critics' Reviews—1965,* 294.

The New Layman's Parallel Bible. Grand Rapids, Mi.: Zondervan Bible Publishers, 1981.

"New Plays on Broadway." *Time,* 14 December 1959, 77.

Nightingale, Benedict. "Obscene Child." *New Statesman,* 9 November 1979, 735.

———. "Some Immortal Business." *New Statesman,* 13 February 1970, 227.

———. "*The Royal Hunt of the Sun* at Chichester." *The Guardian,* 8 July 1964, 7.

Oakes, Philip. "Philip Oakes Talks to Peter Shaffer." *The Sunday Times,* 29 July 1973, 33.

"One Family Split Four Ways." *Life,* 21 March 1960, 93, 97.

Oppenheimer, George. "A Playwright's Critique." *Newsday* (Long Island), 6 November 1965, 37W.

Panter-Downes, Mollie. "Letter From London." *The New Yorker,* 10 March 1980, 138–40.

———. Untitled Review of *Five Finger Exercise. The New Yorker,* 6 September 1958, 121.

"Pantomime by Stealth." *The Times,* 20 December 1963, 5.

Pennell, Charles A. "The Plays of Peter Shaffer: Experiment in Convention." *Kansas Quarterly* 3, no. 2 (1971): 100–109.

"Peter Shaffer Restores the Spectacle." *Evening Standard,* 8 July 1964, 6.

"Peter Shaffer's Personal Dialogue." *The New York Times,* 6 October 1963, sec. 2, pp. 1, 3.

Pit. "Show Abroad." *Variety,* 11 December 1985, 138.

———. "Shows Abroad." *Variety,* 8 August 1973, 44.

———. "Shows Abroad." *Variety,* 14 November 1979, 90, 92.

Plunka, Gene A. "The Existential Ritual: Peter Shaffer's *Equus,*" *Kansas Quarterly* 12, no. 4 (1980): 87–97.

———. "Roles, Rites, and Rituals: Peter Shaffer's *The Royal Hunt of the Sun.*" *Ball State University Forum* 27, no. 3 (1986): 71–79.

Podol, Peter L. "Contradictions and Dualities in Artaud and Artaudian Theater: *The Conquest of Mexico* and the Conquest of Peru." *Modern Drama* 26, no. 4 (1983): 518–27.

Pree, Barry. "Peter Shaffer." *The Transatlantic Review* 14 (Autumn 1963): 62–66.

Prescott, William H. *The Conquest of Mexico*. 2 vols. London: J. M. Dent and Sons, 1933.

Prideaux, Tom. "The Royal Hunt of Virtue." *Life,* 10 December 1965, 137–38.

———. "Things That Go Bump in the Dark." *Life,* 10 March 1967, 70A–70D.

"The Private Ear and *The Public Eye." Newsweek,* 21 October 1963, 104.

Raynor, Henry. *Mozart*. London: Macmillan, 1978.

Rich. "Show Abroad." *Variety,* 13 March 1968, 3.

———. "Shows Abroad." *Variety,* 23 July 1958, 58.

Rich, Frank. "The Theater: *Amadeus* by Peter Shaffer." *The New York Times,* 18 December 1980, in *New York Theater Critics' Reviews—1980,* 64.

Richardson, Jack. "English Imports on Broadway." *Commentary,* June 1967, 43.

———. "The English Invasion." *Commentary,* 1975 February, 76–78.

Rosenwald, Peter J. *"Amadeus:* Who Murdered Mozart?" *Horizon* 23, no. 2 (1980): 33.

Ross, Don. "Peter Shaffer Is an Enemy of 'Togetherness.' " *New York Herald Tribune,* 3 January 1960, sec. 4, p. 3.

Rutherford, Malcolm. "The Christ That Died." *The Spectator,* 17 July 1964, 82, 84.

Sadie, Stanley. *Mozart*. New York: Crown Publishers, 1970.

Schickel, Richard. "Showman Shaffer." *Time,* 11 November 1974, 117, 119.

Schonberg, Harold C. "Mozart As 'A Silly Little Man.' " *The New York Times,* 2 March 1980, sec. 2, pp. 21, 27.

———. "Mozart's World: From London to Broadway." *The New York Times,* 14 December 1980, sec. 2, pp. 1, 35.

———. "The Villain of *Amadeus* in Real Life." *The New York Times,* 1 February 1981, sec. 2, pp. 1, 17.

Sellin, Eric. *The Dramatic Concepts of Antonin Artaud*. Chicago: University of Chicago Press, 1968.

Sheed, Wilfrid. "Conquests." *Commonweal,* 19 November 1965, 215.

Shorter, Eric. "Exotic Epic Play by Peter Shaffer." *Daily Telegraph,* 8 July 1964, 16.

———. "Gielgud and Magee As Mouthpieces of Ideas." *Daily Telegraph,* 6 February 1970, 16.

Shulman, Milton. "Arguments without Soul." *Evening Standard,* 6 February 1970, 24.

———. "Cinderella Is Fine—for Grown-Ups." *Evening Standard,* 20 December 1963, 4.

———. "Dark Laughter. . . ." *Evening Standard,* 22 February 1968, 4.

———. "It's a Mad, Mad Romp. . . ." *Evening Standard,* 28 July 1965, 4.

———. "Milton Shulman at the Old Vic." *Evening Standard,* 27 July 1973, 28–29.

———. "Mr. Culver Gets the Treatment." *Evening Standard,* 17 July 1958, 10.

———. "Mr. Shaffer—First Sex-War Reporter." *Evening Standard,* 11 May 1962, 21.

———. Review of *The Royal Hunt of the Sun. Evening Standard,* 8 July 1964, 4.

———. "A Search for Faith in a Feast of Spectacle." *Evening Standard,* 9 December 1964, 14.

Simard, Rodney. *Postmodern Drama: Contemporary Playwrights in America and Britain*. Lanham, Md.: University Press of America, 1984.

Simon, John. " 'Amadequus,' Or Shaffer Rides Again." *New York,* 29 December 1980/5 January 1981, 62–63.

———. "Hippodrama at the Psychodrome." *The Hudson Review* 28, no. 1 (1975): 97–106.

———. "Theater: The Blindness Is Within." *New York,* 11 November 1974, 118.

Sitwell, Sacheverell. *Mozart.* Freeport, N.Y.: Books for Libraries Press, 1970.

Slutzky, Jacob E. "*Equus* and the Psychopathology of Passion." *International Journal of Psychoanalytic Psychotherapy* 5 (1976): 489–500.

Sontag, Frederick. "God's Eyes Everywhere." *Christian Century,* 17 December 1975, 1162, 1164.

Stacy, James R. "The Sun and the Horse: Peter Shaffer's Search for Worship." *Educational Theatre Journal* 28, no. 3 (1976): 325–37.

"Stage Challenge to Production." *The Times,* 9 December 1964, 9.

Stamm, Julius L. "Peter Shaffer's *Equus*—A Psychoanalytic Exploration." *International Journal of Psychoanalytic Psychotherapy* 5 (1976): 449–61.

T., J. R. "New Players Encouraged to Ape." *The Times,* 22 February 1968, 13.

Taubman, Howard. "About a *Royal Hunt.*" *The New York Times,* 14 November 1965, sec. 2, p. 1.

———. "The Theater: Pizarro, Gold and Ruin." *The New York Times,* 27 October 1965, in *New York Theater Critics' Reviews—1965,* 296.

———. "The Theater: 2 Comedies by Shaffer." *The New York Times,* 10 October 1963, in *New York Theater Critics' Reviews—1963,* 251.

Taylor, John Russell. *Anger and After.* London: Methuen, 1963.

———. *The Angry Theater.* New York: Hill and Wang, 1969.

———. *Peter Shaffer.* Writers and Their Work Series, no. 244. Harlow, Essex: Longman Group, 1974.

———. *The Second Wave: British Drama for the Seventies.* New York: Hill and Wang, 1971.

———. "Shaffer and the Incas." *Plays and Players,* April 1964, 12–13.

Terrien, Samuel. "*Equus:* Human Conflicts and the Trinity." *Christian Century,* 18 May 1977, 472–76.

Timm, Neil. "*Equus* As a Modern Tragedy." *Philological Papers* (West Virginia University) 25 (1978): 128–34.

"*Tiny Alice* in Inca Land." *Time,* 5 November 1965, 77.

Tobias, Tobi. "Playing without Words." *Dance Magazine,* May 1975, 48–50.

"Total Darkness Lit by Brilliant Gags." *The Times,* 28 July 1965, 14.

Trewin, J. C. "Eyes and Ears." *The Illustrated London News,* 26 May 1962, 860.

———. "Noisy Weekend." *The Illustrated London News,* 21 February 1970, 26.

———. "When the Light Is Dark Enough at Chichester." *The Illustrated London News,* 7 August 1965, 36.

Turner, W. J. *Mozart: The Man & His Works.* New York: Tudor Publishing, 1938.

"TV: Cloak and Dagger." *The New York Times,* 28 January 1958, 55.

Tynan, Kenneth. "Fathers and Sons." *The Observer,* 20 July 1958, 13.

———. "London Can Keep it." *The Observer,* 13 May 1962, 25.

———. "Roses and Thorns." *The Observer,* 12 December 1959, 100–102.

Vandenbroucke, Russell. "*Equus:* Modern Myth in the Making." *Drama and Theater* 12, no. 2 (1975): 129–33.

"Variations on a Triangle." *The Times,* 11 May 1962, 12.

Vidal, Gore. "Strangers at Breakfast." *The Reporter,* 7 January 1960, 36–37.

Vinson, James, ed. *Contemporary Dramatists.* New York: St. Martin's Press, 1982.

Walls, Doyle W. "*Equus:* Shaffer, Nietzsche, and the Neuroses of Health." *Modern Drama* 27, no. 3 (1984): 314–23.

Wardle, Irving. "Philosopher of Peace." *The Times,* 6 February 1970, 13.

———. "Shaffer's Variation on a Theme." *The Times,* 27 July 1973, 15.

Watt, Douglas. "*Amadeus* Questions the Gift of Genius." *Daily News,* 18 December 1980, in *New York Theater Critics' Reviews—1980,* 68.

———. "*Equus* Is a Smashing Psychodrama." *Daily News,* 25 October 1974, in *New York Theater Critics' Reviews—1974,* 201–2.

Watts, Richard, Jr. "Comedy of Light in Darkness." *New York Post,* 13 February 1967, in *New York Theater Critics' Reviews—1967,* 372.

———. "A Powerful New Play From England." *New York Post,* 3 December 1959, in *New York Theater Critics' Reviews—1959,* 208.

———. "Two Delightful London Comedies." *New York Post,* 10 October 1963, in *New York Theater Critics' Reviews—1963,* 251.

———. "With Pizarro in Inca Peru." *New York Post,* 27 October 1965, in *New York Theater Critics' Reviews—1965,* 295.

Webb, W. L. "Committed to Nothing But the Theatre." *The Manchester Guardian,* 27 August 1959, 4.

Westarp, Karl-Heinz. "Myth in Peter Shaffer's *The Royal Hunt of the Sun* and Arthur Kopit's *Indians,*" *English Studies* 65, no. 2 (1984): 120–28.

Wilson, Edwin. "Conflicting Elements in a Human Soul." *Wall Street Journal,* 28 October 1974, in *New York Theater Critics' Reviews—1974,* 203.

———. "Peter Shaffer's Astigmatic View of God." *Wall Street Journal,* 19 December 1980, in *New York Theater Critics' Reviews—1980,* 25.

Winegarten, Renee. "The Anglo-Jewish Dramatist in Search of His Soul." *Midstream* 12 (October 1966): 40–52.

Witham, Barry. "The Anger in *Equus.*" *Modern Drama* 22, no. 1 (1979): 61–66.

Worsley, T. C. "Give Me a Good Play." *New Statesman,* 26 July 1958, 112–13.

———. "Merry Roosters' Panto." *Financial Times,* 20 December 1963, 18.

———. "The Private Ear: The Public Eye." *Financial Times,* 11 May 1962, 26.

Young, B. A. "*Amadeus.*" *Financial Times,* 5 November 1979, 15.

———. "The Battle of Shrivings." *Financial Times,* 6 February 1970, 3.

———. "The Royal Hunt of the Sun." *Financial Times,* 8 July 1964, 24.

Index